"PERSONAL" PROPERTY OF
EDWARD G. VERLANDER

Law for Business Managers
The Regulatory Environment

Law for Business Managers

The Regulatory Environment

THOMAS J. HARRON
Central Connecticut State College

HOLBROOK PRESS, INC.　　　BOSTON

© 1977 by Holbrook Press, Inc., 470 Atlantic Avenue, Boston. All rights reserved. No part of the material protected by this copyright notice may be reproduced or utilized in any form or by any means, electronic or mechanical, including photocopying, recording, or by any informational storage and retrieval system, without written permission from the copyright owner. Printed in the United States of America.

Library of Congress Cataloging in Publication Data

Harron, Thomas J
   Law for business managers.

   Includes index.
   1. Commercial law—United States. 2. Labor laws and legislation—United States. 3. Securities—United States. 4. Administrative procedure—United States. I. Title.
KF889.H27   346'.73'07   76-46576
ISBN 0-205-05743-8

Contents

List of Illustrations ix
Preface xi

PART ONE   INTRODUCTION TO THE STUDY OF LAW   2

Chapter 1. The Definition and Meaning of Law   5

Introduction · Definition of Law · Origins and Functions of Law · Limits to Law · World Legal Systems · Classification of Laws · Sources of American Law · Constitutional Basis of Business Regulation · Notes on Case Study · Review Questions

Chapter 2. The Judicial Process   26

Introduction · Definition of a Court · Court Classifications · American Court Structure · Jurisdiction · Trial Procedures · Class Action Suits · Review Questions

Chapter 3. The Administrative Process   42

Introduction · Development of Administrative Agencies · Advantages of the Agency Form · Powers of Administrative Agencies · Types of Administrative Agencies · Agency Operations · Agency Procedures · Review Questions

Chapter 4. Some Problems With Administrative Agencies   68

Introduction · Constitutional Questions · Political Influences · Economic Costs · Regulatory Errors · Freedom of Information Act · Review Questions

PART TWO   LAWS AND REGULATIONS AFFECTING THE SECURITIES MARKETS — 90

Chapter 5. Stockholder Rights and Liabilities — 93

Introduction • Rights to Corporate Records • Meeting Rights • Dividend Rights • Minority Rights • Other Rights • Stockholder Liabilities • Review Questions

Chapter 6. Securities Act of 1933 — 111

Introduction • Definitions of a Security • Registration Requirements • Exemptions from Registration • Liabilities • Management Guidelines • Review Questions

Chapter 7. Securities Exchange Act of 1934 — 132

Introduction • Registration and Reporting Requirements • Inside Reports • Short Swing Trades • Margin Trading • Tender Offers • Rule 10(b)(5) • Securities and Exchange Commissions • Liabilities • Other Federal Securities Laws • State Securities Laws • Management Guidelines • Review Questions

PART THREE   LAWS AND REGULATIONS AFFECTING BUSINESS GROWTH AND PRODUCT DISTRIBUTION — 154

Chapter 8. Common Law Background — 159

Introduction • Interference with Business Relations • Contracts in Restraint of Trade • Trademarks and Tradenames • Patents and Copyrights • Trade Secrets • Disparagement • Computers and the Law • Review Questions

Chapter 9. The Sherman Antitrust Act — 179

Introduction • Section 1, the Rule of Reason • Per Se Violations • Section 2 • Proving a Sherman Act Violation • Liabilities • Review Questions

Chapter 10. The Clayton Act and the Federal Trade Commission Act — 194

Introduction • Exclusive Dealings Arrangements • Mergers • Unfair Methods of Competition • Liabilities • Exemptions • Enforcement Procedures • Management Guidelines • Review Questions

Chapter 11. Consumer Protections — 220

Introduction • Price Discrimination • Other Pricing Restrictions • FTC Act Protections • Warranty • Consumer Product Safety • Other Federal Laws • Management Guidelines • Review Questions

PART FOUR   LAWS AND REGULATIONS AFFECTING LABOR — 242

Chapter 12. Collective Bargaining — 245

Introduction • Employee Rights • Employer Unfair Labor Practices • Union Unfair Labor Practices • Dispute Settlement Procedures • Review Questions

Chapter 13. Union Management Relations — 267

Introduction • Strikes • Picketing • Union Democracy • Union Reports • Officer Reports • Penalties • Pension Reform • Management Guidelines • Review Questions

Chapter 14. Occupational Injuries — 288

Introduction • Workmen's Compensation • Collection Procedures • Employer Defenses • Occupational Safety and Health Laws • Employer Duties • Employer Rights • Employee Rights and Duties • Management Guidelines • Review Questions

Chapter 15. Employment Discrimination — 314

Introduction • Civil Rights Laws • Remedies • State Civil Rights Laws • Affirmative Action Programs • Reverse Discrimination • Management Guidelines • Review Questions

PART FIVE BUSINESS AND SOCIETY 342

Chapter 16. Ethical Problems in American Business 347

Introduction • Criminal Conduct • Altruistic Crimes • Abuse of Position • Misuse of Power • Social Irresponsibility • Multinational Power • Summary • Review Questions

Chapter 17. Social Responsibility of Business 361

Introduction • Criminal Enforcement • Civil Remedies • Self-Regulation • Enforcement Techniques • Professional Liability • Social Responsibility • Summary • Review Questions

APPENDIXES 382

   I. How To Find and Use the Services of an Attorney 385
  II. Table of Cases 393
 III. Glossary 397

Index 421

Illustrations

TABLES

1.1	Major Federal Business Regulatory Laws	19
1.2	The Risks Executives Face Under Federal Laws	20–21
1.3	State Court Citations	23
2.1	American Court Structure	31
2.2	Federal Court Citations	32
2.3	Trial Stages	37
3.1	Administrative Agencies	50–51
3.2	Administrative Agency Procedural Stages	66
4.1	Due Process Rights Depend Upon the Proceeding	78–79
4.2	Government Forms	82
6.1	Registration Statement and Prospectus	115
11.1	Major Functional Offices in the Consumer Product Safety Commission	237
12.1	Major Functional Offices in the National Labor Relations Board	263
13.1	Minimum Pension Vesting Standards	282
14.1	Major Functional Offices in the Occupational Safety and Health Review Commission	304
15.1	Summary of the Civil Rights Acts Relating to Employment	316
15.2	Major Functional Offices in the Equal Employment Opportunity Commission	321
17.1	Annual Cost of White Collar Crime	363
17.2	National Association of Purchasing Management: Standards and Ethics of Buying and Selling	376

FIGURES

1.1	The Legal System	11
3.1	Interstate Commerce Commission	54
5.1	Shareholder Rights	107
7.1	Securities Exchange Commission	144
10.1	Federal Trade Commission	215
13.1	Department of Labor	274

Preface

American managers are earning more than ever, but along with their traditional work load and responsibilities, they face a new—and more perilous—burden. The shield that protects them from individual accountability for corporate acts of negligence and lawlessness seems far less impregnable than it used to be. Even now, managers at several levels—from chief executive officers to plant managers—are feeling the heat as new regulatory laws go on the books and established regulatory agencies take a harder line toward those who err. ("The Law Closes in on Managers," *Business Week*, May 10, 1976, p. 110.)

The modern business manager is confronted with an increasing body of laws. These laws affect the manager in three ways: first, they permit shareholders and consumers to sue for monetary damages for improper activities; second, they permit courts to impose damages and criminal fines on managers for improper activities done on behalf of their firms; and third, they create regulatory agencies to police all aspects of business operations, from designing a product to distribution of profits.

The volume of lawsuits filed against managers and their firms by disgruntled shareholders and consumers have been increasing over the years. This increase resulted from new laws permitting actions against businesses and also from a greater awareness by individuals of their rights to sue. Substantial monetary damages have been awarded against firms and individual employees of those firms guilty of wrongdoing. For serious violations, courts are now more likely to apply criminal sanctions. In one recent case, the president of a large corporation was fined because the manager of one of his food warehouses failed to prevent rodent infestation. Fines for individuals working in a corporation can go as high as $100,000 and jail terms up to several years can be imposed for some business violations.

Regulatory agencies are now more anxious to supervise business operations in an effort to prevent wrongdoing before the public is harmed. Congress and the states have been creating new agencies to regulate business and giving new powers to the existing agencies. The volume of regulations made by agencies has been increasing at a substantial rate. One indication of this regulatory growth is the size of the *Federal Register*. This journal contains all new regulations issued by the federal agencies. When it was first published in 1936, it contained 2,411 pages, by 1974 it had grown to 45,422 pages, and in 1975 it was 64,000 pages. In one year, the *Federal Register* grew by 42 percent.

The challenge facing today's business manager and those preparing for a career in management, is obvious. They must find ways to cope with increasing legal responsibilities. Without developing some system for understanding and complying with the laws, rules, regulations, and decisions affecting business, the manager may incur substantial costs and penalties for his firm and its personnel. This book is designed to help people who are interested in management to develop such a system. It deals with how the courts and the government administrative agencies regulate business operations. It discusses, among other things, how the Securities and Exchange Commission, the Federal Trade Commission, the National Labor Relations Board, the Equal Employment Opportunity Commission, and the Occupational Safety and Health Administration affect a manager's decision about financing company operations, business expansion, marketing of products, and hiring employees. Regulatory actions affecting consumer safety and pension reform are also discussed.

This book is for the person who does not have a detailed knowledge of law but wants exposure to the broad areas of business regulations. It contains five parts which correspond to the five groups a business manager deals with: government (Part 1), stockholders (Part 2), customers and competitors (Part 3), employees (Part 4), and the public (Part 5). The first part discusses the importance of law, its sources, the court system of the United States, and the administrative agency. The reader should compare the regulatory process with court procedures, and evaluate the impact of agencies on American Law. Part 2 discusses the administrative regulation of the capital markets, including a detailed discussion of some recent developments in capital formation, officer and director responsibilities, and stockholder rights and duties. The third part explains those laws and regulations affecting business growth and expansion, marketing of products, and consumer product safety. Part 4 surveys the laws of collective bargaining, worker safety, job discrimination, and pension reform. The final part raises some questions about why administrative agencies must regulate business. The chapters discuss the social responsibility of managers, their ethical duty to employees, customers, and the public.

Selected cases illustrate the points of law discussed in each chapter. These cases have been carefully edited to stress the basic concepts of the opinions without burdening the reader with excessive legal terminology. Questions at the end of each chapter not only review the material but also raise new issues for the reader to consider. Each chapter follows a uniform format, beginning with an introduction explaining the purposes and importance of the chapter, followed by a survey of the relevant law and its interpretations by the courts and administrative agencies.

"Management Guidelines" at the end of most chapters summarize the law in the chapter in an easy-to-follow format. There is an extensive legal glossary at the end of the book, as well as a section on how to find and use the services of an attorney and a table of cases.

Although numerous persons assisted me in the preparation of this manuscript for publication, final responsibility for accuracy, content, and style rests with the author. Some persons who have been helpful include: David E. Loss, Associate Dean of the School of Business at Central Connecticut State College who consistently encouraged me to complete this work; Miss Nancy Molinari, Mrs. Peggy Kornichuk, and Mrs. Donna Miles who helped to type the manuscript; and those reviewers whose comments improved the contents of this book, specifically, Professors Carol Caul of Arizona State University, Gerald R. Ferrera of Bentley College, and Daniel Scioletti of Northeastern University.

Law for Business Managers
The Regulatory Environment

TOPICS

CHAPTER 1. THE DEFINITION AND MEANING OF LAW
Introduction • Definition of Law • Origins and Functions of Law • Limits to Law • World Legal Systems • Classification of Laws • Sources of American Law • Constitutional Basis of Business Regulation • Notes on Case Study • Review Questions

CHAPTER 2. THE JUDICIAL PROCESS
Introduction • Definition of a Court • Court Classifications • American Court Structure Jurisdiction • Trial Procedures • Class Action Suits • Review Questions

CHAPTER 3. THE ADMINISTRATIVE PROCESS
Introduction • Development of Administrative Agencies • Advantages of the Agency Form • Powers of Administrative Agencies • Types of Administrative Agencies • Agency Operations • Agency Procedures • Review Questions

CHAPTER 4. SOME PROBLEMS WITH ADMINISTRATIVE AGENCIES
Introduction • Constitutional Questions • Political Influences • Economic Costs • Regulatory Errors • Freedom of Information Act • Review Questions

PART ONE

INTRODUCTION TO THE STUDY OF LAW

The aim of this book is to develop a broad understanding of how administrative agencies of the federal government regulate the operations of business firms, and of how these agencies affect the decision-making processes of business managers. These interactions between business and government regulatory law are of great importance to business managers, consumers, and citizens.

Government regulations now touch every phase of a business firm's operations. Internal Revenue Service rulings affect profits, labor laws regulate employee relations, consumer product safety acts and environmental laws limit manufacturing, securities laws influence capital formation, and antitrust laws restrict business growth. Decisions made by managers must take account of these regulations, as violators can be fined, imprisoned, and sued. See Table 1-2.

The manufacture and sale of products are regulated by laws and governmental agencies, which give persons injured by defective products or by unfair sales tactics rights to recover money. But legal procedures must be followed to enforce those legal rights. Without some knowledge of law, a consumer may not know how to enforce his or her rights or even that a right was violated.

Administrative agencies have changed our traditional system of government and altered the rights citizens have when accused of misconduct by government officials. These changes came about gradually. The average citizen is unaware that any change took place at all. But for democracy to function effectively, citizens must be aware of government actions and capable of evaluating new policies. This requires that citizens be informed about regulatory laws.

For us to understand business regulatory laws, we must first know what law is and see its importance to our society. This means we must examine the nature of law, the role courts play in our country, and how courts differ from administrative agencies. The first chapter of this book defines law and explains its functions and sources. The second chapter discusses the American court systems and the conduct of a trial. An analysis of the administrative agency, its development, operations, and problems rounds out the discussion.

1

THE DEFINITION AND MEANING OF LAW

Although hundreds of lawyers and legislators studied the revised New York divorce law before it was passed in 1966, no one noticed what turned out to be the improper choice of preposition. One of the new grounds for divorce is "the confinement of the defendant to prison for a period of three or more years..." A woman filed for divorce because her husband had been sentenced "to" prison for more than three years, but whose sentence had been suspended. The lawmakers, who clearly meant confinement in prison and not confinement to as is the case with suspended sentences, have since substituted "in" for "to" in the law. (New York Times, January 4, 1970.)

Law is a unique field of knowledge. It is special partly because the people who work in the legal profession often use ordinary words in a technical and precise way. If we want to learn about legal rules and concepts, then we must accept legal terminology as legal practitioners use it. It is impossible to have an accurate understanding of law if we do not make this minimal effort at bridging the language barrier. A few examples illustrate this difficulty.

A major rule of American law says that all persons are presumed to know the law. Obviously, this is impossible because the law of the United States is too complex for anyone to know. But the word "know" has a very precise meaning in this context. It means that a person has actual knowledge of the law or should have knowledge of the law. Thus to a lawyer, the statement means that all persons know or should know the law of the United States.

The quotation at the beginning of this chapter shows again how precise words can be in law. For the nonlawyer, the prepositions "in" and "to" are interchangeable. Going to the store or going in the store appear to mean the same thing: "I went in the store to buy a book" or "I went to the store to buy a book." A lawyer looking at the sentences would see a difference. Going to a store does not mean entering the store. The books could be purchased either inside the store or outside of it.

When we read about the law, we must study carefully the words used in laws, court cases, and other legal writings. We must remember that a word may be used by a lawyer in a different way from the way we would use the same word in everyday conversation. You must tune yourself into the jargon of the attorney if you want a clear understanding of our laws.

One word that we will be using frequently in these chapters has a unique meaning. It is the word "law." The word requires some explanation because it is used so often by different people to mean different ideas. For example, economists speak of the law of diminishing returns to signify inefficiency, sportscasters describe the umpire's decisions as the law of the game, political scientists refer to America as a government of laws not of men, and historians tell us that democratic as well as totalitarian societies have laws. Obviously, the word law in each of these phrases means something different to the person using it.

The definition of law is not a simple one. *Webster's Collegiate Dictionary* gives more than nine different meanings to this word. But before we can begin our study of administrative regulation of business, we must clarify our definition of law. To do so, we will study the meaning of law in its contacts with individuals, explain its functions in society, survey world legal systems, and discuss the sources of American business regulatory law.

DEFINITION OF LAW

Members of the legal profession do not agree among themselves as to the exact meaning of the word law. This fact should not be surprising, because law has developed through its use as a way of solving problems, not through scholarly dissertations. Law is a practical subject, not a theoretical one. Consequently, academic definitions have not been important for the existence of law. Individuals often develop personal meanings for the word. Some of the meanings people associate with law are:

Rules

Many persons think of law as a list of rules and regulations that must be obeyed. Traffic and criminal laws seem to fall within this area—a motorist must not pass a red light, businesspersons must not agree among themselves to fix the prices of their products, a wage earner must not avoid paying federal income taxes, and so on.

Enforcement

Some people believe the rules and regulations themselves are not as important as how they are enforced. For example, a traffic law prohibits speeds in excess of fifty-five miles per hour on interstate highways. But police in most states allow motorists to exceed this limit by a reasonable margin, perhaps by five miles per hour, before stopping the driver. In this example, the speed limit is really sixty miles per hour. Also, judges interpret laws differently. This difference can change the meaning of a law. For example, many judges will suspend a jail sentence for first-time offenders. Thus a law imposing a jail term on a business manager guilty of price fixing often means that in practice only those convicted two or more times will be jailed. For some people, law means only those rules that are enforced by the police and judges.

Purpose

Law must exist for some purpose. It is meaningless to create a legal structure with a system of rules and regulations unless some worthwhile goal is sought. Some people emphasize this aspect of law, giving the word its third meaning—law is a path leading to an agreed-upon objective. For most people, the purpose of the law is an important part of law. If a rule or regulation does not lead to the desired end, then it should not be followed. In the 1960s, some civil rights activists refused to obey segregation laws because they considered such laws in conflict with the objectives of our society. In the 1970s, some war resisters ignored draft laws because they considered them a hindrance to society's goals.

Authority

A final meaning some people give to law is authority. Law can only be imposed by someone who has the right to impose it. That right implies the power to compel obedience to established rules and regulations. Some people, therefore, associate law with the power that creates it. For them, law is any command from the government. Since most laws now seem to come from the federal, state, or local governments, some people feel the government is the law. But in our society, government derives its powers from the people. They are the authority from which law comes.

In summary, we can accept as our definition of law the four basic meanings given to it by most individuals who come into contact with it. Law is a system of rules and regulations, established and enforced by some authority, to help society accomplish its goals. This definition tells us what law is, but it does not tell us anything about where law comes from or why laws are necessary. To answer these questions, we should look at the origins and functions of law.

ORIGINS AND FUNCTIONS OF LAW

Philosophers do not agree on the basic origins of law, but two theories concerning basic roots to law are worth discussing here. Some say law arises from the nature of human beings. Each person has certain basic rights which exist merely because he or she exists. These rights must be respected by other persons. Law only commands others to respect basic natural rights; it does not confer rights on people. For example, each person has a right to live and to acquire property. Those rights come to a person because he or she exists. A law ordering others not to kill or steal is merely a formal expression of duties that already exist in nature. This philosophy of law is called the natural law theory, and it is the basis of American legal philosophy. The Declaration of Independence states that all men are endowed by their creator with certain inalienable (natural) rights.

Other philosophers say law comes from human behavior, not human nature. Humans can agree among themselves to pass any laws thought necessary for governing their society. There are no limitations on this power, and any law desired by the people is valid. A person has no basic, natural rights. Individuals have only those rights given them by other members of the society. Thus, people will pass laws forbidding killing or stealing so that each member of society will be protected from the other. This concept of law, called the social compact theory, is the philosophical justification of law in a pure democracy.

A better insight into the meaning of law can be obtained by looking at the functions and purposes of a system of laws. Some current functions of law are:

To Preserve Society

People live together in families, tribes, states, or nations for some purpose. They may want to acquire property, improve their social position, experience mystical satisfactions or attain some other goal. To accomplish their goals, these people must remain together and protect their society from any disruptions. They require rules and regulations—laws—to preserve their society. Without self-preservation, no progress toward obtaining any of their objectives is possible. Laws providing for national defense, criminal laws punishing anti-social behavior, and laws preserving family units are examples of the use of law to preserve society.

To Settle Disputes

When people are living together, conflicts are inevitable. There will be accidents which cause frictions among the persons involved, and there will always be some people seeking advantages over others. To solve these problems caused by people in society, there must be some procedure to settle disputes peacefully. If no procedure exists, then the persons involved in the dispute will settle it by themselves. Their settlement procedures may mean the use of force, and frequently all members of the society are brought into the fight. Warring factions often defeated society's goals more than each other. A legal system must provide some mechanism to settle disputes peacefully. It must establish a system to which disputing parties will go voluntarily to solve their problems. Use of this procedure rather than the battlefield will allow society to continue and its members to reach their goals. Laws creating a court system and those providing for trials and appeals to higher courts are possible means of establishing dispute-settling procedures.

To Preserve Social Values

People living in a society develop habits and these habits turn into customs. A custom is any behavior pattern or way of acting in the society. As most people in a society come to follow certain customs, they begin to expect all people to follow the same behavior patterns. Laws are then adopted to require persons to observe certain customs. Violations of society's customs offend the majority and some action will be taken against the few who disregard the majority's will. Such violations could disrupt society. So protection of social values is necessary to keep society together and enable it to accomplish its goals. Examples of this type of law are obscenity statutes limiting vulgar speech and dress, restrictions on deviant social conduct, prohibitions on certain sexual acts between consenting adults, and limitations on abortions.

To Promote Justice

Fulfilling its goals is the basic purpose of any society. These objectives should include improving the well-being of all members of society. Each person in society should have a sense that his or her life is improving. If not, living becomes futile and society's existence becomes unimportant. Punitive action may be taken against other members of society who appear to be in a better social or economic position. Class warfare could develop. To keep society peaceful, some social progress must be made by all members of society. Some examples of laws attempting to promote social justice are the civil rights acts to encourage equal opportunity for all citizens, labor laws requiring employers to negotiate with their employees for a fair sharing of economic gains, and voting laws permitting the widest possible participation in government by all citizens.

LIMITS TO LAW

Law is not an all-powerful force, capable of performing any function assigned to it. Lawmakers must operate within certain limits. They can only do that which is possible for law to do. They cannot make laws that violate the fundamental rules of society or nature. Demands for new legislation should be evaluated in light of the limitations on law. Some of these limitations are:

Economic Rules. Economists have identified several forces at work in our economy. The law of diminishing returns states that at some point, any more resources committed to a project will actually cause output to decrease. Also, the law of supply and demand affects prices of products through the market system. Lawmakers can regulate and influence economic rules, but they can never repeal them.

Physical Rules. Nature has its own laws for governing the universe. The law of gravity requires all objects to move toward each other. A legislature cannot repeal that law for its territory. Similarly, laws cannot increase the amount of raw materials available in the soil. A law passed by Congress to cure cancer would be meaningless since the physical tools necessary are unavailable.

Customs. Social customs develop through years of acceptance and practice, perhaps originating in religious beliefs, social mores, or moral doctrines. Any law changing these customs will be met with resistance. Police must either ignore the violations or enforce the law with repressive force. Both consequences will be harmful since a lack

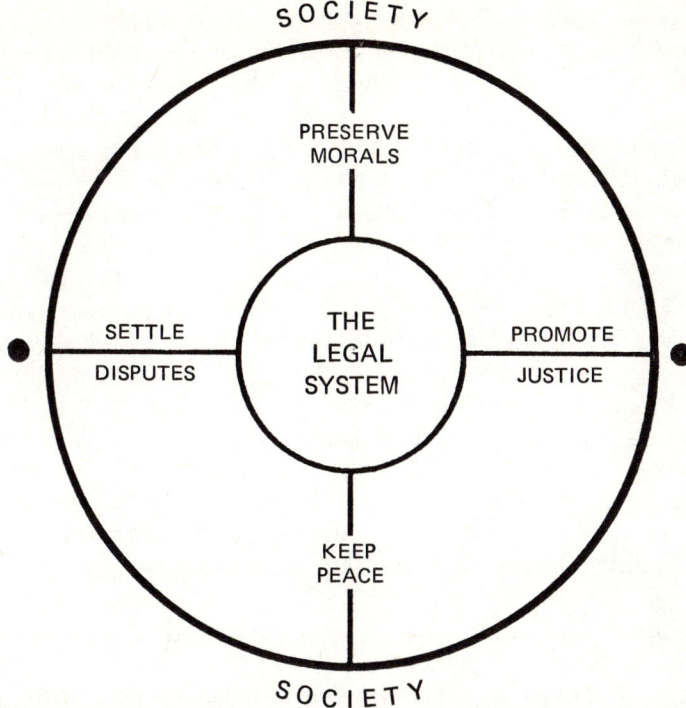

FIGURE 1—1: The Legal system is the center of organized society. Its functions help to keep society orderly.

of respect for some laws will encourage disrespect for all laws. An example of an attempt to force a change in customs was alcoholic prohibition in the 1920s.

Political Rules. Frequently, political realities paralyze a government into inaction. In this situation, legislatures are helpless giants, having the ostensible power to act but unable to do so. Such cases arise where members of the legislature are evenly divided over an issue and unable to compromise on one acceptable solution. Political paralysis can arise also from a minority's skillful use of parliamentary procedures. Filibustering is an example of this situation.

WORLD LEGAL SYSTEMS

Law is not unique to America or to the Western world. It must exist in every organized society. Even though legal systems appear to be different, they all have certain elements in common. Those common elements are the functions that law carries out. For example, several law teachers from the People's Republic of China recently stated that law in China serves three purposes—to punish those who would destroy the government, to protect the property of the communes, and to settle disputes between citizens. Although our systems of government are different, both America and China agree on these purposes of law, if not on the goals of society.

In the world today, there are several types of legal systems. Some of the major ones are:

Civil Law. This legal system arises from the Roman Empire. In that government, and in those following its example, one comprehensive series of laws sets out the basic rights and duties of people in all legal disputes. Frequently, religious law, customs, court structures, social and business regulation, and legislative procedures are combined in one code. Any change in this code must be made by the legislature. Courts merely apply the law as it exists. The civil law system is the dominant one in the world today, existing in Europe, South America, and parts of Asia and Africa.

Common Law. This law system evolved from England. It is based on a system of court-made laws rather than on legislatively enacted ones. Judges interpret the religious beliefs and social customs of the people as a basis for settling disputes among them. If the interpretations by the judges in one case are reasonable, then other judges in similar cases will follow the same interpretations. This is called precedent. Using precedent to decide future cases gives predictability and stability to law. The common law system is the second most prominent world legal system, existing in England and those areas settled by English colonists—North America, India, and parts of Africa and Asia.

Religious Laws. In some societies, law is part of the people's religion and it is impossible to separate them. Some of these societies are the Moslem world, the Confucian order, and Brahmanic civilizations. Moslem law consists of those things Allah revealed to Mohammed. It sets up religious duties, business regulations, and social customs. All aspects of a person's life are regulated by the religious law and all disputes among individuals must be settled in conformity with the doctrines expressed in the Koran, the Islamic bible. This system of law exists throughout the Moslem world, ranging from Asia through the Middle East and across central and north Africa.

The Confucian order establishes principles of human conduct and social order through the philosophy of Confucius. Law develops through observation and obedience to the natural order of things, and becomes a ritualistic observance of ancient customs. This system exists in central Asia. By contrast, Brahmanic law is the traditional law of the Hindu religious communities. Elaborate rules govern judicial procedure, the settling of disputes, and political control. Custom and tradition determine how the law will be used. This system exists in India, coexisting with the common law.

CLASSIFICATION OF LAWS

To see the types of laws we will be studying, it may be helpful to classify law into some common groups.

Crimes, Torts, and Contracts. Early law is divisible into three basic areas—crimes, torts, and contracts. From these roots grew our present legal system. In the law of crimes, society defines specific acts as harmful to its people and imposes punishment on anyone who intentionally does one of these acts. At first, society made violations of religious doctrines criminal acts. Today, legislatures make criminal any act that they think could harm the public interest if carried out on a wide scale by others. From criminal laws, society developed investigatory methods, arrest procedures, prosecution rules, and punishment techniques.

The law of torts developed out of criminal law. This branch of law permits a person injured by someone's criminal acts to sue for compensation. The lawsuit did not seek punishment of the wrongdoer, merely money from the person who caused injuries. Courts and legislatures expanded tort law by creating standards by which every person must act. Now, if one person injures another or another's property by not living up to these standards of care, then the injured person can sue in a tort action for damages. Under tort law, standards exist for the protection of a person's physical body, reputation, personal property, and business property.

Contract law developed from the need to protect promises made between persons. During the early development of business, merchants relied upon a person's promise as the basis for commercial transactions. The proper functioning of their economy required rules for upholding promises. Courts soon developed certain requirements for making contractual promises, interpreting contract terms, and enforcing contractual obligations. From general contract law came laws regulating specific types of business contracts, such as sales contracts, negotiable instruments, insurance, securities, and others. Most business regulatory laws developed out of a need to protect parties making contracts.

Public and Private Law. Public law is that branch of law dealing with the government, its organization, and its relationship to people living under its authority. Some examples are constitutional law dealing with the setting up of governmental powers, criminal law limiting antisocial conduct, and administrative law regulating agency operations. Private law is that branch of law that regulates the conduct of individuals in their relations with each other. Some examples are contract law permitting persons to make enforceable business agreements, commercial laws providing for the formation of business organizations and setting up procedures for business dealings, and property law encouraging people to create and own wealth.

Substantive and Procedural Law. Substantive laws create legal rights and duties for persons in a society. For example, the law of torts gives a person the right to sue for money damages if injuries are inflicted by another, and contract laws give a person the right to recover damages if he or she is the victim of a breach of contract. Procedural law establishes a method of enforcing a substantive right. The law of evidence, for example, sets up a method for proving a claim for damages, and appellate law creates a mechanism for having a court decision reviewed for error by a higher tribunal.

Written and Unwritten Law. Written laws are rules and regulations adopted by the legislature. Congress makes written laws when it passes a new civil rights act, imposes a tax on oil imports, or establishes wage and price controls. Unwritten laws are interpretations of the written laws by the courts. In our legal system, courts have the power to explain laws passed by the legislatures. These interpretations often give new meanings to written laws. For example, the Constitution of the United States says no law shall be passed by Congress restricting the right of free speech. Yet the Supreme Court has interpreted this to mean Congress can pass reasonable laws restricting free speech. Thus a law can be valid that prohibits a person from shouting a false alarm of fire in a crowded theater. All persons must obey the written and unwritten laws of the United States.

We will be studying the public, substantive, and unwritten laws of the United States. We will read about how courts have interpreted the rights and duties of businesspeople in their dealings with various administrative agencies. These rights and duties have evolved from many different sources. A look at some of the major sources of these substantive rights can give us another insight into the meaning of law.

SOURCES OF AMERICAN LAW

Some major sources of law are:

Constitutions. A constitution is a system of fundamental laws for the operation of a nation or other grouping of individuals. It is the authority by which a government acts. The United States Constitution states that it is the supreme law of the land. Therefore, all disputes must be settled in conformity with it. Each state has a constitution and it becomes the supreme law for that state. Conflicts between the federal and state constitutions are decided in favor of the federal one.

Treaties. A treaty is any contract made between two sovereign nations. The U.S. Constitution gives the President powers to make treaties, subject to the advice and consent of the Senate. Treaties become part of our internal law so that a dispute arising within this country must be settled in conformity with them. In addition to formal treaties, the President can make "executive agreements," not requiring the consent of the Senate. These also regulate the settlement of disputes. Business can be regulated by a treaty. For example, foreign aid agreements often specify the types of American products an underdeveloped nation must purchase in order to receive money. Depending on the type of loan agreement, different segments of business may be helped or hurt. States are prohibited by the Constitution from entering into agreements with foreign nations.

Statutes. Based upon the powers given it by the constitution, a legislature may enact laws to carry out the policy of government. All legislatures have set up a procedure for making laws. If proper procedures for passing a law are not followed, then the courts can declare the law invalid. Both state and federal legislatures have enacted many laws regulating business. Some examples of federal laws important to business are: the Internal Revenue Code establishing the tax law for business firms, trusts, and individuals; the Securities Act of 1933 and the Securities Exchange Act of 1934 regulating stock and bond sales; the Sherman and Clayton Acts limiting the size of business; the National Labor Relations Acts encouraging collective bargaining between labor and management; and the Civil Rights Acts prohibiting discrimination in employment. State statutes regulate many of the same areas of business as do federal statutes. In the event of conflict, the federal Constitution and its laws and treaties take priority over state laws. State statutes regulate contracts made within state borders, the legality of checks, stock transfers, and sales of merchandise. The major state business regulatory law is the Uniform Commercial Code, a comprehensive law regulating certain aspects of business operations.

Ordinances. Governmental units other than federal and state are municipal corporations. They include cities, counties, towns, school districts, zoning boards, and special authorities for harbor facilities, turnpikes, and water districts. Each of these municipal corporations has powers delegated from the state legislature to govern within their areas of responsibility. Disputes arising within the jurisdiction of one of these units must be decided according to its laws, called ordinances. A municipal corporation's authority is limited by the state's delegation of power and by the geographic limits of its territory. Some examples of local ordinances affecting business are zoning laws regulating the types of buildings in each neighborhood, building codes specifying the types of construction necessary for commercial buildings, and traffic laws limiting the size and weight of trucks on certain highways.

Administrative Law. The Congress and the legislatures of the various states establish regulatory bodies, called administrative agencies, to handle some aspects of the legal process. Generally, these agencies have powers to carry out details of law administration delegated to them by their legislatures, in order to provide flexibility and expertise in the implementation of laws. On the federal level, some examples of these agencies are the Federal Trade Commission, the Securities and Exchange Commission, and the Interstate Commerce Commission. On the state level the names vary, but there is usually a liquor control authority, a workman's compensation board, and an insurance commission. Each of these various agencies can have power to hear and decide disputes, make findings of factual questions, and issue rules and regulations pertaining to its authority. Thus a dispute must be settled in agreement with the pronouncements of the appropriate administrative agency. A discussion of these agencies and how they operate is the basic purpose of this text.

Courts. These bodies are a primary source of law in the country today. Federal and state courts have the power to decide upon the constitutionality of all laws enacted by the legislature, the legality of any actions taken by the executive branch of the government, and the validity of any rulings made by an administrative agency. In this respect, courts act as a "conscience" of the governmental system. Also, courts have the authority to hear and decide cases or controversies brought before them by individuals. In deciding these disputes, the courts must interpret and apply laws. By interpreting and applying a law, courts frequently add new meanings to it. Also, when no statutory law exists to determine the outcome of a dispute, the court will apply the common law as a means of settling the dispute. By the concept of precedent, all other courts in the same governmental unit must apply the same decision to cases having similar characteristics. Thus, if we wanted to know the law governing a particular problem, we would have to consult all the judicial decisions pertaining to the matter, as well as appropriate statutes, ordinances, treaties, and constitutions.

Common Law. The common law is the foundation upon which American law rests. Essentially, it is a system by which judges formulate basic legal principles, based upon the general custom, usage, or common consent of the people, and followed by them for a prolonged period of time. It is an expanding body of rules, continually adapting to the changing behaviorial patterns of people in society. Courts interpret these general customs and apply them when there is no written law regulating the issues in dispute. Thus, when the legislature has failed to enact provisions governing a particular problem, the court can apply the common law to settle the dispute. Although the common law relies on precedent, it is not a static, unchanging body of rules. Its rules can be changed by judges or legislatures when any good reason shows the need for change. All legal disputes must be settled in conformity with the common law unless it has been specifically changed by statute.

The Supreme Court summarized the meaning of the common law in a case arising between two states. In *Kansas* v. *Colorado*, 206 U.S. 46 (1907), the Court stated: "What is the common law? ... [It] includes those principles, usages, and rules of action applicable to the government and security of persons and property, which do not depend for their authority upon any express and positive declaration of the will of the legislature. As it does not rest on any statute or other written declaration of the sovereign, there must, as to each principle thereof, be a first statement. Those statements are found in the decisions of courts, and the first statement presents the principles as certainly as the last. For after all, the common law is but the accumulated expressions of the various judicial tribunals in their efforts to ascertain what is right and just between individuals in respect to private disputes."

Through the use of precedent, the common law courts derived a number of categories, called actions, through which lawsuits customarily were started. Overreliance on precedent soon developed into such rigidity that if a case did not fit into one of these actions, no relief was available. To remedy this defect in the common law system, persons unable to obtain adequate remedies at common law began petitioning the king. The king, through his chancellor, granted remedies which seemed fair and equitable to reconcile the disputes. A separate system of courts began developing, known as equity courts. These courts adjudicated disputes that the common law courts were unable or unwilling to settle. Since the parties asked the king for some remedy, no jury was present. Also, the king had different possible remedies for settling a dispute from those available to common law courts. For example, at common law, only money damages could be awarded, whereas in equity injunctions and specific performance were available. In the United States today, law and equity courts are the same. No distinction is now made between them.

Private Law. In reconciling disputes, courts will also look to the agreements made by the disputing parties themselves as a source of law for settling the controversy. When parties form a contract, the terms of their contractual relationship will govern, as much as possible, the settling of their disputes. Where no contract exists between the parties, the court will apply the current practices of the business in which the parties work to settle the dispute. Hence, the court looks, as a source of law, to the prior dealings between the parties themselves, their contractual agreements, and the customary usages of their business to settle the dispute. Of course, these sources are consulted only after the other sources mentioned above are examined and found inapplicable.

CONSTITUTIONAL BASIS OF BUSINESS REGULATION

An important source of business regulatory laws is Article I, Section 8, of the federal Constitution. This section lists the powers of Congress. If a federal business regulation cannot be based upon one of the following powers, then it is an invalid use of congressional powers. Some of these powers of importance to us are:

Interstate Commerce. Congress has the power to regulate all aspects of interstate commerce, including any part of manufacturing, transportation, or sales that has either an indirect or direct effect on commerce between two or more states or between the states and

TABLE 1-1. MAJOR FEDERAL BUSINESS REGULATORY LAWS

Year	Law	Purpose
1887	Interstate Commerce Act	Regulates transportation services
1890	Sherman Antitrust Act	Prohibits restraints of trade
1914	The Clayton Act	Prohibits specific business practices
1914	Federal Trade Commission Act	Regulates marketing, created FTC
1933	Securities Act	Requires financial disclosures in securities sales
1934	Securities Exchange Act	Regulates stock exchanges and trading practices
1935	National Labor Relations Act	Encourages unionization and collective bargaining
1947	Labor Management Relations Act	Limits union powers
1959	Labor Management Reporting and Disclosure Act	Requires reports from and democratic rules in unions
1970	Environmental Quality Act	Establishes pollution control policy
1972	Equal Employment Opportunity Act	Assures equal job opportunities
1972	Consumer Product Safety Act	Creates product safety standards
1974	Employee Retirement Income Security Act	Encourages pension reform

TABLE 1-2. THE RISKS EXECUTIVES FACE UNDER FEDERAL LAW

Agency	Year Enforcement Began	Complaint May Name Individual	Maximum Individual Penalty	Maximum Corporate Penalty	Private Suit Allowed Under Applicable Statute
Internal Revenue Service	1862	Yes	$5,000, three years, or both	$10,000, 50% assessment, prosecution costs	No
Antitrust Div. (Justice Dept.)	1890	Yes	$100,000, three years, or both	$1 million, injunction, divestiture	Yes
Food & Drug Administration	1907	Yes	$1,000, one year, or both for first offense; $10,000, three years, or both thereafter	$1,000 for first offense; $10,000 thereafter; seizure of condemned products	No
Federal Trade Commission	1914	Yes	Restitution, injunction	Restitution, injunction, divestiture, $10,000 per day for violation of rules, orders	No
Securities & Exchange Commission	1934	Yes	$10,000, two years, or both	$10,000, injunction	Yes

Equal Employment Opportunity Commission	1965	No	Injunction, back pay award, reinstatement	Yes
Office of Federal Contract Compliance	1965	No	Suspension, cancellation of contract	Yes
Environmental Protection Agency	1970	Yes	$25,000 per day, one year, or both for first offense; $50,000 per day, two years, or both thereafter	$25,000 per day, first offense; $50,000 per day thereafter; injunction	Yes
Occupational Safety & Health Administration	1970	No*	$10,000, six months, or both	$10,000	No
Consumer Product Safety Commission	1972	Yes	$50,000, one year, or both	$500,000	Yes
Office of Employee Benefits Security (Labor Dept.)	1975	Yes	$10,000, one year, or both; barring from future employment with plan; reimbursement	$100,000, reimbursement	Yes

*Except sole proprietorship

Reprinted from *Business Week*, May 10, 1976, by permission.

21

foreign governments. This power is the legal basis for regulating most phases of business activities, from raising capital to marketing products. State governments also have the power to regulate interstate commerce in areas where Congress has not prohibited the states from doing so by preempting the regulatory power. Any state regulation of interstate commerce must not put an unreasonable burden or barrier to the interstate activities of a business. Courts determine when state regulations are reasonable and when Congress has preempted the area of regulation.

Taxing Power. Congress can raise money for government expenditure by imposing taxes on business and people. By putting high taxes on some activities and low taxes on others, Congress can influence business operations. For example, Congress puts a lower tax on profits made from oil and mineral exploration than on the profits of manufacturing companies to encourage investors to put money into development of raw materials. Tax concessions to stimulate exports and to encourage growth of certain types of farm products are common.

Miscellaneous Powers. Several other powers given Congress regulate aspects of business operations in the country. The power to grant patents and copyrights stimulates creative inventions and artistic works by giving the holder of a patent or copyright exclusive use and royalties from the use of the protected work. Government power to borrow, spend, and print money is an important source of business regulation. For example, by changing the money supply, the government can expand or restrict the growth of business. Also, it can channel government spending into one segment of business and away from others. Money taken from welfare and spent for military research aids companies in the defense business but hurts hospitals and charitable institutions.

Necessary and Proper. Congress has the authority to make all laws that are necessary and proper for carrying out any of the above-mentioned powers. This is a broad grant of power. The government can enact any law it thinks suitable or appropriate for regulating interstate commerce, taxing business, spending or making money, and granting patents.

NOTES ON CASE STUDY

As mentioned before, a significant source of material for understanding the law comes from judicial decisions. To learn the law dealing with a particular problem, we must read all those decisions pertaining to the problem. But with fifty state courts and the federal courts handing down decisions almost daily, the volume of potential decisions pertaining to a problem is staggering. Therefore, some system of indexing these cases is necessary.

Two methods are used, one by the court giving the decision, the other by private companies. Courts will file cases chronologically by the date of case and by the court giving the decision. Thus, 119 CONN 53 means this is a case decided in Connecticut by its highest court and can be found in volume 119 on page 53 of its court reports. Further qualifying letters would indicate a court other than the highest court, e.g., 122 N.Y.S. 332 indicates that the case comes from a lower New York court. Federal cases are reported in a similar fashion but with "U.S." signifying the Supreme Court, "F" and "F

TABLE 1-3. STATE COURT CITATIONS

WEST PUBLISHING COMPANY

Region	Abbreviation	States	
Pacific	P.	Alaska	Montana
		Washington	Idaho
		Oregon	Wyoming
		California	Nevada
		Hawaii	Utah
		N. Mexico	Arizona
		Colorado	Kansas
		Oklahoma	
South Western	S.W.	Texas	Arkansas
		Missouri	Kentucky
		Tennessee	
Southern	S.	Louisiana	Alabama
		Mississippi	Florida
South Eastern	S.E.	Georgia	N. Carolina
		S. Carolina	Virginia
		W. Virginia	
North Eastern	N.E.	Illinois	Ohio
		Indiana	New York
		Massachusetts	
North Western	N.W.	N. Dakota	Minnesota
		S. Dakota	Iowa
		Nebraska	Wisconsin
		Michigan	
Atlantic	A.	Maryland	Connecticut
		Delaware	Rhode Island
		N. Jersey	Vermont
		Pennsylvania	New Hampshire
		Maine	District of Columbia

Supp." indicating lower courts. Legal dictionaries list the abbreviations of court decisions.

West Publishing Co., a private company, groups the reported cases together by geographic region, instead of by states, and publishes a comprehensive index to find cases. Thus, a case referred to as 73 NW 289 tells us the case is in volume 73 on page 289 in a set of books for the northwestern region of the country. Here we will find cases from other states within the same region. Comprehensive indexes are available where we can find other cases from the same region relating to our problem. By following the same method in books for the other regions we can find nearly all the reported cases relating to our problem. Similar methods are available for finding federal court decisions as well as foreign case decisions. This means of referring to a case is called citations.

Decisions given by judges are more than just solutions to disputes between individuals. Our legal system permits judges to interpret laws and develop new interpretations of custom. Since our law is based on precedent, these decisions become binding on future courts. It is important for someone learning the law to read and understand these decisions. But reading court decisions is difficult. Cases are drafted in legal language and frequently only briefly sketch the facts of the case. Court opinions assume the reader knows about the law and case already. Those of us without this knowledge must piece together the major parts of the case from the information given by the judge. This can be difficult. To make it easier, we can use a method of case analysis called briefing.

To brief a case, we must first read the entire case. Then we should note the name, date, and place of the case. This information gives us a basis for referring to the case and shows its relevancy today. Second, we would note the key facts of the case. Key facts are those the judge considers important in reaching a decision. These facts are important because other disputes having similar facts should be decided in the same way as this case. Third, we should find the legal problem in the case. This problem, referred to as the issue of the case, is the legal question the court must answer. Fourth, we should note the decision of the case, the side for whom the court ruled. Last, we should list the reasons given by the judge. These reasons are important because they explain why the court decided as it did. If the reasons are not good ones, the case will not be followed as precedent. The following is an example of a case brief:

NAME OF CASE
(Court, Date)

FACTS:

ISSUE:

DECISION:

REASON:

From this brief survey of law, we can see why it is a unique subject to study. The words used in law can have different meanings to different people. Even the word law has different meanings, depending upon whether a person means its source, purposes, functions, or characteristics. For our study of administrative regulations of business, the nature of law is not as important as its effectiveness. As we read the following chapters, we should ask ourselves if the law works as a method of solving disputes fairly. If it does, then the law is good; if not, then it is bad and should be changed.

REVIEW QUESTIONS

1. Give examples of your daily contact with the law. Why should a person study law?
2. Why is it difficult for someone to begin studying law?
3. Explain the different meanings associated with the word law. What does it mean to you?
4. Give a definition to the word law.
5. Explain the functions common to all legal systems.
6. Show how the various world legal systems accomplish each of these functions.
7. Contrast public, private, substantive, procedural, written, and unwritten law. What is our study primarily concerned with?
8. List and explain the major sources of American law.
9. Indicate the constitutional authority for regulation of business activities by the federal government.
10. What is the common law, how did it develop, and what does it mean to our legal system?

2

THE JUDICIAL PROCESS

Go not in and out in the court of justice, that thy name may not [be defamed]. (The Wisdom of Anii, 900 B.C.)

Historical records show that people did not always respect law courts. People expressed resentment against courts by making laws restricting public use of them, and by showing apathy toward court problems and open contempt toward judicial powers. These attitudes among people are unfortunate because courts must exist to carry out the functions of a legal system. For example, to settle disputes peacefully, a judge or some other official must see that remedies are applied fairly and correctly. Also, courts work for social justice by acting as a conscience for government, overruling actions that abuse people's rights. Courts help to preserve society by punishing those who disrupt it. Finally, courts protect society's social values by limiting laws that violate the people's customs. To fulfill the purposes of a legal system, it is necessary to have a functioning and respected court system.

In this book, we will learn about our substantive rights before administrative agencies. Laws dealing with how these rights are enforced will be left to professionally trained attorneys to learn and use. But we must know something about procedural law.

First, we will be reading many law cases about disputes between government and business. It is helpful to know the procedures these parties used to settle their differences.

Second, since administrative agencies operate differently from courts, we should contrast the methods of the two. To make intelligent comparisons, we must know about court operations.

Third, we must understand how procedural laws can affect our substantive rights. A violation of a procedural rule can nullify a substantive right. As one example, the statute of limitations is a procedural rule requiring lawsuits to be started within a certain period of time. If not, the right to sue may be lost.

In this chapter, we will study the judicial process. We will examine the definition of a court, the types of courts existing, and the six stages of a trial. In the next chapter, we will compare courts with administrative agencies.

DEFINITION OF A COURT

The judicial process means the courts and the rules by which they operate. Technically, a court is a judicial tribunal engaged in the administration of justice. This means a court is any place where laws are applied to settle disputes fairly. Some key elements are contained in this definition.

First, a court must be officially established by some competent authority. In our system, only a government can create a court and only a government can enforce its decisions.

Second, the court must meet at a regular place and at a regular time. This lets people know where and when they can make use of court procedures.

Third, courts administer laws to settle disputes. As stated in one court case, *Vecki* v. *Sorensen*, 340 P. 2d 1020 (1959), "... courts exist primarily to afford a forum for the settlement of litigable matters between disputing parties. Over the long and bitter history, this method of adjudication has replaced other and primitive, and indeed physical, means of resolution."

Fourth, a court must try to settle disputes fairly. Rules of law are merely guides for adjusting claims between parties. They should not become barriers to justice. "The primary function of our courts is to see that justice is done and the framework of law is just a means to that end." (*Greguski* v. *Oyster Bay*, 187 N.Y.S. 2d 432, 1959.) To deny parties the use of a court because one of them did not follow a technical rule of law is not justice.

In every court, there are at least three participants: the plaintiff, who complains of some injury; the defendant, who is asked to pay for that injury; and the judge, who must examine the truth of the complaint and apply the relevant rules of law to settle the dispute. Judges may use other people to assist in performing these functions. For example, a jury may determine disputed facts; a marshall or sheriff can bring people into the court, keep order during court proceedings and carry out its decisions; technical experts may advise on complex matters; probation officers can supervise orders made by the judge; a stenographer records testimony and evidence offered during a trial; and a clerk processes court papers and documents.

COURT CLASSIFICATIONS

Grouping courts into several categories gives a better understanding of what courts do. Most courts must keep official journals of their proceedings. These courts are courts of record. Those courts that do not keep official transcripts are not courts of record. Generally, only courts of record impose fines or imprison people. However, both kinds of courts have authority to settle certain types of noncriminal cases. Authority to hear and decide cases is jurisdiction.

A court of original jurisdiction has authority to hear a case when it is first brought to court. Those courts having power to review a case for errors are courts of appellate jurisdiction. Only a court of record can have appellate jurisdiction, and normally appeals can be taken only from decisions of a court of record. If a court has the power to decide only certain types of cases brought to it, it has special jurisdiction. Courts having power to decide all types of cases are general jurisdiction courts.

Another classification of courts is based on the types of cases brought to trial. A criminal court hears cases involving wrongful acts committed by persons against the public. Civil courts deal with cases concerning private rights and duties. Some examples of civil courts are probate courts, juvenile courts, and bankruptcy courts. In our legal system, courts have jurisdiction in law and equity cases. A law case requests certain specific remedies, but equity cases permit a judge to award those remedies considered appropriate to accomplish justice between the parties.

AMERICAN COURT STRUCTURE

An understanding of the American judicial system permits us to contrast court procedures with the administrative agency system. Our courts are based upon the English court system. Although English courts have changed over time, their basic structures remain the same. A brief analysis of them will help us to understand American courts.

The English created a multilevel system of courts, allowing a person to bring a case in one court and permitting a different court to study it for any errors. The lowest court was the hundred, a court of general jurisdiction where trials began. Appeals went to the County Court and then to the Witena Gemote, the king's advisory council. Minor and special interest courts existed for particular cases. For example, a magistrate's court decided petty criminal offenses, a justice of the peace court handled local matters, family court decided domestic relations cases, and an admiralty court settled law suits arising from accidents at sea. In America, we have two court systems, the federal courts and the state courts.

Federal System

Article III of the Constitution creates one Supreme Court and such inferior courts as the Congress wants to create. In exercising this delegated power, the Congress established two inferior courts and several special interest courts.

The lowest federal court is the district court. At least one of these courts exists for each of the states and territories. It is a court of record and has original jurisdiction. Appeals go to the court of appeals. Eleven of these courts exist throughout the country. These courts have appellate jurisdiction only. A final appeal may be taken to the Supreme Court in Washington, D.C. This court of last resort has appellate jurisdiction over all federal courts and original jurisdiction in cases affecting ambassadors and disputes among the states. Also, Congress set up several special jurisdiction courts. The Tax Court decides questions arising under the Internal Revenue Code; a Customs and Patent Appeals Court hears cases involving import duties and patents; and a Court of Claims settles suits against the United States government. See Table 2-2.

State System

Courts in the state system also follow the English pattern of multi-level structures. However, the names, organizational patterns and jurisdictional authority differ among the fifty states. Only general observations can be made about state courts.

All states have courts of original jurisdiction, often called circuit court, county court, court of common pleas, or district court. These courts may have powers to hear civil and criminal cases, award legal and equitable remedies, fine and imprison people. Appeals go to some intermediate court of appeal. Frequently, this court is not a separate entity, but exists as a part of the lower court. The appellate division of the district court is one example of such a court. These courts have appellate jurisdiction, but in some states they may have original jurisdiction in certain matters. A court of last resort, from which no appeal can be taken, must exist in each state. It may be called the supreme court, supreme judicial court, or the supreme court of errors. Numerous special interest courts exist in the states as well. Probate courts supervise the collection and distribution of a deceased's property, traffic courts apply motor vehicle laws, and family courts decide questions of divorce and child custody. Many states have small claims courts, where individuals with small damage suits can argue their own cases before a judge.

JURISDICTION

Jurisdiction is the power of a court to decide certain types of cases. Before a court can accept a case, it must have authority from the Constitution or the legislature over the subject matter of the case. Also, the disputing parties or their property must be within the territorial limits of the court. If either of these elements is missing, the case will be dismissed by the court because it lacks authority to hear and decide the case. Learning something about jurisdiction will show us how the government regulates the types of disputes its courts will settle, and will enable us to contrast court jurisdiction with administrative agency jurisdiction.

Federal Court Jurisdiction

A federal court has jurisdiction to hear three broad types of cases: those involving a federal question, diversity of citizenship cases where the amount in dispute exceeds $10,000, and cases removed to it. A federal question case is one arising from the federal Constitution, laws passed by Congress, or treaties made by the United States. Diversity of citizenship cases in federal jurisdiction are those in which the plaintiff and defendant are from different states and the suit is for more than $10,000. Cases can be removed to federal courts by a defendant who is sued in a state court where he or she is a nonresident. Federal courts possess the last two types of jurisdiction in order to reduce local bias against out-of-state defendants. Cases not falling within one of these three subject areas must be brought to state courts.

State Court Jurisdiction

Within the states, each court has jurisdiction to hear certain types of cases. A lawsuit must be brought to the appropriate court having jurisdiction over the case. For example, the state of Connecticut has two lower courts, the Superior Court and the Court of Common Pleas. Common Pleas has authority to hear civil cases up to $15,000 and criminal cases where the fine or imprisonment does not exceed $5,000 or five years. All other cases must begin in the Superior Court. A person must consult the laws of each state to determine the

TABLE 2-1. AMERICAN COURT STRUCTURES

Typical Court System	Federal Courts	Connecticut Courts	New York Courts	California Courts
Court of Last Resort	Supreme Court	Supreme Court	Court of Appeals	Supreme Court
Intermediate Court of Appeals	Court of Appeals	Appellate Session of the Superior Court	Appellate Division of the Supreme Court	District Court of Appeals
Trial Court	District Court	Court of Common Pleas Superior Court	Supreme Court	Superior Court
Special Courts	Tax Court Court of Claims Court of Customs and Patent Appeals	Small Claims Court Probate Court Juvenile Court	Family Court Surrogates Court City Court County Court	Municipal Court Justice Court

31

TABLE 2-2. FEDERAL COURT CITATIONS

Court	Abbreviation
Supreme Court	U.S.
	L.Ed
	S.Ct.
Court of Appeals	F.
District Court	F.Supp.

appropriate court in which to begin a lawsuit. Picking the wrong court results in a dismissal.

Jurisdiction Over the Person or Property

Both federal and state courts must have jurisdiction over the person, or in some cases over the property, involved in the case. This type of jurisdiction guarantees that the court will have the power to enforce its decisions. For a criminal case, the defendant must be physically within the court's geographic territory before any trial can start. If the defendant is convicted, the penalty will be applied directly against his or her person. In those cases where the remedy will be against the property of the defendant, actual presence before the court is not necessary. For example, if a lawsuit seeks to seize property to pay an overdue debt, it is directed against the defendant's property, not the defendant personally. Thus, only that property must be within the territory of the court. A person without property in a court's territory or who is not physically present in the court cannot be sued in that court. An exception exists for out-of-state business corporations.

Jurisdiction Over Nonresident Corporations

Most states have enacted "long-arm" statutes. These laws permit a resident of one state to sue, in the state court, a corporation or individual from another state. The suit can be brought even if no property is in the state. Certain conditions must exist before the suit can be heard by the local state court. Some business must be transacted by the defendant in the plaintiff's state. As a result of that business, the plaintiff must have suffered some injury. If the plaintiff wins the case, the decision can be enforced in the defendant's home state by those courts. The theory that permits this exception is that a business consents to be sued in whatever state it transacts business.

A typical state long-arm statute reads: Any person, whether or not a citizen or resident of this state, who in person or through another, transacts any business within this state, thereby submits to the jurisdiction of the courts of this state as to any cause of action arising out of any of the business transacted here.

A state law similar to this was the basis for a lawsuit in an Illinois state court against a corporation from Wisconsin. This corporation sent its employee into Illinois to deliver certain appliances. While unloading the merchandise, the employee pushed some of it onto the plaintiff's hand, crushing it. In permitting the suit in the Illinois courts, the Supreme Court of that state ruled that since the employee received the benefits of Illinois law while in the state, the corporation should be subject to the jurisdiction of the Illinois court. The court added that no mechanical test exists for determining jurisdiction over a nonresident corporation. The only requirement is that the law subjecting the corporation to suit be reasonable and give adequate notice to the defendant of the claim against it.

TRIAL PROCEDURES

Courts have the power to establish the procedures for bringing cases before them. Since we have a great number of courts in the United States, trial procedures will differ considerably throughout the country. But since our legal systems all developed from English roots, there are some similarities in the procedures of all courts. We will examine these elements common to all court proceedings. In the next chapter, court procedures will be contrasted with administrative agency procedures. Six stages exist in the judicial system:

1. Jurisdiction

The plaintiff must show the legal basis upon which the case comes into the court. This means he or she must show federal or state court authority to hear the case, and power of the court over the person or property of the defendant.

2. Pleadings

Once the jurisdictional requirements are satisfied, the plaintiff must tell the court and defendant about the case. This is done by the complaint, a summary of the facts and law of the controversy with a request for some remedy. Copies of the complaint are sent to the court and to the defendant. Also given to the defendant are a summons ordering an appearance at trial and a subpoena requesting documents needed by the court. The procedure for giving the complaint, summons and the subpoena to the defendant is service of process.

Upon receipt of the complaint, the defendant must file an answer. In this response, the defendant must admit, deny, or raise any defenses to the allegations contained in the complaint. Various motions can be made by either party to test the strength of the complaint and answer. Some motions are procedural: questioning the method of serving the complaint on the defendant, attacking the authority of the court to hear the case, or alleging that the wrong persons are sued. Other motions are substantive: attacking the legal theory of the case or protesting the sufficiency of information contained in the complaint or answer. The judge allows the other party a reasonable opportunity to respond to each motion raised before he or she rules on it. The judge may order corrections in the documents filed with the court or order the case to proceed. The complaint, answer, and motions are referred to as the pleadings.

3. Pretrial Conference

After the pleadings are completed, the judge should have a good understanding of the nature of the case and of the areas of agreement and disagreement between the parties and an estimate of the chances for compromise. The areas of disagreement are the issues of the case, and it is these issues that are assigned to the trial for settlement. However, most courts now require cases to go to a pretrial conference. This conference attempts to get the parties to settle their dispute without a formal trial. It consists of a meeting between the judge and the lawyers for the parties. They discuss the case informally, seeking a compromise. If none is possible, the judge will determine a list of all disputed facts contained in the complaint. These factual disputes will be left for the jury to settle. Then, each disputed meaning of a law in the case is listed. These will be decided by the judge at a later time. This conference encourages compromise and speeds up the trial process.

4. The Trial

Upon completion of the pleadings and pretrial conference, the case is ready for trial. A trial is a study of the facts and law in a case for the purpose of deciding the disputed issues. It is an adversary proceeding, where the judge's role is passive. Lawyers for the parties present their arguments on behalf of their clients, hoping to persuade the judge and jury. Competition between lawyers will enable the court to sort out the truth and arrive at a just solution of the dispute. This adversary system is an outgrowth of the ancient trial by battle. Instead of placing individual litigants in physical combat, today's system puts lawyers in verbal combat.

The trial begins with jury selection. A list of potential jurors comes from voting lists. Lawyers ask each potential juror certain questions to see if he or she has any bias that could influence the outcome of the case. Those persons with bias are excused. With the appropriate number of jurors chosen, the clerk of the court then makes jurors take an oath to carry out their legal duties in a fair manner. Then each attorney makes an opening statement summarizing the case to the jury. Evidence must then be presented to prove each of the disputed issues of fact and law. The opposing attorney has the right to challenge the truthfulness of each piece of evidence presented. This is cross-examination.

When both sides finish the presentation of evidence and the cross-examination, each attorney makes a closing statement to the jury. These statements summarize what took place during the trial and what remedies the jury and judge should give. The judge will then instruct the jury on how they should reach a conclusion to the case and what laws they must apply. This is the judge's charge to the jury. The jury then retires for deliberation of the case and formulation of a verdict. All jury discussions are secret. When they have completed their deliberations, the jury announces the verdict to the court. The judge will accept this verdict if it appears reasonable and issue the judgment, confirming the jury's verdict and ordering appropriate remedies to the winning party. The losing party either accepts this judgment or requests a stay in the execution of remedies pending an appeal to a higher court.

5. Appeal

The losing party may appeal to a higher court, requesting it to review the case for errors. Higher courts exist to guarantee the fairness of a trial and to clarify any ambiguities in the law resulting from the trial. To get an appeal, the losing party must show that some material error occurred during the trial that may have made a difference in the outcome of the proceeding. Some grounds for appeal would be the judge's failure to apply the law correctly, a defective charge to the jury, improper evidence submitted in the trial, incorrect court procedures, or newly discovered evidence. In some cases, the losing party has a right to appeal regardless of any errors in the trial. Also, some court procedures permit a judge to send a case to a higher court for settlement if he or she is unable to reach a judgment on the law.

Appellate procedures differ from those followed in the trial. First, the judge examines only legal issues from the trial, not facts decided by the jury. Second, lawyers for the parties present their arguments to the appellate court without witnesses, documents, or other evidence. Third, sometimes more than one judge sits on the appellate court. They listen to the arguments, review the trial records, and reach a decision. This decision may affirm the trial court, reverse it, or send the case back to the trial court for additional work. Any decision must be supported by an opinion giving reasons for the ruling. This opinion is important because it analyzes the law of the case and any prior precedents and becomes a guide for deciding similar cases in the future. A final appeal would be to the court of last resort. Its decision becomes the final stage of the appellate procedure.

Two concepts in the law make the judgment of the court of last resort final—res judicata and the "full faith and credit" clause of the United States Constitution. Res judicata means "the thing is litigated" and provides a conclusive ending to the dispute. The suit can never be brought to court again, thus preventing the losing party from taking chances a second time in a different court. "Res judicata prevents the relitigation of issues disposed of in an earlier case." (*Muller Corp.* v. *Gazocean International*, 394 F. Supp. 1246, 1975.)

The Constitution states that each state must give full faith and credit to the court decisions of another state. This means that if one state court reaches a final decision in a particular case, all other state courts must enforce it. This prevents an unsuccessful defendant from moving to another state merely to avoid paying court judgments. If the defendant flees to a foreign country, enforcement of American court decisions depends upon whether a treaty between the United States and the foreign nation requires enforcement.

6. Enforcement

After completion of all appellate remedies, the judgment becomes final, and enforcement will follow. Let us assume the plaintiff received a judgment of $5,000 for injuries incurred as a result of a defendant's wrongful conduct. The defendant must pay over this amount. If not, the court can issue an order of execution, directing the seizure of defendant's property to pay the judgment. If not enough property exists, then the court can order a garnishment, requiring someone who owes the defendant money to pay it to the plaintiff instead. The plaintiff can recover any property transferred out of the defendant's name. A defendant can avoid paying the judgment by declaring bankruptcy or not paying the judgment until expiration of the statute of limitations.

A judgment may call for more than just the payment of money. It may order specific performance. This compels a person to do some act, such as sell property to the plaintiff. Also the court may issue an injunction. This orders the defendant to stop some specific act, often one that is illegal, deceptive, or fraudulent.

CLASS ACTION SUITS

At times, the wrongful acts by a defendant injure more than one person. For example, a company may overcharge its customers by price fixing and injure thousands of people. If each of these persons sued separately, the costs and time for trial would be too great for most people to assume. To remedy this problem, courts allow a class action suit. This legal device allows all plaintiffs who have similar disputes to combine their separate suits into one case. It is a quicker and less expensive technique for deciding cases involving similar facts

TABLE 2-3. TRIAL STAGES

Jurisdiction:	Federal or state court system
	Proper court within the system
	Person or property before the court
Pleadings:	Complaint (facts, law, and remedy requested)
	Answer (admit, deny, and defenses)
	Motions (procedural and substantive)
Pretrial Conference:	Compromise
	Issues determined
Trial:	Jury selection
	Opening statements
	Evidence and cross-examination
	Closing arguments
	Charge to jury
	Jury verdict
	Judgment
Appeal:	Grounds for appeal
	Arguments
	Decision and opinion
	Res judicata
	Full faith and credit
Enforcement:	Property seizure
	Garnishment
	Injunction
	Specific performance

and seeking similar remedies. The class action suit is popular in securities and antitrust proceedings against business and its managers. But certain conditions must exist before this device can be used.

Eisen v. Carlisle and Jacquelin
94 S. Ct. 2140 (1974)

Mr. Justice Powell.

On May 2, 1966, Eisen filed a class action on behalf of himself and all other odd lot traders on the New York Stock Exchange. The complaint alleged that Carlisle and Jacquelin overcharged such traders by imposing a surcharge on the standard brokerage commission. The differential was twelve and one-half cents per share on stocks trading above forty dollars. A critical fact in this litigation is that Eisen's individual stake in the damage award he seeks is only seventy dollars. No competent attorney would undertake this complex case to recover so minor an amount. Economic reality dictated that this suit proceed as a class action or not at all.

The District Court ruled the suit could proceed as a class action and, after finding that two and a quarter million members of the class could be identified by name and address, ordered notification to be sent to each of them. This would cost $225,000. The District Court also ordered the defendant to share in the costs of mailing out the notices of the class action. The Court of Appeals held that the law required individual notice to all identifiable class members and that the costs of the notice expense should fall on Eisen. We affirm.

We find the District Court's resolution of the notice problem was erroneous in two respects. First, it failed to comply with the notice requirements; and second, it imposed part of the notice expense on defendants. The law provides that in any class action suit, each member of the class shall be advised that he has the right to exclude himself from the action on request or to enter an appearance through counsel; and further, that the judgment will bind all class members not requesting exclusion. To this end, the court must send to class members the best possible notice practicable under the circumstances, including individual notice to all members who can be identified through reasonable effort. Publication notice in newspapers is not adequate where the names and addresses of the class members are known. In the present case, the names and addresses of 2,250,000 class members are easily ascertainable, and there is nothing to show that individual members cannot be notified through the mails. Eisen's effort to impose part of the cost of notice on the defendants must fail. The usual rule is that a plaintiff must initially bear the cost of notice to the class.

Where, as here, the relationship between the parties is truly adversarial, the plaintiff must pay for the cost of notice as part of the ordinary burden of financing his own suit. Since Eisen has consistently refused to pay for the costs of individual notice, we remand the case with instructions to dismiss the class action.

Dissent. When there is a question of law or fact common to persons of a numerous class, one or more of them, whose claims or defenses are representative of the claims or defenses of all and who will fairly and adequately protect the interests of all, may sue or be sued on behalf of all. Such a rule would provide six requirements for a class action: a class, numerous members, common questions of law or fact, impracticability of joinder, representative claim or defense, and fair representation.

A class action serves not only the convenience of the parties but the prompt, efficient administration of justice. I think in our society there are bound to be innumerable people in common disasters, calamities, or ventures who would go begging for justice without the class action but who could with all regard to due process be protected. The class action is one of the few legal remedies the small claimant has against those who command the status quo.

CASE QUESTIONS

1. *Describe the practical limitations on the use of the class action suit.*
2. *How does "justice go begging" in this case?*
3. *When must the defendant share in the expenses of notifying class members?*

Before moving to the next chapter, some further comments about the trial process are worth noting. The outcome of a trial should be the truth. Trials must proceed according to constitutional safeguards, some of which are discussed in the following chapter. The judgment of the court should be based on a rational analysis of the facts and law of the case. It should not be decided on arbitrary applications of law or through overpowering physical strength. Yet at times, jury decisions are based on extraneous factors, such as a lawyer's behavior or the conduct of witness, or on overall impressions. As an example of jury misconduct, consider the case of a young man accused of stealing an automobile. At the trial, evidence against him was overwhelming, but he was nice looking and friendly, while the automobile owner was oppressive and hostile. The jury deliberated and found the defendant not guilty, provided that he return the car. One humorist characterized a jury's performance in a criminal case as follows: "When th' case is all over, the jury'll pitch th' testimony out iv the window an' consider three questions—Did the [man] look as though he'd kill his wife? Did his wife look as though she ought to be kilt? Isn't it time we wint to supper?" (Peter Finley Dunne, *Mr. Dooley in Peace and War*, "On Expert Testimony," 1898.)

To the extent that a jury acts in the ways described above, trials are defective. But it is a defect that cannot be cured. We have established rules for the conduct of a trial, admission of evidence, grounds for appeal, etc. But we have no way of preventing a jury from deciding cases on irrelevant features of the case or subconscious biases, or even from falling asleep during the course of a trial. There is, however, no known substitute for the trial-by-jury system. When a factual dispute arises—one person's word against another's—who is best able to decide the truth? In the absence of divine intervention, collective judgment by our fellow citizens seems more appropriate to determining the truth than does leaving the choice up to the judge, a computer, a governmental board, or a lie detector test. With all its defects, the jury system has sustained a long life and seems to have accomplished justice in a substantial majority of the cases brought before it.

REVIEW QUESTIONS

1. Why have the courts failed to meet some of the demands currently made on them? Explain how their failures can be remedied.
2. How does a court carry out each of the functions of law?
3. Define a court and explain some of its major characteristics.
4. Describe the participants in a court and the role each plays.
5. Contrast the following:
    a. court of record
    b. court not of record
    c. general jurisdiction
    d. special jurisdiction
    e. original jurisdiction
    f. appellate jurisdiction

    g. federal courts
    h. state courts

6. Diagram the courts of your state and indicate the authority of each court to hear cases.

7. Define jurisdiction and explain its different meanings.

8. Explain each trial stage and show how each stage is important in settling disputes between the parties.

9. Explain the meaning of "res judicata" and "full faith and credit."

10. Define a class action suit and explain its importance to settling disputes.

3

THE ADMINISTRATIVE PROCESS

One of the commissioners attending a session of an administrative agency asked the chairman to excuse him from attending the meeting because he couldn't hear well out of one ear. "The request denied," ruled the chairman. "You only need one good ear. This is an investigative hearing and it will be listening to just one side of the case anyway."

This chapter begins our study of the administrative process—authority and procedures of government commissions whose members have the duty of carrying out business regulatory laws. These commissions are administrative or regulatory agencies. A study of their purposes and operations is important for us because of the significant impact agencies have on business and on the American system of government. To see how important these agencies are for us, consider some of the effects they have on our society.

The Constitution of the United States creates three branches of government—a legislature to make laws, a judiciary to explain the meaning of those laws, and an executive branch to enforce the laws. This division of government functions is called the separation of powers. It is unique to our system and is intended to limit the possible abuse of power by government officials. Each branch of government restricts the power of the other branches. However, the administrative agency is not a part of the three original branches of government. It is not created by the federal Constitution but established by the legislature, and it unites all three governmental powers into one commission.

Most administrative agencies have legislative powers to make rules and establish rates, executive powers to enforce their orders, and judicial powers to hold hearings and settle disputes over the meaning of their own orders and decisions. In overruling a challenge to an order of the Interstate Commerce Commission, a federal administrative agency, the Court of Appeals stated, "... administrative bodies, such as the ICC, created by Congress to carry into effect legislative policies ... act in part legislatively and in part judicially (and carry out executive functions) and the authority of Congress, in creating agencies, cannot well be doubted." (*ICC* v. *Chatsworth*, 347 F.2d 821 1965.) The unification of these separate powers into one tribunal alters our system of government. Administrative agencies become a fourth branch of government, without the restrictions on possible abuse of power by government officials that apply to the other branches.

Although most people are unaware of their importance, agencies have a direct effect on the daily life of every American. Agencies help to decide the kind of television viewers see, the types of products consumers can buy, the fares paid for shipping merchandise and transporting people, the amount of credit available to borrowers, and the cost to homeowners for their electricity, gas, and other utilities.

Administrative agencies affect all phases of business operations. The key steps for a manufacturing company are to design a product, raise capital to build it, hire employees, acquire physical facilities, manufacture the product, market it, and return a profit to the owners. At each step, the manager must make critical decisions affecting capital, labor, product, and customers. Administrative regulations have a direct effect on the manager's decision-making processes. Procedures must be established to insure that decisions are in conformity with agency rules and regulations.

In this chapter, we will study the operations of administrative agencies. Comparisons with the judicial process will be made. When reading the text and cases, we should see the importance of the agencies to consumers affected by agency decisions, to business people required to comply with agency rules, and to citizens whose liberties may be endangered by agency operations. A brief historical summary of agency development shows us how agencies came into existence.

DEVELOPMENT OF ADMINISTRATIVE AGENCIES

Some historians trace the origins of administrative agencies to the medieval guilds. Guilds, associations of merchants and craftsmen, were organized to promote the welfare and protection of their members. Funds paid money to sick or disabled members, a police force protected trading caravans from attackers, and regulatory codes attempted to insure product quality, fix production quotas, and stabilize prices. In addition guilds established internal enforcement procedures to punish members who violated regulatory codes.

In many ways, the guilds acted like modern administrative agencies. They made laws, enforced them, and settled disputes involving the members. But guilds were private organizations, separate from governments. Administrative agencies are public commissions, acting as a part of government.

Perhaps the earliest governmental administrative agency in the English legal system was the Curia Regis (Kings Council). The Curia had governmental powers that were delegated to it from the king. It helped make laws for the English people and aided in the enforcement of those laws. Early settlers in this country followed the concept of the Curia. For example, commissions determined colonial borders in the western territories. By the end of the eighteenth century, the states had administrative agencies; for example, Vermont set up a special magistrate to regulate prices charged by ferry boats operating within its waterways. After the Civil War, intensive lobbying by the Grange Movement influenced many states to establish agencies regulating railroads. The Grange was a national organization of farmers concerned over the high costs charged for shipping agricultural products to the cities and the poor service given shippers. Most states created railroad regulatory commissions to supervise the operations of railroads and to adopt rules eliminating unfair practices toward farmers.

Although states created numerous agencies, the national government created very few. Most politicians feared centralizing too much power in the federal government, and most problems facing the country were local, not national. But as America industrialized, national problems emerged. Railroads became large multistate businesses, making state regulation of them ineffective. Large business corporations accumulated substantial capital which enabled them to control state governments. Congress responded to these new challenges by creating several regulatory agencies. It created the Interstate Commerce Commission in 1887 to regulate railroad rates and service on interstate transportation. In 1914, Congress set up the Federal Trade Commission to supervise the expansion of business corporations.

With the stock market crash of 1929 and the resulting depression, the country faced different problems. To prevent business from using fraud or deception in raising money for its operations, Congress established the Securities and Exchange Commission to police the stock and bond markets. Other agencies formed by Congress regulated banking, labor, electrical power, agriculture, and unemployment. Currently, the trend toward creating special agencies to solve national problems continues. Questions of racial discrimination in our society, riots, campus disorders, product hazards, and presidential assassination are turned over to agencies rather than to the courts for solutions. Since the trend is increasing, we should attempt to understand why national problems are sent to the administrative agency.

ADVANTAGES OF THE AGENCY FORM

Legal experts give several reasons for the wide use of administrative agencies. We should evaluate the merits of each reason in relation to the costs to our system of government. Some advantages are:

Flexibility

The size and complexity of modern business operations makes effective business regulation extremely difficult. Regulating corporations requires a streamlined organization with the speed to act before some threatened injury to the public takes place and to make regulatory policy without extensive delays. The organization needs an ability to conduct its proceedings informally and to enforce its own orders. It must be able to supervise the daily, routine operations of a company.

Neither the courts nor the legislature can perform all of these functions. A court makes its decisions based upon complaints from an injured person. Its hearings are formal, conducted according to precise rules of procedure and evidence. When one party in a lawsuit is more powerful than the other party, a lawsuit is inappropriate since delays and the resulting costs can nullify justice. The legislature makes broad guidelines for governmental action. It cannot be occupied with routine, minor matters affecting only one or a few companies. Also, wealthy corporations can influence legislators better than individual members of the public can. Our modern administrative agency is the streamlined organization created to assume these extensive powers. It combines the three governmental functions of making, interpreting, and enforcing laws concerning business regulation.

Expertise

To make regulation effective, regulators must know the details of the regulated business. An administrative agency can hire technical experts who have prior knowledge of the regulated industry and an understanding of company problems. These experts can devote all their working time to investigating and remedying particular problems. For example, solutions to aircraft safety problems require a detailed knowledge of aerodynamics. The layman lacks this knowledge, but an administrative agency can hire staff who already know this field. It is more expedient for them to make and enforce rules in their areas of expertise than for a judge or legislator to do so. In a trial, the judge is impartial without any precise knowledge of industry problems. Legislators lack the time to acquire detailed knowledge of industry problems.

Experimentation

An administrative agency has the option of trying out a solution for a business problem on one company before using that solution for all companies and can adapt a solution after testing it on a company. Neither a legislature nor a court has the time to observe and modify proposed solutions to problems affecting one segment of the national economy.

Localized Remedies

An administrative agency can apply national policy to meet local conditions. For example, Congress established a national policy toward recognition of unions as bargaining agents for employees. But Congress left to the National Labor Relations Board, an administrative agency, the duty of determining when a particular union is the representative of employees at a company plant. Labor policy is uniform throughout the country, but is applied by the NLRB to meet local needs. Often localized administration can permit the modification of national policy to fit the needs of one region of the country. Under price controls, an agency can adjust prices for each part of the country to reflect different labor, transportation, and raw material costs.

In summary, administrative agencies have become popular with political scientists because they can carry out a systematic plan of business regulation where the need for flexible, expert, and local administration cannot be met by the traditional methods of the judicial, legislative, and executive branches of government. As stated by the Supreme Court of Connecticut, "The [agency] is [part] of the state. Throughout the years, the number of such agencies has increased in both the federal and the state governments because the problems facing legislative bodies are such that without the agency many important laws beneficial to the public could not be administered." (*Roan v. Connecticut Industrial Building Commission*, 189 A.2d 399, 1963.) To see how important administrative agencies are to our society, an analysis of the different types of agencies can be helpful. Agencies can be differentiated by their powers, their level of government operation, their status, and by the proceedings they can conduct.

POWERS OF ADMINISTRATIVE AGENCIES

The powers given to an agency are set forth in the law establishing the agency. That law must be read to find out the exact authority of an agency. But every agency can have one or more of the powers listed below. As you read about these powers, you should remember that the law defines these powers broadly. Also, courts frequently give the agency broad discretion in carrying out its powers. Consequently, most agencies have the power to act as a legislator, making rules; a prosecutor, investigating violations of its rules; a judge and jury, determining the guilt of persons violating agency rules; and a police officer, enforcing agency orders.

Legislative Powers

The legislature is the official law making body. It cannot delegate this power to other bodies of government. But the courts allow the legislature to transfer some of its lawmaking powers to an administrative agency if guidelines are given to the agency. "In creating an agency to administer a law complete in itself and designed to accomplish a particular purpose, the legislature must establish precise standards to carry out the law or lay down an intelligible principle to which the agency must conform, although the agency may be authorized to adopt rules and regulations to execute the provisions of the law." (*Roan* v. *Connecticut Industrial Building Commission*, 189 A.2d 399, 1963.)

A legislature cannot delegate lawmaking authority but there can be a transfer of "rule-making" powers. There is a fine line separating these powers. Agencies can make rules, rates, and regulations that have the force and effect of law if given a detailed policy statement on how to make its orders comply with legislative policy. The agency must keep its rules, rates, and regulations within the limits of the detailed policy statement. And, Congress must make "... a proper regard for the protection of the public interest and afford a resort to the courts for the protection of both public and private rights." (*Jennings* v. *Connecticut Light and Power Co.*, 103 A.2d 535, 1954.) Some examples of a proper transfer of rule-making authority to an agency are: the power to set up requirements for a license; the right to formulate rules for paying the minimum wage; the determination of standards for product safety; the right to fix charges for services; and the power to order changes in fixed standards. But agencies cannot be given lawmaking powers to determine what acts are crimes, establish zoning standards, or fix tax rates.

Investigative Powers

An agency can act as a prosecutor, obtaining evidence of possible violations of agency rules by a person or business. It can then file charges against the violators. These powers are part of its investigative authority. An agency can investigate to obtain facts necessary to make rules and set rates in an informed manner. It can also conduct investigations to see if its orders are being carried out. This means an agency can subpoena witnesses to appear before its investigators and require them to turn over business documents relevant to its inquiry. Information obtained during this investigation can be used against the accused person or business in a later hearing before the agency or in a court trial. Usually, proceedings are conducted under oath. Any failure to comply with an agency investigation can result in criminal penalties. As part of their investigative powers, agencies can require businesses to keep records in a prescribed form and turn them over to the agency at any time in the future. This information can be used to recommend new laws to the legislature and as a basis for new rules adopted by the agency.

Judicial Powers

An administrative agency can act as both judge and jury. Judicial powers are delegated to an agency so it can decide if charges filed against a person or business are valid. Since many of the proceedings before an agency are technical in nature, calling a jury to decide disputed facts would be time consuming and expensive. Combining fact finding and law interpretation in one place expedites the determination of guilt or innocence. When an agency acts in its judicial capacity, it must follow due process rules. But due process before an agency is not the same as before a court. Cases discussed in the next chapter clearly illustrate this distinction.

Enforcement Powers

The typical administrative agency has police powers to enforce its rules and orders. Public opinion is one common method. News releases issued to the media call public attention to a violation of agency orders by a person or business. The community often pressures the violator into complying with an agency order. This technique is effective when the violation does not cause any immediate harm to the public. Jawboning against companies raising prices and pollution alerts by local environmental protection agencies are some examples.

If this method is unsuccessful, court action may be necessary. The laws creating most administrative agencies give them the power to issue cease-and-desist orders and to seek injunctions from courts to stop violations of agency orders. Noncompliance with either remedy can be punished by the court's contempt power. The National Labor Relations Board frequently requests an injunction to stop unfair labor practices by either an employer or a union.

Some laws give private persons the right to sue for the violation of an agency order. If successful, the person obtains a money judgment from the violator. For example, if the Federal Trade Commission finds a company in violation of certain sections of the antitrust laws, a person injured by the company can sue for three times any financial losses suffered. See Table 1-2.

If a violation of an agency order poses an immediate threat to the public health or safety, some agencies can take emergency action to stop the threat. Their inspectors can seize or destroy any property causing the danger. They can require immediate repairs to reduce the hazard. This action can be taken before the agency or a court determines if there is a real threat to the public. In cases of suspected food contamination, inspectors from the Food and Drug Administration can take impure foods off the market before allowing an agency hearing or a court appeal. Also, inspectors from the Occupational Safety and Health Administration can order immediate repairs to hazardous job conditions at a factory. If the repairs are not made, the factory can be closed before a hearing determines if any safety hazard exists.

TYPES OF ADMINISTRATIVE AGENCIES

Several methods of classification of agencies are possible:

1. Level of Government

Administrative agencies exist on the federal, state, and local levels of government. Agencies at each level of government can regulate activities of business that fall within their jurisdiction. A business manager must comply with all regulations issued by agencies at each government level. Compliance can be difficult when we consider the variety of agencies in existence. Some major agencies and their authorities are shown in the following chart:

TABLE 3-1. ADMINISTRATIVE AGENCIES

A. Federal Agencies. Every segment of our national economy is regulated by a federal agency.
   1. Transportation
      - Department of Transportation (DOT), administers transportation policy and regulates highway safety.
      - Interstate Commerce Commission (ICC), regulates truck, railroad, and pipeline transportation between states.
      - Civil Aeronautics Board (CAB), regulates airline routes and fares.
      - Federal Aviation Administration (FAA), regulates aircraft and airport safety, certifies pilots.
      - Federal Maritime Commission (FMC), regulates shipping on all navigable waterways.
   2. Utilities
      - Federal Energy Administration (FEA), establishes oil and gas allocation system.
      - Nuclear Regulatory Commission (NRC), supervises atomic energy plants and procedures.
      - Federal Power Commission (FPC), regulates electrical industry.
      - Tennessee Valley Authority (TVA), generates and sells electrical power.
   3. Finance
      - Department of the Treasury, carries out financial transactions for the United States and manages the federal debt.
      - Securities and Exchange Commission (SEC), regulates sales of stocks and bonds and financial markets.
      - Federal Reserve System (FRS), regulates banking and credit.
      - Comptroller of the Currency, shares regulatory authority over banking with the FRS.
      - Federal Deposit Insurance Corporation (FDIC), insures savings accounts.
      - Small Business Administration (SBA), extends financial help and management expertise to small businesses.
   4. Employment
      - Department of Labor, administers labor laws, supervises job safety and pension plans, collects employment data.
      - National Labor Relations Board (NLRB), regulates union-management relations.
      - Occupational Safety and Health Administration (OSHA), regulates employment safety.
      - Equal Employment Opportunity Commission (EEOC), regulates job discrimination.
      - Federal Mediation and Conciliation Service (FMCS), aids settlement of labor disputes.
   5. Agriculture
      - Department of Agriculture (DOA), establishes crop subsidies and allocations, administers food stamps, and carries out farm policies.
      - Rural Electrification Administration (REA), regulates electrical power in rural areas.

6. Manufacture
    - Department of Commerce, administers business policies, gathers statistical data, encourages manufacturing and exports.
    - Consumer Product Safety Commission (CPSC), tests products for hazards and establishes product safety standards.
    - Environmental Protection Agency (EPA), coordinates government policy toward pollution control.
7. Marketing
    - Federal Trade Commission (FTC), regulates business expansion and marketing of products.
    - Food and Drug Administration (FDA), establishes health standards for food, drugs, and cosmetics.

B. State Agencies. The names and authority of state agencies vary widely but some typical ones are:
1. Workmen's Compensation Board, determines the money to be paid injured workers.
2. Motor Vehicle Department, regulates use of state highways, truck weights, and safety.
3. Alcoholic Beverage Control, regulates the sale of liquor in the state.
4. Public Utility Boards, regulates the rate charged by telephone, water, electricity, and gas companies.

C. Local Agencies. The names and authority of agencies existing in cities and towns also vary widely. Some representative local administrative agencies are:
1. Zoning Boards, regulates the types of buildings which can be erected in parts of the city or town.
2. Consumer Protection Agency, regulates business practices within the local area.
3. Municipal Inspectors, enforces building codes for the safety of buildings, conducts health and fire inspections.

It should be noted that some agencies have overlapping jurisdiction. A business can have the same action regulated by three different levels of agencies, each one regulating a part of the same action. For example, an electric utility wanting to raise its rates may have to consult with the city consumer protection agency, the state public utility board, and the Federal Power Commission. Also, some agencies on the federal level may regulate different aspects of the same business action. A company hiring new workers must comply with regulations of the NLRB regarding union membership, the EEOC regarding discriminatory hiring practices, and the OSHA regarding safe working conditions.

2. Status of the Agency

Agencies can be classified by their legal status. Those that are called independent exist and operate separate from any other branch of government. Members of independent agencies are appointed by the President and confirmed by the Senate. Each member has a fixed term of office. Members of dependent agencies are appointed by the head of the branch of government in which the agency exists. Members generally do not have a fixed term of office. Some important independent agencies are the ICC, NLRB, SEC, FTC, and the EEOC. Some major dependent agencies are: the Internal Revenue Service, a part of the Executive Department; General Accounting Office, a part of the Congress; and the Administrative Office of the United States, a part of the Supreme Court. In theory, the independent agency is less subject to political influence than is the dependent agency and therefore has more discretion and power to carry out business regulations. Independent agencies are not directly responsible to either the President or Congress for their actions. But Congress can influence agency action by limiting its appropriations, and the President can appoint new members sympathetic to the administration's views when vacancies occur.

3. Type of Proceeding

Administrative agencies may hold either investigative or adjudicative proceedings. The type of proceeding determines the powers and limits of agency actions. When making rules or setting rates, the agency must obtain facts to make an informed decision. It then holds investigative hearings where any interested party can present evidence. When the agency settles disputes between parties, it must also obtain evidence to make an informed decision. It then holds adjudicative hearings where the disputing parties can present evidence to prove a complaint and answer charges. When an agency holds adjudicative hearings, it is acting like a court and must follow due process rules. But when holding an investigative hearing, the agency does not affect the substantial rights of any parties, and therefore its proceedings can be more informal than those of a court. Cases in the next chapter show the practical effects of this distinction.

AGENCY OPERATIONS

There are more than fifty different agencies on the federal level and an uncounted number at the state and local levels of government. Each agency has its own system of operations. But there are some similarities in the way all agencies act.

1. Every agency owes its *existence* to some legal source. Some are created by specific references in a constitution, others by statutes passed by the legislature. There is no specific Constitutional authority for federal administrative agencies; the legal basis for every federal agency's existence is an act of Congress. Article I, Section 8, of the Constitution gives Congress the power to regulate interstate commerce and to pass all laws necessary and proper for carrying out this regulation. In creating agencies, Congress declares them to be necessary and proper for regulating some aspect of interstate commerce. The exact authority of each agency is determined by the law creating it.

2. Employees of administrative agencies consist of two types—members serving as commissioners and staff to assist the members. The *members* are appointed to their positions or elected by voters. One of the members becomes chairman of the agency. Most federal independent agency members are appointed by the President and confirmed by the Senate. Members of dependent agencies are appointed by the President, the Congress, or the Supreme Court, depending upon which branch of government they are a part of. Most state and local agency members are appointed by either the governor or the mayor, but a few are elected. For example, some states require election of public utility members, and voters in some cities elect zoning board members.

3. Most agencies employ *staff* to assist the members in carrying out agency work. The general counsel is an attorney hired to advise the agency on legal matters, to process lawsuits involving the agency, and to suggest new laws to improve agency effectiveness. The general counsel often employs other lawyers to work on research and case assignments. Also, law judges conduct hearings for the agency. Most agencies use technical experts to make investigations and advise the agency on scientific matters. Qualifications for these people depend upon the purpose of the agency. The job safety administration (OSHA) employs industrial physicians to determine health hazards in industry. The EPA uses environmental engineers to monitor industrial pollution. Economists work in the FTC on such matters as determining the effects of a business merger on the economy. Finally, each agency hires supporting staff—such as controllers, policy planners, public relations experts, secretaries, and clerks—to help perform its duties.

4. Each agency also has its own *organizational structure*. The law creating the agency will specify the organizational chart for it. Most federal agencies are similar, and the structure of the ICC is typical of the agencies we will study.

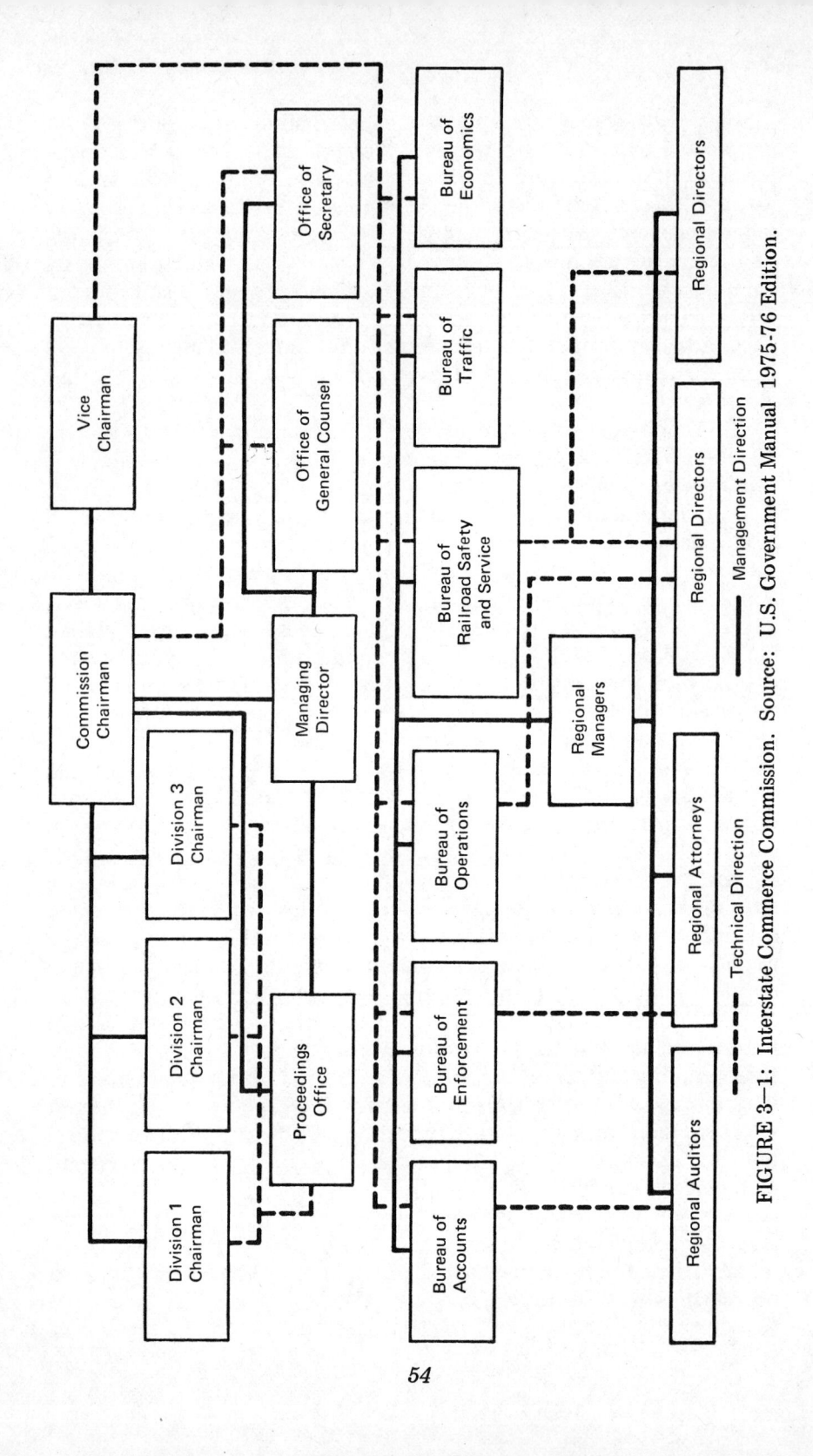

FIGURE 3–1: Interstate Commerce Commission. Source: U.S. Government Manual 1975-76 Edition.

AGENCY PROCEDURES

Federal agencies must follow the procedural rules contained in the Administrative Procedures Act (APA). Congress passed this law in 1946 to create a uniform system for agency procedures, eliminating the confusion of each agency adopting its own rules. However, this uniform law does not apply to state or local agencies. Their procedures are outlined in state and local laws. Since the Administrative Procedures Act is so important for an understanding of how agencies work, we will look at its major sections.

1. Hearings

Administrative agencies can conduct either adjudicative or investigative hearings. The APA allows different procedures for the two types of hearings.

A. Adjudication

> Section 554. "... in every case of adjudication required by statute to be determined on the record after opportunity for an agency hearing... persons entitled to notice of an agency hearing shall be timely informed of the time, place and nature thereof, the legal authority and jurisdiction under which the hearing is held and the matter of fact and law asserted.... The agency shall give all interested parties opportunity for the submission and consideration of facts, arguments... and ... hearing and decision upon notice...."

This section deals with the judicial functions of an agency. It requires an agency to notify all parties of an adjudicative hearing and to follow an orderly system for reaching a decision. This section does not tell us when this type of hearing is necessary. That is left to the courts to decide.

Sections 556 and 557 set out the hearing procedures. These procedures are similar to those followed in a court trial. Generally speaking, the adjudicative process begins with a complaint against a business. It tells the firm the accusations against it, the laws allegedly violated, the legal authority for the hearing into the allegations, and the time and place of the hearing. The complaint may be filed by the agency itself, a member of the general public, the person injured by the alleged violation, or the Attorney General of the United States. Both the complaint and a subpoena are sent to the accused.

Upon receipt of the complaint, the person must respond. This response may contain legal objections to the jurisdiction of the agency or its complaint or outline defenses to the accusation. For example, the response may allege that the agency has no authority to decide this type of accusation or that the hearing notice was inadequate or give reasons for the alleged violation.

After the response, agency procedures differ from court procedures. The agency investigates the facts of the complaint without waiting for a trial to produce evidence. Experts from the agency interview the parties involved in the proceeding. On-site inspection may be ordered. If this preliminary investigation reveals no basis for the complaint, it will be dismissed. But if the allegation seems true, the agency may decide to hold a hearing. An administrative law judge from the agency will meet with both parties and allow each to present evidence and witnesses to support their positions. No jury is present because the law judge is an expert in the field regulated by the agency. The hearing is not conducted before the full membership of the agency.

The law judge will make a recommendation at the conclusion of this hearing. In this decision, the law judge may uphold the complaint and grant the remedies requested, or dismiss it. Reasons must accompany the recommendation. Either party may ask for an appeal to the members of the agency. If it is granted, the members of the agency will review the entire proceeding. Its decision will either affirm, reverse, or modify the law judge's recommendations.

Hearings conducted by the law judge or the agency members do not follow the same rules as court trials. The agency can act more informally than a court, and thus arrive at its decision in a shorter time period. As stated in the case of *Rhodes Pharmacal Co.* v. *FTC*, 208 F.2d 382 (1954), "We recognize that the rule is well established that evidence which would be excluded in an ordinary lawsuit may, under many circumstances, be received on hearings before an administrative agency. The Supreme Court has stated ... 'technical rules for exclusion of evidence applicable in jury trials do not apply to proceedings before federal administrative agencies in the absence of a statutory requirement that such rules are to be observed.' "

The APA encourages a voluntary settlement of disputes. At any stage of these proceedings, the agency may accept a negotiated compromise in the case and issue a consent decree. This decree contains a settlement agreeable to the government and the accused person and binds all parties involved in the case. Acceptance of a consent decree does not mean the accused party admits violating the law.

B. Investigation

Section 553 b. "General notice of proposed rule making shall be published in the Federal Register.... The notice shall include a statement of the time, place and nature of public rule making proceedings ... and either the terms ... of the proposed rule or a description of the subjects and issues involved...."

This section deals with the legislative functions of administrative agencies. It requires agencies to notify all persons of every new rule or rate proposed. This notice is given in the *Federal Register*, a daily newspaper published by the government containing information about its activities. This section does not tell us when a hearing must be held before the new rule becomes effective. Generally, hearings are not needed if the agency determines a hearing to be impracticable, unnecessary, or contrary to the public interest. Courts must decide if the agency improperly adopted a new rule without adequate hearings.

Pharmaceutical Manufacturers Association v. Finch
307 F. Supp. 858 (1970)

Latchum, District Judge

The Pharmaceutical Manufacturers Association (PMA), on behalf of its members, seeks a preliminary injunction restraining the Secretary of Health, Education and Welfare (the secretary) and the Commissioner of Food and Drugs (the commissioner) from taking any action in reliance upon the regulations contained in the commission's order of September 19, 1969 (the September regulations). The September regulations set up new standards for proving the effectiveness of drug products and applied those standards retroactively so as to place in jeopardy the continued marketing of thousands of drug products sold with Food and Drug Administration (FDA) approval, and the effectiveness of which FDA has not yet challenged. The regulations were adopted without a public hearing.

PMA contends that the regulations are invalid because they were issued without notice and opportunity for comment in violation of the requirements of the Administrative Procedure Act.

PMA's contention is well taken. The Administrative Procedure Act requires that rule making by an agency be preceded by "general notice of proposed rule making" in the *Federal Register* at least thirty days before the effective date of the proposed rule, and further requires that the agency give interested persons an opportunity to participate in the rule making through submission of written data, views, or arguments with or without opportunity for oral presentation. That procedure was not followed in this case. The September regulations were made effective by the commissioner upon their publication in the Federal

Register without prior notice or an opportunity for submission of comments by interested parties.

Exempt from the general requirements of notice and opportunity for comment are interpretative rules, general statements of policy, or rules of agency organization, procedure, or practice. The commissioner has characterized the September regulations as procedural and interpretative. But the label placed on the September rules by the commissioner does not determine whether the notice and comment provisions are applicable. It is the substance of what the commission has purported to do and has done that is decisive. When a proposed regulation of general applicability has a substantial impact on the regulated industry, or an important class of the members or the products of that industry, notice and opportunity for comment should first be provided. The September regulations have an immediate and substantial impact on the way PMA's members conduct their everyday business. The regulations apply to more than 2,000 drug products marketed since 1938 with FDA approval, and place all of them in jeopardy, subject to summary removal by order of FDA.

The substantial impact which the September regulations have upon the drug industry, and in turn upon prescribing physicians and their patients, makes it imperative that the commissioner comply with the notice and comment provisions before such regulations become effective. Because the minimal procedural rights of notice and opportunity for comment were not given in the present case, the promulgation of the September regulations was invalid and a preliminary injunction will be granted.

CASE QUESTIONS

1. Describe the effects of the September regulations.
2. Why does PMA contend these regulations are invalid?
3. On what legal basis did the commissioner exempt the regulations from the APA hearing requirement?
4. How does this court rule? Why?

Investigative agency hearings do not follow procedures as demanding as those for adjudicative hearings. Interested parties may submit written data, but not oral evidence unless the agency permits it. Formal hearings are not necessary and cross-examination does not exist. After considering the relevant matters presented by the parties, the agency can issue its rules and state the purpose and legal basis of the new rules. Even this procedure can be a burden or nuisance for some agencies. To avoid these requirements, some agencies try to make new rules for an entire industry through an adjudicative hearing. This procedure avoids giving parties an opportunity to comment on the new rules. Its use was condemned in *NLRB* v. *Wyman-Gordon Co.*, 349 U.S. 759 (1969):

> The Administrative Procedures Act contains specific provisions governing agency rule making, which it defines as "an agency statement of general or particular applicability and future effect." The NLRB asks us to hold that it has discretion to promulgate new rules in adjudicatory proceedings, without complying with the requirements of the Administrative Procedure Act.
>
> Rule making provisions of that Act were designed to assure fairness and mature consideration of new rules of general application. They may not be avoided by the process of making rules in the course of adjudicatory proceedings. There is no authority for the NLRB to replace the statutory scheme with a rule making procedure of its own invention. Apart from the fact that the device fashioned by the NLRB does not comply with statutory command, it obviously falls short of the substance of the requirements of the Administrative Procedure Act.
>
> Most administrative agencies, like the NLRB here, are granted two functions by the legislation creating them: (1) the power under certain conditions to make rules having the effect of laws, that is, generally speaking, quasi-legislative power; and (2) the power to hear and adjudicate particular controversies, that is quasi-judicial power. The line between these two functions is not always a clear one and in fact the two functions merge at many points. For example, in exercising its quasi-judicial function an agency must frequently decide controversies on the basis of new doctrines, not theretofore applied to a specific problem, though drawn to be sure from broader principles reflecting the purposes of the statutes involved and from the rules invoked in dealing with related problems. If the agency decision reached under the adjudicatory power becomes a precedent, it guides future conduct in much the same way as though it were a new rule promulgated under the rule-making power. The Act does specify the procedure by which the rule-making power is to be exercised, requiring publication of notice for the benefit of interested parties and provision of an opportunity for them to be heard, and, after establishment of a rule as provided in the Act, it is then to be published in the Federal Register. Congress had a laudable purpose in prescribing these requirements, and it was evidently contemplated that administrative agencies like the NLRB would follow them when setting out to announce a new rule of law to govern parties in the future. In this same statute, however, Congress also conferred on the affected administrative agencies the power to proceed by adjudication, and Congress specified a distinct procedure by which this adjudicatory power is to be exercised.

2. Judicial Review

Any party dissatisfied with the outcome of an administrative proceeding can appeal to the courts.

A. Standing to Appeal.

Section 702. "... a person suffering legal wrong because of agency action... is entitled to judicial review thereof."

Appeals from an administrative agency go to the federal court of appeals for the circuit in which the agency meets or where the business is located. Appeals may be made by business, the government, or in some cases a party not a direct participant in the proceedings. But the party appealing must have "standing" to appeal.

Sierra Club v. Morton
405 U.S. 727 (1972)

Mr. Justice Stewart.

The Mineral King Valley is an area of great natural beauty nestled in the Sierra Nevada Mountains in California, adjacent to Sequoia National Park. It has been part of the Sequoia National Forest since 1926. Though once the site of extensive mining activity, Mineral King is now used almost exclusively for recreational purposes. Its inaccessibility and lack of development limit the number of visitors each year, and at the same time have preserved the valley's quality as a quasi-wilderness area largely uncluttered by the products of civilization.

The United States Forest Service gave consideration to Mineral King as a potential site for recreational development. Walt Disney Enterprises received a three-year permit to conduct surveys and explorations in the valley in connection with its preparation of a complete master plan for the resort.

Representatives of the Sierra Club, who favor maintaining Mineral King largely in its present state, followed the progress of recreational planning for the valley with close attention and increasing dismay. In June of 1969 the club filed this suit in the United States District Court for the Northern District of California, seeking a declaratory judgment that various aspects of the proposed development contravene federal laws and regulations governing the preservation of national parks, forests, and game refuges, and also seeking preliminary and permanent injunctions restraining the federal government from approving or issuing permits in connection with the Mineral King project. The Sierra Club sued because it has "a special interest in the conservation and sound maintenance of the national parks, game refuges, and forests of the country," and invoked the judicial review provisions of the Administrative Procedure Act.

The District Court granted an injunction, but the Court of Appeals reversed.

The first question presented is whether the Sierra Club has alleged facts that entitle it to obtain judicial review of the challenged action. Whether a party has a sufficient stake in a controversy to obtain judicial review has traditionally been referred to as the question of standing to sue. The question of standing depends upon whether the party has alleged such a personal stake in the outcome of the controversy, as to ensure that the dispute will be presented in an adversary context and in a form historically viewed as capable of judicial resolution.

The Sierra Club relies upon the judicial review section of the Administrative Procedure Act (APA). This section permits a person to appeal if he or she suffers some legal wrong because of an agency action. But the impact of the proposed changes in the environment of Mineral King will not fall upon members of the Sierra Club. The alleged injury will be felt directly only by those who use Mineral King and Sequoia National Park, and for whom the aesthetic and recreational values of the area will be lessened by the highway and ski resort. The Sierra Club failed to allege that it or its members would be affected in any of their activities or pastimes by the Disney development. Nowhere in the pleadings or affidavits did the club state that its members use Mineral King for any purpose, much less that they use it in any way that would be significantly affected by the proposed actions of the respondents.

The requirement that a party seeking judicial review of agency actions must allege facts showing that he is himself adversely affected does not insulate executive action from judicial review, nor does it prevent any public interest from being protected through the judicial process. It does serve as at least a rough attempt to put the decision as to whether review will be sought in the hands of those who have a direct stake in the outcome. That goal would be undermined if we construed the APA to authorize judicial review at the behest of organizations or individuals who seek to do no more than vindicate their own value preferences through the judicial process. The principle that the Sierra Club would have us establish in this case would do just that.

Affirmed.

CASE QUESTIONS

1. What is a declaratory judgment, and why does the Sierra Club want it?
2. Define standing and show what it means in this case.
3. Explain the requirements for standing under the APA.
4. Why does the Sierra Club lack standing to sue?

B. *Time for Appellate Review.* The appellate court can review only certain specified actions of an agency.

Section 704. "Agency action made reviewable by statute and final agency action for which there is no other adequate remedy in a court are subject to judicial review. A preliminary, procedural ... ruling [is] not directly reviewable...."

The law allows the court to review only final actions by the agency. Before appealing, a party must exhaust all of the internal procedures of the agency. Preliminary orders of an agency are not appealable. For example, a temporary cease-and-desist order is not reviewable by the court because the agency itself may revoke it. Recommendations by a law judge cannot be appealed because the agency may modify or review them. This section prevents premature intervention into agency operations by the courts.

C. Scope of Appellate Review.

Section 706. "To the extent necessary [for] decision and when presented the reviewing court shall decide all relevant questions of law, interpret constitutional and statutory provisions and determine the meaning or applicability of the terms of agency action."

This section limits the scope of judicial review. An appellate court can review only questions of law presented to it, not questions of fact. Findings of fact are not reviewable because members who made the findings are experts in their fields. Judges do not have the special knowledge to reverse them. But an appeals court can overturn agency findings of fact if they are not supported by substantial evidence. Other legitimate issues to appeal are an agency violation of constitutional rights, particularly the right of due process, and agency actions beyond the scope of its jurisdiction.

Federal Power Commission v. Florida Power and Light Co.
404 U.S. 453 (1972)

Mr. Justice White.

The Federal Power Commission (FPC) determined that the transfer of power from Florida Power & Light Co. (FP&L) to another Florida utility's "bus" (a transmission line into which subsidiary lines connect) and the simultaneous transfer of power from that utility's bus to a Georgia company gave the FPC jurisdiction over FP&L, under Section 201(b) of the Federal Power Act. This section confers jurisdiction on the FPC over the transmission of electric energy in interstate commerce and the sale of electric energy at wholesale in interstate commerce. The FPC concluded that FP&L energy was commingled with that of the other Florida utility, and thus was transmitted in interstate commerce.

We are asked to determine whether the Federal Power Commission exceeded its statutory authorization when it asserted jurisdiction over the Florida Power and Light Company. The FPC hearing examiner and the commission itself utilized two scientific tests. They determined that the Florida Power and Light Company generates energy which is transmitted in interstate commerce. They therefore held the company was subject to the commission's jurisdiction. FP&L argues that an alternative test better represents the flow of its electricity: by use of this model it purports to demonstrate that its power has not flowed in interstate commerce. The Fifth Circuit Court of Appeals rejected the FPC's tests.

We granted certiorari to determine if either of the FPC's tests provide an acceptable basis at law and a sufficient basis in fact for the establishment of jurisdiction.

The conclusion of the FPC that FP&L energy commingled with that of another utility company and was transmitted in commerce rested on the testimony of expert witnesses. The major points expounded by these witnesses were probed, and in our opinion not undercut, by the hearing examiner's questions, FP&L's cross-examination, and testimony of FP&L witnesses. The hearing examiner found the testimony convincing. A majority of the commission endorsed these conclusions.

A court must be reluctant to reverse results supported by the weight of considered and carefully articulated expert opinion. Particularly when we consider a purely factual question within the area of competence of an administrative agency created by Congress, and when resolution of that question depends on engineering and scientific considerations, we recognize the agency's technical expertise and experience, and defer to its analysis unless it is without substantial basis in fact.

An appreciation of such different institutional capacities is reflected in the congressional directive defining the terms of judicial review of FPC action—the finding of the commission as to the facts, if supported by substantial evidence, shall be conclusive. The rule is no different because the questions involve matters of scientific knowledge and the evidence consists largely of the opinion of experts.

The court may not, for that reason, ignore the conclusions of the experts from the commission and put itself in the absurd position of substituting its judgment for theirs on controverted matters of engineering. It is in just such matters that the findings of the commission, because of its experience and the assistance of its technical staff, should be given the greatest weight and the courts should be hesitant to substitute their judgment for that of the commission.

Recognizing that the men responsible do not now fully understand electricity, though they know how to use it, and use it on an ever-expanding basis, we do not demand more of the commission than that its conclusions be substantially supported by expert opinion that is in accord with the facts known for certain. The commission has done enough to establish its jurisdiction.

The decision of the Court of Appeals is reversed and the case is remanded for reinstatement of the order of the Federal Power Commission.

CASE QUESTIONS

1. On what basis can a court overturn the findings of fact made by an administrative agency?
2. Does the result of this case differ from the appeal procedure followed in court trials?

The APA also limits appeals from discretionary acts of the regulators. The following case illustrates this rule.

Citizens to Preserve Overton Park, Inc.
v.
Volpe, Secretary, Department of Transportation
401 U.S. 402 (1971)

Mr. Justice Marshall.

The Secretary of Transportation may not authorize federal funds to finance construction of highways through public parks if a feasible and prudent alternative route exists. If no such route is available, he may approve construction only if there has been all possible planning to minimize harm to the park. Petitioners contend that the secretary has violated these statutes by authorizing a six-lane interstate highway through a Memphis public park. The decision of the secretary was accompanied by no factual findings. The District Court and the Court of Appeals found that formal findings were not required.

A threshold question—whether petitioners are entitled to any judicial review—is easily answered. The Administrative Procedure Act provides that the action of each authority of the government of the United States, which includes the Department of Transportation, is subject to judicial review except where there is a statutory prohibition on review or where agency action is committed to agency discretion by law. In this case, there is no indication that Congress sought to prohibit judicial review and there is most certainly no showing of clear and convincing evidence of a legislative intent to restrict access to judicial review.

Similarly, the secretary's decision here does not fall within the exception for action committed to agency discretion. This is a very narrow exception. The legislative history of the Administrative Procedure Act indicates that it is applicable in those rare instances where statutes are drawn in such broad terms that in a given case there is no law to apply. Under the law, the secretary cannot approve the destruction of parkland unless he finds that alternative routes present unique problems. Plainly there is law to apply and the exemption does not apply.

A court's powers on appeal are limited. The court is first required to decide whether the secretary acted within the scope of his authority. This determination naturally begins with an analysis of the scope of the secretary's authority and discretion. Although this inquiry into the facts is to be searching and careful, the ultimate standard of review is a narrow one. The court is not empowered to substitute its judgment for that of the agency.

The next inquiry is whether the secretary's action followed the necessary procedural requirements. He cannot act arbitrarily, capriciously, or in abuse of discretion or otherwise violate the law.

It is necessary to remand this case to the District Court for full review of the secretary's decision and reasons. That review is to be based on the full administrative record that was before the secretary at the time he made his decision.

Reversed and Remanded.

CASE QUESTIONS

1. On what basis did the Secretary of Transportation permit highway construction through the park, and why does the citizens group object?
2. Under the APA, when can a court review administrative agency decisions?
3. Can the court review the action of the Secretary? Why?

REVIEW QUESTIONS

1. Describe the impact of administrative agencies on the American economy.
2. List and explain the advantages and disadvantages of administrative regulation.

66   Introduction to the Study of Law

3. Why does modern government use the administrative agency rather than the courts as the instrument for solving national problems?

4. The District of Columbia desired to build a subway system to connect its downtown areas with the suburbs. Federal funds for the project were blocked by a Congressman, who wanted the Secretary of Transportation to authorize construction of a new highway bridge in the District. To build the bridge required the use of parkland. Under the Federal Highway Aid Act, the secretary had to make a finding that there was no other feasible and prudent use for the park than for the highway bridge. Is his determination reviewable by the courts?

5. Several motor carriers requested an increase in freight rates charged shippers for transporting merchandise in the United States. The Interstate Commerce Commission held hearings to determine if the requested rates were reasonable. Evidence submitted by the carriers to support the increase was inconclusive. The ICC gave the carriers an extension of time to file additional evidence. Pending the new evidence, the carriers were allowed to increase their rates provided they returned the increase to shippers if the commission ruled the rates excessive. Did the ICC exceed its authority as an administrative agency in making this determination?

6. A witness before an administrative agency gave evasive answers to several questions asked of him at the hearing. The agency instituted criminal prosecution against the witness for obstructing the due and proper administration of the law that authorized the hearing. Can this criminal action be brought by the agency?

7. The Secretary of Agriculture issued new regulations requiring all poultry processors to put on their packages labels describing ingredients used in the processing of this food product. The evidence relied upon by the secretary as a basis for the new regulations was kept confidential. Can Smith, a poultry producer, require a hearing to challenge the evidence relied upon by the secretary?

8. Two of five members of the Federal Trade Commission issued an order requesting a company to divest itself of certain properties acquired by it in violation of the antitrust laws. The company refused to comply with the order and challenged its validity in court. The company argued that a majority of the members must concur in the order before it becomes effective. Should the court uphold the company's challenge?

TABLE 3-2. ADMINISTRATIVE AGENCY PROCE-
DURAL STAGES

1. Complaint	Public
	Agency
	Government
2. Investigation	Informal by staff
	Findings
3. Hearing	Investigative or Adjudicative
	Administrative Law Judge
	Recommendations
4. Appeal to Agency	Review prior proceedings
	Order - Affirm
	Reverse
	Remand
5. Appeal to Courts	Standing
	Reviewable Matter
	Decision - Affirm
	Reverse
	Remand

4

SOME PROBLEMS WITH ADMINISTRATIVE AGENCIES

The might and power of the Federal Government have no equal.... Our Constitution was drawn on the theory that there are certain things government may not do to the citizen and that there are other things that may be done only in a specific manner. (Dissenting opinion of Mr. Justice Douglas in Hannah v. Larche, *363 U.S. 420, 1960.)*

The number of administrative agencies in the United States is growing and the types of problems agencies are asked to solve is expanding. More than fifty agencies now exist in the federal government and countless more in state and local governments. Administrative agencies now regulate all segments of our economy and parts of every phase of business operations. This growth is a mixed blessing for our society.

Agencies do provide a quick way for solving some problems. These solutions can be applied by expert administrators in a flexible manner to remedy the problems. But such extensive powers as these can lead to abuses. Whenever power transfers from the people to the government, restrictions must be placed on the use of that power. This principle is basic to our system of government. Yet administrative agencies seem to violate this rule. Power conferred on agencies is not limited by the traditional restrictions implied in our governmental system of separation of powers and checks and balances. This chapter discusses some of the problems arising from this lack of control over agency actions. The problems arise in five areas: constitutional questions presented by agency procedures, political influences among agency personnel, economic costs to our society by regulation, regulatory errors, and control over confidential information obtained by agency investigations. It is essential to understand the problems caused by administrative agencies, in order to formulate possible solutions to them.

CONSTITUTIONAL QUESTIONS

In several areas, administrative agencies present constitutional problems for our nation. Agencies do not follow the procedures concerning taking away a person's life, liberty, or property that have been established by court interpretations of our Constitution. By requiring some contracts to meet guidelines that they establish, agencies place limitations on the right to make contracts. Also, agencies may encourage discrimination among citizens. Several examples will illustrate these problems. Whether these actions by administrative agencies are serious enough to present dangers to our society is a question that must be answered by each individual.

1. Due Process

The Fifth Amendment to the Constitution says the federal government cannot take away a person's life, liberty, or property without due process of law. The Fourteenth Amendment puts the same restriction on state governments. Neither amendment defines due process. The Constitution leaves its definition up to the Supreme Court. Today, the Supreme Court divides due process into two categories: procedural due process and substantive due process.

A. Procedural Due Process. At first, the Court defined due process to mean those procedures followed by courts in criminal cases. These procedures are not constant. They change as the Court sees the needs for society's protection changing. At all times, however, procedures must be fair and appropriate. Under current Supreme Court rulings, procedural due process in criminal cases consists of nine major elements:

- an accused must be informed of his or her rights to remain silent and to seek legal advice, *Miranda* v. *Arizona*, 384 U.S. 436 (1966),
- an accused must be formally charged with a crime before a proper court official within a reasonable time after arrest, *Mallory* v. *United States*, 354 U.S. 449 (1948),
- an accused must be furnished free legal assistance if he or she cannot pay for a lawyer, *Gideon* v. *Wainwright*, 372 U.S. 335 (1963),
- an accused can prevent the use in a trial of any evidence obtained by police during an unreasonable search and seizure, *Mapp* v. *Ohio*, 367 U.S. 643 (1961),
- an accused can prevent the use at trial of any information or

evidence that he or she unwillingly gave to the police, *Malloy* v. *Hogan*, 378 U.S. 1 (1964),
- an accused can demand a prompt trial before an unbiased judge and jury, *Powell* v. *Alabama*, 287 U.S. 45 (1932),
- an accused can demand to know who his or her accusers are and to cross-examine evidence offered by the government, *Dowdell* v. *United States*, 221 U.S. 325 (1911) and *Williams* v. *New York*, 337 U.S. 241 (1949),
- an accused has the right to appeal to a higher court for review of the entire proceeding, *Hysler* v. *Florida*, 315 U.S. 411 (1942),
- an accused can demand reasonable punishment if the conviction is affirmed on appeal, *Robinson* v. *California*, 370 U.S. 660 (1962) and *Williams* v. *Illinois*, 399 U.S. 235 (1970).

Administrative agencies are not subject to the same procedural rules as the courts are. For example, investigative agencies gather facts, not to impose any punishment, but to make recommendations to others. Therefore, these agencies do not follow the nine elements of due process listed above. However, the effects of an investigative agency's recommendations can have a significant effect on a person's liberty or property. The *Hannah* case illustrates this.

B. *Substantive Due Process.* Today, the Supreme Court has added a second meaning to due process. Not only must government procedures be fair, but the purpose of a law must also be reasonable. Substantive due process prohibits laws whose effects arbitrarily take away a person's life, liberty, or property even though the way the law does this is reasonable. The Supreme Court decides when a particular law violates substantial due process. Many objections by business firms to administrative agency actions deal with this aspect of due process.

Hannah v. Larche
363 U.S. 420 (1960)

Mr. Chief Justice Warren.

The Civil Rights Commission received some sixty-seven complaints from individual blacks who alleged that they had been discriminatorily deprived of their right to vote. Based upon these complaints, and pursuant to its statutory mandate to investigate allegations in writing under oath or affirmation that certain citizens of the United States are being deprived of their right to vote by reason of their color, race, religion, or national origin, the commission began its investigation into the Louisiana voting situation by making several attempts to acquire information.

The voting registrars refused to answer the questions of investigators. A hearing was then called by the Civil Rights Commission. If the commission were to find at this hearing that the voting registrars were practicing discrimination, they could be removed from their positions and federal registrars would assume their functions. The voting registrars refused to cooperate with the hearings. It was alleged, among other things, that the commission's rules of procedure governing the conduct of its investigations were unconstitutional. These rules provide that the identity of persons submitting complaints to the commission need not be disclosed, and that those summoned to testify before the commission, including persons against whom complaints have been filed, may not cross-examine other witnesses called by the commission. The District Court held that the commission was not authorized to adopt these rules of procedure and therefore issued an injunction prohibiting the commission from holding any hearings. The commission requested this Court to review the District Court's decision.

The specific question that we must decide is whether those rules violate the due process clause of the Fifth Amendment.

Since the requirements of due process frequently vary with the type of proceeding involved, we think it is necessary at the outset to state the nature and function of this commission. The duties performed by the commission consist of (1) investigating written, sworn allegations that anyone has been discriminatorily deprived of his right to vote; (2) studying and collecting information concerning legal developments constituting a denial of equal protection of the laws under the Constitution; and (3) reporting to the President and Congress on its activities, findings, and recommendations. As is apparent from this brief sketch of the statutory duties imposed upon the commission, its function is purely investigative and fact finding. It does not adjudicate. It does not hold trials or determine anyone's civil or criminal liability. It does not issue orders. Nor does it indict, punish, or impose any legal sanctions. It does not make determinations depriving anyone of his life, liberty, or property. In short, the commission does not and cannot take any action that will affect an individual's legal rights. The only purpose of its existence is to find facts which may subsequently be used as the basis for legislative or executive action.

The specific constitutional question, therefore, is whether persons whose conduct is under investigation by a governmental agency of this nature are entitled, by virtue of the due process clause, to know the specific charges that are being investigated, as well as the identity of the complainants, and to have the right to cross-examine those complainants and other witnesses. Although these procedures are very desirable in some situations, we are of the opinion that they are not constitutionally required in the proceedings of this commission.

"Due process" is an elusive concept. Its exact boundaries are undefinable, and its content varies according to specific factual contexts. Thus, when governmental agencies adjudicate or make binding determinations that directly affect the legal rights of individuals, it is imperative that those agencies use the procedures that have traditionally been associated with the judicial process. On the other hand, when governmental agencies do not adjudicate, it is not necessary that the full scope of judicial procedures be used. Due process embodies the differing rules of fair play, which through the years have become associated with differing types of proceedings. Whether the Constitution requires that a particular right be considered in a specific proceeding depends upon: (1) the nature of the alleged right involved, (2) the nature of the proceeding, and (3) the possible burden on that proceeding.

It is probably sufficient merely to indicate that the rights claimed by respondents are normally associated only with adjudicatory proceedings, and that since the commission does not adjudicate, it need not be bound by adjudicatory procedures. The investigative process could be completely disrupted if investigative hearings were transformed into trial-like proceedings, and if persons who might be indirectly affected by an investigation were given an absolute right to cross-examine every witness called to testify. Fact-finding agencies without any power to adjudicate would be diverted from their legitimate duties and would be plagued by the injection of collateral issues that would make the investigation interminable. Even a person not called as a witness could demand the right to appear at the hearing, cross-examine any witness whose testimony or sworn affidavit allegedly defamed or incriminated him, and call an unlimited number of witnesses of his own selection. This type of proceeding would make a shambles of the investigation and stifle the agency in its gathering of facts.

When these agencies are conducting nonadjudicative, fact-finding investigations, rights such as appraisal, confrontation, and cross-examination generally do not obtain.

Reversed and Remanded.

Dissent. The Civil Rights Commission, it is true, returns no indictment. Yet in a real sense the hearings on charges that a registrar has committed a federal offense are a trial. Moreover, these hearings before the commission may be televised or broadcast on the radio. In our day we have seen on television the proceedings of Congressional committees probing into alleged criminal conduct of witnesses. This is in reality a trial in which the whole nation sits as a jury. Their verdict does not send men to prison. But it often condemns men or produces evidence to convict and even saturates the nation with prejudice against an accused so that a fair trial may be impossible. If several million television viewers see and hear a politician, a businessman, or a movie actor subjected to searching interrogation, without ever having an opportunity to cross-examine his accusers or offer evidence in his own support, that man will stand convicted, or at least seriously compromised, in the public mind, whatever the later formal findings may be. The use of this procedure puts in jeopardy our traditional concept of the way men should be tried and replaces it with a new concept of guilt based on inquisitorial devices.

Complaints have been filed with the commission charging respondents, who are registrars of voters in Louisiana, with depriving persons of their voting rights by reason of color. If these charges are true and if the registrars acted wilfully, the registrars are criminally responsible under a federal statute which subjects to fine and imprisonment anyone who wilfully deprives a citizen of any right under the Constitution by reason of his color or race.

The investigation and hearing by the commission are therefore necessarily aimed at determining if this criminal law has been violated. The serious and incriminating nature of the charge and of the disclosure of facts concerning it are recognized by the Congress, for the act requires certain protective procedures to be adopted.

CASE QUESTIONS

1. Describe the procedures established by the Civil Rights Commission and state why they were needed in this situation.
2. What are the functions of the commission, and how do they affect its procedures?
3. Describe the meaning of due process and show how it is important to our system of liberty.
4. Contrast judicial due process with investigative due process.
5. What is the result of this case? Explain the reasons for the dissent.

Rules of business regulatory agencies limit the rights persons have when appearing before an investigative hearing. For example, rules of the Federal Trade Commission require it to give persons summoned to appear before its investigative hearings only general notice of the purpose and scope of the investigation, and deny the person's counsel a right to participate in the investigation. Investigative agencies can obtain evidence from persons showing they committed a crime, then turn it over to criminal prosecutors for use against the persons. The constitutional prohibition of self-incrimination does not apply in this circumstance.

California v. Byers
402 U.S. 424 (1971)

Mr. Chief Justice Burger.

This case presents the narrow but important question of whether the constitutional privilege against compulsory self-incrimination is infringed by California's so-called "hit and run" statute that requires the driver of a motor vehicle involved in an accident to stop at the scene and give his name and address. Similar "hit and run" or "stop and report" statutes are in effect in all fifty states and the District of Columbia.

On August 22, 1966, Byers was charged with two misdemeanor violations of the California Vehicle Code: he passed another vehicle without maintaining a safe distance and was involved in an accident but failed to stop and identify himself.

California law requires:

> "The driver of any vehicle involved in an accident resulting in damage to any property including vehicles shall immediately stop the vehicle at the scene of the accident and shall then and there . . . locate and notify the owner or person in charge of such property of the name and address of the driver and owner of the vehicle involved. . . ."

It is stipulated that both charges arose out of the same accident.

Byers demurred on the grounds that the "hit and run" law violated his privilege against compulsory self-incrimination. His demurrer was sustained by the California Supreme Court. That court held that the privilege protected a driver who reasonably believes that compliance with the statute will result in self-incrimination.

We reverse.

An organized society imposes many burdens on its constituents. It commands the filing of tax returns for income; it requires producers and distributors of consumer goods to file informational reports on the manufacturing process and the content of products and on the wages, hours, and working conditions of employees. Those who borrow money on the public market or issue securities for sale to the public must file various information reports; industries must report periodically the volume and content of pollutants discharged into our waters and atmosphere. Comparable examples are legion.

In each of these situations there is some possibility of prosecution—often a very real one—for criminal offenses disclosed by or deriving from information that the law compels a person to supply. Information revealed by these reports could well be "a link in a chain" of evidence leading to prosecution and conviction. But under our holdings the mere possibility of incrimination is insufficient to defeat the strong policies in favor of a disclosure called for by statutes like the one challenged here.

Although the California law imposes some criminal sanctions, the statute is essentially regulatory, not criminal. The California Supreme Court noted that the law was not intended to facilitate criminal convictions but to promote the payment of civil liabilities arising from automobile accidents. In gambling cases, the Court declared unconstitutional statutes requiring gamblers to apply for a license because almost everything connected with gambling is illegal under state and federal statutory laws. The Court noted that in almost every conceivable situation compliance with the statutory gambling requirements would have been incriminating.

In contrast, the California law, like income tax laws, is directed to all persons—here all persons who drive automobiles in California. Driving an automobile, unlike gambling, is a lawful activity. Moreover, it is not a criminal offense under California law to be a driver involved in an accident. An accident may be the fault of others; it may occur without any driver having been at fault.

The disclosure of inherently illegal activity is inherently risky. But disclosures with respect to automobile accidents simply do not entail the kind of substantial risk of self-incrimination involved in gambling cases.

Although identity, when made known, may lead to inquiry that in turn leads to arrest and charge, those developments depend on different factors and independent evidence. Here the compelled disclosure of identity could have led to a charge that might not have been made had the driver left the scene; but this is true only in the same sense that a taxpayer can be charged on the basis of the contents of a tax return or failure to file an income tax form. There is no constitutional right to refuse to file an income tax return or to flee the scene of an accident in order to avoid the possibility of legal involvement.

The judgment of the California Supreme Court is vacated and the case is remanded for further proceedings not inconsistent with this opinion.

CASE QUESTIONS

1. Why did Byers refuse to stop and report the accident as required by law?
2. Under what circumstances can a person refuse to give information to administrative agencies?

The prior cases and discussions dealt with investigative agencies and the procedures they must follow. But adjudicative agencies act differently. Before an adjudicative agency can take away or change any of the property rights of an individual or business, it must follow some of the due process rules required in court proceedings. Specifically, adjudicative agencies must hold a hearing before acting. This hearing must include the following elements: timely notice detailing the reasons for the hearing, an opportunity to defend oneself by confronting witness and by presenting evidence, counsel who may advise and participate in the proceedings, an impartial decisionmaker, a decision based upon legal rules and evidence developed at the hearing, and reasons for the decision. However, a jury does not decide factual issues and appellate rights are limited to a review of the law or procedures followed at the hearing. The following case discusses when and why a hearing may be required.

Matthews v. Eldridge
96 S. Ct. 893 (1976)

Mr. Justice Powell.

Eldridge was awarded disability benefits under the Social Security Act. Approximately four years later, he received a questionnaire from the government asking information about his medical condition. Eldridge filled out the form and the agency then investigated his medical condition. It found that Eldridge was no longer disabled and reported its findings to the Social Security Administration. Disability benefits stopped. Eldridge filed this action requesting a hearing before his benefits are terminated.

The issue in this case is whether the due process clause of the Fifth Amendment requires a hearing before the government ends Social Security disability benefits. The District Court concluded Eldridge's rights were violated and the Court of Appeals affirmed. We reverse.

In determining when due process requires a hearing before a government agency may act, courts must balance the public interest with the person's request for a hearing. The public interest means the cost and administrative burden on government for having to hold hearings before taking actions. A great number of hearings would be too costly. Also, the benefit to an individual of an additional safeguard may be outweighed by the cost.

Further, the differences in the origin and function of administrative agencies preclude wholesale transplantation of the rules of procedure, trial, and review that have evolved from the history and experience of the courts. The judicial model of a hearing is neither a required nor even the most effective method of decision making in all circumstances. The essence of due process is the requirement that an accused person be given notice of the case against him and the opportunity to meet it. All that is necessary is that the procedures be tailored, in light of the decision to be made, to the capacities and circumstances of those who are to be heard, to insure that they are given a meaningful opportunity to present their case. In assessing what due process is in this case, substantial weight must be given to the good faith judgments of the individuals charged by Congress with the administration of the agency that the procedures they have provided assure fair considerations of individuals' claims.

We conclude that a hearing is not required prior to the termination of benefits and that the present administrative procedures comply with due process.

Affirmed.

CASE QUESTIONS

1. Why were benefits halted in this case?
2. Why does the court deny Eldridge a hearing in this case?
3. Why does the court decide that hearings are not required in all cases involving agency actions?
4. Are there any dangers in denying a hearing in this case?

2. Freedom of Contract

The Constitution guarantees citizens freedom of contract. Article I, Section 10, states that the government cannot pass any law which impairs the obligation of contracts. Private citizens are guaranteed the right to make contracts without fear of having them changed by government laws. Yet administrative agencies frequently adopt regulations which have the effect of changing contractual terms. The National Labor Relations Board establishes the legal framework for making collective bargaining contracts. The Consumer Product Safety Commission can prevent the sale of hazardous products even if a contract for this sale exists. The Department of Labor can set guidelines for the administration of private pension plans negotiated by a company with its employees. These restraints on the right of contract are legal if necessary to protect the public welfare or safety. The limits on government action to protect its citizens have not been determined.

TABLE 4-1. DUE PROCESS RIGHTS DEPEND UPON THE PROCEEDING

Criminal Court	Investigative Agency	Adjudicative Agency
To determine guilt or innocence of a person accused of a crime	To determine facts prior to making recommendations to others for action	To settle disputes affecting a person's property
specific notice of reasons for an arrest	general notice of the purpose and scope of an investigation, the time and place of any hearings	timely notice of the time and place of a hearing and notice of its purpose
inform accused of all rights	no duty to inform person of any rights before the agency	no duty to inform person of any rights before the agency
formal charges filed with an appropriate court	no criminal charges filed	no criminal charges filed
right to legal counsel, paid for by government if indigent	counsel may advise persons at a hearing but may not participate in the hearing as a matter of right, not paid by government	counsel has rights to participate in the hearing and advise persons at the hearing, not paid by government

no unreasonable searches and seizures of evidence	subpoena all relevant documents and reports	subpoena all relevant documents and reports
no self-incrimination	evidence obtained at an investigative hearing can be used in criminal proceedings	evidence obtained at an adjudicative hearing can be used in criminal court proceedings
prompt trial before a judge and jury	prompt hearing before commission, no judge or jury present	prompt hearing before commission, no judge or jury present
confrontation and cross-examination	no right to confrontation and cross-examination	right to confrontation and cross-examination
appeal	appeals from final agency actions on law or procedures followed, not on factual determinations	appeals from final agency actions on law or procedures followed, not on factual determinations
reasonable punishment	no punishment but public opinion can be adverse	can order remedies in favor of complainant: seize property, fine, issue cease-and-desist order, and require reports

3. Equal Protection

The Fourteenth Amendment also guarantees all citizens the equal protection of the laws of the United States. This clause prevents the government from passing laws either for or against any person or class of persons. The law must treat all citizens equally. But administrative agencies seem to treat certain classes of persons or businesses differently. For example, affirmative action programs of the Equal Employment Opportunity Commission encourage employers to hire minority workers in proportion to their numbers in the community. Indians and veterans have employment preferences in Civil Service. This type of class legislation is legal where there is a reasonable basis for discriminating among citizens.

POLITICAL INFLUENCES

Several problems exist in this area. The tremendous power concentrated in administrative agencies produces some political corruption. Business executives anxious to win agency approval for their actions sometimes give money, property, or other things to agency members and their staff. A recent airlines executive admitted to giving large sums of money to a political party, hoping to influence actions by the Civil Aeronautics Board. Other examples can be mentioned:

1. Some decisions made by agencies may be legally correct, yet too unpopular for the public to accept. For example, the Environmental Protection Agency recently caused a plant to close because it was polluting a nearby lake. If the plant closed, thousands of people would be adversely affected. Public pressure caused politicians to speak out against the EPA action. A higher court eventually overturned the agency action. The economic consequences of some agency actions may be too great for elected politicians to accept.

2. Appointments of members and staff to administrative agencies cause additional problems. Personnel are appointed because they have technical expertise in the area of the agency's authority. Their expertise comes through education and frequently practical experience working in the industry regulated by the agency. When they are appointed to the agency, their prior working experience can lead to charges of biased administration. Also, when a member leaves an agency, he or she usually looks for employment in the industry regulated by the agency. Awareness of this future need for employment may encourage an agency member to favor one of the regulated businesses. Recent disclosures at the Federal Energy Administration show that some of its staff members received substantial payments

and promises of employment from their employers when they were first appointed to the agency. Their former employers were oil companies, subject to FEA regulation.

3. In yet another case, some officials threatened to use agency inspectors to shut down a business unless the managers made political campaign contributions. Transcripts of conversations in the White House revealed that politicians considered sending OSHA inspectors to factories and plants of any company whose president refused to donate to their political campaigns. The inspectors would issue safety violation citations requiring the companies to make expensive repairs or shut down. Fortunately, these plans were not carried out. The abuses to which agencies can be subjected is obvious, however.

ECONOMIC COSTS

One of the original purposes in creating administrative agencies was to protect the public's interest. They were to bring fairer prices to the consumer, eliminate business abuses, and equalize the economic power of the buyer and seller. Agencies were the first consumer-oriented organizations in our country. But today, agencies seem to promote industry interests rather than consumer needs. The result is higher prices to purchasers and inferior products or services in return. Consider some examples.

1. The Interstate Commerce Commission wanted a national system of truck transportation in the United States. To make sure trucking companies located throughout the country, a rule prohibits some truckers from carrying merchandise on return trips. "Deadheading" caused higher shipping rates, ultimately passed on to the consumer in the form of higher prices. Some practices of the ICC and CAB are costing the American family as much as $2,000 annually. Regulations from the CAB caused airline fares to be forty percent higher than necessary.

2. A recent study of agencies by the Tax Foundation (*Tax Review*, August, 1975) showed that the costs of making, complying with, and enforcing administrative agency rules are staggering. Government costs for an administrative workforce in excess of 63,000 persons total approximately $2 billion a year. This is paid for by the public through taxes. But the costs to industry are even greater. Consumers must pay the added expenses incurred by business firms in complying with government directives. A direct cost of government regulation is the growing paperwork burden imposed on business firms. There are now 6,828 different types of government

TABLE 4-2. GOVERNMENT FORMS

Government Department	Number of Forms Issued	Forms Completed (in Millions)
IRS	3,500	122.0
HEW	957	176.0
LABOR	270	42.2
TREASURY	133	37.4
AGRICULTURE	795	31.0
COMMERCE	571	22.6
TRANSPORTATION	285	18.3
JUSTICE	167	16.7
CIVIL SERVICE COMM.	150	16.4

Source: Internal Revenue Service and Office of Management and Budget

forms, some of which have to be prepared by every business. The costs of hiring workers to gather the information required on these forms, fill them out, and appeal to the courts because of problems with them is passed on to consumers. One large corporation estimates its costs of completing government reports at almost $5 million annually.

3. Another type of cost to the consumer cited by the Tax Foundation is a reduction in the rate of technological advancement. It takes a long time for a new product or new manufacturing process to be approved by government regulators. The longer the approval process takes, the less likely it is that companies will make any change. Ultimately, the consumer suffers. For example, FDA testing procedures may delay the sales of new drugs by about four years after other countries are using them safely. Also, new proposals from OSHA and EPA to reduce noise in factories will cost industry $13.5 billion. That investment will not be spent on new product research, but on noise reduction technology.

4. A recent study of government regulation of business conducted by the National Commission on Productivity and Work Quality concluded that, "A major problem associated with government regulation is that many of the rules, policies, and standards imposed by regulatory authorities do not provide for adequate recognition of their impact on costs. In particular, we need to understand the very real trade-offs and balances which exist between achieving such objectives as clean air and water and the maintenance of other national priorities such as low costs to the consumer and high overall rates of employment. There is a particular need to promote this greater awareness of and concern about the economic impact of

regulations among regulatory agencies themselves." Source: *A National Policy for Productivity Improvement* (Washington: U.S. Government Printing Office, 1975), p. 31.

REGULATORY ERRORS

No human organization can be free of error. All people will make mistakes at some time, and regulatory agencies are no better than the people who work for them. But the consequences of error by these agencies can have drastic and far-reaching effects on companies and the economy. A few examples can illustrate this point.

1. The case of Marlin Toy Products Company is now a classic example of agency mistakes. This firm made plastic toys for children. The FDA ruled that one of its products was unsafe. Marlin made corrections, and the agency removed its ban on their sale. But the Consumer Product Safety Commission put the product on its list of banned products, although there was no reason to prohibit their sale. Retailers refused to purchase this toy from Marlin and the company eventually went bankrupt. Later the agency admitted its mistake, calling it an "editorial error."

2. Some people cite the ban on cyclamates as another example of regulatory mistake. In 1969, the Secretary of Health, Education and Welfare ordered this sugar substitute off the market because it was suspected of causing cancer in animals. Under the law, any food ingredient linked to causing cancer must be removed from the food market. Removal of cyclamates cost more than $150 million for food producers, contributed to a 400 percent increase in sugar prices, and deprived diabetics of this sugar substitute. Now, the biochemist who conducted the original tests on cyclamates admits the link between this product and cancer was inconclusive. Other scientists agree that his tests did not justify the ban on cyclamates. Studies performed in European countries did not confirm the American test results and no ban was imposed there.

3. Even more costly to the American economy and public comfort are the mistakes made over the automobile safety equipment. Purchasers of new cars produced in the United States in 1974 paid over $3 billion extra for the equipment and modifications needed to meet federal safety requirements. One year after the Department of Transportation ordered mandatory seat buzzers on cars, Congress removed them by statute. The costly catalytic converter ordered installed on new model cars to reduce air pollution now seems to cause an even more dangerous type of auto exhaust. Premature

action by government regulators may have contributed to the decline of domestic automobile sales.

4. More serious are government regulations which contradict each other. For example, OSHA safety rules require alarms to sound when construction vehicles are backing up. Regulations also require workers to wear earplugs to deaden the sound of heavy construction machinery. But those earplugs prevent the wearers from hearing the safety alarms. In another situation, federal regulations require a fire retardancy chemical on all children's pajamas, while a New York state rule prohibits use of phosphates in detergents. Phosphates in the wash water preserve the fire retardant chemical required by the federal government. Washing the pajamas "in an ecologically sound manner may risk washing away its fire resistant properties," according to Dr. Murry L. Weidenbaum, Director of the Center for the Study of American Business at Washington University in St. Louis, Missouri. "What does a conscientious mother do," he asks, "avoid dressing her child in nightclothes that could burn up? Smuggle in the forbidden detergent? Commit an illegal act of laundry?"

FREEDOM OF INFORMATION ACT

Administrative agencies accumulate significant information about the companies and individuals regulated by them. This information can be stored in computer banks, and retrieved at a later time for use by other investigators. Such data banks can endanger personal liberties. Information contained in them may be erroneous, only half true, or taken out of context. Persons with access to the data can use it to blackmail individuals, to defame reputation, to coerce, or for other improper purposes. Some controls are necessary to protect the public. One control technique is the Freedom of Information Act, a part of the Administrative Procedures Act. It requires government agencies to make public their rulings, records, and proceedings but to keep confidential their documents on individuals. It also gives individuals the right to inspect certain agency records about them.

> *Disclosure.* Section 552(a)(1). "Each agency shall make available to the public information as follows... rules of procedure, substantive rules of general applicability adopted as authorized by law, statements of general policy or interpretations of general applicability...."

Disclosure of material in government files has now become the rule rather than the exception. This act increases public access to agency records by forcing liberal disclosure rules on agency staff. Requested information must be disclosed regardless of the motive, interest, or intent of the person requesting the material. Under this section, an individual can request information about him or herself, a firm can ask for information about investigations of it, and companies can obtain government findings about their competitors. Some materials that must be disclosed include: FAA reports on airworthiness of planes, IRS rulings and advice to taxpayers, Defense Department audit rules, and draft board memoranda.

> *Exemptions.* Section 552(b). This section does not apply to matters that: ... [pertain] to national defense ..., related solely to internal personnel rules ..., trade secrets ..., memorandums ... not available by law ..., investigatory records compiled for enforcement purposes [if disclosure would result in an unfair trial, invade privacy, invade a personal privacy or reveal a confidential source].... Any reasonable segregable portion of a record shall be provided to any person requesting [it] after deletion of [exempt] portions."

Narrowly construed exemptions limit the materials that can be disclosed. A court determines when an exemption applies. It is presumed that all records must be disclosed unless the agency can show that the material requested is specifically exempted. A mere statement by an agency staff member or commissioner is not enough to earn an exemption. Instead, the agency must show particular and specific reasons for seeking an exemption. Judges will rule on each request on a case-by-case basis. Some materials ruled exempt from disclosure are: OSHA training manuals for its inspectors, evidence from the Kennedy assassination, IRS investigatory files where a case is pending against a taxpayer, and names of government informers.

Another limitation on disclosure of government information is important for the protection of an individual's reputation. No agency can disclose any record about a person until he or she gives consent to the disclosure in writing. But disclosure can be made without this consent in eleven situations. These deal mostly with requests made by the courts, Congress, and government agencies that are required by law to compile data (such as Census or the Government Accounting Office).

Safeguards. Section 552(e) requires each agency that keeps records to gather information and store it in a certain manner. This procedure helps protect individual rights. Agencies can keep information about a person only if it is needed to accomplish a legitimate purpose of the agency. If possible, the agency must collect that data directly from the individual. The individual must be told why the information is requested, the things it can be used for, and the effects for the person of refusing to cooperate. Although no record system is perfect, agencies must strive for accuracy in their record-keeping systems and take reasonable efforts to guarantee that any disclosures are accurate and relevant. Persons handling these records must be trained in their proper use, and safeguards must be established to insure the confidentiality of these records. Also, agencies must establish rules by which individuals can inspect any files on themselves.

Inspection. The Freedom of Information Act permits individuals to inspect records kept on them and allows them to see certain other documents which agencies maintain. Each agency must establish procedures by which a person can obtain this information. Although these procedures can vary among agencies, all must follow the same outline established by Congress. This inspection procedure requires:

1. Agencies must publish in the *Federal Register* every year a notice about the types of records they keep, stating the names and locations of these records, the types of persons likely to be listed in them, the uses for the records, all policies regarding storage, access, and control over them, who can be contacted in order to inspect them, and how requests for inspections can be made.

2. To obtain information in agency records, the individual must file a request with the appropriate person in the agency, explaining the type of information desired. That information must be reasonably described by the person requesting it. A broad categorical request may not be granted. Within ten working days, the agency must decide to give or withhold the requested information. If the agency does not release the information, the person may appeal. Within twenty working days of the appeal, the agency must make its final decision. The agency processes all appeals internally. Each agency now has rules and procedures to process these requests and appeals. Reasonable fees to cover the costs of locating and copying records may be charged persons requesting record searches.

3. An individual must be allowed to look at the records once the agency decides to disclose them. He or she may inspect these records with an attorney or other person, copy them, and suggest corrections to them. The agency must make the changes requested by the person or within a reasonable time inform him or her of its refusal to amend its records. This denial must explain why the changes were not made and show how the person can appeal the agency's decision. The person's objections must be noted in the record system and disclosed along with the record to others entitled to see it.

Penalties. Section 552(g) permits any individual who was denied access to information by an agency to bring a civil action in the district courts. Those courts can order the agency to disclose the information, to change its procedures or record keeping, to amend the individual's record, and to have attorney fees and court costs paid by the government. Of course, the courts can also uphold an agency's refusal to disclose information.

If the agency wilfully violated an individual's inspection rights, it can be sued for the actual damages suffered by that individual. Also, any agency employee who knowingly violates any agency rules regarding the privacy of these records can be guilty of a misdemeanor and fined not more than $5,000. A similar penalty can be imposed on any agency employee who knowingly maintains a system of records that violates this act. Any person who uses false pretenses to request information on another can also be fined not more than $5,000.

Summary. Despite these constitutional, political, and economic problems, administrative agencies form a significant part of our governmental system. They exist to fill a vacuum created by the need to regulate business in a legal system developed before business became a significant part of our economy. The Constitution was written in 1789 when America was a small, rural nation. Most people lived on farms they owned and worked in nonmechanical, agriculture communities. Today, many Americans live in urban and suburban areas, renting apartments and working in large corporations at automated tasks. The changes in our society created new problems for Americans. Congress responded to these problems by enacting numerous laws to regulate business and by creating numerous administrative agencies to apply them. Some abuses by agencies prompted Congress to enact the Freedom of Information Act. The theory of this act is simple—full disclosure of agency activities may stop wrongdoing. The remaining parts of this book will examine those agencies that have the most impact on business and its needs for capital, markets, and employees. Specifically, we will study the operations of the SEC, FTC, NLRB, OSHRC, and EEOC. Some reference will be made to the Consumer Product Safety Commission and the Environmental Protection Agency.

REVIEW QUESTIONS

1. Contrast due process before the courts with that followed by investigative agencies. Why is there a difference?

2. Show how agencies can come under political influences. Can they be immune from politics?

3. Agencies can cause higher prices for the consumer. But are there any benefits from these higher costs? Consider the total cost of airline fares if carriers could drop service to unprofitable markets and serve populated markets only.

4. To what extent can errors by regulatory agencies be prevented? To what extent are "errors" really just experiments?

5. Outline the main sections of the Freedom of Information Act. How does it help eliminate the problems of administrative agencies? Is something more required?

6. A state health board determined that there were too many doctors practicing their profession in metropolitan areas of the state but not enough of them in its rural areas. To remedy this imbalance, the board passed a regulation requiring all new doctors to practice in specified rural areas of the state. Is this regulation constitutional?

7. Jones was under investigation by the Internal Revenue Service for tax evasion. As part of the preparation of his court trial, he requested all the documents kept by the IRS on him and the manual tax agents used in negotiating settlements with taxpayers. Both types of information were sought under the Freedom of Information Act. On what basis could the IRS deny access to this information. Are these exemptions relevant here?

8. Employees were upset with collective bargaining efforts with their employer. To make the employer more responsive to their wage demands, they requested reports from the Federal Trade Commission about the pricing policies of the employer's products and intended to threaten to release this information to the public. Can the FTC refuse this request because of their purpose?

TOPICS

CHAPTER 5. STOCKHOLDER RIGHTS AND LIABILITIES
Introduction • Rights to Corporate Records • Meeting Rights • Dividend Rights • Minority Rights • Other Rights • Stockholder Liabilities • Review Questions

CHAPTER 6. SECURITIES ACT OF 1933
Introduction • Definitions of a Security • Registration Requirements • Exemptions from Registration • Liabilities • Management Guidelines • Review Questions

CHAPTER 7. SECURITIES EXCHANGE ACT OF 1934
Introduction • Registration and Reporting Requirements • Inside Reports • Short Swing Trades • Margin Trading • Tender Offers • Rule 10(b)(5) • Securities and Exchange Commissions • Liabilities • Other Federal Securities Laws • State Securities Laws • Management Guidelines • Review Questions

PART TWO

LAWS AND REGULATIONS AFFECTING THE SECURITIES MARKETS

Investing money in business is a complicated act. It requires careful analysis of financial information about companies and continued attention to every investment decision. To make sure useful, accurate data is available and to make it possible for the public to check on their investments, laws are necessary to protect the investing public from the deception and dishonesty of a few people in the securities industry. They benefit the investor and the economy. Without them, money would not be channeled into corporations, business would stagnate and the economy would suffer. In Part II, we will study laws and regulations for investor protections. First, we will look at some stockholder rights and duties. Then, we will analyze federal securities regulation and conclude this section with a general overview of state securities laws. Selected cases illustrate how securities laws and regulations affect decision making by financial managers.

5

STOCKHOLDER RIGHTS AND LIABILITIES

> *... majority shareholders ... have a fiduciary responsibility to the minority and to the corporation to use their ability to control the corporation in a fair, just and equitable manner. Majority shareholders may not use their power to control corporate activities to benefit themselves alone or in any manner detrimental to the minority. Any use to which they put the corporation or their power to control the corporation must benefit all shareholders proportionately and must not conflict with the proper conduct of the corporation's business.* (Jones v. Ahmanson & Co., 460 P.2d 464, 1969.)

The corporation is the dominant form of business organization in the United States today. Other forms of business may be more numerous but the corporate business form produces the largest portion of our national output. A corporation is an artificial person, invisible, intangible, and existing only in contemplation of law. This means the corporation is separate and distinct from the persons who own it. Corporation owners have transferable shares of stock representing their ownership in the business. Owners of these certificates are stockholders. The stockholders elect directors to supervise the operations of the corporation and the directors appoint officers to run the corporation. State law, the corporation's charter, and its bylaws list stockholder rights and duties. Each of these must be read to see what rights a stockholder has in a particular corporation.

> There can be no doubt that the relation between a corporation and its stockholders is contractual. But it is equally true that the statutes of the state governing corporations and their organization are also a part of the contract. And all of the provisions of the charter are likewise to be considered in determining the true agreement. (*Berger* v. *Amana Society*, 95 N.W. 2d 909, 1959.)

In this chapter, we will study the general rights and duties that stockholders may have in any corporation.

RIGHTS TO CORPORATE RECORDS

Stockholders have invested money in their corporation. They are the owners of the business. As owners and as investors they must have access to the records and reports of their corporation. Corporation managers are sometimes reluctant to turn over these documents to stockholders. Managers may fear the information contained in the reports may show mismanagement and be used to discharge them. Often the managers wish to keep corporate information secret to avoid its use by competitors. But stockholders do have some rights to see relevant corporation information. Courts must balance the corporation's need for secrecy with the stockholders' right to know how their investments are managed.

Stockholders have the right to inspect all corporate books and records, shareholder lists, financial records, and the physical properties of the corporation. However, stockholders must use this right of inspection only for a legitimate purpose. For example, a request to inspect the names and addresses of other stockholders to send them information about the corporation is a legitimate purpose. But a request to inspect corporate trade secrets to sell them to a competitor, or a request for the stockholder list to send them advertisements are improper purposes.

To enforce this right of inspection, a stockholder must first ask the corporation for the documents. The corporation can require the stockholder to state his or her purposes and require the inspection to take place at reasonable times and places. If the stockholder is refused permission to inspect, or if unreasonable conditions are imposed, the stockholder can sue the corporation in court. The court will determine if the stockholder has the right to inspect corporate records or if the conditions imposed by management are reasonable. Enforcing this right may be expensive and time consuming.

MEETING RIGHTS

The laws of most states require corporations to hold annual meetings of the stockholders. At these meetings, stockholders elect directors of the corporation, who then appoint officers. The stockholders ratify business activities of the past year, authorize new activities for the next year, and discuss other corporation matters. Special meetings may be called by the corporation whenever emergencies justify them. Stockholders must be notified in advance of annual and special meetings. Corporate bylaws state the requirements for this notice.

"Even when there is no provision in statute or by-laws for notice, it has been held that common law principles require corporate meetings to be called by reasonable notice to stockholders." (*Toombs* v. *Citizens Bank of Waynesboro*, 281 U.S. 643, 1930.) This notice generally must be in writing and state the time, place, and purpose of the meeting. Only stockholders whose names are recorded with the corporation receive this notice. If proper notice is not given, actions taken at the meeting may be void. Some states permit stockholders to waive notice.

Special and annual meetings are conducted according to rules specified in the corporation's bylaws. A quorum must be present to transact business. A presiding officer, usually the president, calls the meeting to order, determines if a quorum exists, and then takes up the meeting agenda.

Stockholders have the right to participate fully in these meetings. They have rights to speak at the meeting, present resolutions, question officers and directors, and vote. The extent of a shareholder's voting rights depends on the corporation's charter and bylaws. Generally, corporations can issue voting and nonvoting classes of stock. Persons listed on the corporate records as owners can vote or give a proxy to others. This proxy must be in writing and can give broad or limited authority to another to vote the stock. A proxy can be revoked at any time but often expires within one year. Each share of stock has one vote, either personally or by proxy. Fractional shares do not vote.

In some corporations, stockholders have cumulative voting rights. This special voting right only applies to the election of directors. It gives stockholders the option of casting more than one vote for the same candidate, distributing among the candidates a number of votes equal to the number of candidates to be elected. Cumulative voting gives the minority shareholders an opportunity to elect their representatives to the board of directors. The following case illustrates stockholder voting rights when cumulative, fractional shares are outstanding.

Benson v. 1120 St. Charles Co.
422 S.W. 2d 297 (1967)

Barrett, Commissioner.

The Gitts, Bensons, and Mandels are the owners of all the common stock of the Eleven-Twenty St. Charles Company. In this action, the Gitts and Bensons sought to have declared void the election of Mandel and his son, Burton, as directors of the corporation. The trial court's findings of fact and conclusions of law were against the plaintiffs, and they have appealed. Both parties assert that jurisdiction is in this court because the appeal involves the construction of Article 11, Section 6, of the Missouri Constitution relating to cumulative voting of fractional shares for corporate directors.

In very brief summary the facts are that in 1947 Mandel and his then friends, Dr. Gitt and George Benson, formed Eleven-Twenty Corporation with a capitalization of ten shares of stock, five of which were issued to Mandel, two and one-half to Dr. Gitt and two and one-half to Benson. The Gitts have transferred one-quarter share to their minor son, David, and one-quarter share to their daughter, Barbara Ann. The purpose of this corporation was to purchase a multistory parking garage at 1120 St. Charles Street.

This lawsuit came out of the annual meeting of stockholders of the Eleven-Twenty Corporation on February 7, 1964. As of that date Mandel was the record owner of five shares of stock; Benson, 2½ shares; Dr. Gitt, of one share; Charlotte Gitt, of one share; and ¼ share was issued in the names of J.J. Gitt and Charlotte Gitt as trustees for David, and one-quarter share in their names as trustees for Barbara. Benson and Gitt did not attend the annual stockholder's meeting; instead, their two attorneys appeared with proxies from Benson and Gitt and attempted to cast, cumulatively voting, 7½ votes for each of their nominees for director. Mandel ruled, however, that fractional shares could not vote and, casting his votes for himself and his son, Burton, elected two directors. Gitt's and Benson's counsel declined to cast their votes. Thus is presented the question of whether under Missouri law fractional shares of stock are entitled to cumulative voting in the election of corporate directors.

In support of their contention that fractional shares are entitled to vote, the appellants point to the language of the constitutional and statutory provisions concerning cumulative voting of stock for directors and managers—"Each shareholder shall have the right to cast as many votes in the aggregate as shall equal the number of shares held by him;" and "Each outstanding share entitled to vote under the provisions of the articles of incorporation shall be entitled to one vote on each matter submitted"—and urge that "each shareholder" and "shares" in the constitution do not mean "each full share" but include "fractional shares." They urge that under the statute and the constitution stock ownership carries the right to vote, and this right may not be destroyed by denial of the right to vote "fractional shares."

On the other hand, the respondents point to eleven sections of the General and Business Corporation Law of Missouri and urge that the words "share" or "shares" do not and cannot mean "fractional shares." The bylaws provide that "Each stockholder shall have one (1) vote for each share of stock having voting power, registered to his name on the books of the corporation." The respondents, of course, rely on this provision of the bylaws and the rule that fractional shares of stock cannot be voted in the absence of express legislative authorization to that effect.

The legislature authorized the issue of certificates for fractional shares, but it did not authorize voting based on such shares. It could have done so, and it may even have intended to do so, but the fact is it did not do so. For the reasons indicated and upon this record fractional shares may not be voted for director and accordingly the judgment is affirmed.

CASE QUESTIONS

1. Explain how the fractional shares came into being in this case.
2. Under what circumstances could fractional shares be permitted to vote?

In some corporations, stockholders have preemptive rights. These rights give stockholders the opportunity to buy the same proportion of new stock issued as the proportion they now have in the corporation. For example, if a stockholder now owns thirty percent of existing outstanding shares, he or she may buy thirty percent of any new shares of stock issued by the corporation in the future. This right allows a stockholder to preserve his or her relative position of voting control in the corporation.

Katzowitz v. Sidler
249 N.E. 2d 359 (1969)

Keating, Judge.

Isador Katzowitz is a director and stockholder of a close corporation. Two other persons, Jacob Sidler and Max Lasker, own the remaining securities and, with Katzowitz, comprise Sulburn Holding Corporation's board of directors. Sulburn was organized in 1955 to supply propane gas to three other corporations controlled by these men. Sulburn's certificate of incorporation authorized it to issue 1,000 shares of no par value stock for which the incorporators established a $100 selling price. Katzowitz, Sidler, and Lasker each invested $500 and received five shares of the corporation's stock.

Two directors called a special meeting of the board on December 1, 1961. The only item on the agenda for this special meeting was the issuance of seventy-five shares of the corporation's common stock at $100 per share. The offer was to be made to stockholders in "accordance with their respective preemptive rights for the purpose of acquiring additional working capital." The amount to be raised was the exact amount owed by the corporation to its shareholders. The offering price for the securities was one-eighteenth the book value of the stock. Only Sidler and Lasker attended the special board meeting. They approved the issuance of the seventy-five shares.

Notice was mailed to each stockholder that they had the right to purchase twenty-five shares of the corporation's stock at $100 a share. Katzowitz did not exercise his option to buy the additional shares. Sidler and Lasker purchased their full complement, twenty-five shares each. This purchase by Sidler and Lasker caused an immediate dilution of the book value of the outstanding securities. On August 31, 1962, the directors unanimously voted to dissolve the corporation. Upon dissolution, Sidler and Lasker each received $18,885.52 but Katzowitz only received $3,147.59.

The plaintiff instituted a declaratory judgment action to establish his right to the proportional interest in the assets of Sulburn in liquidation, less the $5,000 which Sidler and Lasker used to purchase their shares in December, 1961.

The concept of preemptive rights was fashioned by the judiciary to safeguard two distinct interests of stockholders—protection against dilution of their equity in the corporation and protection against dilution of their proportionate voting control. It is clear that directors of a corporation have no discretion in the choice of those to whom the earnings and assets of the corporation should be distributed. Directors, being fiduciaries of the corporation, must, in issuing new stock, treat existing shareholders fairly.

Though there is very little statutory control over the price that a corporation must receive for new shares, the power to determine price must be exercised for the benefit of the corporation and in the interest of all the stockholders. When new shares are issued, at prices far below fair value in a close corporation or a corporation with only a limited market for its shares, existing stockholders who do not want to invest or do not have the capacity to invest additional funds can have their equity interest in the corporation diluted to the vanishing point.

The defendant directors here make no claim that the price set was a fair one. No business justification is offered to sustain it. Admittedly, the stock was sold at less than book value. The defendants simply contend that, as long as all stockholders were given an equal opportunity to purchase additional shares, no stockholder can complain simply because the offering dilutes his interest in the corporation.

The defendants' argument is fallacious.

One part of a stockholder's right to maintain his proportionate equity in a corporation by purchasing additional shares is the right not to purchase additional shares without being confronted with dilution of his existing equity if no valid business justification exists for the dilution. A stockholder's right not to purchase is seriously undermined if the stock offered is worth substantially more than the offering price. Any purchase at this price dilutes his interest and impairs the value of his original holding. A corporation is not permitted to sell its stock for a legally inadequate price at least where there is objection. Plaintiff has a right to insist upon compliance with the law whether or not he cares to exercise his option. He cannot block a sale for a fair price merely because he disagrees with the wisdom of the plan but he can insist that the sale price be fixed in accordance with legal requirements.

Here the obvious disparity in selling price and book value was calculated to force the dissident stockholder into investing additional sums. No valid business justification was advanced for the disparity in price, and the only beneficiaries of the disparity were the two director-stockholders who were eager to have additional capital in the business.

Accordingly, the order of the Appellate Division should be reversed, with costs, and judgment granted in favor of the plaintiff against the individual defendants.

CASE QUESTIONS

1. Why was new stock issued and what was its value?
2. How did the new issue affect the plaintiff?
3. How does the court protect the minority rights in a close corporation?

DIVIDEND RIGHTS

A corporation exists to make a profit and to distribute a portion of that profit to stockholders. A distribution of profits to stockholders is called a dividend. It may be paid in the form of cash, property, or stock. Before any amounts can be paid, the corporation must have funds available for a dividend. No dividend can be paid stockholders if the distribution causes the corporation to go bankrupt or insolvent. Some states require dividends to be paid only from the corporation's earned surplus, undistributed profits earned through regular operations. Other states permit dividends to be paid from a corporation's paid in surplus, excess assets arising from sources other than profits. A careful reading of state law is necessary to determine what funds are available for distribution in a particular corporation. If an illegal dividend is paid, stockholders may have to return it to the corporation or to any of its creditors.

If funds are available for a dividend, the directors must declare one before stockholders have the right to receive it. Directors have the discretion to declare a dividend, according to their business judgment. This means the directors do not have to pay out a dividend just because money is in the corporation treasury. They can reinvest the surplus money in the corporation for future expansion. However, a stockholder can sue the directors, forcing them to pay a dividend, if they unreasonably accumulate money in the corporation. Stockholders have the burden of proving unfair use of the money, and courts seldom overrule the director's decision.

Once directors declare a dividend, all stockholders must receive the same amount of money for each share of stock owned. But the directors do not have to pay the same dividend to each class of stock. For example, some corporations issue preferred stock, which generally has a first claim to any dividends paid by the corporation. Preferred stockholders receive their dividends before other stockholders receive any money. Sometimes corporations issue cumulative preferred stock. This stock gives the owner a first preference to dividends and a future claim on the corporation's earnings for any dividends not paid. Suppose a corporation has three classes of stock—cumulative preferred, preferred, and common; yearly net profits of ten dollars per share of all stocks; no dividends paid last year; and the preferred stock entitled to a two dollar dividend. If the corporation votes a dividend of nine dollars to the three classes of stock, it would be distributed as follows: four dollars to the cumulative preferred, two dollars to the preferred stock and three dollars to the common stock.

A dividend payment must be voted on by the entire board of directors. Once it is declared, the dividend becomes a debt of the corporation owed to its stockholders. If the corporation refuses to distribute a declared dividend or goes bankrupt, the stockholders become creditors of the corporation. Only persons whose names are registered with the corporation as owners of the stock receive the declared dividend. Since it takes several days from the time stock is sold until it is registered with the corporation, the seller of stock may receive the dividend after he or she sells the stock to another person.

Wabash Ry. Co. v. Barclay
280 U.S. 197 (1930)

Mr. Justice Holmes.

The railway company was organized in 1915 under the laws of Indiana with three classes of capital stock: (1) shares with a par value of $100, of Five Percent, Profit Sharing Preferred Stock A; (2) shares with the same par value of Five Percent, Convertible Preferred Stock B; and (3) shares with the same par value of

Common Stock. At the date of the case there were 693,330.50 shares of A, 24,211.42 B and 66,977.75 common. From 1915 to 1926 there were net earnings on most of the years, but for a number of years no dividend was paid on Class A, while $16,000,000 net earnings that could have been used for the payment were spent on improvements and additions to the property and equipment of the road. It is agreed that these expenditures were proper and were made in good faith. The company now is more prosperous and proposes to pay dividends not only upon A but also on B and the common stock. The preferred stockholders say that it is not entitled to do so until it has paid to them unpaid preferential dividends for prior fiscal years in which it had net earnings that might have been used for dividends but were not.

The dividend obligations of the company appear in its instrument of incorporation and in the certificates of Preferred Stock A in substantially the same words. "The holders of the Five Per Cent Profit Sharing Preferred Stock A of the Company shall be entitled to receive preferential dividends in each fiscal year up to the amount of five per cent, before any dividends shall be paid upon any other stock of the Company, but such preferential dividends shall be non-cumulative." In the event of a liquidation, the holders "shall be entitled to be paid in full out of the assets of the Company the par amount of their stock and all dividends thereon declared and unpaid before any amount shall be paid out of said assets to the holders of any other stock of the Company." The holders "are not entitled, of right, to dividends, payable out of the new profits accruing in any particular year, unless the directors of the Company formally declare . . . a dividend payable out of such profits."

We believe that it has been the common understanding of lawyers and businessmen that noncumulative stock is entitled to a dividend only if declared out of annual profits. If the directors use earnings for capital improvements and no dividend is declared within the year, the claim for that year is gone and cannot be asserted at a later date. But recently doubts have been raised that seem to have affected the minds of the court below. We suppose the ground for the doubts is the probability that the directors will be tempted to abuse their power in the usual case of a corporation controlled by the holders of the common stock. Their interest would lead them to use earnings for improvements rather than to pay dividends on stock they do not own. But whether the remedies are adequate or not, and apart from the fact that the control of the Wabash seems to have been in Class A, the class to which the plaintiffs belong, the law has long advised them that their rights depend upon the judgment of men subject to just that possible bias.

When a man buys stock instead of bonds he takes a greater risk in business. No one suggests that he has a right to dividends if there are no net earnings. But the investment presupposes that the business is to go on, and therefore even if there are net earnings, the holder of stock, preferred as well as common, is entitled to have a dividend declared only out of such part of the earnings as can be applied to dividends consistently with a wise administration of a going concern. When, as was the case here, the dividends in each fiscal year were declared to be noncumulative and no net income could be so applied within the fiscal year referred to in the certificate, the right for that year was gone. If the right is extended further upon some conception of policy, it is enlarged beyond the meaning of the contract and the common and reasonable understanding of men.

Decree reversed.

CASE QUESTIONS

1. Distinguish between common and preferred stock.
2. Why are the preferred stockholders bringing this case?
3. When are the preferred holders entitled to their dividends?
4. What discretion do directors have regarding dividends?

MINORITY RIGHTS

The majority stockholders have the right to control their corporation. But the majority also has a duty to run the corporation in the best interests of all the stockholders. They have a fiduciary duty to the minority stockholders. This means the majority cannot use control of the corporation to benefit themselves alone and cannot engage in any activity that conflicts with the proper running of the corporation. If the majority violates this duty, the minority stockholders can sue them for violation of their minority rights. Courts generally do not interfere with the internal operations of a corporation. But if the majority stockholders violate the rights of the minority, then the court can order whatever remedy is necessary to stop this wrong. The remedy may be to dissolve the corporation, substitute new managers for the majority stockholders, or order the majority to pay damages to the minority stockholders.

Perlman v. Feldmann
219 F. 2d 173 (1955)

Clark, Chief Judge.

This case is brought by minority stockholders of Newport Steel Corporation to compel accounting for, and restitution of, allegedly illegal gains that the defendants received from the sale in August, 1950, of their controlling interest in the corporation. Feldmann was the dominant stockholder, the chairman of the board of directors, and the president of the corporation. Newport operated mills for the production of steel products. The buyers, Wilport Company, consisted of steel users who were interested in securing a source of supply in a market becoming ever tighter in the Korean War. Plaintiffs contend that the money paid for the stock included compensation for the sale of a corporate asset, a power held in trust for the corporation by Feldmann as its fiduciary. This power was the ability to control the allocation of the corporate product in a time of short supply. Plaintiffs argue that in the situation here disclosed the vendors must account to the minority stockholders for that share of their profit that is attributable to the sale of the corporate power.

The lower court dismissed the suit. Reversed.

Both as director and as dominant stockholder, Feldmann stood in a fiduciary relationship to the corporation and to the minority stockholders as beneficiaries thereof. His fiduciary obligation must in the first instance be measured by the law of Indiana, the state of incorporation of Newport.

Directors of a business corporation act in a strictly fiduciary capacity. Their office is a trust. When a director deals with his corporation, his acts will be closely scrutinized. Directors of a corporation are its agents and they are governed by the rules relating to honesty and fair dealing in the management of the affairs of the corporation. They must not, in any degree, allow their official conduct to be swayed by their private interest, which must yield to official duty. In a transaction between a director and his corporation, where he acts for himself and his business at the same time, it is presumed that self-interest will overcome his fidelity to his business. Absolute and most scrupulous good faith is the very essence of a director's obligation to his corporation.

We do not find compliance with the corporate fiduciary duty. We do not mean to suggest that a majority stockholder cannot dispose of his controlling block of stock to outsiders without having to account to his corporation for profits. But when the sale necessarily results in a sacrifice of corporate good will and in unusual profit to the fiduciary who has caused the sacrifice, he should account for his gains. So in a time of market shortage, where a call on a corporation's product commands an unusually large premium in one form or another, we think it sound law that a fiduciary may not take for himself the value of this premium. Such personal gain at the expense of the other stockholders seems particularly reprehensible when made by the trusted president and director of a company. In this case the violation of duty seems to be all the clearer because of this triple role in which Feldmann appears.

Hence, to the extent that the price received by Feldmann included such a bonus, he is accountable to the minority stockholders who sue here.

CASE QUESTIONS

1. Explain the duty owed by Feldmann to the minority shareholders.
2. How was his duty violated?
3. Explain the rights of a minority shareholder.

Stockholders' minority rights may be enforced through an individual lawsuit, a stockholders' class action lawsuit, or a derivative action. An *individual* stockholder can sue when a wrongful act done to the corporation injures only the stockholder and the rights of other stockholders and creditors will not be affected by the suit. For example, if all but one stockholder are officers of the corporation who are taking excessive salaries, the non-officer stockholder can bring an individual lawsuit to recover some of those salaries. Individual legal action can enforce any of a stockholder's rights discussed in this chapter. Where a wrongful act harms the entire corporation, a stockholder cannot sue individually but must use either a class action or derivative action.

The *class action suit* is appropriate where a number of stockholders have a right or claim to enforce against the same person. Courts permit the stockholders to join all of their individual lawsuits into one law case to recover for all stockholders. This device saves all persons involved in the legal action substantial time and money. Each court determines rules for a class action suit. Generally, there must be similar facts and similar legal issues among each of the separate stockholder complaints. A small number of stockholders act as representatives for all the stockholders, and each stockholder must share the legal expenses of the class action. Any recovery made must go to all stockholders fairly.

Stockholders can bring a lawsuit for the benefit of their corporation when the directors refuse to sue for some wrongful act done to the corporation. This law suit is a *derivative action* and it can be directed against officers or directors of the corporation or any outsiders who caused some injury to the corporation. For example, a corporation may refuse to sue its president for a wrongful use of corporate funds because the president is a personal friend of the directors, or a corporation might refuse to sue its customer for nonpayment of a debt because the customer is a friend of the officers. In both examples, a stockholder can bring a derivative action against the president or customer. The stockholder has this right to sue on behalf of the corporation—the stockholder derives the right to sue when the corporation refuses to sue. Any money recovered normally goes to the corporation, less expenses. To maintain this action, the stockholder must own stock in the corporation at the time the wrongful act occurred and must request the corporation to sue for the wrongful act. Stockholder approval of the corporate policy may nullify the derivative action.

Smith v. Brown-Borhek Company
200 A.2d 398 (1964)

Bell, Chief Justice.

Plaintiff owns 516 out of a total of 8,000 shares of stock in the Brown-Borhek Company. He brought this stockholder's derivative suit to recover for the corporation $605,507, the amount of the loss allegedly resulting from negligent mismanagement by the individual defendants, who are officers and directors. The defendants denied plaintiff's allegations and alleged the stockholders ratified their acts. The Court of Common Pleas granted defendants' motion for judgment and this appeal followed.

The transactions complained of are a series of sales on credit by Brown-Borhek Company to a large customer, Raydel Homes Corporation, and an eventual compromise of Raydel's debt.

Raydel's debt of $605,507 to Brown-Borhek was compromised by an agreement under which Brown-Borhek received $363,300 worth of Raydel five percent noncumulative preferred stock with a par value of ten dollars a share and a promissory note for $242,207, with interest at six percent. Shortly after this transaction, Raydel went bankrupt.

Plaintiff does not allege fraud nor personal profit by the defendants but alleges that the above transactions occurred when the individual defendants knew or should have known (a) that Raydel's liabilities greatly exceeded its assets, (b) that it was unable to meet its current obligations, and (c) that defendants had no reasonable expectation that the indebtedness would be paid.

Defendants claimed immunity from this suit because stockholders ratified the transaction.

The general rule is well established that stockholders can ratify any action of the board of directors that they themselves could have lawfully authorized. This general rule is subject, however, to the limitation that the majority stockholder may not, as against the corporation and minority stockholder, dissipate or waste its funds, or fraudulently dispose of them in any way, either by ratifying the action of the board of directors in voting themselves illegal salaries or by any other similar act.

> Courts are reluctant to interfere in the internal management of a corporation, since that is a matter for the discretion and judgment of the directors and stockholders, unless a minority stockholder's rights are jeopardized or injured by fraud or waste of company assets, or an overreaching, actual or legal.

In the instant case the stockholders were fairly and fully informed that the actions of the officers and directors in connection with the Raydel Account were to come before the annual meeting for consideration and approval. There was no fraud or concealment. Judgment affirmed.

CASE QUESTIONS

1. What acts of negligent mismanagement are alleged in this case?
2. Describe the defenses put forth by management.
3. Under what circumstances can shareholders ratify acts of bad management?

OTHER RIGHTS

Some corporate transactions require special procedures before they can be carried out. Stockholders have a right to see that these procedures are followed. For example, a change in the corporation's charter generally requires advance notice to all stockholders, and a certain percentage of stockholders must approve these changes. Also, a merger of the corporation with another, or a sale of a substantial portion of its assets, or a termination of the corporation must be approved by stockholders, often by a higher percentage vote than a mere majority. Some state laws give stockholders appraisal rights. This means a corporation must buy back stock from those stockholders who are dissatisfied with corporate policy.

Jaquith Co. v. Island Creek Coal Co.
219 A.2d 514 (1966)

Weintraub, Chief Justice.

This action arises out of a corporate merger. Plaintiffs, claiming to have dissented from the merger, brought this action for the appointment of appraisers to fix the value of their shares and for the payment of the sums so fixed. The critical question is whether plaintiffs gave written notice of their dissent as required by the statute. The trial court held for plaintiffs. We certified defendant's appeal. Affirmed.

The statute requires a corporation to buy shares from a stockholder (1) if he does not vote for the merger, and (2) if he, at any time prior to the vote on such merger, gives to the corporation in which he is a stockholder written notice of his dissent. Plaintiffs voted by mail against the merger. Thus the question is whether this letter can tell the company that the shareholder dissents.

The statute does not specify the form or content of the required "dissent." It does not require a statement of an intent to seek an appraisal. It requires no more than a written notice of disagreement. A letter with a mandate for a vote "Against" the proposal surely expresses the shareholder's disagreement. If the letter were produced for the first time at the stockholders' meeting, it could readily be disputed that it sufficed as written notice to the corporation of a dissent prior to the vote. But here the letter was solicited by management and received by it well before the vote. In its solicitation the corporation, speaking of the subject of "dissenting stockholders," said that under the New Jersey

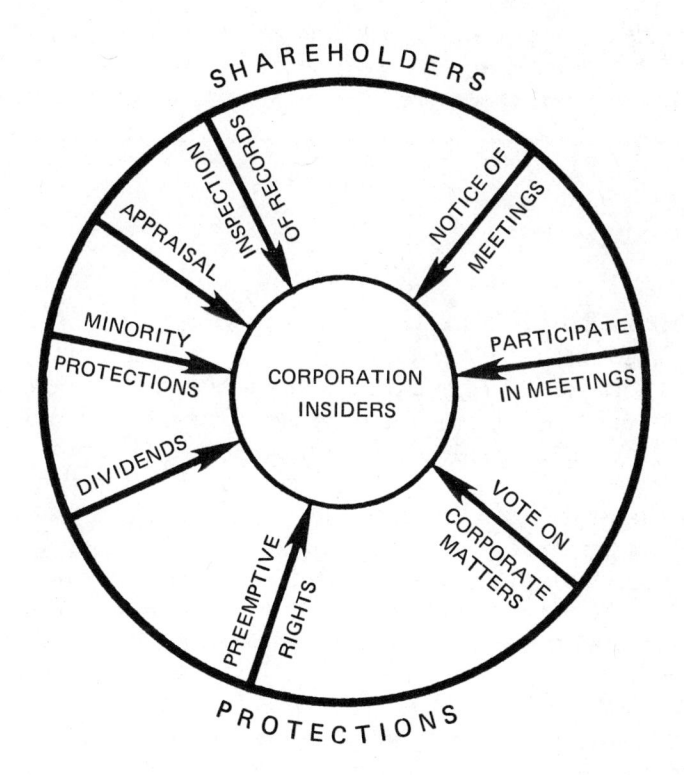

FIGURE 5–1: Shareholder rights are essential to protect outside owners from insiders controlling corporations.

statute "any stockholder of West Kentucky dissenting from the Joint Agreement of Merger and shall give to West Kentucky written notice of his dissent at any time prior to the vote on the Joint Agreement of Merger and shall not vote in favor of the Joint Agreement of Merger" will have a right of appraisal. A shareholder could readily assume that the letter gave the company written notice of his dissent prior to the vote.

Thus the corporation complicated the scene by what it did and by what it failed to say. It created a situation in which a vote "Against" became ambiguous. One shareholder could think a vote against the merger was not a demand for appraisal and payment if the proposal should be carried. Another shareholder could as readily think, as plaintiffs here contend, that his or her vote, if returned to the company in advance of the vote, informed the company that appraisal and payment were sought if the merger ensued. The ambiguity was of the company's making and should be resolved against it.

CASE QUESTIONS

1. What right does a shareholder have if dissatisfied with a merger?
2. Explain the procedure for enforcing this right. Show the role of the letter in this procedure.

STOCKHOLDER LIABILITIES

Many stockholder liabilities can be inferred from the previous discussion of stockholder rights. For example, a stockholder who knowingly receives an illegal dividend may be forced to return it to the corporation. A majority stockholder has a duty to run the corporation for the benefit of all stockholders. Some states impose liability on stockholders for debts of the corporation if they used the corporation to deceive or defraud creditors. Stockholders may be liable for corporate debts if the corporation exceeded its powers in contracting debts with creditors. The next two chapters will show examples of stockholder liabilities for violations of the federal securities laws. These liabilities broaden the traditional liability of stockholders. Today, stockholders have liability limited by the amount paid for their stock, unless a court decides stockholders should have greater liabilities to creditors, minority stockholders, or the public.

REVIEW QUESTIONS

1. Define a corporation and state why it is important to the American economy.
2. Describe the importance of the corporation charter and bylaws.
3. List the rights stockholders have in a corporation.
4. Summarize stockholder liabilities in a corporation.
5. Ajax purchased five shares of stock in fifteen different corporations. Each of the corporations made war products used by the Department of Defense. Ajax requested a list of stockholder names and addresses from each corporation to mail them information opposing the continued manufacture of these items and to seek their support in voting for a change in production to more profitable items. This request was denied by the corporations and Ajax seeks a court order compelling them to disclose the names. Should the court honor Ajax's right of inspection?
6. Corporate bylaws require fifteen days notice to all shareholders of any meeting called by the directors of the corporation. The bylaws also require an annual meeting on the third Wednesday of September. No notice of the annual meeting went to stockholders. The directors argued none was necessary because constructive notice of the annual meeting was in the bylaws. Is this argument correct?
7. Boston Corporation issued stock that carried with it preemptive rights. Carlson purchased a substantial block of this stock, giving her thirty-percent ownership of the corporation. The directors wanted to exclude her from any effective control, so they voted to issue substantially more stock. Carlson was given the option of subscribing to her thirty percent of the new stock. But with an offering price of ten dollars per share, she was unable to purchase any shares. Carlson sues the directors, complaining they denied her the preemptive rights to which she was entitled. How should the court rule?
8. Smith and Jones, two shareholders in a small close corporation, instituted a derivative action against Bundwell for damages caused to the business. Evidence at the trial established that Bundwell contracted to sell oil to the corporation at a fixed price. World economic and political conditions caused the price of oil to increase substantially over the contract price and Bundwell refused to sell at the agreed-upon price. The corporation

refused to sue him, arguing that to do so could impair the delivery of oil, even at the higher price. The trial court ruled in favor of the shareholders and Bundwell appealed. On what basis could the appellate court overrule the trial court?

9. Jackson was the owner and principal stockholder in Jackson Construction Corporation, formed to build homes on a tract of land he owned. As each home was constructed and sold, Jackson would dissolve the corporation and create a new one. Taylor purchased one of these homes while it was still under construction. When the house was finished, Taylor noticed several defects in it. Since the workmanship was guaranteed by the builder, Taylor sued Jackson Construction Corporation. The court dismissed the complaint because the business was dissolved. What remedy does Taylor have against Jackson?

6

SECURITIES ACT OF 1933

*This Act indicates the Congressional purpose to require an accompanying registration statement of securities with the offer or sale of a conventional issue of securities to the general public; to exempt isolated transactions from the burden of registration requirements; the imposition of liability for the failure to register nonexempt transactions; to ensure the full and truthful disclosure of all pertinent facts to undisclosed and unidentified prospective purchasers; and to leave the fraud remedies to the more isolated transactions involving known purchasers. (*Woodward v. Wright, *266 F.2d 108, 1959.)*

State laws, the corporation charter, and its bylaws give the stockholder certain rights. But to enforce these rights, a stockholder must hire a lawyer and sue the corporation in court. The stockholder must assume the financial burden of suing. However, not all stockholders may feel they have suffered a serious enough wrong from their corporation to justify the time and money costs of suing. Many stockholders do not care if the corporation acts improperly as long as the value of their shares increases. And the investing public has none of the rights discussed in the last chapter until they become stockholders. To protect potential investors and stockholders from misrepresentation and manipulation and to establish fair trading practices in the securities markets, Congress passed several securities laws. These laws help the investing public to make informed investment decisions. But it is the investor, not the government, who must make the ultimate judgment about a security's worth.

In this chapter, we will study the major sections and the current interpretations of the first important federal securities law, the Securities Act of 1933. This law requires a corporation to furnish investors with relevant financial, and other information concerning securities offered for sale and prohibits fraudulent acts in the sale of securities. The law accomplishes these objectives by requiring government registration of certain securities before they can be advertised or sold. Registration requires public disclosure of specific information. Violations of this law may result in civil and criminal penalties.

DEFINITION OF A SECURITY

Securities must be registered before they can be sold. Stocks and bonds are the most common types of securities but not the only ones. The Securities Act of 1933, Section 2(1), defines a security as: "... any note, stock, treasury stock, bond, debenture, evidence of indebtedness, certificate of interest or participation in any profit sharing agreement, collateral trust certificate, preorganization certificate or subscription, transferable share, investment contract, voting trust certificate, certificate of deposit for a security, fractional undivided interest in oil, gas or other mineral rights, or, in general, any interest or instrument commonly known as a security...."

This is a far-reaching definition, including as a security any investment in which the owner expects some profit primarily coming from the efforts of other people rather than through the investor's own work. Some examples of securities contracts are contracts for the sharing of profits from the sale of the offspring of animals and produce from citrus groves where others must raise or care for the property, franchise operations, and mineral exploration contracts. Courts do not look merely at the name of a business venture to determine whether it is a security. Instead, courts examine the elements of the transaction. To become a security, the venture must be started with the intention of dividing up profits according to ownership, represented by transferable shares. In a recent Supreme Court case, *United Housing Foundation, Inc.* v. *Forman*, 421 U.S. 837 (1975), the Court ruled that stock in a cooperative housing project did not become a security even though investors expected a profit when they sold their stock. The project was a nonprofit operation giving living space to the purchasers of the stock. The following case is a classic definition of a security under the Securities Act.

S.E.C. v. Howey
328 U.S. 293 (1946)

Mr. Justice Murphy.

The SEC sued to stop respondents from using the mails and instrumentalities of interstate commerce in the offer and sale of unregistered and non-exempt securities in violation of Section 5(a) of the Securities Act. The District Court denied the injunction and the Fifth Circuit Court of Appeals affirmed. We granted certiorari.

The respondents, W.J. Howey Company and Howey in the Hills Service, Inc., are Florida corporations under direct common control and management. The Howey Company owns large tracts of citrus acreage in Florida. It has planted 500 acres annually, keeping half of the groves for itself and offering the other half to the public to help finance additional development. Howey in the Hills Service, Inc., cultivates the groves and markets the crops.

Each prospective customer was offered both a land sales contract and a service contract, after having been told it is not feasible to invest in a grove without a service contract. Purchasers of land receive a deed, but the service company leases the land back. For a fixed fee plus the cost of labor and materials, the company has full discretion and authority over the cultivation of the groves, the harvest and marketing of the crops. The company then allocates the net profits to the owners. All business is done in the company name.

It is admitted that the mails and instrumentalities of interstate commerce are used in the sale of the land and service contracts and that no registration statement or letter of notification has ever been filed with the commission in accordance with the Securities Act of 1933 and its rules and regulations.

Section 2(1) of the act defines the term "security" to include the commonly known documents traded for speculation or investment. This definition also includes securities of a more variable character, such as "certificate of interest or participation in any profit sharing agreement," "investments contract," and "in general, any interest or instrument commonly known as a security." The legal issue in this case is whether the land sales contract, deed, and service contract together constitute an investment contract within the meaning of Section 2(1). The lower courts, in reaching a negative answer to this problem, treated the contracts and deeds as separate transactions involving no more than an ordinary real estate sale and an agreement by the seller to manage the property for the buyer.

The term investment contract is undefined by the Securities Act or by relevant legislative reports. But the term was common in many state "blue sky" laws in existence prior to the adoption of the federal statute. Although the term was also undefined by the state laws, it had been broadly construed by state courts so as to give the investing public a full measure of protection. Form was disregarded for substance and emphasis was placed upon economic reality. An investment contract thus came to mean a contract or scheme for the placing of capital or money to get income or profit from its employment. This definition was uniformly applied by state courts to a variety of situations where individuals invested money in a common enterprise with the expectation that they would earn a profit solely through the efforts of the promoter or of someone other than themselves.

By including an investment contract within the scope of Section 2(1) of the Securities Act, Congress used a term whose meaning was fixed by prior judicial interpretation. In other words, an investment contract for the purposes of the Securities Act means a contract, transaction, or scheme whereby a person invests his money in a common enterprise and is led to expect profits solely from the efforts of the promoter or a third party, it being immaterial whether the shares in the enterprise are evidenced by formal certificates or by nominal interests in the physical assets employed in the enterprise. This definition is a flexible rather than a static principle, one that is capable of adaption to meet the countless and variable schemes devised by those who seek the use of the money of others on the promise of profits.

The transactions in this case clearly involve investment contracts. The companies are offering something more than land, something different from a farm or orchard coupled with management services. They are offering an opportunity to contribute money and to share in the profits of a large citrus fruit enterprise managed and partly owned by Howey. They are offering this opportunity to persons who reside in distant localities and who lack the equipment and experience needed to cultivate, harvest, and market the citrus products. Such persons have no desire to occupy the land or to develop it themselves; they are attracted solely by the prospects of a return on their investment. Indeed, individual development of the plots of land that are offered and sold would seldom be economically feasible due to their small size. Such tracts are useful as citrus groves only when cultivated and developed as parts of a larger area.

Reversed.

CASE QUESTIONS

1. Explain the investment nature of Howey's business.
2. Define a security.
3. Is it necessary for profits to come solely from the efforts of others?

REGISTRATION REQUIREMENTS

Before a corporation can offer its securities to the public, a registration statement must be filed with the government. When the statement becomes effective, the securities can be offered for sale. Registration requires disclosure of relevant information so that investors can appraise the merits of a security. To that end, investors must be given a prospectus, containing a summary of the information in the registration statement.

In general, the registration statement must contain: a description of the corporation's property and business, a detailed statement of the capital structure and the terms of the security offering, information about corporate management, a description of the uses to which proceeds from the sale will be put, the terms of all contracts between the corporation and those hired to sell the security, a copy of the prospectus, and detailed financial statements certified by independent public accountants. This registration statement must be signed by the officers and directors of the corporation, any expert named in the statement who helped prepare it, and others who participated in

---

TABLE 6-1. REGISTRATION STATEMENT AND PROSPECTUS

In general, the registration statement must contain the following information:

1. the name of the business,
2. a description of its activities and assets,
3. a listing of all managers and promoters,
4. its earnings and capital structure,
5. the plan for selling this security,
6. the proposed uses for any money raised by the sale,
7. an explanation of any securities sold other than for cash,
8. a list of all major stockholders in the firm,
9. managers' stock ownership in the firm,
10. compensation and stock options for officers and directors,
11. a list of all pending legal actions by and against the firm,
12. an audited financial statement,
13. the stock marketing experience of every issuer and distributor,
14. explanations about financial relationships between the experts preparing the registration statement and the firm,
15. a list of all prior sales of unregistered securities and other special security sales,
16. a list of all subsidiaries, franchises, and concessions,
17. financial statements,
18. a list of all major contracts,
19. signatures of all directors, officers and experts preparing the registration statement, and
20. an auditors certified opinion.

The prospectus must contain the first twelve items.

its preparation. These may include attorneys, accountants, engineers, and other technical experts.

The registration statement and prospectus become public immediately upon being filed with the government. It is unlawful to sell or offer to sell the security until the statement becomes effective. The Securities Act provides that registration statements shall become effective on the twentieth day after filing, but the government can extend this time. After filing but before the effective date, the securities can be publicized orally or by a written summary of the information in the registration statement. This preliminary written statement is a red herring prospectus. Corporations may also put brief announcements in the press about a new security. These are called tombstone ads. All other publicity about the security prior to the effective date is prohibited.

S.E.C. v. Manor Nursing Centers, Inc.
458 F.2d 1082 (1972)

Timbers, Circuit Judge.

Ira Feinberg was sole owner of a corporation known as 133 County Road, Inc., operating a nursing home in Tenafly, New Jersey. Exrine, a securities lawyer, persuaded Feinberg to sell to the public securities in the nursing home. A new corporation was organized in 1969, called Manor Nursing Centers, Inc. It acquired the assets of 133 County Road and issued approximately 1.2 million shares of common stock to Feinberg. He then sold 62,000 shares to certain relatives and friends, and 138,000 shares to two corporations controlled by Ezrine. Three hundred fifty thousand shares were to be sold to the public to raise over $3 million for the business.

Ezrine prepared the registration statement and arranged for underwriting. The SEC alleged that there were several errors and misrepresentations in the registration statement and prospectus. The District Court agreed with the SEC, ruling that defendants violated the securities laws.

With respect to this appeal, it is important to note statements made concerning the terms of the offering. First, it was presented on an "all or nothing" basis. This meant, according to the prospectus, that unless all shares were sold, the offer would terminate and money would be returned. Secondly, the prospectus stated that subscribers funds will be maintained in escrow and will not be available for other use. Thirdly, the registration statement indicated that shares sold in the offering would be sold only for cash. Finally, the statement did not disclose that certain purchasers would be offered special compensation for their agreement to participate in the offering.

The offering of Manor shares began on December 8, 1969, the effective date of the registration statement. No escrow account was established. From the very outset, Manor shares could not be sold. Feinberg met with representatives of Carlton Cambridge & Company, a stock brokerage firm. They were given 15,000 shares at no cost but agreed to sell 142,000 shares to the public. Part of this block was sold to the public. Also, at the same time the public was buying this stock, others were purchasing the stock for substantially less than the price announced in the prospectus.

The District Court correctly held that the defendants had violated the prospectus delivery requirement of Section 5(b)(2) of the 1933 Act. This section prohibits the delivery of a security unless the security is accompanied or preceeded by a prospectus that meets the requirements of Section 10(a). To meet these requirements, a prospectus must contain a summary of the information contained in the registration statement. In turn, the registration statement, pursuant to Section 7 of the 1933 act, must set forth certain information specified in the 1933 act. Among the items that the registration statement and the prospectus must contain are the use of proceeds, the estimated net proceeds, the price at which the security will be offered to the public, and all commissions or discounts paid.

The Manor prospectus did not disclose the information required. The evidence showed that developments after the effective date of the registration statement made the information contained in the prospectus false and misleading. Moreover, Manor and its principals did not amend or supplement the prospectus to reflect changes that made the information inaccurate.

Manor contends, however, that Section 5(b)(2) does not require a prospectus to be amended to reflect material developments that occur subsequent to the effective date of the registration statement. This contention is based on the assumption that the prospectus spoke only as of the effective date of the statement and that the prospectus contained no false or misleading statements as of the effective date. This claim is without merit. The antifraud provisions of the 1933 act require that the prospectus reflect post-effective developments that make the prospectus misleading in any material respect.

We hold that Manor was under a duty to amend or supplement its prospectus to reflect post-effective developments, and their failure to do so stripped the Manor prospectus of compliance with the law.

CASE QUESTIONS

1. *Explain the underwriting function and describe its use in this case.*
2. *Define prospectus and summarize some of its contents.*
3. *What was false and misleading about the prospectus in this case?*

When a registration statement is filed, officials examine it to see if it complies with the disclosure requirements of the 1933 act. If the statement appears to be incomplete or inaccurate, the corporation must file amendments. If the statement contains false or misleading information, the government can refuse or suspend its effectiveness by issuing a stop order. This order does not bar permanently the effectiveness of a registration statement or the future sale of the security. It can be removed when corrections are made. This examination process contributes to the general reliability of the registration disclosures, but it does not guarantee the accuracy of any information contained in the statement. Also, government review does not indicate any opinion about the worth of the securities or their future worth in any public trading. In fact, the government cannot deny registration to a security offering because it thinks that the price is too high or that other investments are better. The act merely prohibits false and misleading statements and gives the stockholder important rights to sue for any losses incurred because of defective registration statements.

EXEMPTIONS FROM REGISTRATION

The registration requirement applies to securities sold by foreign and domestic corporations. There are, however, certain exemptions from the registration requirement. Some of these are:

Private Offerings. If the proposed sale of a security is to a small group of people who have access to the kind of information required in a registration statement, then no filing is necessary. But this stock cannot be resold to the public without registration.

**Hill York Corp. v. American International Franchises, Inc.
448 F.2d 680 (1971)**

Clark, Circuit Judge.

Freemans and Browne developed a franchise promotion scheme designed to funnel funds from the sale of stock in certain franchise sales centers to themselves as stockholders of American International Franchises, Inc. The concept involved marketing two restaurant franchises called Hickory Corral and Italian Den. American would find local investors to incorporate a statewide or regional franchise sales center. Upon payment of a fee, the owner had the exclusive right to sell franchises in the territory. The local investors in the franchise sales contract centers would sell stock to a small number of persons who would most likely furnish supplies and services to the restaurants.

Freemans and Browne formed Florida Franchise Systems, Inc., as a state franchise sales center. Shepherd, Quinn, and McDaniel were incorporators, who in turn sold stock in Florida Franchise to the plaintiffs. Sales information and aids were furnished by American International. Also, Florida Franchise was required to pay $25,000 to American International for the right to sell franchises in Florida and $1,000 per month as a franchise fee. Plaintiffs allege these activities are an illegal scheme and sue to recover their investments under Section 12(1) and (2) of the Securities Act of 1933. Defendants argue their transactions were exempt from the act as a private offering. The District Court ruled for the plaintiffs.

The SEC has stated that the question of public or private offering is one of fact and must depend upon the circumstances of each case. We agree with this approach. The following specific facts are relevant to deciding whether an offering is private:

1. The number of offerees and their relationship to the issuer and to each other. No particular number is required. If the offerees know each other and the issuer from prior business dealings, then it is more likely to be a private offering.
2. The number of units offered. There is no fixed number, but the smaller the offering the less likely it is a public offering.
3. The size of the offering. The smaller the amount of money raised from the sale, the more likely it is a private offering.
4. The manner of the offering. A private offering is more likely made directly to the offerees than through public distribution.

The way we interpret these factors is in light of the statutory purpose. The design of the Securities Act of 1933 is to protect investors by promoting full disclosure of information for informed investment decisions. Thus the ultimate test is whether the particular class of persons affected needs the protections of the act.

The distribution here was nationwide, and the offerees did not have the sophistication to obtain from the defendants the type of information that would be included in a registration statement. There is no evidence showing how many offerees were involved or the experience of those persons. The defendants did not prove the defense of a private offering. Affirmed.

CASE QUESTIONS

1. *Explain how the franchise system worked. Why is it a security?*
2. *Summarize the requirements of a private offering.*
3. *Why was this offering a public offering?*

Intrastate Offerings. The registration requirement applies to securities sold to residents of states different from that of the issuing corporation or to sales made through the mails. If the issuer and the purchasers are residents of the same state, registration is not required. Rights to resell the stock are limited until a registration statement is made.

S.E.C. v. McDonald Investment Co.
343 F. Supp. 343 (1972)

Neville, District Judge.

The SEC sued McDonald Investment Company and H.J. McDonald, the company's president and treasurer and the owner of all the company's outstanding common stock. The SEC requests that the defendants be permanently enjoined from offering for sale and selling securities without complying with the registration requirements.

All parties agree to the following pertinent facts. The defendant company was incorporated in Minnesota, where its principle place of business is located and where all of its books and records are kept. Prior to 1971, the defendants registered an offering for $4,000,000 of the company's own installment notes with the state of Minnesota. Sales of these notes were made to Minnesota residents only. The company now plans to lend the proceeds from the sales of these notes to land developers with security taken from them in the form of mortgages. The installment note buyers will not have any direct ownership in the mortgages nor in the business of the developers.

No registration statement for the installment notes was filed with the SEC. Section 5 of the 1933 act in general makes it illegal to offer or sell a security unless a registration statement containing the prescribed information has been filed with the commission. Section 3(a)(11) of the act exempts intrastate sales of securities from registration: "Any security which is a part of an issue offered and sold only to persons resident within a single State or Territory, where the issuer of such security is a person resident and doing business within or, if a corporation, incorporated by and doing business within such State or Territory."

In order to qualify for this exemption, the issuer must offer and sell his securities only to persons within a single state and the issuer must be resident of that same state. In addition to this, the issuer must conduct a predominant amount of his business within the same state. This refers to the income-producing activities of the business. Here, the income-producing activities of the issuer will be located in other states.

The legislative history of the Securities Act clearly shows that this exemption applies only to local financing that may practically be consummated completely within the state or territory in which the issuer is both incorporated and doing business. The exemption should not be relied upon if the financing is for expansion outside the state, to merge with out-of-state firms, or where the issuer performs only minor clerical tasks in the local state. The success of the installment notes in this case depends upon the success of land development outside the state. Therefore, the exemption is lost. Injunction granted.

CASE QUESTIONS

1. Why were these installment notes sold?
2. When is a security issue exempt from registration as an intrastate offering?

Government Securities. Securities of municipal, state, and other government agencies do not register with the federal government. However, states may have laws requiring registration with a state agency.

Small Offerings. The government specifies the amount of money which must be raised from the sale of securities before registration is necessary. This amount varies, but now stands at $500,000.

Other. Corporations regulated by other agencies of the federal government. Some of these corporations include banks, railroads, utilities, and airlines. Each of these companies will file statements with the administrative agency responsible for their regulation. Charitable institutions, religious associations, and insurance companies, are also exempt, each regulated to some degree by state laws. Also, registration applies only to issuers of securities, underwriters, and dealers, not to any other persons selling securities. The following case shows how confusing it may be to determine who is an issuer, underwriter, or dealer.

S.E.C. v. Datronics Engineers, Inc.
490 F.2d 250 (1973)

Bryan, Senior Circuit Judge.

The SEC sought a preliminary injunction to restrain Datronics Engineers, Inc., its officers and agents, as well as related corporations from continuing in alleged violation of the registration and antifraud provisions of the act. The alleged violations were committed in the sale of unregistered securities. Summary judgment went for the defendants and the commission appeals. We reverse.

Specifically, the complaint charged that Datronics violated the statutes by using the mails to distribute to its stockholders unregistered stock it owned in other corporations. The pattern of these distributions was as follows:

Datronics would organize a subsidiary corporation. This subsidiary would then merge with a small privately owned corporation. The sellers received stock in the subsidiary although Datronics kept a minority stock interest in the subsidiary as compensation for its services in arranging the merger. Then Datronics would distribute its stock in the subsidiary to stockholders of Datronics. None of this subsidiary stock was registered with the SEC, but Datronics used the mails to distribute the stock. This practice was repeated nine times.

Primarily, in our judgment, each of these stock distributions violated the Securities Act, in that Datronics used the mails to deliver an unregistered security. Datronics was actually an issuer and not exempted. Datronics and the other corporations contend, and the District Court agreed, that this type of transaction was not a sale. The argument is that it was no more than a dividend parceled out to stockholders from the corporation's portfolio of investments. But this argument fails because it does not recognize the definition of a sale contained in Section 2(3) of the act: "When used in this subchapter, unless the context is otherwise, . . . the term sale shall include every contract of sale or disposition of a security for value. The term offer for sale shall include every attempt to dispose of or solicitation of an offer to buy a security for value . . . ."

Concurring opinion. I note that the opinion of the court may not be broad enough read to cast doubt upon the legitimate business acquisition of one company by another or the legitimate business merger of two companies, although a market for securities sold as a consequence of the transfer may be created; for, as the opinion of the court recites, the market created by Datronics distributions was done without any business purpose of its own.

CASE QUESTIONS

1. *How was the distribution used to sell securities in this case?*
2. *Why did this transaction qualify as a sale of a security?*

3. Why are distributions of stock in a merger exempt from registration?

LIABILITIES

The Securities Act of 1933 imposes civil and criminal liability. A fine up to $10,000 and/or five years in jail for each wilful violation of the act or rules issued under it can be imposed. An investor who finds the registration statement contained false or misleading statements or failed to state a material fact can sue for any losses incurred by trading in that security. Those who may be liable are all who signed the registration statement, all directors, every expert who helped prepare the statement, underwriters, and even public relations people advertising the security. Each of these persons may defeat liability if they exercised due diligence in preparing the registration statement. The due diligence defense requires that each person who participates in the filing of the statement must make a reasonable investigation into the truth of the facts contained in it.

The act also prohibits the use in selling securities of any device or scheme that defrauds investors. This rule applies to registered and unregistered securities. Finally, the act requires persons who publicize a security in the media to disclose any compensation received for advertising it.

Escott v. Barchris Construction Corp.
283 F.Supp. 643 (1968)

McLean, District Judge.

This is an action by purchasers of five and one-half percent convertible subordinated fifteen year debentures of Barchris Construction Corporation. Plaintiffs purport to sue on their own behalf and on behalf of all other present and former holders of the debentures. When the action was begun on October 25, 1962, there were nine plaintiffs. Others joined. At the time of trial, there were over sixty.

The action is brought under Section 11 of the Securities Act of 1933. Plaintiffs allege that the registration statement of the debentures filed with the SEC contained material false statements and material omissions. The defendants fall into three categories: the persons who signed the statement, the underwriters, and the auditors.

Barchris built bowling centers. These were elaborate affairs, containing lanes, bars, and restaurants. The company was started by Vitolo and Pugliese in 1946. But with the introduction of automatic pin-setting machines in 1952, the business grew. Bowling rapidly became a popular sport, and bowling centers began to appear throughout the nation. Barchris installed about 3% of all lanes built in the United States. Its method of operation was to enter into a contract with a customer, receive from him at that time a comparatively small down payment on the purchase price, and proceed to construct and equip the bowling alley. When the work was finished, the customer paid the balance in notes, due over a number of years. Barchris discounted these notes with a factor and received part of their face amount in cash. The factor held part as a reserve.

In 1961, Barchris needed additional working capital. It decided to sell debentures to fill that need. A registration statement was prepared and filed with the SEC. It became effective in 1961 and the debentures were sold within two weeks. By that time, Barchris was experiencing difficulty in collecting amounts due from some of its customers. In 1962, the company filed bankruptcy and defaulted on the interest due on the debentures.

The registration statement contained a description of Barchris's business and its real property and remarks about its affairs. It also contained financial information, specifically a balance sheet audited by Peat, Marwick. It also contained unaudited figures on net sales, gross profit, and net earnings for the first quarter of 1961. Unfilled orders, contingent liability, and other information was in the registration statement.

The court found that Barchris had in the prospectus overstated sales, earnings, and current assets. It also understated its contingent liabilities, overestimated backlogs, and erroneously listed the amounts of loans outstanding to officers. The prospectus failed to state that a major portion of the debenture proceeds was used to pay off past debts rather than for expansion.

Section 11(b) of the act provides that:

"... no person, other than the issuer, shall be liable ... who shall sustain the burden of proof—... (3) that (A) as regards any part of the registration statement not purporting to be made on the authority of an expert ... he had, after reasonable investigation, reasonable ground to believe and did believe, at the time such part of the registration statement became effective, that the statements therein were true and that there was no omission to state a material fact required to be stated therein or necessary to make the statements therein not misleading ... and (C) as regards any part of the registration statement purporting to be made on the authority of an expert (other than himself) ... he had no reasonable ground to believe and did not believe at the time such part of the registration statement became effective, that the statements therein were untrue or that there was an omission to state a material fact required to be stated therein or necessary to make the statements therein not misleading ...."

Section 11(c) defines "reasonable investigation" as follows: "In determining ... what constitutes reasonable investigation and reasonable ground for belief, the standard of reasonableness shall be that required of a prudent man in the management of his own property." Every defendant has pleaded this affirmative defense.

Persons who signed the statement. Russo was the chief executive officer of Barchris, a member of the executive committee, and familiar with all aspects of the business. He could not have believed that there were no untrue statements or material omissions in the prospectus. Russo has no due diligence defenses.

Vitolo and Pugliese were the founders of the business. Although they exercised little control over the business, they were each directors and each signed the registration statement. Their liability does not depend upon whether they read it or understood it. They must make an investigation into the facts contained in the statement. They have not proved their due diligence defense.

Kircher was treasurer of Barchris, a certified public accountant, and an intelligent man. He was familiar with all aspects of the company's financial affairs. He must have known that in part the registration statement was untrue, and therefore he did not prove his due diligence defense.

Trilling was not a member of the executive committee; he was a minor figure. He may have been unaware of the errors in the statement. But as a signer, he could not avoid responsibility by leaving it up to others to investigate. He did not sustain the burden of proving his due diligence defense.

Birnbaum was a young lawyer, working as house counsel and assistant secretary of Barchris. He probably did not know of the errors in the statement but he made no investigation. Thus he did not have reasonable grounds to believe the statements were true. He did not satisfy his due diligence defense.

Auslander was an outside director, not an officer of the company. He signed the registration statement while it contained blank pages, not knowing its purpose. Section 11 imposes liability on a director no matter how new he is. He is presumed to know his responsibility when he becomes a director. He can escape that liability only by using the reasonable care to investigate facts that a prudent man would employ in the management of his own property. In my opinion, a prudent man would not act in an important matter without any knowledge of the relevant facts, in sole reliance on others who are strangers. Auslander has not established his due diligence defense.

Rose was another outside director who relied solely on the statements of Peat, Marwick and upon Barchris officers. What has been said about Auslander applies equally to Rose. He has not satisfied his due diligence defense.

Underwriters. The underwriters made no investigation of the accuracy of the prospectus. They say it is the company's prospectus, not theirs. Doubtless this is the way they customarily regard it. But the Securities Act makes no distinction. The underwriters are just as responsible for the registration statement and prospectus as the company, if either is false. If they may escape liability by taking at face value representations made to them by management, then the inclusion of underwriters among those liable under Section 11 affords the investors no additional protection. To effectuate the statute's purpose, the phrase reasonable investigation must be construed to require more effort on the part of the underwriters than the mere accurate reporting in the prospectus of the data presented to them by the company. The underwriters must make a reasonable attempt to verify the data submitted to them. They may not rely solely on the company's officers or on the company's counsel. A prudent man in the management of his own affairs would not rely on them.

Auditors. Section 11(b) provides "... no person ... shall be liable ... who shall sustain the burden of proof—(3) that ... (B) ... as regards any part of the registration statement purporting to be made upon his authority as an expert ... he had after reasonable investigation, reasonable ground to believe and did believe, at the time such part of the registration statement became effective, that the statements therein were true and that there was no omission to state a material fact required to be stated therein or necessary to make the statements therein not misleading ...." This defines the due diligence defense for an expert and Peat, Marwick has pleaded it.

Peat, Marwick's work was in general charge of a member of the firm, Cummings, and more immediately, Logan. Most of the actual work was performed by a senior accountant, Berardi, who had junior assistants, one of whom was Kennedy. Berardi was about thirty years old, was not yet a CPA, and had no previous experience with the bowling industry. This was his first job as a senior accountant. It is unnecessary to recount everything that Berardi did in the course of the audit. But he did incorrectly report the 1960 figures in the prospectus, failed to discover that some assets had been sold, erred in computing the contingent liability on leaseback arrangements, failed to discover errors in 1961 figures and other errors. What Berardi did do was accept figures prepared by the management of Barchris, examine only the trial balance prepared by the company, and talk with Trilling. He did not examine the minutes of the executive committee.

Accountants should not be held to a standard higher than that recognized in their profession. I do not do so here. Berardi's review did not come up to that standard. He did not come up to the standards recommended by Peat, Marwick. He did not spend an adequate amount of time on the audit. Most important of all, he was too easily satisfied with glib answers to his inquiries. Generally accepted accounting principles require a more complete investigation under these circumstances. The burden of proof is on Peat, Marwick and they did not satisfy it.

Section 11(a) provides that when a registration statement contains an untrue statement of a material fact or omits to state a material fact, "any person acquiring such security ... may sue." Each plaintiff must prove his claim separately in court. This opinion merely expresses findings of fact and law common to all plaintiffs.

So ordered.

CASE QUESTIONS

1. Describe the errors contained in the registration statement.
2. Contrast the duty of an expert and a nonexpert signer of a registration statement.
3. Show how this duty was neglected by each of the defendants in this case.

MANAGEMENT GUIDELINES

The federal securities laws, SEC regulations, and court interpretations have created new degrees of liability for financial managers and others concerned with raising capital. Accordingly, every corporation should establish some guidelines to assist personnel in avoiding or minimizing their liability. The following are some suggestions:

1. A rule should be established that whenever any member of the corporation considers any dealings affecting the stock, bonds, or other securities of the business, professional assistance should be obtained. Raising money is a complex transaction involving many variables and alternatives. Experts in law, accounting, finance, and brokerage should evaluate the ramifications of any proposed securities financing.

2. A committee composed of experts in each of the areas mentioned above should be formed. Generally, the corporation's attorney, its certified public accountant, investment banker, and members of the financial management should be included. The committee should coordinate information, evaluate alternative financing plans, and make recommendations to top operating management. A spokesperson should be designated for liaison with the financial news organizations, and all other corporate employees should be instructed to avoid any discussions about the company to the media.

3. All managers involved in the financing should be advised of their duties and liabilities under the securities laws. The committee should work with these managers to avoid possible embarrassment to the corporation and serious legal penalties to the manager.

4. The committee should encourage all managers to obtain relevant information in preparation of the registration statement. All employees should be urged to cooperate with the committee by furnishing members all requested information. Each person intending to sign the registration statement should be urged to take an active role in obtaining and evaluating information furnished the committee. One member of the group should be designated as liaison officer with other employees.

5. The committee must decide upon the type of information to be disclosed about the company. Recent government directives require detailed financial statements, a summary of all legal actions involving the company, an explanation of

environmental and consumer issues affecting the business, and even a discussion of political involvement by the corporation, its officers and directors.

6. Preparation of the registration statements should be done by the corporation's legal counsel in cooperation with the committee. The statement must give full and fair disclosure about all aspects of the business affecting an investor's decision to commit funds to it. The SEC supplies forms that indicate the type of information required. When completed, the forms are sent to the SEC for examination. It either accepts, rejects, or requires additional information. Conferences with SEC officials can clarify any disputes.

7. When the statement becomes effective, securities can be sold to the public. Advice from the corporation's brokers and investment bankers is helpful at this point. While the statement is pending with the SEC, the committee should refrain from making any public statements about the corporation. Press releases or publicity during this period may be construed as advertisements to sell unregistered securities, a punishable offense. The committee can release a red herring prospectus and tombstone ad.

REVIEW QUESTIONS

1. Why was the Securities Act of 1933 necessary, and what are its principal requirements?

2. Explain the importance to an investor of each item required in a registration statement.

3. Explain the rationale for each exemption from the registration requirement.

4. Discuss the penalties for managers who do not comply with the Securities Act and indicate some ways a manager can avoid this liability.

5. Perlman was a wealthy doctor seeking to minimize his tax liability. His accountant suggested he invest in a tax shelter, a device by which assets can be put into a business with profits paid at a later time when Perlman would be in a lower tax bracket. To accomplish this, Perlman bought into a cattle-breeding farm. A manager of the farm would use Perlman's money to buy animals, breed them, and sell any offspring. Any profits made would be distributed to Perlman at a later time. The farm operation did not turn out to be profitable and Perlman sues. On what basis can he sue?

6. Fuller Corporation was a small corporation which sold shares of stock to residents of New York state. Some of the stock was sold to Oliver Corporation, a Connecticut-chartered business. The sales were made in New York. Was this transaction exempt from the Securities Act of 1933?

7. As part of a bonus system for its employees, Merrill Jones, Inc., sold at a discount ten shares of its stock to each employee who achieved a certain quota of sales. The firm did not register the securities offering with the SEC, alleging it was an exempt private offering. Is this correct?

8. As part of a public offering of its securities, Brown Corporation registered one million shares. It prepared a registration statement with the assistance of Peabody, its lawyer. While gathering information about the corporation, Peabody learned some of the directors made illegal cash contributions of corporate money to administrative agency members and political candidates. The lawyer did not report these transactions to the government and did not include them in the registration statement. He did instruct the directors to stop this illegal activity. Two years later,

the government learned of the contributions and fined the corporation. Amundson, an investor who purchased shares in Brown at the time of its public offering, sued the lawyer for losses he suffered and to recover the amount of the contributions and the fines paid by the directors. Is the lawyer liable?

9. In the above problem, part of the registration statement was signed by Siblis, an engineer who described some of the technical aspects of environmental requirements recently imposed on the corporation. She did not know about the illegal gifts. To what extent is she liable?

7

SECURITIES EXCHANGE ACT OF 1934

By this Act, Congress proposed to prevent inequitable and unfair practices and to insure fairness in securities transactions generally, whether conducted face to face, over the counter or on exchanges. (SEC v. Texas Gulf Sulpher, 401 F.2d 833, 1969.)

Companies issue securities with the intent of selling them to investors. To make sales easier, markets exist where representatives of buyers and sellers can meet to exchange money for securities. These markets are called exchanges. Congressional investigations revealed many abuses on securities exchanges. Insuring fair trading practices on these markets is as necessary to protecting investors as requiring a disclosure of information about securities. Congress responded to this challenge by enacting the Securities Exchange Act of 1934. This act broadened the disclosure requirements for securities, developed rules for trading practices on exchanges, and created the Securities Exchange Commission (SEC) to regulate the securities industry. In this chapter, we will study the relevant sections of this act.

REGISTRATION AND REPORTING REQUIREMENTS

Any corporation that wants its securities listed and traded on any of the public exchanges must file a registration application with the exchange and the SEC. A corporation listing its securities on the over-the-counter market must file a similar application if the corporation's assets exceed $1 million and the stockholders number 500 or more. These registration applications contain information similar to but not as extensive as the registration statements required under the Securities Act of 1933. Companies do not have to give investors this data. It can be inspected by any member of the public at the exchanges, however.

To keep its securities registered with the exchange, the corporation must file periodic reports with the government. These reports are an annual report (10K), a quarterly report (10Q), and sometimes a current report (8K). The 10K report must include audited financial statements for the year plus any current information about the conduct of business, its management, and the status of its securities. This report keeps the 1934 Act registration statement up to date. The 10Q report requires a summary of quarterly financial changes in the corporation. It does not have to be audited. At times, the 8K report must be filed with the government. This report details the effect of any changes in the amount of the corporation's securities outstanding, any default on some of its securities, any sale or purchase of assets, any changes of corporate control, and any other important event occuring in the life of the corporation since the last annual report.

Another provision of these reporting requirements governs the solicitation of proxies from holders of registered securities. A proxy is a written permission from a stockholder in a corporation allowing another person to vote the stockholder's shares. Proxies may be given for the election of directors and for the transaction of any corporate business. Some stockholders may ask for proxy votes from other stockholders. This request is a solicitation. In any solicitation, all material facts concerning the matters on which stockholders are asked to vote must be disclosed. Frequently, a proxy solicitation must contain an audited annual report. Where a contest for control of the corporation exists, the rules require disclosure of the names and interests of all parties to the contest, including their employment contracts, fringe benefit agreements, and a summary of all other business dealings they may have with the corporation.

Either management or outside groups can solicit proxies. Often management and outsiders will solicit proxies jointly from stockholders, using one form. Regardless of how proxies are solicited, each side can comment on the proposals made by the other, and stockholders have the opportunity of voting either "yes" or "no." Management can omit from proxies proposals that require the corporation to take action in excess of its powers. Also, management can omit any proposal on which stockholders have already voted on in the past three years. If misleading or false statements are made in proxy solicitation, the votes may be declared void and penalties imposed on the persons who are responsible.

A recent case discussed the use of proxy solicitations and the types of proposals which management must include. A public interest group purchased stock in Dow Chemical Company, then its chairman wrote a letter to the company expressing concern over Dow's policy of making napalm for use in war. This letter also requested that the company include in its next proxy solicitation a proposal to limit the sale of napalm. Dow refused to include this item in its proxy, citing Rule 14(a)(8) of the SEC. It exempts a proposal:

> If it clearly appears that the proposal is submitted by the security holder primarily for the purpose of enforcing a personal claim or redressing a personal grievance against the issuer or its management, or primarily for the purpose of promoting general economic, political, racial, religious, social or similar causes; or if the proposal consists of a recommendation or request that the management take action with respect to a matter relating to the conduct of the ordinary business operations of the issuer.

The court upheld the company's right to exclude this proposal for procedural reasons. But the dissenting opinion of one Supreme Court justice explained that modern corporations have tremendous economic power and the proxy enables the small stockholder to exercise some control over this power. (*SEC* v. *Medical Committee for Human Rights*, 404 U.S. 403, 1972.)

TRADING RULES

In addition to registration, reporting, and proxy rules, the act includes requirements for registration with the SEC of all national securities exchanges and all stockbrokers. To obtain registration, exchanges must agree to comply with governmental regulations and adopt rules insuring fair dealing to protect investors. For example, exchange rules must discipline members for improper conduct, and exchanges must establish and enforce a voluntary code of business ethics for its members and employees. Stockbrokers must conform their business practices to these standards as well as to those in the law and SEC regulations. Violations of these standards by brokers can result in suspension or termination of their right to sell securities. Both brokers and exchanges are subject to a number of trading rules established by the SEC. Some of these are:

Insider Reports. The act requires all directors, officers, and persons owning ten percent or more of a corporation's securities that are registered with the SEC to file a statement disclosing the amount of their stock ownership in the corporation. Every month, they must report all changes in their stock holdings.

Short-swing Trades. All directors, officers, and ten-percent stockholders of a corporation registered with the SEC who make a profit by trading in the securities of their corporation must turn the profit over to the corporation if it occurs within a six-month period. This section of the act prevents insiders from profiting from the use of any confidential information learned because of their inside role with the corporation. The Supreme Court exempts purchases and sales of stock within six months if there was a legitimate reason for making the short swing and no inside information was used. In *Reliance Electric Co.* v. *Emerson Electric Co.*, 404 U.S. 418 (1972), the Court explained this exemption. Here, Emerson purchased more than thirteen percent of the stock in Dodge Manufacturing Company, attempting to take it over through a stock merger. Instead, Dodge stockholders approved a merger with Reliance, and Emerson began selling out its stockholdings. Some of the sales were made within six months of their purchase, and Reliance sued to recover profits made by this transaction. The Court disallowed recovery, saying Emerson's sales were made in two parts: four percent within the six-month period and the remainder after six months. Liability for short-swing profits cannot be imposed merely because an investor structured the transaction with the intent of avoiding liability under the law when the investor had no confidential information.

Margin Trading. The act contains provisions governing margin trading in securities. It authorizes the Board of Governors of the Federal Reserve System to set limits on the amount of credit banks can give for purchasing securities.

Tender Offers. A tender offer is an offer to stockholders to buy their stock in exchange for money or other securities. In the late 1960s, a wave of corporate mergers alarmed the government, so it created new rules for tender offers. Any person seeking more than five percent of a corporation's securities for a merger must file with the SEC and give stockholders information about the offerer, any agreements with other stockholders, sources of the money used for the merger, the purpose of the merger, and future plans for the corporation that is to be taken over.

Rule 10(b)(5). This is a very broad rule whose limits have not been fully defined by the SEC or the courts. Basically, it prohibits any manipulative or deceptive act in violation of any rule the SEC may establish. Specifically, the rule states: "It shall be unlawful for any person, directly or indirectly, by use of any means or instrumentality of interstate commerce or of the mails, or any facility of any national securities exchange, (a) to employ any device scheme or artifice to defraud, (b) to make any untrue statement of a material fact or to omit to state a material fact necessary in order to make the statements made, in the light of the circumstances under which they were made, not misleading, or (c) to engage in any act, practice, or course of business which operates or would operate as a fraud or deceit upon any person, in connection with the purchase or sale of any security."

This rule applies to "any security," including nonregistered securities, over-the-counter securities, registered securities, and privately sold securities. Some examples of rule 10(b)(5) violations are: sales of stock when only one of the parties knows material confidential information about the stock or corporation; publication of misleading information about a corporation to encourage investors to buy its stock; reducing dividends to lower stock prices; using employee pension funds to buy stock simply to raise the stock's price; selling stock without filing required reports to the SEC; and buying stock without stating that the purpose of the purchase was for corporate control. Either the SEC or the investor can sue for violations of this rule. But before an investor can recover any damages, the U.S. Supreme Court now requires proof that a defendant had the intent to deceive, manipulate or defraud. *Ernst & Ernst* v. *Hochfelder*, 47 L. Ed. 668 (1976).

Three recent cases illustrate the current interpretations courts now give to rule 10(b)(5).

Superintendent of Insurance of the State of New York as Liquidator of Manhattan Casualty Company

v.

Bankers Life and Casualty Company
404 U.S. 6 (1971)

Mr. Justice Douglas.

Manhattan Casualty Company, now represented by New York's Superintendent of Insurance, was defrauded in the sale of certain securities in violation of the Securities Exchange Act of 1934. The District Court dismissed the complaint and the Court of Appeals affirmed.

Bankers Life agreed to sell all of Manhattan's stock to Begole for $5,000,000. It is alleged that Begole conspired with Bourne and others to pay for this stock, not out of their own funds, but with Manhattan's assets. They obtained a $5,000,000 check from Irving Trust, although they had no funds on deposit there at the time. On the same day they purchased all the stock of Manhattan from Bankers Life for $5,000,000, and as stockholders and directors installed Sweeny as president of Manhattan.

Manhattan then sold its U.S. Treasury Bonds for $4,854,552.67. That amount, plus enough cash to bring the total to $5,000,000, was credited to an account of Manhattan at Irving Trust and the $5,000,000 Irving Trust check was charged against it. As a result, Begole owned all the stock of Manhattan, having used the $5,000,000 of Manhattan's assets to purchase it.

Though Manhattan's assets were depleted, its books reflected only the sale of its government bonds and did not show that its assets had been used to pay Begole for his purchase of Manhattan's shares.

Manhattan was the seller of Treasury bonds and, it seems to us, clearly protected by Section 10(b). This makes it unlawful to use in connection with the purchase or sale of any security any manipulative or deceptive device or contrivance in contravention of the rules and regulations of the SEC. There certainly was a fraudulent act or practice within the meaning of Rule 10(b)(5) that operated as a fraud or deceit on Manhattan. To be sure, the full market price was paid for these bonds, but the seller was duped into believing that it, the seller, would receive the proceeds. We cannot agree that no investor was injured.

The fact that fraud was performed by an officer of Manhattan is irrelevant to our problem. Section 10(b) bans the use of any deceptive device by any person. And the fact that the transaction is not conducted through a securities exchange is irrelevant to the coverage of the section. Likewise irrelevant is the fact that the proceeds of the sale were misappropriated.

Since deceptions constantly vary and practices legitimate for some purposes may be turned to illegitimate and fraudulent means, the SEC must have broad discretionary powers. Hence, we do not read 10(b) narrowly. It must be read flexibly, not technically and restrictively. But Congress did not seek to regulate transactions that comprise no more than internal corporate mismanagement.

The crux of the present case is that Manhattan suffered injury as a result of deceptive practices touching its sale of securities as an investor. When a person who is dealing with a corporation in a securities transaction denies the corporation's directors access to material information known to him, the corporation cannot make an informed judgment on the part of its board regarding the merits of the transaction. In this situation the corporation can sue under Rule 10(b)(5). We reverse and remand the proceedings for action consistent with this opinion.

CASE QUESTIONS

1. Describe the fraudulent acts committed by Bankers Life, Begole, and Bourne.
2. To what types of transactions does 10(b) apply? Why is it applicable to this case?
3. What further action is necessary in this case?

In the next case, the court holds managers responsible for disclosing misleading information about their corporation. This liability can extend to all persons responsible for issuing the misleading information and to those who knowingly used it to make a profit by trading in the corporation's stock.

S.E.C. v. Texas Gulf Sulpher Co.
401 F.2d 833 (1969)

Waterman, Circuit Judge.

This action was started in the District Court by the SEC against Texas Gulf Sulpher (TGS) and several of its officers, directors, and employees, to enjoin conduct by TGS and the individuals said to violate Section 10(b) and Rule 10(b)(5).

The complaint alleged (1) that defendants purchased TGS stock from November 12, 1963, through April 16, 1964, on the basis of material inside information concerning the results of TGS drilling in Timmins, Ontario, while such information remained undisclosed to the investing public generally or to the sellers; (2) that defendants gave this information to others for use in purchasing TGS stock while the information was undisclosed to the public and the sellers; (3) that defendants accepted options to purchase TGS stock on February 20, 1964, without disclosing the material information to either the stock option committee or the TGS board of directors; and (4) that TGS issued a deceptive press release on April 12, 1964.

The factual setting. This action arises out of explorations by TGS begun in 1957 on the Canadian Shield in eastern Canada. In March of 1959, aerial surveys were made over more than 15,000 square miles of this area by Mollison, a mining engineer and a vice president of TGS. The group included Holyk, TGS's chief geologist; Clayton, an electrical engineer; and Darke, a geologist. These operations showed some promising minerals near Timmins. On October 29 and

30, 1963, Clayton conducted ground surveys of this area which confirmed the presence of minerals and then ordered drilling. Drilling for core samples started on November 8 and ended on November 12 at a depth of 655 feet. Visual inspection indicated copper and zinc content. This estimate convinced TGS to acquire the land in this area, and TGS's president, Stephens, instructed the group to keep its findings confidential. Later chemical assays of the test materials revealed the presence of copper, zinc, and silver in quantities so remarkable that none of TGS officers had ever heard of comparable finds. By March 27, 1964, the land acquisition program was complete and drilling resumed.

During this period, certain individual defendants and others said to have received tips from them purchased TGS stock. Prior to these transactions, these persons owned 1,135 shares of TGS stock; after these transactions, they owned 8,235 shares. On February 20, 1964, TGS issued stock options to twenty-six of its officers and employees whose salaries exceeded a specified amount. At this time, neither the stock option committee nor the board of directors knew of the test results. Rumors of a major ore discovery began circulating. Some rumors were published in the newspapers.

With the aid of Carroll, a public relations consultant, Fogarty, the vice president, drafted a press release and issued it on April 12. It read in part:

> The following statement was made today by Dr. Charles Fogarty, executive Vice President of TGS in regard to the company's drilling near Timmins. "In the past few days, the exploratory activities of TGS have been widely reported in the press. These reports exaggerate the scale of operations and mention statistics of size and grade of ore that are without factual basis. The facts are as follows. TGS has been exploring in Timmins for six years as part of its overall search in Canada. During the course of this work, TGS conducted exploration entirely on its own. Numerous projects have been investigated and a large number of cores drilled. No inference as to grade can be drawn from this procedure. Most of the areas drilled in Eastern Canada have revealed either barren rock, a few have resulted in discoveries of small ore bodies. Recent drilling on one area near Timmins has led to preliminary indications that more drilling would be needed. The drilling done has not been conclusive. The work done to date has not been sufficient to reach any definite conclusions and any statement as to size and grade would be premature and misleading. When we have reached the point where reasonable and logical conclusions can be made, TGS will issue a definite statement to its stockholders and to the public."

The effect of this release on the investing public was questionable. While drilling activity continued, TGS officials were taking steps toward ultimate disclosure of the discovery. A statement drafted by Mollison was given to the Canadian media. It was released at 9:40 on the sixteenth of April. About one hour later, it was released to American news media.

Between the first press release and the release of the April 16 news, Clayton, Crawford, and TGS director Coates purchased stock in TGS. Coates purchased stock through his broker. The broker also purchased stock for his customers. During the period TGS stock rose in value, beginning at seventeen and three-eighths when the drilling started, going to twenty and seven-eighths when the assays were made and reaching twenty-six when land acquisition started. After the first press release, the stock rose to thirty but tapered off to twenty-nine. Following the news release on April 16, the price rose to thirty-seven, and by May 15, TGS stock was selling at fifty-eight and one-quarter.

Rule 10(b)(5). This rule was made by the SEC from its authority in the Securities Exchange Act of 1934. By that act Congress wanted to prevent inequitable and unfair practices and to insure fairness in securities transactions, whether conducted face to face, over the counter, or on exchanges. The act and the rule apply to the transactions here, all of which were made on exchanges. The rule is based on the policy that all investors trading on impersonal exchanges have relatively equal access to material information. The essence of the rule is that anyone who, trading for his own account in the securities of a corporation, has access, directly or indirectly, to information intended to be available only for a corporate purpose and not for the personal benefit of anyone, may not take advantage of such information knowing it is unavailable to those he is dealing with, *i.e.,* the investing public.

Insiders, such as directors or management officers, are, of course, precluded by this rule from so unfairly dealing, but the rule also applies to anyone knowing the information. Thus, anyone in possession of material inside information must either disclose it to the investing public, or, if he cannot disclose it without betraying a corporate confidence or because he chooses not to do so, he must not trade in or recommend the securities concerned while such inside information remains undisclosed. It is no justification for insider activity that disclosure would increase the cost of the land surrounding the exploration site. If the information was material, then the TGS officers should not have purchased any stock.

Material inside information. An insider is not, of course, always foreclosed from investing in his own company merely because he may be more familiar than an outside investor with company operations. An insider's duty to disclose information or to abstain from dealing in his company's securities arises only in those situations that are essentially extraordinary in nature and are reasonably certain to have a substantial effect on the market price of the security if the situation is disclosed.

Nor is the insider obligated to confer upon outside investors the benefit of his superior financial or other expert analysis by disclosing his educated guesses or predictions. The only regulatory objective is that all investors have access to material information. This objective requires nothing more than the disclosure of basic facts so that outsiders may draw upon their own evaluative expertise in reaching their own investment decisions with knowledge equal to that of the insiders.

The basic test of materiality is whether a reasonable man would attach importance in making his choice of action in the transaction. This of course encompasses any fact that in reasonable and objective contemplation might affect the value of the corporation's stock or securities. Thus, material facts include not only information disclosing the earnings and distributions of a company but also those facts that affect the probable future of the company and those that may affect investors' decisions to buy, sell, or hold the company's securities.

Our survey of the facts established that knowledge of the results of the test drilling and assay would have been important to a reasonable investor and might have affected the price of the stock. We hold therefore that all transactions in TGS stock by individuals apprised of the test results were made in violation of Rule 10(b)(5). Insiders must keep out of the marketplace until the established procedures for public release of information are carried out instead of hastening to make transactions in advance of the release. They must wait until the news could reasonably be expected to appear over the media of widest circulation.

CASE QUESTIONS

1. Explain the knowledge each of the corporate officers had at the time of the August 12 press release.
2. What motives did Fogerty have in issuing this statement?
3. Under what circumstances can this information be material?
4. Who are insiders?
5. What consequences follow from the use of material inside information by these persons in question 4?
6. Explain the effects of this case for corporate public relations departments.

False or misleading statements issued by a corporation about its activities may discourage a person from investing in the firm's securities. Price increases do not go to these persons because they do not own the stock. The question arises if the lost opportunity to invest enables a person to sue for damages. That question is answered in the next case.

Blue Chip Stamps v. Manor Drug Stores
42 L.Ed 2d 264 (1975)

Under an antitrust consent decree, New Blue Chip had to offer a substantial number of common stock shares in its new trading stamp business to retailers like the Manor Drug Stores. New Blue Chip devised a scheme to dissuade Manor from buying. It issued materially misleading statements containing an overly pessimistic appraisal of the business. If Manor did not buy, then Blue Chip could sell those shares to the public at a higher price. Manor brought this class action for damages for violation of the provisions of Section 10(b) of the Securities Exchange Act of 1934 and Rule 10(b)(5), which makes it unlawful to use deceptive devices or make misleading statements in connection with the purchase or sale of any security.

The District Court dismissed this suit. It acted on the basis of the rule enunciated in 1952 in *Birnbaum* v. *Newport Steel Corporation*. This rule states that a person who is neither a purchaser nor a seller of securities may not bring an action under Section 10(b) of the act or the SEC's Rule 10(b)(5). The Court of Appeals reversed, concluding that this case was an exception to the rule.

During the early days of the New Deal, Congress enacted two landmark statutes regulating securities. The Securities Act of 1933 was described as an act to provide full and fair disclosure of the character of securities sold in interstate commerce and through the mails and to prevent fraud in the sale of these securities. The Securities Exchange Act of 1934 was described as an act to provide for the regulation of securities exchanges and of over-the-counter markets operating in interstate commerce and through the mails and to prevent inequitable and unfair practices on such exchanges.

The various sections of the 1933 act dealt at some length with the required contents of the registration statement and expressly provided for private civil causes of action. Section 11(a) gave a right to sue "to any person acquiring the security," and Section 12 gave a right to sue the seller of a security who had engaged in proscribed practices "to the person purchasing the said security from him." Section 10 of the 1934 act made it unlawful to use deceptive practices in "connection with the purchase or sale" of any security. While this section does not give an express civil remedy for its violation, courts inferred a private right to sue for violations of the rule. Such suits are entirely consistent with the Court's recognition that private enforcement of the SEC's rules is a necessary supplement to SEC action.

But private damage actions under Section 10(b) and Rule 10(b)(5) are limited to the actual purchasers and sellers of securities. The 1934 act uses words directed toward injuries suffered in connection with the purchase or sale of securities. This wording is in contrast to the broader language of the 1933 act (Section 17-a), which prohibits fraud in the offer or sale of securities. The 1934 act limits recovery to actual damages suffered. A plaintiff who neither purchases nor sells securities but sues instead for intangible economic injury such as loss of a noncontractual opportunity to buy or sell is more likely to be seeking a largely artificial and speculative recovery in which the number of shares involved will depend on the plaintiff's subjective hypothesis.

Three principal classes of potential plaintiffs are presently barred by this rule from suing: first, potential purchasers of shares who allege they decided not to purchase the securities on the basis of gloomy misrepresentations; second, actual shareholders in the issuer who decide not to sell their shares because of an unduly rosy misrepresentation; third, shareholders and creditors who suffered loss in the value of their investment due to corporate or insider activities, in connection with the purchase or sale of securities, that violate Rule 10(b)(5).

Limiting suits to persons who suffered actual damages in the purchase or sale of a security prevents legal harassment suits, started merely to compromise the defendant without going to trial. Also, Congress has not passed a law giving persons in the above three classes the right to sue.

Manor is neither a purchaser nor a seller as those terms are used in the 1934 act. We therefore hold that Manor was not entitled to sue for violation of Rule 10(b)(5) and the judgment of the Court of Appeals is reversed.

CASE QUESTIONS

1. For what reason did Manor decline to purchase stock in Blue Chip?
2. Why are they prevented from suing? Explain the reasons for limiting suit to actual purchasers and sellers.
3. List the classes of persons not entitled to sue under the rule followed in this case.

SECURITIES AND EXCHANGE COMMISSION

The 1934 act establishes the SEC. It is an independent, bipartisan regulatory agency set up to administer laws in the securities and finance fields and to provide protection to investors. The commission has five members, not more than three of whom may be members of the same political party. Members of the SEC are appointed by the President with the advice and consent of the Senate, to serve a five-year, renewable term. The President selects one member to serve as chairman. Congress conferred broad authority on the SEC to collect registration forms, require reports from individuals and corporations, police securities trading practices on exchanges, initiate investigations, hold hearings, bring legal actions to enforce securities laws, and make rules for the investment community.

The SEC investigates complaints of possible law violations in securities transactions. Complaints can be filed by a stockholder, a member of the investing public, a corporation, or the SEC itself. Upon receiving the complaint, staff assistants from the SEC will investigate allegations made in it. These investigations are privately conducted, through informal inquiries, interviews with witnesses,

FIGURE 7–1: Securities Exchange Commission. Source: U.S. Government Manual, 1975-76 Edition.

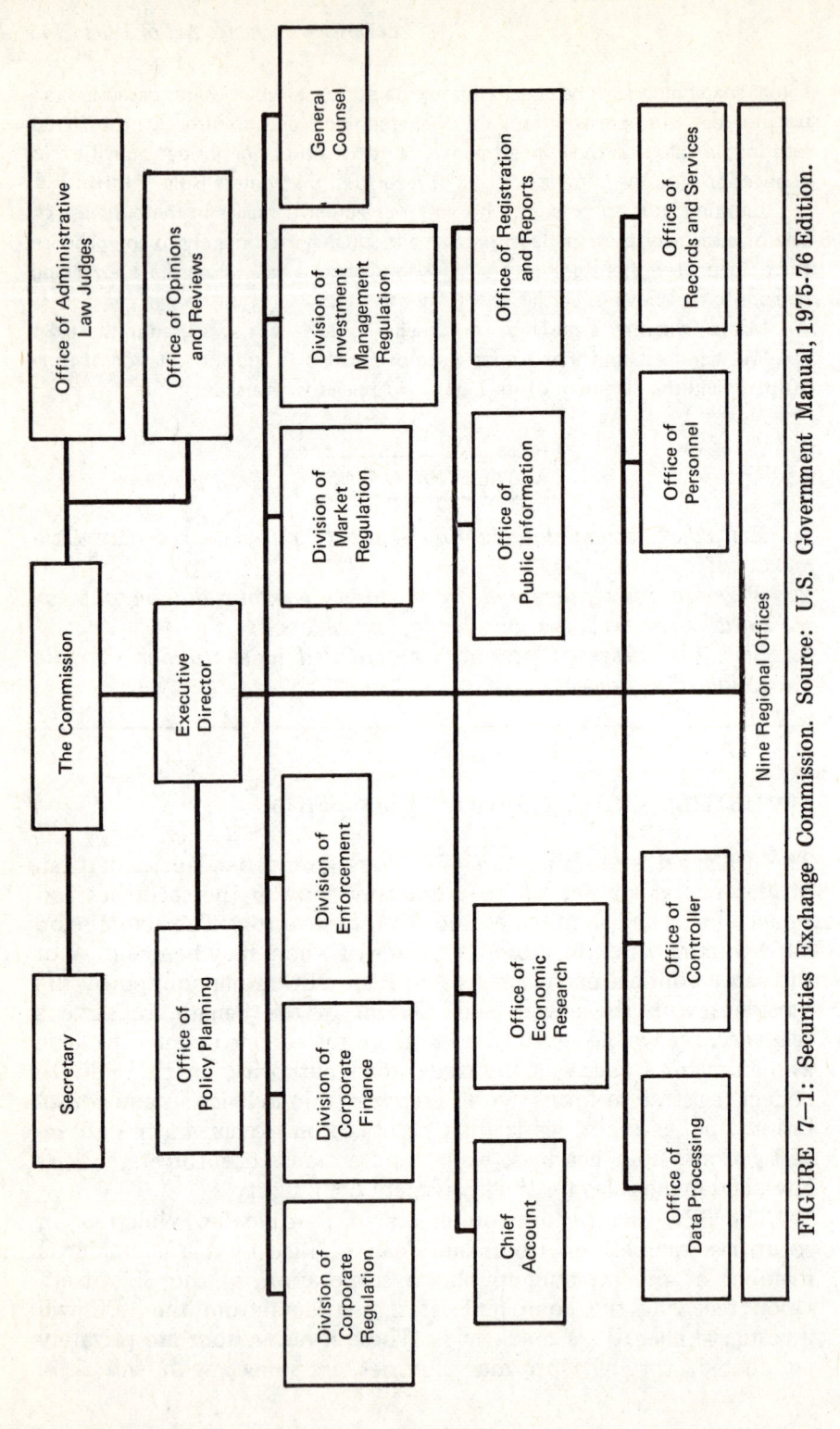

examinations of brokerage records and other documents, reviews of trading data, and other similar means. The SEC can issue subpoenas requiring sworn testimony and the submission of books, records, and other documents pertaining to the investigation. Evidence obtained by these assistants can be turned over to the Department of Justice for criminal prosecution.

Some typical investigations made by the SEC deal with investor complaints, surprise inspections of stockbroker books and records to see if their business practices conform to agency rules, and inquiries into any excessive market charges in particular stocks. The subject matter of these investigations generally deals with the sale of unregistered securities, misrepresentation or omission of material facts when securities are traded, manipulation of market prices of securities, and misappropriation of customer funds by brokers.

Facts acquired by the staff investigation go to the commission for its action. The commission may hold a formal hearing to determine the accuracy of evidence gathered by its investigators. All formal administrative proceedings of the SEC are conducted according to its rules and the Administrative Procedures Act. In an adjudicative hearing, due process safeguards must be observed. This means that notice of the hearing and of the charges made must be given. Also, the right of an accused to appear at the hearing, to present evidence, and to cross-examine must be recognized. All hearings are held before an administrative law judge, appointed by the SEC. This judge rules on all issues and charges raised by the parties and reports findings to the SEC for their approval. The law judge's report must set out the factual findings made by the judge and contain an order, either upholding the staff investigation or dismissing the complaint. Any party to the proceeding can appeal to the full commission for a review of the order, and from there to the courts.

Assuming the facts show a possible law violation, the SEC may do several things. It may ask for an injunction from a United States district court to stop those acts found to be in violation of the law. Or it may refer the facts to the Justice Department with a recommendation for criminal action. Also, the SEC may issue orders suspending or expelling members from the securities industry. The SEC can suspend trading in any security when it needs more time to investigate alleged fraudulent conduct. Frequently, the SEC uses public pressure to obtain voluntary compliance with its orders.

In its investigative and enforcement actions, the SEC cooperates with other federal, state, and local government agencies and with private organizations like the Better Business Bureau. These organizations share information. Facts uncovered by the SEC can be used by individual shareholders in their law suits for fraud. But the SEC does not sue on behalf of stockholders; it is not a collection agency.

Another aspect of the commission's work is the making and interpreting of rules for the securities business. To do this, the commission consults with representatives from the industry and with others. Their views are incorporated into new or amended rules. The commission constantly reviews its rules and the reports filed with it to determine if any new rules are required. Hearings must be held before these rules are adopted if they affect more than just internal procedures of the agency. Since these hearings are not adjudicatory, courtlike due process rules are not followed.

LIABILITIES

Violations of the Securities Exchange Act of 1934 may result in civil and criminal penalties. Stockholders can sue for any losses they suffered because of the violation. Any wilful violator of the act or of SEC rules can be fined up to $10,000 or sent to prison for up to five years or both. If an exchange violates securities rules, it can be fined up to $500,000.

Two recent cases show the cost to a company when their managers violate securities laws. In one case, shareholders sued officials of ITT who traded shares of stock in that corporation using inside information about an antitrust settlement. The court ordered ITT to set up a fund of $3.2 million to reimburse certain stockholders who suffered losses as a result of the managers' trades. It also required those officers who made the illegal trades to pay $350,000 to the corporation. In another recent case, a court ordered the Penn Central Company to pay $12.6 million to stockholders because some of its officers and directors issued false financial statements about the company to investors. More than fifty individual company employees must pay $10.6 million, and the remainder will come from an insurance company.

Criminal liability imposed under the act can be severe. In one recent case, a CPA was held criminally liable for his reckless audit of data in a proxy statement filed with the SEC that included information from reports that he knew or should have known were misleading. Conviction can bring about a fine, imprisonment, suspension from the securities business and from his accounting practice.

Civil and criminal penalties are imposed after investors suffer financial harm. The SEC would like to find out about wrongdoing in a corporation before investors suffer any damage. Lawyers and accountants who advise corporate managers often learn about securities fraud through their professional roles as counselors and auditors. The SEC has proposed that these professionals report such irregularities to the government.

S.E.C. v. National Student Marketing Corp. (NSMC)
360 F.Supp. 284 (1972)

In this proceeding the commission has set forth a complaint which contains four claims. The first claim outlines an alleged mammoth securities fraud scheme caused by the principal officers, directors, and accountants of NSMC and details the purchase and sale of over eleven million shares of NSMC stock between 1968 and 1970. Lying at the heart of this alleged scheme was the preparation, issuance, dissemination, and promotion of false and misleading financial statements which artifically inflated the price of NSMC stock and enabled NSMC to fraudulently acquire approximately twenty-five companies in exchange of its own stock.

A significant portion of the remainder of the complaint concerns the October, 1969, acquisition of Interstate by NSMC. During the spring and summer of 1969, Interstate explored the possibility of merging with NSMC, which at the time was a District of Columbia corporation. Interestate hired the investment banking firm of White, Weld and Company to make an investigation into the background, history, and finances of NSMC, and to make recommendations on the merger. A preliminary report on NSMC was generally favorable to the merger. Interstate was to receive from NSMC's counsel, White and Case, an opinion letter satisfactory to its lawyers, Lord, Bissell and Brook, that NSMC had completed all transactions in connection with the merger. Peat, Marwick and Mitchell, NSMC's accountants, would issue an opinion, called a comfort letter, stating that NSMC's unaudited nine-month financial statements for the period ending May 31, 1969, were prepared in accordance with standard and accepted accounting procedures.

After receiving and having the opportunity to review the proxy material mailed to them, which included copies of the proposed merger agreement, shareholders of each corporation approved the merger at a specially held meeting in early 1969. The material mailed to Interstate's stockholders included the required nine-month financial statements of NSMC, which reflected a profit of almost $700,000. The closing meeting took place at the office of White and Case in New York on Friday afternoon, October 31, 1969.

On the date of closing but prior to consummation of the merger, Peat, Marwick wanted to change its opinion about NSMC's earnings. The change showed that NSMC's unaudited financial statements for the nine-month period would not show a profit but rather a net loss and that the operations of NSMC would show a break-even as to net earnings for the entire year. White and Case did not inform the others of this information. Despite the unexpected revelations of the comfort letter and without its contents being disclosed by any of the defendants who had knowledge of such, the merger was completed on schedule.

The basis of the SEC's charges against the attorney defendants, as they relate to this case are: As part of the fraudulent scheme, White and Case and Lord, Bissell and Brook issued their opinions without revising the NSMC's earnings. Also, they did not advise shareholders of this and continued representing their clients. Under the circumstances, they should have told the SEC about the misleading nature of the nine-month financial statements.

The complaint reveals that these attorneys are charged with specific acts in connection with their active participation in the alleged fraud. Their role as characterized by the commission was not a passive one, nor was their involvement simply that of lawyers representing their clients. Accordingly, the persons and firms could be held liable for securities fraud. Motion to dismiss the complaint is denied.

CASE QUESTIONS

1. Describe the role played by the attorneys in this case.
2. To whom does the professional advisor, such as an attorney or certified public accountant, owe a duty? Contrast their traditional duty with that imposed by the SEC.
3. What further legal proceedings are necessary in this case?
4. Discuss the impact of this case on a professional's liability under the securities laws.

OTHER FEDERAL SECURITIES LAWS

Several other laws protect investors. The *Trust Indenture Act of 1939* imposes special duties in certain types of bond transactions. A trust indenture is a bond where a trustee manages the invested money. Under this law, the trustee cannot have any conflicting interests that might intereferre with the performance of its duties to the bond purchasers. It requires the trustee to be a corporation with a certain minimum capital. It imposes a fiduciary duty on the trustee and requires periodic reports by the trustee to the bondholders.

The *Investment Company Act of 1940* regulates those firms that sell securities to the public and reinvest that money in securities of other businesses. These companies must register with the SEC and disclose their financial condition and reinvestment policies to the investors. The law prohibits such companies from changing their business or policy without approval of the stockholders, and it bars persons guilty of securities fraud from serving as officers or directors. All stockholders and underwriters must approve contracts between the corporation and its managers. The SEC can initiate court action if any of the activities by investment companies are unfair to their stockholders. In addition, these companies are subject to all regulations under the Securities Acts of 1933 and 1934.

A related law is the *Investment Advisers Act of 1940*. It requires persons or firms who advise others about their securities transactions to register with the SEC and comply with its regulations. The law prohibits fraud, requires advisers to disclose the nature of their interest in any transaction for their clients, and requires advisers to keep records of all transactions for their clients. Investment advisers may be suspended or expelled from the SEC's registration list if they violate securities laws. A hearing must be held before any sanctions can be applied. An adviser is disqualified automatically if convicted of a serious crime, mail fraud, or any wilful filing of false reports to the SEC.

The *Public Utility Holding Company Act of 1935*, and the *Bankruptcy Act* give the SEC additional authority over certain types of corporations. Congress enacted the Public Utility Act to correct many abuses in the financing and operation of electric and gas public utility holding company systems. Under the Bankruptcy Act, the SEC acts as an adviser to the court, recommending reorganization plans for bankrupt companies that are fair to the creditors and securities holders.

STATE SECURITIES LAWS

Securities regulations by the states are not as effective as those of the federal government. Geographic boundaries limit their power to regulate securities; they can only regulate the intrastate activities of business. Since most corporations are multistate operations, states are powerless to correct major securities abuses. Also, limited financial budgets of states restrict their enforcement powers. However, most states have securities acts, and corporations must comply with them in addition to the federal laws. State laws fall into several categories.

Some states impose *restrictions on the sellers* of securities, requiring them to be licensed by the state, to disclose relevant facts to investors, and to maintain certain levels of financial responsibility.

The second type of state law requires *registration* of securities with the state. This law operates much like the federal law. A third type of state law imposes *penalties* for fraud in the sales of securities and gives the state broad authority to investigate alleged fraudulent transactions, prevent unfair practices, and prosecute those guilty of fraudulent conduct. The Uniform Securities Act exists in certain states. It combines all three types of state laws, requiring registration of securities and persons who sell them, prohibiting fraudulent conduct by persons in the securities industry, and authorizing prosecution for any improper conduct.

MANAGEMENT GUIDELINES

To protect its managers from inadvertent violations of the Securities Exchange Act of 1934, each company should establish some guidelines for those managers involved with financial operations. The following is a brief guide for such corporate policy:

1. Establish an audit committee to review financial controls and accounting procedures, all financial reports, and all press releases, and to maintain liaison with independent auditors. A policy on who should answer news media questions and what information to disclose should be formulated.

2. Appoint outside directors who are knowledgeable in corporate business affairs and who will actively take an independent role in supervising corporate activities. These people should be given adequate compensation and staff to enable them to perform their function.

3. Create a stockholders relations office to supervise all communications with stockholders, to conduct proxy solicitations, and to prepare corporate responses to stockholder requests for proposals included on proxy materials.

4. Impose a strict ethical code of responsibility for those employees coming into contact with confidential corporate information that could affect the market price of its stock. The code should prevent them from using that information for personal gain, and it should be enforced by vigorous legal action against any employee violating it.

5. Conduct periodic meetings with those managers and employees who come into contact with confidential information that could affect the market price of its stock. These meetings should review the latest developments in securities laws affecting corporate managers and employees.

REVIEW QUESTIONS

1. Explain the major differences between the Securities Act of 1933 and the Securities Exchange Act of 1934.
2. Outline the major sections of the 1934 act.
3. Explain how proxies can be an important management tool to retain control over a corporation and show how the SEC regulates their use for the protection of shareholders.
4. Discuss some of the trading rules established by the SEC to protect investors.
5. Explain the scope of Rule 10(b)(5) and give some current examples of its use by the SEC.
6. Show how the SEC investigates complaints made by investors.
7. Summarize other federal laws to protect investors.
8. Contrast state and federal securities laws. Can a company be subject to both sets of regulations? When do state securities regulations become invalid restrictions on interstate commerce?

TOPICS

CHAPTER 8. COMMON LAW BACKGROUND
Introduction • Interference with Business Relations • Contracts in Restraint of Trade • Trademarks and Tradenames • Patents and Copyrights • Trade Secrets • Disparagement • Computers and the Law • Review Questions

CHAPTER 9. THE SHERMAN ANTITRUST ACT
Introduction • Section 1, the Rule of Reason • Per Se Violations • Section 2 • Proving a Sherman Act Violation • Liabilities • Review Questions

CHAPTER 10. THE CLAYTON ACT AND THE FEDERAL TRADE COMMISSION ACT
Introduction • Exclusive Dealings Arrangements • Mergers • Unfair Methods of Competition • Liabilities • Exemptions • Enforcement Procedures • Management Guidelines • Review Questions

CHAPTER 11. CONSUMER PROTECTIONS
Introduction • Price Discrimination • Other Pricing Restrictions • FTC Act Protections • Warranty • Consumer Product Safety • Other Federal Laws • Management Guidelines • Review Questions

PART THREE

LAWS AND REGULATIONS AFFECTING BUSINESS GROWTH AND PRODUCT DISTRIBUTION

There are two general ways by which a country's economic resources can be developed for its people. Each method represents a terminal point on a broad spectrum of economic theories for the allocation of products and services. At one end is the monopoly, where an organization is so powerful that it can control the selling prices for its products or services and the amount of them available for sale, and prevent any competition to itself. Under this system, the seller determines who can buy, how much they can buy, and the price they must pay. There is no choice to purchase from another because no other exists.

A free competition system is at the opposite end of the economic spectrum. In this system there are so many sellers of a product or service that no one of them can determine the prices or quantities of their products or prevent others from coming into the market. Consumers set prices for products by shopping around for the lowest price, they regulate supply by buying or not buying the products available, and they determine how many sellers exist by demanding more or less of the product. Certainly, neither system exists today and neither could exist in its purest form. However, in the United States, the economic system leans more toward free competition than monopoly. Monopoly is rejected because it leads to higher prices, shortages of products, a corrupting social system, and a general lack of consumer protection.

To keep the American economic system as freely competitive as possible, legislatures enacted a series of antitrust and consumer protection statutes. These laws regulate business growth, the distribution of products, and unfair business practices. Part III explains the major federal laws in each of these areas. A person must know them to minimize liability and to evaluate their effects on decisions made by marketing managers and business planners. Violations of these laws can result in criminal and financial penalties for the business manager and the company.

The first major federal antitrust law passed by Congress was the Sherman Act (1890), to dissolve large corporations dominating the economy. In 1914, Congress enacted the Clayton Act, to make certain business practices illegal. In that same year, Congress adopted the Federal Trade Commission Act, to prohibit unfair methods of competition and to set up a regulatory agency supervising antitrust and related laws. During the 1960s, state and federal governments created new laws to protect the consumer.

To understand these laws and why they were needed, it is

necessary to see what laws existed before government enacted the antitrust and consumer protection laws. Chapter 8 outlines the common law of regulating unfair business practices. Chapters 9 and 10 discuss the three basic federal laws regulating business growth. Chapter 11 discusses some consumer protection laws.

8

THE COMMON LAW BACKGROUND

> *The law of competition ... takes little note of the ordinary rules of good neighborhood or abstract morality. Nonetheless, there is an outer perimeter to permissible conduct. The tradesman must be assured that his competitors will not engage in conduct which falls below the minimum standard of fair dealing.* (Testing Systems Inc. v. Magnaflux Corp., 251 F.Supp. 286, 1966.)

It is important for us to know something about the law of business regulation predating our antitrust and consumer protection laws. Common law rules show us the strengths and weaknesses of the law before Congress enacted modern laws. Also, since these laws still exist, they describe for us some additional remedies a person has if injured by improper business conduct.

Under the common law, specific types of business torts evolved. The word tort comes from the Latin word "tortus," meaning twisted. In law, a tort is any form of lawsuit for monetary damages because of an injury committed to the person or property of another. Some examples of personal torts are: assault, causing some fear of bodily harm; battery, actual bodily harm to another; and libel, printing false statements causing damage to another's reputation. Examples of property torts are: conversion, the wrongful taking of another's property; and business torts, a collective term referring to acts causing damage to another's company or its products. This chapter discusses some important business torts. The common law relied upon these to prevent unfair business practices. We will see the problems of relying upon these remedies as the exclusive way of regulating business.

INTERFERENCE WITH BUSINESS RELATIONS

This tort arises where one person causes another person to either break a contract or to break off business negotiations leading to a contract. Interference with contractual relations is a tort where one person intentionally and unjustifiably causes another person to breach a valid contract with some third person. For example, Joe and Sam have a valid contract for the sale of a car. Peter can be sued by Joe for this tort if he wrongfully and intentionally tells Sam to reject the contract. Examples of wrongful conduct are the use of fraud, violence or intimidation to cause another to breach a contract.

Some states allow damage actions for interference with prospective business relations that have not yet been written into a contract. To be guilty of this tort, a person must intentionally and wrongfully cause another person to break off business discussions with a third person. Courts do recognize the furthering of one's own business interests as a justification for interfering with another's prospective relations. For both of these torts, the person inducing the break must have acted with the intent to cause harm to the other person.

Hannigan v. Sears, Roebuck and Co.
410 F.2d 285 (1969)

Hastings, Senior Circuit Judge.

The evidence shows that in May, 1956, TruHan Corp. was organized in Illinois by Hannigan. He became its president and majority stockholder. The corporation became a distributor of metal outdoor storage buildings manufactured by Fabricated, Inc. In 1958, Fabricated agreed to manufacture outdoor metal cabinets, developed by Hannigan, exclusively for TruHan, and TruHan agreed to buy and market all such cabinets so produced. Fabricated continued to sell its outdoor buildings to others, including Sears.

In 1959, a buyer from Sears wrote a letter to the president of Fabricated, attempting to persuade its sales manager to sell the cabinets directly to Sears, thus avoiding TruHan's middleman commissions. Sears knew of Hannigan's exclusive sales contract with Fabricated but nonetheless persisted in attempting to get Fabricated to sell direct. Sears threatened to stop buying outdoor storage buildings from Fabricated unless it agreed to change TruHan's contract. Since Fabricated depended heavily upon Sears' business, it agreed. Under the modified contract, Hannigan allowed Fabricated to sell to Sears directly in return for a flat ten percent commission.

Hannigan alleges that Sears wrongfully and intentionally interfered with his contractual rights by inducing Fabricated to change its contract with him. Sears argues the modification was agreed to by Hannigan, that it only dealt with a minor part of the contract, and that it did not result from any coercion. We disagree.

It is evident that if Hannigan had refused to agree to the modification, Fabricated would have lost all of Sears' business. Because of its economic dependency upon Sears, Fabricated would have been forced out of business leaving Hannigan without any source of supply. Hannigan had no choice in the matter but to accept the modification and permit Fabricated to sell directly to Sears.

To us, there is no legally significant distinction between unabashed third party conduct which induces one party to outrightly repudiate and breach its contract with another and subtle third party conduct which achieves essentially the same result through the equally questionable means of coercing a contractual modification. Both approaches are equally tortious in nature and similarly interfere with the contractual relationships of others.

The traditional elements of the tort of inducing breach of contract are: (1) an existing contract between the plaintiff and a third party, (2) defendant's knowledge of this contract, (3) an intentional unjustified inducement to breach the contract, (4) a subsequent breach of the contract by the third party, (5) resulting damages to the plaintiff.

In the instant case, it is undenied that there was an existing contract between Hannigan and Fabricated and that defendant knew of this contract. It is also true that at different times and in varying ways, Sears, for purely private business reasons, encouraged Fabricated to either breach or alter its contract with Hannigan. In its effort to induce Fabricated to sell the cabinets directly to it, Sears threatened Fabricated with severe economic hardships and offered Fabricated greater economic opportunities. Though Sears' overtures did not cause Fabricated to outrightly repudiate and breach its contract with Hannigan, Sears accomplished an equivalent result by economically coercing the parties into modifying their original agreement. As a result of this coercion, Hannigan suffered monetarily.

CASE QUESTIONS

1. Why did Hannigan consent to the modifications?
2. Explain why the law does not permit contractual interference.
3. Explain the elements of this tort.

CONTRACTS IN RESTRAINT OF TRADE

Frequently persons form contracts whereby one of them agrees not to compete against the other. These contracts, called restraint of trade contracts, are dangerous because they deprive one person of a right to make a living, they concentrate economic power in the one person able to perform, and they deprive the public of some services. But the courts also recognize the need for some agreements not to compete. For example, when a professional sells his or her practice to another, the buyer needs some protections from the seller prohibiting the reopening of that practice. Also, when an employee learns confidential information, the employer needs protection to prevent the employee from using those secrets for a competitor. So courts developed a rule of reason. Contracts in restraint of trade are valid if reasonable to the parties in the contract and to the public. If a contract not to compete is for an unlimited time period or too broad a geographic area or is harmful to the public, it is unreasonable and void.

Often employers ask sales personnel and engineers to sign restrictive employment covenants. In these contracts, an employee agrees not to compete with his or her former employer upon leaving the firm. These contracts are valid if necessary to protect the legitimate interests of the employer and if not too restrictive of an employee's rights. Such contracts are valid if competition is restricted only in the area where the former employer operates. Protection to the employer cannot be broader than necessary. And the courts require that the time period when competition is restrained be short enough so that the employee's skills do not become obsolete. Some courts will declare these contracts void if the public has a greater need for the employee's services than the employer has need for protection.

**Central Credit Collection Corporation v. Grayson
499 P.2d 57 (1972)**

Pearson, Judge.

Central employed Grayson for a six-year period to work as a debt collector. In his employment contract with Central, Grayson agreed not to work in any county surrounding Central's location, as either a direct or indirect competitor, for a two-year period of time. The contract further provided that since Grayson received valuable trade secrets and other information from Central, he would not work for any competitor of Central's for two years. Grayson left Central after the six-year period and soon thereafter opened up a competing debt collection agency within seventy-three yards of Central's office. Central brought this action to enforce the restrictive contract. Judgment was entered for Central and Grayson appealed. Affirmed.

It is well settled that covenants not to compete upon termination of employment are valid. But these contracts should not be greater than reasonably necessary to protect the business or the good will of the employer. The contract in this case stated that the employer spent considerable sums of money developing its business and customer accounts. It needed some protections. We think the trial court was right in concluding that the act of Grayson in locating his business so close to Central's was violative of the reasonable area restriction.

The same rationale applies to the time restriction. Where the undisputed evidence offered at trial showed that Grayson opened his business within the two-year prohibited period, an injunction is proper to enforce the restrictive covenant.

CASE QUESTIONS

1. For what purpose would an employer request an employee to sign a post-employment restrictive covenant?
2. When are these types of contracts legal?
3. Explain the public interest in these contracts.

TRADEMARKS AND TRADENAMES

A trademark or tradename is any distinctive mark, symbol, word, phrase, or picture that is associated with a particular corporation or its product so that the public may know who makes them. Trademarks and tradenames are acquired in similar ways, although slight differences can be noted.

A trademark can be acquired by placing some symbol somewhere on each product manufactured and using it with the intention of its being a trademark. The symbol adopted cannot be one that violates public policy, such as an obscene photo. To acquire a tradename, a person must use some word or phrase exclusively for a certain and prolonged period of time, to identify a business or product so that the word or phrase develops a unique and secondary meaning. This means consumers associate the word or phrase with the product. If another person uses the trademark or tradename of another, the public could be confused into thinking someone else made the product. To prevent this confusion, courts give the owner of a trademark and tradename the right to sue to stop others from using it and to recover damages for any lost sales due to the improper use of the symbol, word, or phrase.

The federal Lanham Act, enacted in 1946, permits persons to

register tradenames and trademarks with the Patent Office. Registration gives an owner protection from unauthorized use by another. Protection extends throughout the United States. Without registration, the user of a tradename or trademark must register with each state or prove that it was the first to use the word or symbol, in order to be able to prevent others from using it.

Maternally Yours v. Your Maternity Shop
234 F.2d 538 (1956)

Waterman, Circuit Judge.

Maternally Yours, Inc., the plaintiff, is a New York corporation engaged in the retail merchandising of maternity apparel in the New York metropolitan area. It began using the name "Maternally Yours" in 1945 and registered this name as a tradename in 1949. This was the first shop in New York and perhaps the country to sell these specialty clothes. Your Maternity Shop began operation in a New York suburb in 1946. Plaintiff informed the defendant it was infringing upon its name, but the defendant continued using it. This action was brought to enjoin the defendant from using its name, alleging that the plaintiff had a tradename from 1945 to the present. The complaint asked an accounting for damages including all profits realized from the alleged infringement. The trial court found for the plaintiff and ordered defendant to stop using the name "Your Maternity Shop."

Plaintiff's right to injunctive relief under the Lanham Act depends upon a determination that the defendant's use of "Your Maternity Shop" in connection with the sale and advertising of maternity apparel is likely to cause confusion or mistake or to deceive purchasers as to the source of origin of such goods. It is not necessary to show actual cases of confusion or deception since the test is the likelihood that an appreciable number of ordinarily prudent purchasers will be confused.

The trial judge found that defendant's use of the tradename "Your Maternity Shop" was misleading, caused confusion, and did divert trade from plaintiff and that defendant knowingly used this name similar to plaintiff's. Furthermore, the defendant imitated plaintiff's advertising format, used similar packaging, and adopted confusing telephone listings with the intention of misleading the public and diverting trade. We agree with these findings.

An intent on the part of the alleged infringer is a relevant factor in determining the likelihood of consumer confusion. But it is only one of the factors that should be carefully weighed, such as the degree of similarity between the tradenames, the strengths of the plaintiff's name, the area and manner of concurrent use, and the degree of care likely to be exercised by the purchasers.

In this case, the similarity of the names is not so marked as to itself create the probability that reasonably prudent purchasers would be confused. But considering the geographic market and the narrow specialty market within that area to which the concurrent use was confined, the novelty of the tradename, and the similar signs, labels, boxes, advertising slogans, and telephone listings, the likelihood of confusion is adequately established.

We also agree that plaintiff's chosen name was unique rather than merely descriptive. But the name is entitled to protection even before registered as a tradename if it acquired a secondary meaning by the time of defendant's entry into the market. Here, plaintiff was the first to enter this narrow field and spent substantial sums advertising its name, which the public recognized as unique. We think that these circumstances indicate the plaintiff's name had acquired a secondary meaning by the time of defendant's entry. Where there has been a palming off and confusion to the public, an accounting for profits is justified.

CASE QUESTIONS

1. *Contrast the acquisition of a tradename and trademark.*
2. *What factors are important to determine if there is public confusion over similar names or marks?*
3. *How would a court make an accounting for profits as ordered in this case?*

PATENTS AND COPYRIGHTS

The common law permitted the acquisition of patents and copyrights. Now federal law regulates the field. Patents could be given to use and license for use by others any new and useful invention of a process, machine, product, plant, or an improvement to any of these, if it has not been developed or used by others. A patent could not be obtained on a mere formula, a computer program of general application, any invention not shown to be a useful invention, or something obvious to a person having ordinary skill in the art to which the invention pertains. At common law, a patent could last indefinitely, but federal law now restricts patents to seventeen years. Any person using a patent without permission could be sued for any profits earned from its use and an injunction to prevent future unauthorized use. Similar remedies exist under federal law.

A copyright gives the holder an exclusive right to print, publish, copy, and sell books, periodicals, lectures, plays, music, maps, art works, drawings, photographs, and motion pictures. This monopoly lasted indefinitely at common law, but now federal law restricts it to a twenty-eight-year renewable term. Unauthorized reproduction subjects the copier to a suit for damages and an injunction.

Gottschalk v. Benson
409 U.S. 63 (1972)

Justice Douglas.

Benson developed a method of programming a general-purpose digital computer to convert signals from binary-coded decimal form into pure binary form. A procedure for solving a given type of mathematical problem is known as an algorithm. The procedures developed by Benson were generalized formulations for programs to solve mathematical problems of converting one form of numerical representation to another. From the generic formulation, programs could be developed as specific applications. Benson sought a patent on his method. It was rejected by the Patent Office, but the Court of Customs and Patent Appeals reversed. Gottschalk appealed on behalf of the Patent Office.

The Court has stated that while a scientific truth, or the mathematical expression of it, is not a patentable invention, a novel and useful structure created with the aid of knowledge of scientific truth may be. That statement followed the longstanding rule that an idea of itself is not patentable. A principle, in the abstract, is a fundamental truth, an original cause, a motive; these cannot be patented, as no one can claim in either of them an exclusive right. Phenomena of nature, though just discovered, mental processes, and abstract intellectual concepts are not patentable, as they are the basic tools of scientific and technological work. One who discovers an unknown phenomenon of nature has no claim to a monopoly of it that the law recognizes. If there is to be invention from such discovery, it must come from the application of the law of nature to a new and useful end.

It is argued that a process patent must either be tied to a particular machine or apparatus or operate to change articles or materials to a different state or thing. We do not hold that no process patent could ever qualify if it did not meet the requirements of the above rules. It is said that the decision here precludes a patent for any program servicing a computer. We do not so hold. It is said that we have before us a program for a digital computer but extend our holding to programs for analog computers. We have, however, made clear from the start that we deal with a program only for digital computers. It is said we freeze process patents to old technologies, leaving no room for the revelations of the new, onrushing technology. Such is not our purpose.

It is conceded that one may not patent an idea. But in practical effect that would be the result if Benson's formula could be patented. The mathetmatical formula involved in this case has no substantial application except in connection with a digital computer, which means that if the judgment below is affirmed, the patent would wholly preempt the mathematical formula and in practical effect would be a patent on the algorithm itself.

CASE QUESTIONS

1. *Describe Benson's invention.*
2. *What conditions must exist before a computer program can be patented?*
3. *Why did this program fail to meet those conditions?*
4. *Why does the law allow patents?*

TRADE SECRETS

A trade secret is a plan, process, tool, or mechanism that is of special value to the owner and is known only to a relatively small number of people. Many ideas are not patented or copyrighted because filing with the government gives limited protection and ideas filed with the government are open to public inspection. A trade secret can last forever and may never be seen by the public. Also, some ideas can never be patented. Keeping a process as a trade secret rather than registering it as a patent may give a person more protection.

A person claiming a trade secret must show that the process was kept confidential. This means that some steps were taken to keep knowledge of the secret confined to a few individuals on a "need to know" basis. If the trade secret is accidently discovered by a competitor, the competitor can lawfully use it. But when improper means are used by a competitor to discover the secret, the court can issue an injunction restraining further use of the secret and award damages for any injuries suffered by the owner. Examples of some improper ways to learn another's trade secrets are bribes to those who know the secrets, theft of the property, and financial incentives to hire those employees who know them.

DISPARAGEMENT

This business tort consists of making untrue statements about the quality of products or service given by a competitor that result in damages. To sue for this tort, a person must show that specific customers and specific transactions were lost as a result of the disparaging remarks. Comparisons with competitors' products can be made if such comparisons are not untrue and can be substantiated by objective tests and analysis.

A related legal action is slander of title. In this tort, one person makes false statements to potential buyers about the legal ownership of a competitor's products or about the competitor's right to sell the products. If these statements cause potential buyers to refrain from dealing with the person slandered, then this action can be brought to stop the publication of the false statements and to recover money for any lost sales caused by the defamation. Truth is a defense to this slander action.

Testing Systems, Inc. v. Magnaflux Corp.
251 F. Supp. 286 (1966)

Lord, District Judge.

Testing Systems, Inc., and Magnaflux Corporation were competitors making equipment and chemical products. Testing sued Magnaflux for damages because it orally and in writing disparaged Testing's products. This included statements to customers that Testing's products were no good and that the government was "throwing them out" because they were tested to be only forty percent as good as Magnaflux's products.

The fine line that separates healthy competitive effort from underhanded business tactics is frequently difficult to determine. Apart from the businessman's right to free speech, the public has a genuine interest in learning the relative merits of particular products. To advance these interests the law gives the competitor a wide berth in the conduct of business. The businessman may use any mode of persuasion with a customer that appeals to his self-interest, reason, or even prejudices. But there is an outer limit to permissible conduct. The businessman must be assured that his competitors will not be suffered to engage in conduct that falls below the minimum standard of fair dealing.

Magnaflux's comments in this case presently before this court do not entitle it to the protection given to unfavorable comparison. There is a difference between saying one's product is, in general, better than another's and asserting, as here, that the other's is only forty percent as effective as one's own. The former expresses an opinion while the latter is an assertion of fact implying that the party making it is fortified with facts necessary to prove it.

Judgment for Testing.

CASE QUESTIONS

1. *Summarize the law which permits one competitor to make comparisons with another competitor's products.*
2. *How did Magnaflux violate this law?*
3. *Give some examples of permissible comparisons and impermissible ones.*

COMPUTERS AND THE LAW

A brief study of the computer industry shows some of the difficulties caused by attempting to regulate business today with common law rules. Electronic data processing and office machine technology have revolutionized business procedures. Often, however, the law regulating such innovations has not developed as rapidly. Consequently, courts are sometimes faced with the difficult problem of settling space-age computer problems using ancient common law principles. Frequently, the results are unrealistic. We can see some of these problems by examining four areas of the computer industry: patents and copyright protections, trade secrets, interference with contracts, and computer fraud.

1. Patents and Copyright Protections. The patent statute of the United States (35 USCS 100[b], 101) provides that whoever invents or discovers any new and useful process or machine may obtain a patent on it. Courts define a process as an act or series of acts performed upon some property which change it into something different. A machine is a concrete thing, consisting of parts or devices having a certain mode of operation. In the computer industry, scientists have developed machines to sort information and processes by which these machines operate. Computer machinery is called hardware while computer processes are known as software.

Neither the common law nor the government would issue a patent for the mere function or operation of computer hardware. Effects or results of a machine's operation cannot be the subject of a patent. Only the new and useful way of obtaining that result can be patented. Consequently, computer industry managers must determine the purpose and uniqueness of their machines before seeking patent protections. If a computer is programmed merely to accomplish data sorting faster, to obtain different facts from stored data, or to perform new tasks, no patent could be obtained from the Patent and Trademark Office. However, if new devices or parts are put into the computer to perform any of these functions, then a patent could be obtained.

Manuals with respect to the maintenance and operation of particular computers can be copyrighted. Courts make a distinction between the computer itself, which might not be patented, and the explanation of how to use the machine, which can be copyrighted. "The description of art in a book lays no foundation for an exclusive claim to the art itself. The object of the one is explanation, the object of the other is use. The former may be secured by copyright. The latter can only be secured, if it can be secured at all, by patent." (*Telex Corporation* v. *International Business Machines*, 367 F.Supp. 258, 1973). The doctrine of "fair use" permits the limited use of material copyrighted in computer explanation manuals.

The law on computer software packages requires a similar analysis. As pointed out in the case of *Gottschalk* v. *Benson*, 409 U.S. 63 (1972), basic ideas, abstract principles, or scientific truths cannot be patented. In that case, the Supreme Court ruled that a method for programming any type of general-purpose digital computer to convert binary coded decimal numerals into pure binary numerals is not a process that could be patented. The Court distinguished two types of computer programs: those that were limited to a particular technology or a particular machine and those that were of general use in any type of machine or for any type of purpose. The former are patentable but the latter are not. Thus computer industry managers must determine the nature of their software packages. If the software methodology is so abstract or generalized that it could be used in any machine for any purpose, ranging from the operation of a train to verification of drivers' licenses to researching textbooks, then no patent will be granted. The method is merely an idea with no substantial practical application. Without a patent, legal protections for computer formulas and machines are limited even though substantial time, expertise, and money were invested in their development. Protections for some computer developments must be found in the law of trade secrets.

2. *Trade Secrets.* Computer firms unable to patent some aspect of their products must protect these innovations through trade secret

laws. Although there may be no patent protection for abstract ideas or machine effects, trade secret laws can protect pure mental conceptions that have been put into tangible form. A secret, unpatented formula or device can be protected as a trade secret so long as the inventor takes necessary steps to protect it. To protect a computer innovation as a trade secret, a company must show that its machine or process is known only to it and to those of its employees to whom it is necessary to confide. Also, the computer firm must show that the innovation is the firm's secret, not in the general knowledge of the computer industry.

A firm can lose its ownership of a trade secret in two ways. First, if the employer did not take reasonable steps to insure its confidentiality, the secret will be lost. That means an employer can tell computer secrets only to relatively few employees on a need-to-know basis only. Employees who are told a trade secret must be informed that the information is confidential and must promise not to disclose it to others. Generally, courts require that the employee make a contractual promise not to disclose the secret or that a confidential relationship be created with the employee such that disclosure would violate his or her duty of fidelity. Second, a computer firm can lose its trade secrets if they are discovered by others independently. For example, if the technology of a computer firm is put on the market, anyone may use it to any extent without liability if he or she discovers by personal efforts the secret workings or theory supporting the technology.

If a computer firm has complied with the trade secrets law, then an employee who leaves the firm may take and use only the general knowledge or skill acquired during the course of his or her employment, not the employer's secret processes or devices. An injunction can stop the employee from disclosing such information and the new employer from using it. The computer firm could sue for an accounting, recovery of lost profits caused by the use of the secrets, and damages.

Telex Corporation v. International Business Machines Corp.
367 F. Supp. 258 (1973)

Christensen, Senior District Judge.

This was an antitrust action brought against International Business Machines Corporation (IBM), manufacturers of electronic data processing systems. It was brought by Telex Corporation (Telex), another manufacturer of such systems.

Defendant counterclaimed against Telex, alleging unfair competition and misappropriation of trade secrets and confidential information. (Only that part of the case dealing with the counterclaim is discussed here.)

Telex's business has been largely directed toward offering interchangeable replacements for products manufactured by IBM. Telex charges lower prices for its products than IBM. Their cost savings come from copying as closely as possible the IBM designs. Telex generally has not marketed products of independent design but rather has waited until IBM has designed a product and copied it. Telex tries to determine the specifications and plans for new IBM products as soon as it is able and, if possible, before the products are announced to the public. One of the ways it has found to do this has been by hiring IBM employees or former employees.

Statistically, the number of IBM employees hired by Telex has not been great. Of those personnel who had formerly been employed by IBM, some of them were employed by Telex after intervening employment with third parties and some were employed immediately after the termination of their employment at IBM. In 1970, Telex employed fifty engineers, of whom one was a former IBM employee. In 1971, Telex employed eighty-eight engineers, eighteen of whom were former IBM employees. In 1972, thirty-one out of 145 engineers were former IBM employees. On March 31, 1973, Telex had a total of 1,929 employees of whom 152 had IBM employment experience.

These former IBM employees have furnished an important and vital part of Telex technology and business development. For example, in March, 1970, Telex hired IBM employee Jack James, who possessed substantial confidential information about IBM's future product plans. At the suggestion of Telex Vice President of Sales, Grant, who had worked with James at IBM, Telex contacted James in January, 1970, regarding the possibility of his resigning from IBM and taking a posibion with Telex. He had been employed as the Systems Requirement and Business Manager for the General Systems Division of IBM and was in a position of responsibility over various IBM products and services. In the course of his duties at IBM, James had access to confidential data relating to IBM products under development and to financial information.

While James was still an employee of IBM, but considering employment by Telex, he gave Telex Chairman Wheeler an appraisal of Telex's marketing of terminal products and advice as to what types of products Telex should offer in the future. After a meeting with Telex executives, James returned to IBM and collected a substantial quantity of IBM planning data and shipment forecasts. James was offered the position of Vice President of Finance for Telex Computer Products, Inc., and accepted that position in March, 1970.

James had no contract with IBM for a fixed term of employment and had made no agreement not to accept employment from a competitor of IBM, but he understood that he should not disclose IBM's secret or confidential information or documents, and prior to his leaving IBM he had an interview in which his obligations with respect to IBM trade secrets and business confidential information, such as marketing analysis, product costs, and plans for potential new products were discussed. On March 23, James acknowledged these obligations in writing.

It was natural, proper, and to be expected that James's general knowledge of electric data products of both IBM and its competitors, his knowledge of the markets for these products, his knowledge of equipment pricing factors, and his acquaintance with sales and marketing problems relating to such equipment were the currency of his qualifications for any position he might accept. It was natural and proper also that his general knowledge and opinions respecting the existing and future markets for electronic data processing equipment, and even limited general notes of information or opinions respecting the fields of his work experience would be carried with him into any future employment. Beyond this, it might have been reasonably expected that he would utilize in his new employment all of his general knowledge concerning the EDP industry, his general judgment based upon the sum total of his experience, and his experience and competence derived from dealing with the problems and plans of his former employer.

But beyond this, Telex expected and James intended as a part of his new employment to capitalize on and exploit confidential IBM documents and studies themselves. Prior to leaving IBM James had access to IBM's Plan 25 Forecast and IBM's SCAN Forecast assumptions. James knew these documents were confidential and entitled to protection. He took with him to Telex confidential information copied from the forecasts, including information about the performance of many of IBM's products. Immediately after he was employed by Telex, James prepared memoranda which disclosed IBM's confidential information relating to unannounced products and future plans. They were detailed and specific, negating any idea that they constituted merely general information or opinions based upon his experiences. Both of these documents were registered confidential documents within IBM.

In the ensuing months, James disclosed further IBM confidential information, which was used in forming Telex's product strategy and in determining Telex's development program. Telex's officers and employees thereafter engaged in a concerted effort to recruit IBM engineers and to discover technical and business confidential information through the recruiting process, to gain access to proprietary documents locked in cabinets under the jurisdiction of IBM's maintenance personnel, and otherwise to obtain proprietary information. Such information gave Telex a comparable product to IBM's product line and thereby reduced the competitive advantage of IBM.

The court finds that James deliberately misappropriated IBM confidential information and made that information available to Telex, and that principal officers of Telex knew or should have known that the information made available to Telex was confidential IBM information and that it had been wrongfully misappropriated by James. The court also finds that beginning with the hiring of James and continuing at least until commencement of this lawsuit, Telex followed a practice of acquiring, as an important part of its business, IBM confidential information and trade secrets through the hiring of IBM employees with knowledge of such confidential information and trade secrets. IBM employees experienced and knowledgeable in IBM's plans and designs were sought by Telex through the offer of exceedingly liberal salaries and bonuses, in some cases as much as a quarter of a million dollars.

In all the areas where IBM confidential and trade secret information has been sought or utilized by Telex, the line of demarcation between such use and legitimate utilization of the skills, knowledge, judgment, and expertise of former IBM employees is often difficult, and on some occasions impossible, to define with accuracy or assurance. However, in the areas discussed here, it is quite clear that Telex has had the intent to benefit not only from these appropriate elements of utilization but from confidential information and trade secrets which IBM has had the right to preserve. And IBM did take steps to preserve its secrets and confidential information. It installed magnetic locks on building doors to allow access only to authorized personnel, it started a procedure to control the distribution and use of documents containing IBM trade secrets designed "Registered IBM Confidential Documents," and it signed agreements by which employees agreed not to disclose such information and held exit interviews reaffirming the responsibility of the employee. It has spent money to hire guards, installed television cameras, sensors, locks, safes, and computer-controlled access systems.

Reasonable efforts and precautions to protect trade secrets and confidential information are to be expected on the part of those entitled to their benefit. The expenses of reasonable protection should not be shifted to competitors, whose mere existence motivates such protection. But where the efforts of a competitor to penetrate unlawfully trade secrets require extraordinary measures for their protection, it is not unreasonable for the measures to be paid for by the party so unlawfully causing them.

The facts here go beyond the mere termination of employment and the acceptance of employment from a competitor. Telex hired key IBM employees in order to obtain their skills and knowledge of trade secrets and confidential information about specific products and plans. The information so acquired could not have been discovered independently, was not readily available from other sources, and was not common knowledge in the industry. They were treated as confidential to IBM and entitled IBM to obtain legitimate competitive advantage over competitors not possessing such information and not able reasonably to duplicate it.

The court concludes that IBM is entitled to an injunction ordering Telex:

a. To return to IBM all IBM documents and all Telex documents containing confidential information that are in Telex's custody or under its control.
b. To refrain from hiring or soliciting any IBM employee for a period of two years without the approval from the court.
c. To refrain from soliciting or using any confidential or proprietary information.
d. To refrain from assigning any former IBM employee now or in the future to

the development or manufacture of products functionally equivalent or similar to those on which such employee worked at IBM, for a period of not less than two years following the termination of his employment with IBM.

The court further concludes that IBM is entitled to damages in the following amounts:

a. $4.5 million for losses through December, 1972, in monthly rentals of specific machines caused by accelerated shipments of Telex competing products made possible by the misappropriation of IBM's trade secrets.
b. $13 million in damages arising from the additional advantages secured by Telex in the development of certain computer facilities made possible by the misappropriation of IBM's trade secrets.
c. $3 million for the costs of increased security.
d. $1 million in punitive damages for the wilful, deliberate, and pervasive nature of Telex's unlawful conduct.

(Note. That portion of this case printed here has been affirmed on appeal.)

CASE QUESTIONS

1. What was the nature of Telex's business? How did it relate to IBM?
2. What tactics did Telex use to develop its product line?
3. Describe the work of James at IBM and at Telex. In what ways did James violate his obligations to IBM? Explain the types of information an employee can bring to a new position and the types he cannot bring.
4. What steps did IBM take to preserve its trade secrets? Why were they necessary?
5. Explain how the court can enforce each of its injunctive remedies.

---

3. *Interference with Contractual Relations.* Competitors want to hire key employees of a computer firm. They do this to get their knowledge about the computer industry as well as about their former employer. Competitors hope to learn the trade secrets of other computer firms. To stop this tactic, computer employers have two weapons from the law. First, they could require employees to sign a contract agreeing not to work for a competitor. Post-employment contracts are valid if reasonable in duration and geographic restrictions. Since computer technology develops rapidly, the time period

limiting future competition would be short, perhaps no more than two years. However, since many computer firms are large national companies competing against each other in the entire United States market, competition from former employees could be limited within the entire United States. However, courts frequently require the contract to limit the employee's future employment only to the areas of effective competition with the former employer. Unlimited restraints on an employee's work are void because such restraints are greater than necessary to protect the former employer.

The second approach for computer firms to follow in protecting their employees from raids by competitors is the tort action of interference with contractual relations. To maintain this suit, a computer firm must show that its competitor knowingly induced an employee to break his or her contract of employment by using unjustified means, and this breech caused injury to the former employer. These suits may be difficult to win because the former employer must show specific injury to itself by the employee's breach of contract. And, specific unjustified tactics must be shown. Damages can be established by proving that certain technical knowledge known only to that employee has been lost to the competitor or that trade secrets are now being disclosed. Unjustified means can be proven by showing aggressive acts of recruitment, such as promises of higher wages, better positions, greater amounts of research money, or better job opportunities.

4. Computer Fraud. Many companies use electronic data processing systems to process financial transactions, update and store inventory data on computer records, and print out negotiable instruments. In computer systems, the steps necessary to accomplish these transactions are combined in a few programs. These programs are written and controlled by relatively few programmers in a company. With such power centralized in a few hands, the opportunities for computer fraud are abundant. An employer needs legal protections against dishonest programmers and their managers. An employer's best protection is knowledge about some ways computers can be used for fraudulent purposes. A recent study by Donn Parker at Stanford Research Institute, summarized in the *New York Times Magazine* for September 8, 1974, identifies four types of computer fraud:

a. Financial frauds. A dishonest employee can use computer systems to take money from the employer. In one case, the chief teller at one New York savings bank transferred money from legitimate accounts stored in a computer memory bank to fraudulent accounts he had created, and then withdrew the money.

b. Fraudulent conversion of property. Computerized ordering systems can be used to divert merchandise. In 1972, an engineering student was arrested on charges of stealing $1 million worth of supplies from a company. To accomplish this fraud, he used a set of instructions, found in the firm's trash cans, that gave him the entry code to the company's computer ordering system. The student would enter item numbers from the instructions telling where to make deliveries and vary his orders by size and location.
c. Fraudulent conversion of information. Employees can tap into a computer record system, obtain print-outs of confidential corporate reports, and sell them to competitors.
d. Personal use of company computer systems. Employees often feel they have a license to take some office supplies from their employer for home use. This practice applies to the use of the company computer. Some employees feel they have permission to use the firm's programs and hardware to operate a private consulting business. Other employees have taken stored lists of customers and sold them as mailing lists for private solicitations.

REVIEW QUESTIONS

1. Contrast a monopolistic economy with a freely competitive one.
2. Give some examples of business-related torts.
3. Is free competition a defense to interference with business relations?
4. Distinguish between reasonable and unreasonable post-employment restrictive contracts.
5. How are tradenames and trademarks protected by the Lanham Act?
6. What must an employer do to preserve trade secrets?
7. What parts of computer technology can be patented or copyrighted?
8. Bracket Corporation advertised its products as comparable to or better than those manufactured by Salvia, its chief competitor. Television commercials showed both products and a voice stated: "Bracket tools outperform Salvia's in three tested categories—longer life, better performing, and lower price." Under what circumstances would this advertisement become a disparagement?

9. Rasmussen developed a new process for manufacturing magnetic valves and contacted a leading automobile maker to attempt to sell his invention to them. They refused to purchase it on the basis of their chief engineer's recommendations. Soon thereafter, the engineer left the auto company and began manufacturing valves using Rasmussen's process. Can Rasmussen sue either for infringement of his patent or for violation of his trade secret?

10. James and John entered into a contract whereby James agreed to sell John a stipulated amount of wheat at a fixed price over a two-year period. Peters learned of this contract several months after it was executed. He called John, telling him the same amount of wheat could be purchased from Peters at a ten-percent reduction in price. John cancelled his contract with James and signed a new one with Peters. Discuss James's rights in this case.

11. De Costa was a local entertainer in the New England states. He used the name "Paladin," dressed in a black cowboy suit and used calling cards marked, "Have gun, will travel." De Costa used these procedures for a prolonged period of time. CBS, a television network, began airing a TV program based on the Paladin character. De Costa sued for infringement of his trademark. What must De Costa prove to win his lawsuit?

9

THE SHERMAN ANTITRUST ACT

> ... the main cause which led to the [Sherman Act] was the thought that it was required by the economic conditions of the times; that is, the vast accumulation of wealth in the hands of corporations and individuals, the enormous development of corporate organizations ... and the wide spread impression that their power had been and would be exerted to oppress individuals and injure the public generally. (Standard Oil Co. of New Jersey v. United States, *221 U.S. 1, 1911.*)

Throughout American history, the public feared any concentration of economic power. They believed such power would be used to oppress individuals and injure the public by restricting competition and increasing prices. But by the end of the nineteenth century, a vast amount of wealth became concentrated in the hands of a few corporations and individuals. In fact, a few corporations controlled certain basic industries, such as oil, lead, steel, cotton, and whiskey. Only the common law and state antitrust laws could be used to halt this menace. Both were inadequate to meet the challenge.

Under the common law, a consumer or corporation had to sue in court to stop any unfair business practices. This lawsuit required the individual to take the initiative, hire a lawyer, and prove monetary damages in court. It was costly and time consuming. And at times, it was an ineffective procedure. For example, in the classic case of *Mogul v. McGregor*, 23 Q.B.D. 598, (1889), the court ruled that a conspiracy to drive competitors out of business was legal since conspiracies were a legitimate action in the war between competitors.

Some states enacted antitrust laws declaring monopolistic practices illegal. Any company guilty of forming a monopoly could lose its charter. But states were slow to enforce their laws, and corporations could simply move to a state without antitrust laws.

Confronted with these problems, the average person injured by unfair or monopolistic practices did not bother to sue. A few corporations continued to monopolize commerce. Federal laws were needed, and Congress responded by enacting the Sherman Antitrust Act in 1890. This law attempted to stop the concentration of economic power, by breaking up existing monopolies and by punishing any person who tried to form a monopoly or restraint of trade. Section 1 of the act makes illegal every conspiracy in restraint of trade. Section 2 of the act imposes criminal penalties on any person who monopolizes or attempts to monopolize commerce.

The case of *United States* v. *Topco*, 405 U.S. 596 (1972), summarizes the importance of the Sherman Act:

> Antitrust laws in general, and the Sherman Act in particular, are the Magna Carta of free enterprise. They are as important to the preservation of economic freedom and our free enterprise system as the Bill of Rights is to the protection of our fundamental personal freedoms. And the freedom guaranteed each and every business, no matter how small, is the freedom to compete—to assert with vigor, imagination, devotion, and ingenuity whatever economic muscle it can muster. Implicit in such freedom is the notion that it cannot be foreclosed with respect to one sector of the economy because certain groups believe that such foreclosure might promote greater competitive behavior in a more important sector of the economy.

In this chapter, we will study the major sections and the court interpretations of the Sherman Act.

SECTION 1, THE RULE OF REASON

Under this section, every contract, combination or conspiracy in restraint of trade in interstate or foreign commerce is illegal. Its purpose is simple: to stop monopolies in every industry, regardless of size or effects on the national economy. The law applies to monopolies in mining, manufacturing, production, transportation, and distribution industries.

Interpretations of the Sherman Act restrict its meaning. The Supreme Court held that the act prohibits only unreasonable restraints of trade. Prohibitions against all monopolies would be unjust and an undue burden on the liberties of people, according to the Court. The Sherman Act must be interpreted in this way; if not, nearly every business contract would be illegal since all of them restrain trade to some extent. For example, contracts to sell a product restrain the buyer from purchasing it elsewhere and a patent restrains others from using the patented item. In the case of *United States* v. *American Tobacco Co.*, 221 U.S. 106 (1911), the Supreme Court stated: "only embraced acts or contracts, or agreements or combinations which operated to the prejudice of the public interest by unduly restricting competition . . . either because of their inherent nature or because of the purpose of the acts, etc. injuriously restrain trade . . . ." In the *Topco* case, the Supreme Court explained the rule of reason as follows:

> On its face, Section 1 of the Sherman Act appears to bar any combination of entrepreneurs so long as it is in restraint of trade. Theoretically, all manufacturers, distributors, merchants, sellers and buyers could be considered as potential competitors of each other. Were Section 1 to be read in the narrowest possible way, any commercial contract could be deemed to violate it. The history underlying the formulations of the antitrust laws led this Court to conclude, however, that Congress did not intend to prohibit all contracts, nor even all contracts that might in some insignificant degree or attentuated sense restrain trade or competition. In lieu of the narrowest possible reading of Section 1, the Court adopted a rule of reason analysis for determining whether most business combinations or contracts violate the prohibitions of the Sherman Act. An analysis of the reasonableness of particular restraints includes consideration of facts peculiar to the business in which the restraint is applied, the nature of the restraint and its effects, and the history of the restraint and the reasons for its adoption.

The rule of reason is a concept broad enough to meet the needs of changing economic times. It calls for the use of judicial discretion in determining when a restraint of trade becomes unreasonable. Courts must consider economic evidence to determine whether an act unduly hampers free competition. For example, in the *American Tobacco* case, the Supreme Court used economic surveys to show that the company had a large concentration of capital, used this capital to buy up thirty of its competitors in the United States and abroad, and so dominated the tobacco market that new firms could not enter this industry without the approval of American Tobacco. Its actions were an unreasonable restraint of trade.

Examples of some common reasonable restraints of trade are franchise agreements assigning a sales territory to a person, employee contracts not to compete against a former employer for a limited time period in an appropriate geographic area, post-employment contracts prohibiting solicitation of former customers by a salesperson, and trade associations.

Trade associations are organizations formed by business firms to promote their common interests. They lobby for laws favorable to them, standardize products, improve employee relations, gather statistical data, develop research programs, and promote better public relations for their industry. It is possible for an association to be active in each of these areas without violating the Sherman Act. But once the trade association fixes prices, limits the channel of distribution, allocates customers or markets, or restrains production or sales, it becomes involved in illegal activity. The Supreme Court has ruled that statistical information on production, costs, or prices furnished by a member of an association cannot be disclosed to other members of that association because such data could be used to restrain trade. Business persons attending association meetings or conventions must be careful not to disclose information that could be used by a competitor member of the association to fix prices or limit production.

PER SE VIOLATIONS

The Supreme Court ruled that certain forms of conduct among businesses are automatic violations of the law because their effects are always presumed to be harmful to competition. They are called per se violations of the law. No economic evidence need be looked at to determine whether the acts are proper. In *Northern Pacific R. Co. v. United States*, 356 U.S. 1 (1958), the Supreme Court explained the per se rule as follows:

> There are certain agreements or practices which because of their pernicious effect on competition and lack of any redeeming virtue are conclusively presumed to be unreasonable and therefore, illegal without elaborate inquiry as to the precise harm they have caused or the business excuse for their use. This principle of per se unreasonableness not only makes the type of restraints which are prescribed by the Sherman Act more certain to the benefit of everyone concerned, but it also avoids the necessity for an incredibly complicated and prolonged economic investigation into the entire history of the industry involved, as well as related industries, in an effort to determine at large whether a particular restraint has been unreasonable—an inquiry so often wholly fruitless when undertaken.

The principal per se violations are price fixing and acts leading to it, territorial restrictions, boycotts, tying arrangements, and production quotas.

Price Fixing. A seller may not agree with competitors on the price for which they will sell their products or with customers on their resale prices. Whether the prices so set are reasonable or not is immaterial in determining if there has been a violation of Section 1. Also immaterial is whether the parties to the agreement have any power to set the market price, whether setting prices is needed to yield a reasonable profit, or whether the set prices are only minimum prices to preserve their product's image.

Price-fixing agreements can result from the exchanging, collecting, or compiling of information concerning prices or terms and conditions of a product's sale by competitors, either through a trade association or direct negotiations. Any agreement formed for the purpose of raising, depressing, fixing, pegging, or stablizing prices for a product is illegal per se. The result of such agreements eliminates competition and leads to higher prices.

Some examples of price fixing are pricing systems agreed to by competitors that result in identical delivered prices to each shipping point. Also, price fixing can result from competitor agreements refusing to allow customers to perform part of the delivery function.

United States v. Container Corporation
393 U.S. 333 (1969)

Mr. Justice Douglas.

This is a civil antitrust action charging a price fixing agreement in violation of Section 1 of the Sherman Act. The case is here on appeal. It is unlike any of the other price decisions we have rendered. There was an exchange of price information but no agreement to adhere to a price schedule. There was an exchange of information concerning specific sales to identical customers, not a statistical report on the average cost to all members.

Here, each defendant requested from its competitor information as to the most recent price charged or quoted, whenever it needed such information and whenever it was not available from another source. Each defendant on receiving that request usually furnished the data with the expectation that he would be furnished reciprocal information when he wanted it. That concerted action is of course sufficient to establish the combination or conspiracy, the initial ingredient of a violation of Section 1.

There was of course freedom to withdraw from the agreement. But the fact remains that when a defendant requested and received price information, it was affirming its willingness to furnish such information in return. Price exchanges between the defendants were infrequent and irregular, and often the data was available from the records of the defendants or from the customers themselves. Yet the essence of the agreement was to furnish price information whenever requested. Moreover, although the most recent price charged or quoted was sometimes fragmentary, each defendant had the manuals with which it could compute the price charged by a competitor on a specific order to a specific customer. Further, the price quoted was the current price a customer would need in order to obtain products from the defendant furnishing the data.

The defendants account for about ninety percent of the shipment of corrugated containers from plants in the southeastern United States. While containers vary as to dimensions, weight, color, and so on, they are substantially identical no matter who produces them, when made to particular specifications. The prices paid depend on price alternatives. Suppliers, when seeking new or additional business or keeping old customers, do not exceed a competitor's price. It is common for purchasers to buy from two or more suppliers concurrently. A defendant supplying containers would quote the same price on additional orders, unless costs had changed. Yet where a competitor was charging a particular price, a defendant would normally quote the same price or even a lower price.

The exchange of price information seemed to have the effect of keeping prices within a fairly narrow range. Capacity has exceeded demand and the trend of container prices has been downward. But in the southeast, the industry has expanded. The result of the reciprocal exchange of prices was to stabilize prices at a downward level. Knowledge of a competitor's price usually meant matching that price. Any limitation or reduction of price competition brings the case within the ban, interference with the setting of price by free market forces is unlawful per se. Price information exchanged in some markets may have no effect on a truly competitive price. But the container industry is dominated by relatively few sellers. The product is fungible and the competition for sales is price. The demand is inelastic, as buyers place orders only for immediate, short-run needs. The exchange of price data tends toward price uniformity. Stabilizing prices as well as raising them is within the ban of Section 1 of the Sherman Act. The inferences are irresistible that the exchange of price information has had an anticompetitive effect in the industry, chilling the vigor of price competition.

Price is too critical, too sensitive a control to allow it to be used in an informal manner to restrain competition. Reversed.

CASE QUESTIONS

1. Describe how price information was exchanged in this case.
2. Explain the effect of this exchange on the market for containers.
3. Why is price fixing illegal per se?

Territorial Restrictions. Agreements among producers to divide up the areas in which they sell so that each would have one market to sell in without competition from other producers is an illegal per se violation of the Sherman Act. It is illegal per se for competitors to apportion out their market geographically among themselves. However, a supplier may establish a distributor as the primary although not exclusive marketing agent for a product. Under this arrangement, a supplier can then refuse to deal with any distributor who does not make adequate sales of the product in that assigned territory.

United States v. Sealy, Inc.
388 U.S. 350 (1967)

Mr. Justice Fortas.

Sealy has, for more than forty years, licensed companies to manufacture mattresses and bedding products and to make and sell such products under the Sealy name and trademarks. In this civil action the United States charged that Sealy had violated Section 1 of the Sherman Act by conspiring with its licensees to allocate mutually exclusive territories among such manufacturer-licensees.

The District Court held that the United States had not proved this conduct to be an unreasonable restraint of trade and the United States appealed.

There is no dispute that exclusive territories were allotted to the manufacturer-licensees. Sealy agreed with each licensee not to license any other person to manufacture or sell in the designated area; and the licensee agreed not to manufacture or sell Sealy products outside the designated area. A manufacturer could make and sell his private label products anywhere he might choose.

The territorial restraints were not mere incidents of a lawful program of trademark licensing. The territorial restraints were a part of the unlawful price fixing and policing. As specific findings of the District Court show, they gave to each licensee an enclave in which he could, and did, zealously and effectively maintain resale prices, free from the danger of outside sellers. It may be true, as Sealy argues, that the territorial exclusivity served many other purposes. But its connection with the unlawful price fixing is enough to require that it be condemned as an unlawful restraint and that Sealy be effectively prevented from its continued or further use.

It is argued that we should condone this territorial limitation among manufacturers of Sealy products because there is no showing that it is unreasonable. But here, the arrangements are part of an aggregation of trade restraints including unlawful price fixing and policing. Within settled doctrine, they are unlawful under Section 1 without inquiring into their business or economic justification, their impact in the marketplace, or their reasonableness. Accordingly the judgment of the District Court is reversed and the case remanded for the entry of an appropriate decree.

CASE QUESTIONS

1. *Explain how the licensing system harmed free competition.*
2. *On what basis could territorial allocations be legal?*
3. *A territorial restriction must be combined with what other factors to become a per se violation?*

Boycott. Competitors may not agree among themselves to exclude other businesses from dealing in their products. Such agreements cause the boycotted business to close, thereby reducing competition and leading to higher prices. A good example of a boycott is *Klor's, Inc.* v. *Broadway-Hale Stores, Inc.*, 359 U.S. 207 (1959). In this case, Broadway induced ten manufacturers of household appliances not to sell products to Klor's, a competitor of Broadway. The public suffered no injury because numerous other retail outlets existed where customers could purchase the appliances. But the Court still declared it an illegal per se activity. "Group boycotts or concerted refusals by traders to deal with other traders have long been held to be in the forbidden territory." Private injury is not necessary for these acts to be wrong. They cannot be saved by showing that they were reasonable and did not result in price fixing, production limitations, or destruction of product quality. Group boycotts restrain traders in their ability to sell in accordance with their best judgment.

Some agreements by a manufacturer with its retailers can limit competition in the market without violating the Sherman Act. For example, a franchise agreement gives a person permission to sell a product within a specified territory and exclude others from selling the same product in the assigned territory. The legality of these agreements depends upon several factors. These are discussed in the next case.

United States v. Arnold, Schwinn and Co.
388 U.S. 365 (1967)

Mr. Justice Fortas.

The United States brought this appeal to review the judgment of the District Court in a civil antitrust case alleging violations of Section 1 of the Sherman Act. The complaint alleged a continuing conspiracy since 1952 between defendant and others involving price fixing, allocation of exclusive territories to wholesalers, and confinement of merchandise to franchised dealers. The District Court rejected the charge of price fixing, holding that the territorial limitations were unlawful per se as respecting products sold by Schwinn to its distributors but not unlawful for sales to its franchised dealers. The United States appeals, asking the Court to consider the franchise sales unreasonable restraints of trade.

After World War II, Schwinn had begun studying and revamping its distribution pattern. As of 1951–1952, it had reduced its mailing list from about 15,000 retail outlets to about 5,500. It started franchising approved retail outlets. The franchise did not prevent the retailer from handling other brands but it did require the retailer to promote Schwinn bicycles and to give them at least equal prominence with competing brands. The number of franchised dealers in any area was limited and a retailer was franchised only as to a designated location. Each franchised dealer was to purchase only from or through its distributor authorized to serve the area. He was authorized to sell only to consumers and not to unfranchised retailers. The District Court found that while each Schwinn franchised retailer knows he can sell at any price he wants, he also knows that he is not a wholesaler and cannot sell at a wholesale price or act as agent for a discount house. If he does, Schwinn can cancel his franchise.

Schwinn assigned specific territories to each of its twenty-two wholesale cycle distributors. These distributors were instructed to sell only to franchised dealers and only in their territories.

The agreements are vertical restrictions as to territory and dealers. The source of the restriction is the manufacturer. These are not horizontal restraints, in which the actors are distributors with or without the manufacturer's participation. We have held in such a case, where the purpose was to prevent the distribution of automobiles to or by discounters that a classic conspiracy in restraint of trade results. Nor is this a case of territorial or dealer restrictions accompanied by price fixing, for here the issue of unlawful price fixing was decided against the government and it has not appealed that decision. If it were otherwise, if there were here a finding that the restrictions were part of a scheme involving unlawful price fixing, the result would be a per se violation of the Sherman Act.

At the other extreme, a manufacturer of a product may select his customers, and for this purpose, he may franchise certain dealers to whom alone he will sell his goods. If the restraint stops at that point, if nothing more is involved than vertical confinement of the manufacturer's own sales of the merchandise to selected dealers, and if competitive products are readily available to dealers, the restriction, on these facts alone, would not violate the Sherman Act. It is within these boundary lines that we must analyze the present case.

Under the Sherman Act, it is unreasonable for a manufacturer to seek to restrict and confine areas or persons with which an article may be traded after the manufacturer has parted with dominion over it. Such restraints so obviously destroy competition that their existence is enough to make the practice illegal. If the manufacturer parts with dominion over his product or transfers risk of loss to another, he may not reserve control over the conditions of its resale. To permit this would sanction franchising and confinement of distribution as the ordinary instead of the unusual method of selling.

On the other hand, franchising is not a per se violation. Such a rule might hamper smaller enterprises resorting to reasonable methods of meeting the competition of giants and of merchandising through independent dealers, and it might sharply accelerate the trend towards vertical integration of the distribution process. But to allow franchising where the manufacturer has parted with dominion over the goods, the usual marketing situation, would violate the ancient rule against restraints on alienation and open the door to exclusivity of outlets and limitations of territory further than prudence permits.

Once the manufacturer has parted with title and risk, he has parted with dominion over the product, and his effort thereafter to restrict territory or persons to whom the product may be transferred, whether by explicit agreement or by silent combination or understanding, is a per se violation of the Sherman Act. Accordingly the judgment of the District Court is reversed and the case remanded for the entry of a decree in accordance with this opinion.

CASE QUESTIONS

1. Summarize Schwinn's marketing system in this case.
2. Why did it violate the Sherman Act?
3. Are all franchise agreements invalid under the Sherman Act?

Production Quotas. Agreements by sellers to limit their production directly affect the supply of a product. Under a competitive economic system, the public should receive the benefits of an optimum production at the lowest possible prices. Production quota agreements arbitrarily restrict supply and increase prices; hence, they are not permitted.

In one classic case, the Supreme Court condemned an "open competition plan" because it effectively limited production. Manufacturers of hardwood flooring formed an association to promote industry sales. This association collected data on production goals of each company and their current inventories. It then recommended specific production targets for each producer. Under this plan, the Court said, the association advice actually limited production in order to keep prices high and to limit competition among the members of the association. "This is not the conduct of competitors but so clearly that of men united in agreement to act together and pursue a common goal to restrict production and increase prices." (*American Column and Lumber Co. v. United States*, 257 U.S. 377, 1921.)

Tying Arrangements. Another illegal per se violation of the Sherman Act is a tying arrangement. Under this plan, a buyer must agree to purchase one product or service as a condition before being allowed to buy a desired product. For example, a purchaser wanting to buy a computer may be forced into buying a service contract to repair it and a software package to program it as well. The service and software contracts are tied to the computer. These contracts are illegal. "They deny competitors free access to the market for the tied product not because the party imposing the tying requirement has a better product or a lower price but because of his power or leverage in another market. At the same time, buyers are forced to forego their free choice between competing products. For these reasons, tying agreements are illegal." (*Fortner Enterprises, Inc.* v. *United States Steel Corp.*, 394 U.S. 495, 1969.)

SECTION 2

This part of the Sherman Act makes it a felony to "monopolize, to attempt to monopolize, or combine or conspire with any other person or persons, to monopolize any part of" the interstate or foreign commerce of the United States. This section is a supplement to Section 1, making certain that no monopolistic practices escape the law's penalties. Practices prohibited by Section 2 are any acts that give a person power to control prices or to exclude competitors from a market, done with the intent to use that power. Thus a person could be guilty of violating Section 1 if he or she conspires to form a monopoly, but not guilty of violating Section 2 if there is no intent to use that power. Intent may be presumed from a person's conduct.

PROVING A SHERMAN ACT VIOLATION

The Sherman Act does not define the type or degree of proof needed to convict a person of conspiracy to restrain trade. Under general law, a conspiracy involves two or more persons acting together. Proving concerted action is difficult because most conspiracies are formed secretively and carried out deviously. Thus, courts use the implied conspiracy test to prove concerted action.

Under this test, it is not necessary for the government to show a formal contract or any overt act in violation of the law. Instead, the conspiracy to restrain trade is inferred from things that are actually done. Courts look to the actions of competitors, and if these actions show a pattern of consciously following uniform business behavior, then evidence of a conspiracy exists. But this pattern of uniform behavior is only evidence of guilt, not proof. Before a person can be convicted of restraint of trade, the court must find some prior agreement of the competitors to act together. One competitor merely following the actions of another competitor indicates similar behavior but does not violate the law.

A recent case specifically rejects both conscious parallelism and interdependent consciously parallel behavior as tests for proving restraint of trade by competitors. In *Bogosian* v. *Gulf Oil Corp.*, 393 F. Supp. 1046 (1975), two gasoline service station lessees sued a number of major oil companies. They alleged the companies combined or conspired against them by requiring service station operators to buy their gasoline only from the firm from which they leased their station. Each oil company followed this practice through a course of interdependent consciously parallel action. That meant each firm saw what the others were doing and decided to follow the same conduct. There was no specific agreement among the oil companies to follow this practice. In rejecting plaintiff's argument, the U.S. District Court for Pennsylvania held that interdependent consciously parallel behavior is merely additional circumstantial evidence of an illegal agreement. A violation of the Sherman Act does not arise from facts that show nothing more than parallel business behavior among competitors.

After establishing a combination or conspiracy, the plaintiff must next prove that this agreement was illegal per se or an unreasonable restraint of trade. Per se violations are set out in court decisions and proof means merely showing defendant's conduct falls within the definitions of the prohibited acts. To show unreasonableness, the plaintiff must produce economic evidence to illustrate harmful effects on prices, buyers, or competitors.

Proof of a conspiracy is not required for a Section 2 violation since this section prohibits any person from monopolizing trade. Thus one person acting alone can be guilty. For conviction, the person must have the power to control prices or to exclude competitors, the intent to use that power, and the actual control in a specific market. That power can be acquired by one firm that gets its economic power through natural growth and by agreements with competitors.

LIABILITIES

A fine up to $100,000 and up to three years imprisonment or both may be imposed for each violation of either section of the Sherman Act. Corporations can be fined up to $1 million. The Department of Justice brings criminal proceedings against those who violate Section 2. Court injunctions can stop violations of the act and civil fines up to $5,000 can penalize persons violating either section. Also, any property owned under a contract or conspiracy prohibited by Section 1 can be taken by the government.

Any person injured as a result of violations of the act may sue for treble damages and court costs. In order to sue, the plaintiff must have standing and the defendant must be the direct cause of the injury. Standing, or authority to sue, exists only in those persons who are directly injured by the illegal acts of the defendant. The following case illustrates how courts compute damages in antitrust civil actions.

The Hanover Shoe, Inc. v. United Shoe Machinery Corp.
392 U.S. 481 (1968)

Mr. Justice White.

The Hanover Shoe, Inc., is a manufacturer of shoes and a customer of United Shoe Machinery Corporation, a manufacturer and distributor of shoe machinery. In 1954, this Court affirmed the judgment of the District Court for the District of Massachusetts, in favor of the United States in a civil action against United under the Sherman Act. In 1955, Hanover brought the present treble damage action against United. In 1965, the District Court rendered judgment for Hanover and awarded treble damages, including interest of $4,239,609 as well as $650,000 in counsel fees. On appeal, the Court of Appeals affirmed. Both Hanover and United sought review of the Court of Appeals decision.

Hanover's action against United alleged that United had monopolized the shoe machinery industry in violation of Section 2 of the Sherman Act; that United's policy of leasing and refusing to sell its more complicated and important shoe machinery had been an instrument of the unlawful monopolization; and that therefore Hanover should recover from United the difference between what it paid United in shoe machine rentals and what it would have paid had United been willing to sell those machines.

Two questions are raised here about the manner in which damages were computed by the courts below. Hanover argues that the Court of Appeals erred in requiring the District Court to take account of the additional taxes Hanover would have paid had it purchased the machines instead of renting them during the years in question. The Court of Appeals evidently felt that since only after-tax profits can be reinvested, Hanover was damaged only to the extent of the after-tax profits that it failed to receive. The view of the Court of Appeals is sound in theory, but it overlooks the fact that in practice the Internal Revenue

Service has taxed recoveries for tortious deprivation of profits at the time the recoveries are made, not by reopening the earlier years.

United contends that if Hanover had bought machines instead of leasing them, it would have had to invest its own capital in the machines. United argues that the District Court erred in computing damages because it did not properly take in account the cost of capital to Hanover. The District Court found that in the years in question, Hanover was able to borrow money for between 2 and 2.5% per year and that had Hanover bought machines it would have obtained the necessary capital by borrowing at this rate. It therefore deducted an interest component of 2.5% from the profits it thought Hanover would have earned by purchasing machines. Our review of the record convinces us that the courts below did not err in these determinations.

CASE QUESTIONS

1. Are damages awarded for loss of pretax profits or after-tax profits?
2. What other costs affect damages in this case?
3. Why does the law permit treble damages?

REVIEW QUESTIONS

1. Why did Congress enact the Sherman Act?

2. Explain the differences between reasonable and illegal per se restraints of trade.

3. Outline the per se violations of the Sherman Act.

4. State the liabilities for violating the Sherman Act.

5. Jackman Marine Transport alleges it was denied the right to purchase several transport ships. In its complaint, Jackman alleges that Norfolk Drydock, the leading manufacturer of naval vessels, and Sealand, Jackman's main competitor, agreed not to sell any vessels to Jackman. Norfolk moves for summary judgment in its favor because Jackman failed to allege any unreasonable effects on interstate commerce. Should the court grant this motion?

6. Higgins, the owner of a food manufacturing company, registered his product name with the government pursuant to the Lanham Act. He then licensed certain companies to use his tradename in

selling food products. Does this license agreement violate the Sherman Act?

7. Lance Newspapers sold its paper to readers through independent contractors, who resold to the public. Lance also used its own employees to sell the papers. Independent contractors could sell the papers at any price, but Lance suggested a fair resale price. Madden was an independent contractor selling Lance papers at a higher price than that recommended by the publisher. Persuasion failed to induce Madden to sell at the suggested price so Lance terminated its contract. Madden sued Lance for damages under the Sherman Act. Should any be awarded?

8. Norris had a contract with McAvoy Brewery to be exclusive distributor of its beer products in a certain territory. Norris also carried lines of beer produced by competitors of McAvoy. McAvoy threatened to cancel Norris's contract unless he agreed to stop carrying other beer products. Norris refused and sued McAvoy, requesting an injunction restraining it from carrying out its threat. Should the injunction be granted?

10

THE CLAYTON ACT AND THE FEDERAL TRADE COMMISSION ACT

The economic theories which the [Supreme Court] has read into the Antitrust Laws have favored rather than discouraged monopoly. As a result... big business has become bigger and bigger. Monopoly has flourished.... The full force of the Antitrust Laws has not been felt on our economy.... Niggardly interpretations have robbed those laws of much of their efficacy. (Dissent of Mr. Justice Douglas in Standard Oil Co. of California v. United States, *337 U.S. 293, 1949.)*

The Sherman Act is a broad law prohibiting agreements in restraint of trade. It did not make any specific acts illegal. Court interpretations made some acts illegal per se but also created the "rule of reason" for most other acts in restraint of trade. This rule weakened the enforcement of the Sherman Act. The act was also weakened when the government used it to break up existing monopolies, not to stop emerging ones. For these reasons, business continued to grow and expand into monopolies. To remedy this situation, Congress passed the Clayton Act. This act prevents specific anticompetitive practices. Its three main sections prohibit exclusive dealings arrangements, mergers that may lessen competition, and price discrimination.

At the same time, Congress enacted the Federal Trade Commission Act. This law contains vague language and attempts to eliminate unfair methods of competition. It also establishes the Federal Trade Commission, an administrative agency to enforce antitrust laws. In this chapter, we will study the Clayton Act, the Federal Trade Commission Act, exemptions from antitrust laws, and enforcement procedures. By combining the three major antitrust laws studied in Chapters 9 and 10, we can develop some management guidelines for persons involved with business growth and expansion.

THE CLAYTON ACT

Exclusive Dealings Arrangements

Section 3 of the Clayton Act states:

> That it shall be unlawful for any person engaged in commerce, in the course of such commerce, to lease, or make a sale or contract for sale of goods, wares, merchandise, machinery, supplies, or other commodities, whether patented or unpatented, for use, consumption, or resale within the United States or any Territory thereof or the District of Columbia or any insular possession or other place under the jurisdiction of the United States, or fix a price charged therefore, or discount from or rebate upon such price, on the condition, agreement or understanding that the lessee or purchaser thereof shall not use or deal in the goods, wares, merchandise, machinery, supplies or other commodities of a competitor or competitors of the lessor or seller where the effect of such lease, sale or contract for sale or such condition, agreement or understanding may be to substantially lessen competition or tend to create a monopoly in any line of commerce.

This lengthy section makes it unlawful to sell or lease products where the purchaser or lessee must agree not to use or deal in products from the seller's or lessor's competitor if that agreement may substantially lessen competition. For example, violations of this section can arise where the buyer agrees not to handle the products of a seller's competitors, where the seller agrees not to distribute products through the buyer's competitors, or where a seller agrees to supply all the product requirements of a buyer. Four conditions are necessary for these agreements to violate the Clayton Act:

1. Transaction. Section 3 applies to a lease or sale only, not to relationships between a principal and agent or between a consignor and consignee. The transaction must lock the buyer into dealing with the seller's products only.

2. Probable Effects. These agreements must have some effect on competition. The section uses the words "may be" in describing these consequences. These words prohibit agreements where there is a chance that competition may suffer. This language prevents any arrangements that might lessen competition in the future.

3. Substantial. Not every lessening of competition is prohibited by this section. The probable effects of the agreement must have a substantial impact on competition. Even though an agreement may reduce competition, no violation of this section exists if the impact is only minor. The test is whether a major quantity of commerce is adversely affected by the agreement. A court must weigh the probable effects of the agreement on the relevant market area of effective competition. Factors courts must consider are the relative strengths of the parties, the volume of commerce involved in relation to the total volume of commerce in the market, and the likely immediate and future effects of the agreement.

Substantiality was found by the courts in contracts requiring some 5,900 service station dealers to purchase gasoline and other products exclusively from one supplier, where the arrangement affected 6.7 percent of all gasoline sales, 5 percent of lubricating sales, and 2 percent of tire and battery sales having a total cost of $57 million. But the test of substantiality was not met in a contract to supply the coal requirements for power plants in Florida for twenty years where the coal was less than one percent of the total market.

4. Market. Finally, the court must determine the relevant market area in which the effects of the exclusive dealings arrangements may be to substantially lessen competition. In the Florida coal case, the Supreme Court determined that the relevant market for coal purchased by the power company was not Florida but seven other states, in which the seller and 700 other sellers competed. But in the service station case, the relevant market was the western states, where only a handful of gasoline suppliers competed. The following case illustrates these four conditions.

Standard Oil of California v. United States
337 U.S. 293 (1949)

Mr. Justice Frankfurter.

This is an appeal to review a decree enjoining the Standard Oil Company of California and its wholly owned subsidiary, Standard Stations, Inc., from enforcing or entering exclusive supply contracts with any independent dealer in petroleum products and automobile accessories. The use of such contracts was successfully attacked by the United States as a violation of Section 3 of the Clayton Act.

The Standard Oil Company owns petroleum-producing resources and refining plants in California and sells petroleum products in the western area—Arizona, California, Idaho, Nevada, Oregon, Utah, and Washington. It sells through its own services stations, to the operators of independent service stations, and to industrial users. It is the largest seller of gasoline in the area. In 1946 its combined sales amounted to twenty-three percent of the total taxable gallonage sold there in that year—sales by company-owned service stations constituted 6.8 percent of the total, sales under exclusive dealing contracts with independent service stations were 6.7 percent of the total, and the remainder went to industrial users. Retail service station sales by Standard's six leading competitors absorbed 42.5 percent of the total taxable gallonage; the remaining retail sales were divided among more than seventy small companies. It is undisputed that Standard's major competitors employ similar exclusive dealing arrangements. In 1948 only 1.6 percent of retail outlets were split-pump stations, that is, stations selling the gasoline of more than one supplier.

Exclusive supply contracts with Standard had been entered, as of 1947, by the operators of 5,937 independent stations, or sixteen percent of the retail gasoline outlets in the western area, which purchased from Standard in 1947 over $57 million worth of gasoline and more than $8 million worth of other products. Some outlets are covered by more than one contract so that in all about 8,000 exclusive supply contracts are here in issue. These are of several types, but a feature common to each is the dealer's promise to purchase from Standard all his requirements of one or more products. Two types, covering 2,777 outlets, bind the dealer to purchase from Standard all his requirements of gasoline and other petroleum products, as well as tires, tubes, and batteries. The remaining written agreements, 4,368 in number, bind the dealer to purchase from Standard all his requirements of petroleum products only.

Section 3 of the Clayton Act prohibits specific practices not covered by the broad terms of the Sherman Act. The issue before us, therefore, is whether the requirement of showing that the effect of the agreements "may be to substantially lessen competition" can be satisfied simply by proof that a substantial portion of commerce is affected or whether it must also be proven that competitive activity has actually diminished or probably will diminish.

Requirements contracts may be of economic advantage to buyers as well as to sellers, and thus indirectly of advantage to the consuming public. In the case of the buyer, they may assure supply, afford protection against rises in price, enable long-term planning on the basis of known costs, and reduce the expense and risk of storage in the quantity necessary for a commodity having a fluctuating demand. From the seller's point of view, requirements contracts may lessen selling expenses, give protection against price fluctuations, and offer the possibility of a predictable market. They may be useful to a seller trying to establish a foothold against counterattacks of entrenched competitors.

But these advantages do not offset the illegality of such contracts.

We conclude that Section 3 is satisfied by proof that competition has been reduced in a substantial share of the line of commerce affected. Standard's competitors cannot sell their products to dealers subject to these contracts, and the value of retail sales covered by these contracts is substantial. In view of the widespread use of such contracts by Standard's competitors and the lack of alternative ways to market petroleum products, there is evidence that competitive activity has been reduced. Standard's use of the contracts creates just such a potential clog on competition as it was the purpose of Section 3 to remove wherever it would impede a substantial amount of competitive activity. Affirmed.

CASE QUESTIONS

1. Explain the terms in the exclusive supply contracts used by Standard.
2. What advantages are there in the use of these contracts? Are they illegal per se?
3. Define the relevant market of gasoline sales in this case and explain how competition may be substantially lessened in this market.

Mergers

Section 7 provides:

> That no corporation engaged in commerce shall acquire, directly or indirectly, the whole or any part of the stock or other share capital and no corporation subject to the jurisdiction of the Federal Trade Commission shall acquire the whole or any part of the assets of another corporation engaged in commerce, where in any line of commerce in any section of the country, the effect of such acquisition may be substantially to lessen competition, or tend to create a monopoly.

This section prohibits certain mergers that were not stopped by the Sherman Act. A merger is a union between two or more business firms into one surviving organization. Section 7 restrains mergers by preventing any unions between companies that may lead to a monopoly in the future. It stops potential monopolies in their incipiency rather than waiting until they actually emerge. All types of mergers are covered by Section 7: horizontal mergers among competing firms, vertical mergers among companies in a chain of distribution, and conglomerate mergers of business firms having no relationship among them.

The approach followed under the Clayton Act is radically different from that of the Sherman Act. Clayton Act prohibits emerging monopolies while the Sherman Act prohibits only existing monopolies; Clayton Act considers the probable effects of a merger while the Sherman Act requires actual restraints of trade; and Clayton Act does not require an intent to monopolize while the Sherman Act demands intent to violate Section 2 of the law.

The test for determining whether a merger violates Section 7 has two key parts: first, determine the relevant market and second, estimate the probable effects of the merger.

1. Relevant Market. Courts define the relevant market as the area of effective competition in which the two merging firms operate. It can consist of the product market or the geographic market of competition. To determine the product market in which companies compete, the court must consider the other products which are in competition with those products made by the merging firms. This product market includes those things that are substitutes for a product as well as those that are equivalent. For example, the relevant product market for wood building materials can include concrete building blocks as well as structural glass and vinyl since all can be used in construction. Mergers among companies making products in these areas would fall within Section 7 since they are all competing in one relevant market—building construction materials.

To determine the geographic market in which companies compete, courts look at the area where the products are sold in competition with other, similar products. The area may be a particular section of a state, a region, or even the entire country. The basis for determining a geographic market is a pragmatic analysis of each merger's factual patterns; no precise standards are established by the courts. The boundaries of a geographic market depend on the commercial realities of the industry. For example, two retailers who operate in different sections of the country, one in the east and the other in the west, are not competing in the same geographic market. But if they decide to sell in the midwest, they compete against each other in that market. The following case explains how the product and geographic markets are determined in the context of a bank merger. Only that part of the case dealing with the market area is printed below.

United States v. Phillipsburg National Bank
399 U.S. 350 (1970)

Mr. Justice Brennan.

I: Phillipsburg is a small industrial city on the Delaware River in the southwestern corner of Warren County, New Jersey. The population of the area has been increasing, but not that of the city. Easton, Pennsylvania, lies directly across the river, and its population growth pattern parallels that of Phillipsburg. The combined area has seven commercial banks, four in Easton and three in Phillipsburg. Phillipsburg National Bank and Second National Bank, PNB and SNB respectively, are direct competitors. Both offer the same kinds of banking services, both serve the small depositor, and both serve Phillipsburg. The two banks proposed to merge, reducing the number of commercial banks to six in the area, and two in Phillipsburg. The controller of the currency approved the merger, finding that adequate banking facilities in competition with each other existed in the Lehigh Valley area, which includes Phillipsburg and Easton. More than thirty commercial banks and many other types of banking institutions remained in this area. The United States petitioned the District Court for an injunction stopping the merger under Section 7 of the Clayton Act. The court dismissed the petition and the government appeals.

II: The product market. The cluster of products (various kinds of credit) and services (such as checking accounts and trust administration) called commercial banking is the line of commerce. Commercial banks are the only financial institutions in which a wide variety of financial products and services are gathered together in one place. The clustering of financial products and services in banks makes it easier for all banking customers. Customers of small banks need and use this cluster of services and products. Full-service banking in one institution may be significant to the economy of communities whose populations are too small to support a large array of differentiated savings and credit businesses.

III: The geographic market. In determining the relevant geographic market, the proper question to be asked is not where the parties to the merger do business or even where they compete, but where, within the area of competitive overlap, the effect of the merger on competition will be direct and immediate. This depends on the geographic structure of supplier-customer relations. More specifically, we stated that the area of effective competition in the line of commerce must be charted by careful selection of the market area in which the seller operates and to which the purchaser can practicably turn for supplies.

Commercial realities in the banking industry make clear that banks generally have a very localized business. Convenience of location is essential to effective competition. Most individuals bank in their local community; they find it impractical to conduct their banking business at a distance. In locating the market area in which companies compete, it is important to consider the places from which they draw business, the location of their offices, and where they seek business. Here, the banks drew over eighty-five percent of their business from the Phillipsburg-Easton area and only about ten percent from Easton itself. The entire Lehigh Valley is too broad for a geographic market; it is Phillipsburg only.

(The court concluded the merger violated Section 7.)

The judgment of the District Court is reversed and the case remanded for further proceedings consistent with this opinion.

CASE QUESTIONS

1. How does the Court determine the relevant product market?
2. How does the Court determine the relevant geographic market?

---

2. Effects. After determining the relevant market, courts must then determine the probable effects of the merger to see if it may substantially lessen competition. There is no single test to apply in answering this question. The words in Section 7 are vague, to give courts wide discretion in applying the law to each merger. But there are some guideposts indicating general areas of illegal mergers. For example, courts often consider whether a merger eliminates a substantial competitor, whether the surviving business becomes too powerful over its remaining competitors, whether there is a dangerous lessening of the number of competing firms, or whether the industry in which the firms operate is becoming too concentrated. If the answer to any of these questions is affirmative, then the effects of the merger probably lessen competition substantially.

In the *Phillipsburg National Bank* case, the Court evaluated the effects of the merger as follows: "A merger which produces a firm controlling an undue percentage share of the relevant market and which results in a significant concentration of firms in that market is so likely to lessen competition substantially that it must be enjoined unless evidence clearly shows that the merger is not likely to have those effects. This rule applies in this case. The commercial banking market in Phillipsburg-Easton is already concentrated. Of seven commercial banks in the area, two of them have 49% of the total assets, 56% of the total deposits, 49% of total loans and seven of 16 bank offices. The proposed merger here would significantly concentrate banking further in the area. The resulting bank would have 19% of the area's bank assets, 23% of its total deposits, and 27% of its loans. It would have 12 of the 16 bank offices. Banking alternatives to Phillipsburg residents would be reduced to two and the remaining bank would be three times larger than the other. Thus, we find that the proposed merger is inherently likely to lessen competition substantially."

Thus, in determining the legality of a merger under Section 7, courts make a flexible, case-by-case analysis of the facts. Economics of competition and the history of competition in the industry are factors considered by the courts. Statistical evidence and market surveys can show the trend toward concentration of economic power into a few companies. If the evidence shows that one firm or a small group of firms has a significant share of market power, then future mergers by them may be limited by this section.

Federal Trade Commission (FTC) v. Proctor and Gamble Company (PG)
386 U.S. 568 (1967)

Mr. Justice Douglas.

    This is a proceeding instituted by the FTC charging that PG had acquired the assets of Clorox Chemical Company in violation of Section 7 of the Clayton Act. After hearings before the FTC, the Examiner ordered divestiture and the commission affirmed. The Court of Appeals reversed and directed the FTC's complaint to be dismissed. We find that the commission's findings were supported by the evidence and the Court of Appeals erred.

    This merger may be described as a product extension merger. At the time of the merger, Clorox was the leading manufacturer in the heavily concentrated household liquid bleach industry. It is agreed that household liquid bleach is the relevant line of commerce. The product is used as a whitening agent in washing clothes. It has no substitutes and is sold to consumers through grocery stores and supermarkets. The relevant geographic market is the nation and a series of regional markets. Because of high shipping costs and low sales prices, it is not feasible to ship the product more than 300 miles. Thus most manufacturers are local companies. Clorox is the only firm selling nationally. Purex, its closest competitor, does not sell in the northeast or middle-Atlantic states.

    Since all bleach is the same, advertising and sales promotion is vital. In 1957, Clorox spent almost $4 million on advertising and nearly $2 million on other promotion expenses. PG is a large, diversified manufacturer of low-price, high-turnover household products sold through grocery, drug, and department stores. Prior to its purchase of Clorox, it did not make bleach. Its 1957 sales were in excess of $1 billion and profits exceeded $67 million. Its assets were over $500 million. PG has been marked by rapid growth and expansion. It has successfully developed and introduced a number of new products. Its primary activity has been in the area of soaps, detergents, and cleaners. PG was the dominant producer in this field. The industry is heavily concentrated: Procter and its two competitors account for eighty percent of the market.

    In the marketing of soaps, cleansers, and detergents—as in the marketing of bleach—advertising and sales promotion are vital. In 1957, PG was the leading advertiser, spending more than $80 million on advertising and $47 million on sales promotions. As a multiproduct advertiser, PG enjoys substantial advantages in advertising and sales promotion. It features several products in one commercial, and promotion costs are reduced when products are advertised and promoted together.

Prior to this merger, PG was in the course of developing new product lines. Bleach was a distinct possibility, since packaged detergents and bleach are used together in washing clothes. The decision to acquire Clorox was the result of a study conducted by PG's promotion department designed to determine the feasibility of entering the bleach industry. The report recommended that Clorox be purchased since a larger capital expenditure would be necessary for another product to acquire a market share as large as that possessed by Clorox.

Section 7 of the Clayton Act was intended to arrest the anticompetitive effects of market power in their incipiency. The core question is whether a merger may substantially lessen competition and necessarily requires a prediction of the merger's impact on competition, present and future. The section can deal only with probabilities, not with certainties. And there is certainly no requirement that the anticompetitive power exist before Section 7 can be called into play. If the enforcement of Section 7 turned on the existence of actual anticompetitive practices, the congressional policy of thwarting such practices in their incipiency would be frustrated.

All mergers are within the reach of Section 7, and all must be tested by the same standard, whether they are classified as horizontal, vertical, conglomerate, or other. As noted by the FTC, this merger is neither horizontal nor vertical nor conglomerate. Since the products of the acquired company are complementary to those of the acquiring company and may be produced with similar facilities, marketed through the same channels and in the same manner, and advertised by the same media, the FTC properly called this merger a product-extension merger:

> By this acquisition, PG has not diversified its interests in the sense of expanding into a substantially different market. Rather it entered a market which adjoins those markets in which it is already established and which is virtually indistinguishable from them insofar as the problems and techniques of marketing the product to the ultimate consumer are concerned.

The anticompetitive effects of this can easily be seen: the substitution of the powerful acquiring firm for the smaller but already dominant firm may substantially reduce the competitive structure of the industry by raising entry barriers and by dissuading the smaller firms from aggressively competing; and the acquisition eliminates the potential competition of the acquiring firm.

The judgment of the Court of Appeals is reversed and remanded with instructions to affirm and enforce the FTC's order.

CASE QUESTIONS

1. Distinguish the four types of mergers to which the Clayton Act applies.

2. Explain how this merger violates Section 7 by substantially lessening competition.
3. What merger alternatives do large corporations have after this case?

THE FEDERAL TRADE COMMISSION ACT

Unfair Methods of Competition

Section 5 of the Federal Trade Commission Act declares unlawful "unfair methods of competition in commerce and unfair or deceptive practices in commerce." The act does not define an unfair method of competition; its definition is left for the courts to determine in individual cases. Congressional intent was to leave the phrase vague because it was impossible to determine all the possible unfair acts a businessperson could develop. As explained in one case:

> ... the courts and the law [must] keep pace with the mushrooming increases in business complexity and the concomitant opportunities for chicanery.... Unfair competition is a form of unlawful business injury.... The incalculable variety of illegal commercial practices denominated as unfair competition is proportionate to the unlimited ingenuity that overreaching entrepreneurs and trade pirates put to use. (*Electrolux Corp.* v. *Val-Worth, Inc.*, 6 N.Y. 2d 556, 1959)

At first, Supreme Court cases narrowly construed Section 5, applying it to practices that were against good morals, fraudulent, or against public policy. Gradually, Court opinions broadened its scope. Today, the full meaning of "unfair methods of competition" is not clear. But the following historical summary of interpretations of this phrase may indicate the trend government is following.

Courts first ruled that any violation of the common law, the Sherman Act, or the Clayton Act was an unfair method of competition. Thus a company engaged in price fixing prohibited by Section 1 of the Sherman Act was also guilty of violating Section 5 of the FTC Act. Similarly, a company misrepresenting the products or services of a competitor committed the tort of disparagement and violated Section 5.

Later, other cases applied the phrase to advertisements that were misrepresentations or false statements. A recent case involved the advertising of milk by celebrities, each one stating that "Every *body* needs milk." The FTC contested the ad, complaining that milk is not essential for some persons, such as those with certain health problems caused by excessive fats in the diet. Another example of false advertising now condemned under Section 5 is the improper labeling of products. A recent case prohibited the labeling of Hong Kong–made products as Alaskan Native American–made handicrafts. Similarly, Section 5 would be violated when products assembled in the United States from components produced elsewhere are labeled as American made.

Courts have now extended the meaning of unfair methods of competition to include deceptively large packages for products that could be put into smaller containers and excessive use of graphics on containers to induce people to purchase the products merely because the designs enhances their expectations. Oversized or overly attractive packages can mislead purchasers into thinking they are actually buying a larger product or a more appealing product then they receive. Perhaps the meaning of this phrase "unfair methods of competition" can be summarized by stating that it prohibits any act which runs contrary to generally accepted business ethics.

F.T.C. v. Sperry and Hutchinson Co. (S&H)
405 U.S. 233 (1972)

Mr. Justice White.

In June, 1968, the FTC held that the largest and oldest company in the trading stamp industry, S&H, was violating Section 5 of the Federal Trade Commission Act. The FTC found that S&H attempted to suppress the operation of trading stamp exchanges and other free and open redemptions of stamps. The FTC entered a cease-and-desist order. S&H appealed to the Fifth Circuit Court of Appeals, conceding that it acted as the FTC found, but arguing that its conduct is beyond the reach of Section 5. As S&H sees it, Section 5 gives the FTC power to restrain only such practices as are either in violation of the antitrust laws, deceptive, or repugnant to public morals. The Court of Appeals agreed and reversed the FTC. The FTC petitioned this Court for review. We granted certiorari.

There are two questions in this case. First, does Section 5 empower the FTC to define and prohibit an unfair competitive practice even though the practice does not infringe on the letter or spirit of the antitrust laws? Second, does Section 5 empower the FTC to prohibit practices as unfair or deceptive to consumers when these practices do not lessen competition. We think the statute, its legislative history, and prior cases compel an affirmative answer to both questions.

This conclusion requires us to hold that the Court of Appeals erred in its construction of Section 5. The challenged practices can violate the section even though the acts are not per se violations of the Sherman Act, not violations of the spirit or letter of the antitrust laws, and not violations of any court interpretation of them.

CASE QUESTIONS

1. What activities of S&H allegedly violate Section 5?
2. Summarize the practices that the FTC can prohibit as unfair methods of competition or as unfair or deceptive practices.

ANTITRUST LIABILITIES AND EXEMPTIONS

Liabilities

Section 3 of the Clayton Act imposes a fine of not more than $5,000 or imprisonment of not more than one year, or both, for each violation of the act. A person damaged by any violation of this act can sue for an injunction stopping the violation and for recovery of triple damages for any financial loss caused by the violation. Triple damage actions have increased lately; now more than ten times as many are filed as were filed five years ago. The cost of these suits to companies is staggering. Recently, more than $200 million was paid by one company for Clayton Act violations. By awarding triple damages, the law encourages private citizens to bring these actions against companies to help government enforce the antitrust laws. If the citizen is successful in his or her antitrust action, the court can award attorneys' fees and allowances for court costs. In one recent case, the Supreme Court stated: "The fact that a successful antitrust suit for damages recovers not only the costs of litigation but also attorney's fees, should provide no scarcity of members of the Bar to aid prospective plaintiffs in bringing these suits." (*State of Hawaii* v. *Standard Oil Company of California*, 405 U.S. 251, 1972.)

The FTC Act does not establish any specific penalties for violating Section 5. But if a person or company refuses to obey an order of the FTC that prohibits a specific unfair practice, a fine of up to $10,000 can be assessed. And a consumer injured because of the unfair practices of a company can sue for any damages incurred. Recent legislation gives the FTC power to seek civil penalties of up to $10,000 per day or per violation against any person who violates one of its trade regulation rules, discussed below. In addition, the FTC can now issue orders requiring a business to return money to injured consumers. In one recent case, an FTC aide tentatively ordered a company to make a $44 million restitution to 30,000 persons throughout the United States who paid money into a fraudulent marketing scheme.

Exemptions

Numerous types of businesses are exempt from all or part of the antitrust laws, either because of Congressional law or court policy. Some of the principle exemptions are:

1. Small or Failing Corporations. Where a merger does not have any substantial anticompetitive effects, it is not a violation of the antimerger rules of the Sherman or Clayton Acts. Therefore, the acts do not prohibit mergers between corporations that are economically insignificant or among bankrupt firms. If a firm is not a viable competitor, a merger by it does not eliminate competition. But before mergers among bankrupt firms are permitted, there must be no other purchaser for the firm, and financial rehabilitation of the firm must be impossible. *Brown Shoe Co. v. United States*, 370 U.S. 294 (1962).

2. Investment Purposes. If a business purchases stock in a corporation solely for investment purposes and does not use its stock owership for control or to bring about any lessening of competition, then the acquisition does not violate the merger rules of the Clayton Act.

3. Subject to Other Regulatory Agencies. Also exempted from the Clayton Act are transactions by business firms that are regulated by other administrative agencies, such as the CAB, FCC, FPC, ICC, and SEC. This exemption reduces some problems arising from overregulation of business and allows other regulatory agencies more flexibility to act. The following excerpt from a recent Supreme Court case explains this exemption:

> The agreements questioned by the United States restrict the terms under which the underwriters and brokers-dealers may trade in shares of mutual funds. Such restrictions are concerted refusals to deal and normally constitute per se violations of Section 1 of the Sherman Act. Here however, Congress has made a judgment that these restrictions on competition might be necessitated by the unique problems of the mutual fund industry, and has vested in the SEC final authority to

determine whether and to what extent they should be tolerated "in the interests of the holders of all the outstanding securities of mutual funds."

The SEC, the federal agency responsible for regulating the conduct of the mutual fund industry, urges that its authority will be compromised seriously if these agreements are deemed actionable under the Sherman Act. We agree. There can be no reconciliation of its authority to permit these and similar restrictions with the Sherman's declaration that they are illegal per se. In this instance the antitrust laws must give way if the regulatory scheme established by Congress is to work. We conclude that such agreements are not actionable under the Sherman Act. (*U.S. v. National Association of Securities Dealers*, 42 L Ed 2d 45, 1975)

4. Labor Organizations. The Clayton Act states that the labor of a human being is not an article of commerce, and therefore the antitrust laws do not apply to any labor organization or union. Union members may engage in boycotts, restraints of trade, market division, and price fixing to the extent permitted by labor laws, without violating antitrust laws. But when a labor organization conspires with management of a business to do any of the above-mentioned acts with the purpose of harming a competitor of that management, it forfeits its exemption.

Ramsey v. United Mine Workers
401 U.S. 302 (1971)

Coal mine operators brought this Sherman Act conspiracy action against the union alleging that the union had expressly or impliedly agreed with the major coal producers to impose the terms of the 1950 National Bituminous Coal Wage Agreement on all coal mine operators, knowing that the smaller ones would not be able to meet the terms of this agreement and would be driven out of business. The trial judge dismissed the case.

The mine operators ask us to reconsider our holding in the Pennington case. That case held that under the Clayton and Norris LaGuardia Acts, the union incurs no liability under the antitrust laws when it concludes a wage agreement with the multi-employer bargaining unit and, as a matter of its own policy and not by agreement with all or part of the employers of that union, seeks the same wage from other employers. This we decline to do. The Court made it clear that unilateral conduct by the union of the type protected by the Clayton and Norris LaGuardia Acts does not violate the Sherman Act even though it may restrain trade. These congressionally permitted union activities may restrain trade in and of themselves. There is no denying the fact that many of them do so, both directly and indirectly. But the desirability of such an exemption of labor unions is a question for the determination of Congress. We adhere to this view.

But neither do we retreat from the one line that we can draw while still upholding Congress's purpose. We know that Congress feared the concentrated power of business organizations to dominate markets and prices. A business monopoly is no less such because a union participates, and such participation is a violation of the act. Where a union, by agreement with one set of employers, insists on maintaining in other bargaining units specified wage standards ruinous to the business of those employers, it is liable under the antitrust laws for the damages caused by its agreed-upon conduct.

We reverse the judgment of the lower court and remand the case for further proceedings consistent with this opinion.

CASE QUESTIONS

1. What actions by the union allegedly violate the antitrust laws?
2. When does a labor union lose its antitrust exemption?

---

5. *Intrastate Business.* Business activity conducted entirely within one state is exempt from antitrust laws because the Constitution gives Congress the power to regulate interstate commerce only. However, the Supreme Court has extended Congressional power to regulate local, intrastate business when it has a substantial effect on interstate commerce. *United States* v. *Oregon State Medical Society*, 343 U.S. 326 (1952).

6. *Services.* The Supreme Court exempts from antitrust laws parts of certain service businesses. At first, the court ruled that antitrust laws applied only to commodities, not services. Exempt from the laws were those services that had a detailed self-regulatory code of ethics. For example, lawyers are supervised by state bar associations and subject to a comprehensive code of conduct, called canons, to govern the practice of law. Doctors and certified public accountants have similar standards. Accordingly, these professionals are exempt because they are regulated by states or associations.

But recent court decisions are making some aspects of professions subject to antitrust laws. In *Goldfarb* v. *Virginia State Bar*, 42 L. Ed. 2d 178, (1975), the Supreme Court held that lawyers' minimum fee schedules could violate Section 1 of the Sherman Act. These schedules recommend to lawyers the fees they should charge clients for specified legal services. Lawyers charging less than the schedule allows could be disciplined by the bar. The Court withdrew the traditional exemption of professionals because the fixed fees restrain commerce, adversely affect interstate commerce, and are a form of price fixing.

7. *Professional Sports.* Business firms owning professional sporting teams or leagues are exempt from the antitrust laws. League owners can divide up their territories among franchise owners, assign exclusive territories to certain owners, prevent players from performing in areas not assigned to them by the owners, and engage in other acts not permitted to other types of business firms. *Flood* v. *Kuhn*, 407 U.S. 258 (1973).

ANTITRUST ENFORCEMENT

Enforcement Procedures

The FTC Act is more than just a prohibition on unfair methods of competition. It creates a whole system for investigating and enforcing antitrust laws. The act creates the Federal Trade Commission, a bipartisan administrative agency. This commission consists of five members, each appointed by the President and confirmed by the Senate. One of its members serves as chairman, and the FTC can hire experts to help it carry out its duties. For example, economists determine the extent of monopoly power a business possesses, attorneys bring legal actions against alleged antitrust law violators, and technicians such as physicists and chemists conduct special tests. The FTC shares enforcement with the Antitrust Division of the Department of Justice. Both enforce antitrust laws, but only the Justice Department prosecutes criminal violations.

To enforce its orders, the FTC has several remedies available:

1. Consent Decree. This is a voluntary agreement to accept the complaint, findings, and orders made by the FTC. Lawyers for both sides negotiate the terms of a consent order. Typically, the firm agrees to stop the challenged action and the FTC agrees not to penalize the person for violating the law. The consent order is for settlement purposes and does not admit that a law was violated. A consumer or competitor damaged by the antitrust actions of another cannot use the consent decree as a basis of suing for damages. All consent orders are subject to review by the full membership of the FTC. The following illustrates a typical consent order:

Sterling Drug, Inc.
Federal Trade Commission *News Summary,* **No. 17, 1974.**

A consent order provisionally accepted by the FTC prohibits Sterling Drug, Inc., from making disease prevention claims for Lysol Brand products or any household disinfectants.

Also cited in the agreed to order is Sterling's advertising agency for Lysol's products.

The complaint alleged that the firm's advertising has falsely represented that one should use Lysol to kill influenza virus and other germs and viruses on environmental surfaces and in the air, and that such use will be of significant medical benefit in reducing the incidence and preventing the spread of colds, influenza, and other respiratory diseases.

In reality, the complaint alleged, germs and viruses on environmental surfaces do not play a significant role in transmitting upper respiratory diseases, and using Lysol neither eliminates significant numbers of airborne germs and viruses, which are the known cause of most respiratory disease, nor will be of significant medical benefit in reducing the incidence or preventing the spread of these diseases within the home.

The consent order forbids claims that use of any household disinfectant:

Will be of medical benefit in reducing the incidence or preventing the spread of influenza, colds, or streptococcal throat infection.

Kills airborne viruses or bacteria associated with respiratory diseases. (This does not bar demonstrations of aerosol products as room deodorizers or air fresheners.)

Kills germs associated with disease unless the name of the disease is expressly mentioned, the representation is true, and there is competent and reliable scientific evidence that such use reduces the incidence or prevents the spread of the named disease.

Kills viruses or bacteria associated with respiratory diseases unless the advertisement clearly and conspicuously discloses that there is no evidence that the product portrayed will protect the family against flu or strep throat.

Also prohibited are representations that environmental surfaces play a significant role in transmitting viruses or bacteria associated with influenza, colds, or streptococcal throat infection.

2. *Publicity.* A person suspected of violating an antitrust law may find substantial information about the alleged violation released

to the news media. The FTC has an Office of Public Information, which releases information about actions taken by the commission, complaints filed, answers to the complaints, evidence, testimony, opinions, decisions, and orders. The press can publish this information and the public may exert pressure on the person to comply with FTC requests.

A variation of the publicity approach has recently been developed by the FTC. Questionnaires are sent to companies asking them to define what their practices will be in the future. The unwritten message is to conform those questioned practices to the FTC guidelines for proper business conduct or face a complaint.

3. Trade Conference. This is an informal procedure for obtaining voluntary industrywide compliance with an order of the FTC. From the conference with representatives of the commission and industry, guidelines will issue. These are advisory opinions for the information of businesspersons in that industry. They should eliminate and prevent improper trade practices and unfair methods of competition for an entire industry. These guidelines are voluntary. A recent example is the guide for product endorsements.

Guides Concerning Use of Endorsements and Testimonials in Advertising

These guides deal with major issues peculiar to endorsement and testimonial advertising and state the views of the commission concerning situations and techniques that are frequently presented in such advertising.

Endorsements must always reflect the honest opinions, findings, beliefs, or experience of the endorser. Furthermore, they may not contain any representations which would be deceptive or could not be substantiated if made directly by the advertiser.

Example. A magazine advertisement for cigars shows a picture of a well-known entertainer holding a lighted cigar. In fact, the entertainer does not smoke cigars, but posed for the picture only because of compensation paid to him by the cigar manufacturer. The advertisement conveys the impression that the entertainer actually uses the cigars, and this would be a deceptive endorsement of the cigars by the entertainer.

An advertisement using an endorsement reflecting the experience of an individual consumer will be interpreted as a claim that such experience represents the typical performance of the product under circumstances similar to those depicted in the advertisement. Therefore, if the represented performance is not in fact typical, the advertisement should clearly and conspicuously disclose what the typical or ordinary performance would be in the depicted circumstances. The simple disclosure that not all consumers will get this result is not sufficient.

Example. An appliance manufacturer prints a statement by a satisfied user that the product served adequately for over eight years. Even if it is literally true that a particular customer got eight years of life out of an appliance, the endorsement would be deceptive if the typical life of the product is substantially shorter and such typical life is not revealed.

Whenever an advertisement represents directly or by implication that the endorser is an expert with respect to the endorsement message, then the endorser's qualifications must in fact give him the expertise that he is represented as possessing with respect to the endorsement.

Example. An endorsement of a particular automobile by one described as an engineer implies that the endorser's professional training and experience are such that he is well acquainted with the design and performance of automobiles. If the endorser's field is chemical engineering, the endorsement would be deceptive.

---

4. Trade Regulation Rules. These are similar to the guides but establish rules for business practices. Unlike the guides, these rules have the force and effect of law and must be followed. Notice of the proposed rules must be published in the Federal Register; notice of, and the right to appear at, a hearing must be given to all interested parties. A recent example of a trade regulation rule is the following, dealing with consumer credit sales. This new trade regulation rule changes the rights of a holder in due course. These rights are in Section 3-305 and 306 of the Uniform Commercial Code. Legislatures of forty-nine states adopted this code, but one rule of an administrative agency has changed part of it.

> In connection with any sale or lease of goods or services to consumers, in or affecting commerce ... it is an unfair or deceptive act or practice within the meaning of Section 5 of that Act for a seller, directly or indirectly, to: (a) Take or receive a consumer credit contract which fails to contain the following provision in at least ten point, bold face, type:
> "NOTICE—
> ANY HOLDER OF THIS CONSUMER CREDIT CONTRACT IS

SUBJECT TO ALL CLAIMS AND DEFENSES WHICH THE DEBTOR COULD ASSERT AGAINST THE SELLER OF GOODS OR SERVICES OBTAINED PURSUANT HERETO OR WITH THE PROCEEDS HEREOF. RECOVERY HEREUNDER BY THE DEBTOR SHALL NOT EXCEED AMOUNTS PAID BY THE DEBTOR HEREUNDER."

or, (b) Accept, as full or partial payment for such sale or lease, the proceeds of any purchase money loan (as purchase money loan is defined herein), unless any consumer credit contract made in connection with such purchase money loan contains the following provisions in at least ten point, bold face, type:

"NOTICE—

ANY HOLDER OF THIS CONSUMER CREDIT CONTRACT IS SUBJECT TO ALL CLAIMS AND DEFENSES WHICH THE DEBTOR COULD ASSERT AGAINST THE SELLER OF GOODS OR SERVICE OBTAINED WITH THE PROCEEDS HEREOF. RECOVERY HEREUNDER BY THE DEBTOR SHALL NOT EXCEED AMOUNTS PAID BY THE DEBTOR HEREUNDER." (44 L.W. 2240, 1975)

5. *Advisory Opinions.* The FTC will issue advisory opinions to business firms on the legality of a proposed merger or other trade practice. Business managers find these opinions helpful in avoiding unlawful actions and waste of corporate funds. Advice given by the commission is not binding on the government. It may be revoked at any time. Usually, the FTC will not issue a complaint against a party who relies on an advisory opinion in good faith.

6. *Cease-and-Desist Order.* This leading enforcement technique is similar to an injunction, an order directing some person to stop actions that violate the antitrust laws. The FTC has broad discretion to formulate an order suitable to correct a wrongful action.

7. *Divestiture, Dissolution, and Other Specific Corrective Action.* The FTC can issue orders requiring any of these actions. Divestiture orders one company to sell another because of an improper merger. It is the basic remedy to cure violations of the Sherman or Clayton Acts. It is simple, direct, and easy to administer, although it may be expensive for corporations to follow. To minimize the cost to a firm for complying with its orders, the FTC allows a reasonable time period to conclude any sales. Dissolution is a similar remedy; but instead of a sale, the FTC orders the termination of a business. Its function, like that of divestiture, is to restore competition.

Corrective action tries to reform an unfair method of competition. When a false advertisement does harm to the public, the FTC has ordered a company to publish advertisements correcting the errors and misrepresentations contained in the prior advertisement. Court actions are now challenging this FTC power. With newly

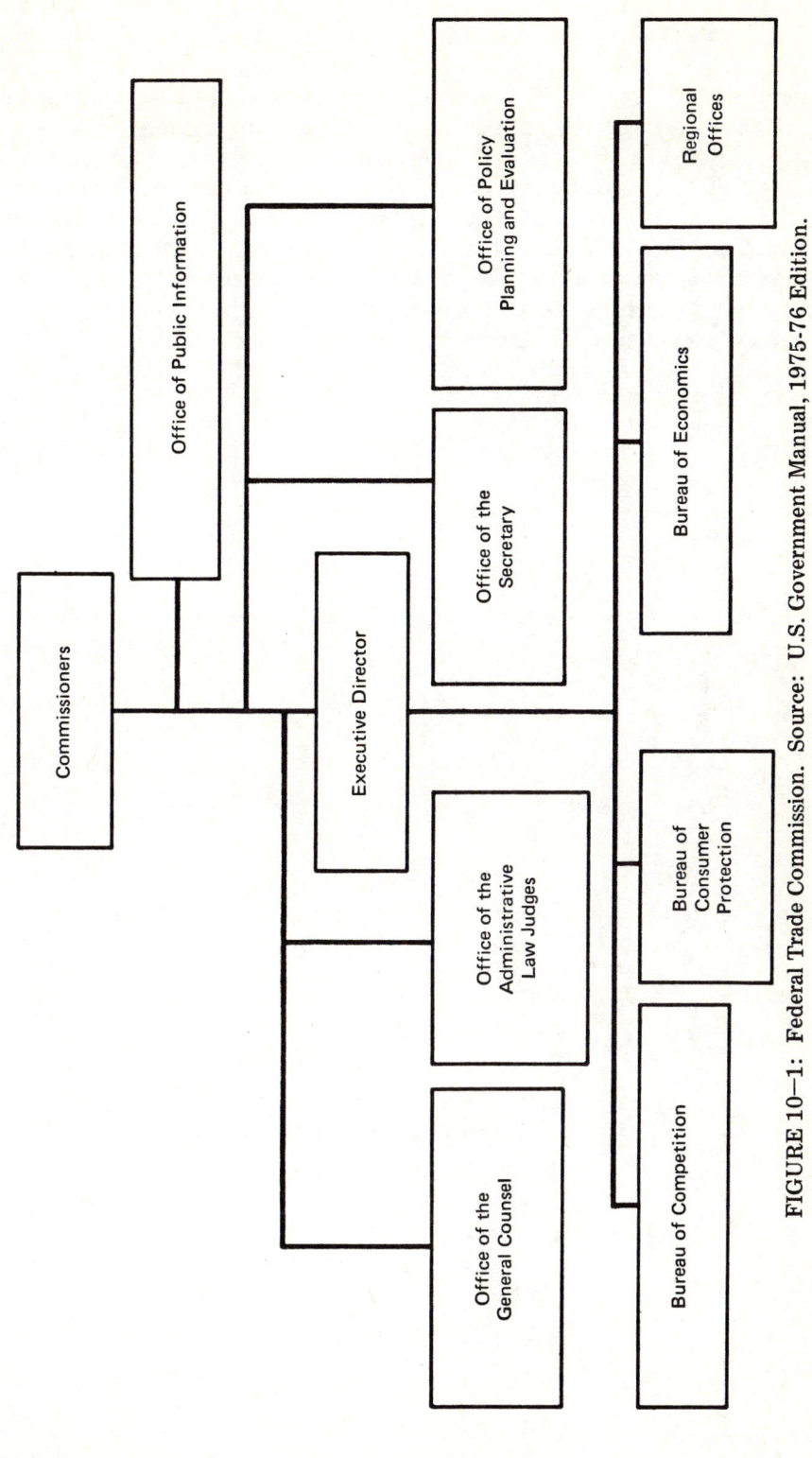

FIGURE 10–1: Federal Trade Commission. Source: U.S. Government Manual, 1975-76 Edition.

215

acquired powers, the FTC can act to stop improper advertisements before a hearing determines them to be false or misleading.

8. Sue. If consumers are injured by some anticompetitive or unfair business act, the FTC can sue in federal or state court on behalf of those victimized by the wrongful acts. It can sue for a cease-and-desist order, obtain damages for injured consumers, seek recision and reformation of any contract made by the injured consumers, and request a refund or a return of property for them.

MANAGEMENT GUIDELINES

The Sherman, Clayton, and Federal Trade Commission Acts impose extensive penalties, fines, and damages on companies and persons who violate antitrust laws. Considerable economic harm may result to a firm if a merger is ruled illegal and divestiture ordered. Unfavorable publicity over an FTC finding of unfair methods of competition may diminish consumer confidence in a company. To minimize these consequences, every company should establish guidelines to direct its employees on how to operate within the laws. Such guidelines should be prepared by the company attorney in cooperation with marketing and other top corporate executives. For reference, two sets of guidelines are listed, one for business practices and the other for mergers. Neither of these lists is exhaustive and they should be altered to suit the needs of a particular company.

1. Business Practices. Certain business practices should be prohibited, others subject to caution. A list should be prepared and distributed to all personnel coming into contact with competitors and customers. Some practices to consider are:

a. No agreements to fix maximum or minimum prices should be made with another person or company that is in competition with the firm. Corporate personnel should not exchange any data that may affect prices or price determinations since a conspiracy may be inferred from even casual discussions.
b. No agreements to divide up a market, territory, or customer list should be made with any competitor.
c. No agreements to limit production should be entered into with competitors.
d. No agreements forcing purchasers to refrain from buying competitors' products should be made.
e. No agreements with a customer to boycott a competitor of the seller or of the buyer should be made.
f. No agreements requiring a buyer, as a condition of purchase, to buy another product or service from the seller should be formed, unless legal advisors approve of the relationship. Some tying arrangements can be justified.

g. No agreements requiring a buyer, as a condition of purchase, to deal with the seller exclusively should be made.

2. Mergers. Laws restricting mergers frequently depend upon the size of the businesses involved and the extent of economic harm to competition. Also, interpretation of these laws changes with the philosophy of antitrust regulators and judges. Consequently, guidelines may vary for each firm and from one time period to another.

a. It is illegal to expand a business to achieve a monopoly, unless the monopoly results from superior merits of a product, a patent, or normal growth.
b. It is illegal for a company with monopoly power to exclude competitors by merging with smaller companies in different fields.
c. It is illegal to buy suppliers, customers, or competitors for the purpose of acquiring a monopoly.
d. It is illegal to acquire the stock or assests of another corpoation if the result might substantially lessen competition.

REVIEW QUESTIONS

1. Summarize the proof needed to show that a firm violated Section 3 of the Clayton Act.
2. Contrast the approach of the Clayton Act with that of the Sherman Act regarding mergers.
3. State the purposes of the FTC Act.
4. Summarize the liabilities under the Clayton and FTC Acts.
5. Under what circumstances is a franchise agreement valid under Section 3 of the Clayton Act?
6. List the exemptions from the antitrust laws and state the reasons for each exemption. To what extent are the reasons justified?
7. Evaluate the effectiveness of each FTC enforcement technique.
8. Discuss some ways managers can avoid violations of antitrust laws.
9. Valentina, a Russian athlete, defected to the United States and soon joined a professional tennis team owned by Tennis Productions, Inc. As a player, she attracted numerous spectators and signed numerous advertisement contracts promoting tennis-related products. After several years, Tennis Productions traded her to another team, but she refused to play there. Pursuant to a rule written by team owners, no team would then employ her. Valentina sued in court, requesting an injunction restraining team owners from enforcing this rule. Should the injunction be granted?
10. Local 507 of the United Car Workers Union and Leffer Corporation were found guilty of conspiring to drive Hicksville Manufacturing Company out of business. Hicksville was a competitor of Leffer. The court issued an injunction restraining the union and Leffer from further action against Hicksville. Hicksville now sues both the union and Leffer asking that the court strip the union of its status as representative bargaining agent of Leffer's employees. Should this remedy be granted?
11. Johnson Corporation, a small producer of sugar, attempted to merge with Peabody, the largest producer of artificial sweetner products. Facts showed that these products are used interchangeably by consumers. Under what circumstances will this merger violate Section 7 of the Clayton Act?

11

CONSUMER PROTECTIONS

> *[The regulation of consumer product safety is necessary because] an unacceptable number of consumer products present unreasonable risks of injury, the complexities of consumer products and the abilities of consumers using them frequently result in an inability of users to safeguard themselves and the public should be protected against unreasonable risks of injury.... (Consumer Product Safety Act, 15 U.S.C.A. 2051.)*

Marketing is an important function of business. In its broadest sense, it means the distribution of products to consumers. Government regulates the marketing function as well as the other aspects of business. These regulations protect the consumer in situations when he or she is unable to use self-protective means. Consumer protection legislation is a radical departure from traditional law. Originally, the consumer had to safeguard his or her own interests. The phrase *caveat emptor* expressed the law's attitude—let the buyer beware. Consumers had to investigate thoroughly the details of any transaction before entering into it. Once a transaction was made, courts would not examine it to see if it were fair or reasonable to all parties. Today, the law has changed.

Consumer interests are protected in four areas: price discrimination laws from the Clayton Act limit a seller's right to price products in two different markets at different prices unless justified; the Federal Trade Commission Act regulates the advertising of consumer products; the Uniform Commercial Code extends warranty protections to purchasers; and the Consumer Product Safety Act creates a new federal regulatory agency to establish and enforce safety standards for certain products. In this chapter, we will study consumer protection laws and interpretations of them in each of these areas, discuss some miscellaneous laws regulating marketing, and conclude with a brief discussion of some ways managers can protect their companies from consumer lawsuits.

PRICE DISCRIMINATION

Section 2(a) of the Clayton Act states:

> That it shall be unlawful for any person engaged in commerce, in the course of such commerce, either directly or indirectly, to discriminate in price between different purchasers of commodities of like grade and quality, where either or any of the purchasers involved in such discrimination are in commerce, where such commodities are sold for use, consumption, or resale within the United States or any Territory thereof or the District of Columbia or insular possession or other place under the jurisdiction of the United States, and where the effect of such discrimination may be substantially to lessen competition or tend to create a monopoly in any line of commerce, or to injure, destroy, or prevent competition with any person who either grants or knowingly receives the benefit of such discrimination, or with customers of either of them: Provided, That nothing herein contained shall prevent differentials which make only due allowance for differences in the cost of manufacture, sale, or delivery resulting from the differing methods or quantities in which such commodities are to such purchasers sold or delivered: Provided, however, That the Federal Trade Commission may, after due investigation and hearing to all interested parties, fix and establish quantity limits, and revise the same as it finds necessary, as to particular commodities or classes of commodities, where it finds that available purchasers in greater quantities are so few as to render differentials on account thereof unjustly discriminatory or promotive of monopoly in any line of commerce; and the foregoing shall then not be construed to permit differentials based on differences in quantities greater than those so fixed and established: And provided further, That nothing herein contained shall prevent persons engaged in selling goods, wares, or merchandise in commerce from selecting their own customers in bona fide transactions and not in restraint of trade: And provided further, That nothing contained herein shall prevent price changes from time to time where in response to changing conditions affecting the market for or the marketability of the goods concerned, such as but not limited to actual or imminent deterioration of perishable goods, obsolescence of seasonal goods, distress sales under court process, or sales in good faith in discontinuance of business in the goods concerned.

This long and complicated section is the anti-price discrimination section of the Clayton Act. It prohibits certain types of pricing policies which can result in a lessening of competition. It protects local sellers of a product from larger, national sellers of similar products who lowered prices to destroy the local, competing sellers while keeping their prices higher elsewhere. In 1936, the section was amended by the Robinson Patman Act, to prohibit large retailers from getting sellers to give them price discounts that were not available to smaller buyers. Both types of price discrimination are now prohibited by the Clayton Act, Section 2(a).

Section 2(a) can be called a consumer protection law because it preserves competition among retail sellers of products. The greater the competition, the smaller the opportunity for price fixing. Product prices will be set by market forces rather than by manufacturers or a few large retailers.

To violate Section 2(a), six key factors must exist: In any line of commerce, the purchase and sale, of commodities of like grade and quality, cannot be made at discriminatory prices, where the effects may be to substantially lessen competition, unless justified. Each of these factors requires some analysis:

1. Any Line of Commerce. The seller must be engaged in interstate or foreign commerce, and the transaction must take place in interstate or foreign commerce. If all sales are local, intrastate transactions, then this section does not apply. Furthermore, the transaction must take place in a distinct product and geographic market. Tests for determining these markets are the same as for Section 7 mergers under the Clayton Act.

2. Purchase and Sale. Discrimination in price must exist between different purchasers in order to violate this section. This means there must be actual sales to and purchases by at least two different buyers from one seller. The law does not prohibit different price quotations to prospective purchasers. Also, a lessee, licensee, or agent are not purchasers; hence, they are not protected from price discrimination by this section. The different purchasers must buy their products from the same seller and purchase them at the same time.

3. Commodities of Like Grade and Quality. "Commodities" refers to items of general manufacture. It excludes services, transportation, and communications. To violate Section 2(a), the price discrimination must concern goods that are similar. They do not have to be identical goods because slight variations in products sold do not make them of unlike grade and quality. Neither do differences in brand names, packaging, or labels make the products dissimilar. A manufacturer cannot avoid this section by selling the same product with slight changes.

4. Discriminatory Prices. A key element of this section is discrimination in price, defined by the Supreme Court to mean a mere price difference. Thus, discrimination exists whenever there is a difference in the price of similar goods sold to different purchasers. A price is the cost to the buyer, including any costs incurred by the buyer to take actual possession of the goods and any indirect costs that affect the accounting cost of the goods. Price therefore includes the cost of items, delivery charges, free samples, discounts, and special options. But price differences are lawful where they result from business considerations not related to the actual cost of the goods, such as the credit status of the buyer or the risk in the market.

5. *Competitive Effects.* The probable effects of the price discrimination must be substantial lessening of competition. Competition may be lessened by price differences that tend to create a monopoly or to injure, destroy, or prevent competition. "Substantial" means that a major injury to competition results. This is determined by an analysis of the economic facts of each case; no mechanical formula can be used. Finally, actual competition does not have to be damaged by the price discrimination; all that is necessary is a chance that it may be reduced.

F.T.C. v. Anheuser Busch, Inc. (AB)
363 U.S. 536 (1960)

Mr. Chief Justice Warren.

AB, a leading national brewer, sells a so-called premium beer, which is priced higher than the beers of regional and local breweries in the great majority of markets, although both the price of AB's beer and the premium differential vary from market to market and from time to time. During the period relevant to this case, AB had three principal competitors in the St. Louis area, all regional breweries: Falstaff, Griesedieck Western, and Griesedieck Brothers. In accord with the generally prevailing price structure, these breweries normally sold their products at a price substantially lower than AB's.

In 1953, most of the national breweries, including AB, granted their employees a wage increase and thereafter put into effect a general price increase. Although many regional and local breweries throughout the country followed suit by raising prices, the three regional breweries in St. Louis maintained their lower price of $2.35 per standard case. Although AB's sales in the St. Louis area did not decline, its national sales fell, along with industry sales in general.

In 1954, AB lowered its price in the St. Louis area from $2.93 to $2.68 per case, thereby reducing the previous fifty-eight cent differential to thirty-three cents. A second price cut occurred later in 1954, this time to $2.35, the same price charged by AB's three competitors. This reduction in price made AB's St.

Louis price lower than its price in other markets, and AB made no corresponding price reductions in any other market. In 1955, AB raised its St. Louis price forty-five cents per case, and the three competitors raised their prices by fifteen cents, which reestablished a substantial differential. This ended the period of alleged price discrimination.

Section 2(a) forbids price discrimination where the effect may be substantially to lessen competition or tend to create a monopoly in any line of commerce or to injure, destroy, or prevent competition with any person who either grants or knowingly receives the benefit of such discrimination or with customers of either of them.

The legislative history of Section 2(a) is plain. The section, when originally enacted as part of the Clayton Act in 1914, was intended to curb the use by financially powerful corporations of localized price-cutting tactics that gravely impaired the competitive position of other sellers. It is, of course, quite true that the 1936 Robinson Patman amendments to the Clayton Act were motivated principally by congressional concern over the impact upon secondary line competition of the burgeoning of mammoth purchasers, notably chain stores. However, the legislative history of these amendments leaves no doubt that Congress was intent upon strengthening the Clayton Act provisions, not weakening them, and that it was not part of Congress' purpose to stop the use of Section 2(a) on price discrimination affecting primary line competition.

The Court of Appeals appears to have rejected this rule. The view of the Court of Appeals was that, before there can be a price discrimination within the meaning of this section, there must be some relationship between the different purchasers that entitles them to similar prices. Such a relationship would exist, the court reasoned, if different prices were being charged to competing purchasers. But the court observed that in this case all competing purchasers paid AB the same price, so far as the records disclosed. Consequently, the court concluded that, even assuming the price cuts were directed at AB's local competition, they were not discriminatory. This is not correct.

The existence of competition among buyers who are charged different prices by a seller is obviously important in terms of adverse effect upon secondary line competition, but it would be merely a fortuitous circumstance so far as injury to primary line competition is concerned. Since, as we have indicated, an independent and important goal of Section 2(a) is to extend protection to competitors of the discriminating seller, the limitation of that protection by the need for competition among purchasers would be improper.

As we read the law, it prohibits price differences subject to certain defined defenses, where the effect of the differences may be substantially to lessen competition. In other words, the statute itself spells out the conditions that make a price difference illegal or legal, and we would change this law if we read other conditions into it. Not only would such action be contrary to what we conceive to be the meaning of the statute, but, perhaps because of this, it would be thoroughly undesirable. As one commentator stated: Inevitably every legal controversy over any price difference would shift from the detailed governing provisions—injury, cost justification, meeting competition, etc.—over into the discrimination concept for resolution apart from specifically pertinent statutory text.

What we have said makes it quite evident, we believe, that our decision does not completely prohibit price differentials, inasmuch as price differences constitute but one element of a Section 2(a) violation. In fact, as we have indicated, AB has vigorously contested this very case on the entirely separate grounds of insufficient injury to competition and good-faith lowering of price to meet competition. Nor is it relevant that the FTC did not proceed upon the basis of AB's price differentials that existed prior to the period in question in this case. This choice is committed to the discretion of the commission; and it may be that the commission did not believe the remaining statutory elements could be established with respect to other differentials. Our interest is solely with this case, and at this stage of litigation that interest in confined exclusively to identifying and keeping distinct the various statutory standards that are part of the Section 2(a) complex.

The judgment of the Court of Appeals is reversed and the case is remanded to that court for further proceedings not inconsistent with this opinion. Reversed.

CASE QUESTIONS

1. Explain the price differentials charged by AB in this case.
2. Explain why the Court of Appeals held that AB's pricing policy did not violate Section 2(a).
3. For what reasons does the Supreme Court reverse this decision?

---

6. Justification. There are several exceptions that permit discrimination even though it lessens competition. First, an allowance or discount can be given to one buyer and not others to reflect differences in the cost of manufacture, sale, or delivery of the goods. This exemption permits a seller to pass cost savings on to buyers if different manufacturing processes or quantities sold produce a cost savings. The seller must prove cost savings. Some examples of legitimate cost savings that can be passed on to buyers are quantity discounts where real savings result because of bulk orders, tax differentials for competing buyers and sales made directly without agent's commissions.

F.T.C. v. Morton Salt Co.
334 U.S. 37 (1948)

Mr. Justice Black.

Morton sells table salt in interstate commerce to wholesalers and retailers on a quantity discount basis available to all customers. Under this system, the purchasers pay a delivered price, and the cost to both wholesalers and retailers of the product differs according to the amount purchased. But only five retail companies could buy in sufficient quantity to take advantage of the lowest discount price offered. Those retailers have been able to sell salt at lower prices, actually cheaper than some wholesalers could buy it for resell to their independent retailers. These independent retailers competed with some of the five large retailers receiving the maximum discount. The FTC ruled that these practices constituted price discrimination under Section 2(a) of the Clayton Act. The Court of Appeals set aside this ruling and the commission appealed. Reversed and remanded.

The legislative history of this section shows that Congress considered it wrong for a large buyer to have a competitive advantage over a small buyer solely because of the large buyer's quantity discount buying power. The act was passed to deprive a large buyer of such advantage except to the extent that a lower price could be justified by reason of a seller's reduced costs because of quantity production or delivery charges, or by reason of the seller's good-faith effort to meet a low price of a competitor.

Under the act, the burden is on the seller to prove that its quantity discount differentials were justified by cost savings. The commission must only prove there is a price difference. The act does not require that the discrimination harm competition, only that there is a reasonable probability that it may have that effect. The finding of the commission that the competitive opportunities of certain merchants were injured when they had to pay Morton more than their competitors had to pay demonstrates sufficient injury to competition. This finding was adequately supported by the evidence in the case. Morton's discount system resulted in price discrimination among competing buyers sufficient to affect the resale price. Such discounts can only be justified by a seller who proves that the full amount of the discount is based on his actual savings in cost. Morton did not prove this in the case.

CASE QUESTION

1. Does this opinion prevent large buyers from receiving lower prices from sellers?

Second, a price differential does not violate Section 2(a) if it was made in a good faith effort to meet the price of a competitor. The lower price can be given to one customer only in response to a specific price offered from a particular competitor. Thus, a cumulative discount could be offered one customer only if necessary to meet a comparable discount given by a competitor.

Third, a seller can sell the same products to different customers at different prices if necessary to prevent immediate destruction of the goods due to their perishable nature, or to prevent certain goods from becoming obsolete. Sales made because of court orders, such as bankruptcy sales, are exempt also.

OTHER PRICING RESTRICTIONS

Section 2(c) of the Clayton Act eliminates the practice of large chain stores demanding price concessions on their purchases to reflect the seller's savings on "middleman" costs, called brokerage fees. Since brokerage savings are a legitimate cost savings, the cost breaks could be passed along to the buyer. But if they were, chain stores would have a significant price advantage over small retailers. The brokerage section of the Clayton Act removes this advantage.

Sections 2(d) and (e) limit the use of advertising and promotional activities as a means for price discrimination. Frequently, chain stores agreed to perform their own advertising of a seller's products and received substantial discounts for the cost savings to the seller. Since smaller retailers could not afford to advertise as much as the chain stores, the discounts were not given to the small retailer. A substantial price advantage resulted to the chain stores which the small retailers could not match. These sections of the Clayton Act require that advertising discounts be available on proportionally equal terms to all competing customers.

Section 2(f) imposes criminal sanctions on any buyer that uses its economic power to force discriminatory price concessions from sellers. It prohibits a buyer from knowingly inducing or receiving price discounts that are discriminatory. A buyer can request discounts, concessions, price reductions, or rebates. But if the buyer knows these are not available to its competitors, then the buyer violates this section.

FEDERAL TRADE COMMISSION ACT PROTECTIONS

The FTC Act, Section 5, prohibits unfair methods of competition and deceptive acts or practices in commerce. Interpretations of this section extend its coverage to false, misleading, or deceptive advertisements. Under this power, the FTC requires advertisers to prove the truth of any claim made in their commercials. It can require that any untrue or misleading commercial be removed and order corrective advertisements to clarify misconceptions resulting from the prior ad. Authority to police advertisements extends to commercials in newspapers, radio, television, and other media. Recent legislation allows the FTC to remove an advertisement from the market when it feels consumer interests will be harmed by it. A hearing is not required before removal, although the advertiser can request a review of the commission's actions.

In Re General Foods
FTC No. 752 3056, July, 1975

The FTC has accepted an agreement containing a consent order that settles a commission complaint alleging that certain advertisements by General Foods Corporation, White Plains, New York, are unfair or deceptive because of their capacity to influence children to engage in harmful activity.

The complaint challenges four television advertisements for General Foods Post Grape Nuts in which Euell Gibbons eats certain wild plants, stating that the particular plant is edible or good tasting.

Specific allegations in the complaint are that:

—The advertisements have the capacity to influence children to eat plants they find growing in natural surroundings.

—Some plants are harmful if eaten, and as children do not have sufficient knowledge or experience to distinguish between those plants which are or are not harmful to eat, the commercials influence children to act in a way that is harmful or involves the risk of harm.

—These ads undercut a commonly recognized safety principle, namely that children should not eat any plants found growing or in natural surroundings, except under adult supervision.

The consent order applies to all General Foods products. The order prohibits representations that a plant can be eaten in its raw state where the impression is that the plant was not grown for human consumption; or where a raw plant is shown being consumed and it is specifically described as a wild plant.

The commission can issue rules and regulations prohibiting deceptive consumer practices. The list of such practices is extensive.

One example of its regulations is the three-day cooling-off period for sales made in a customer's home. Under this policy, a buyer of products from a door-to-door salesperson has three days within which to reconsider the purchase. At any time during this period, a consumer can rescind the purchase and recover any money paid.

Another example of regulations protecting the consumer is the FTC rule that mail order houses ship goods ordered by a customer within a reasonable time. If not, the consumer can request a refund of his or her money, demand alternate products, or wait for the actual delivery of the ordered merchandise.

A third example of the FTC's regulations protecting consumers is a recent one requiring some firms to furnish Spanish-speaking customers with Spanish-language translations of credit contracts. The commission believes the failure to give such customers a Spanish translation deprives them of the opportunity to receive full and adequate disclosure of the terms and conditions they are about to undertake and of their rights and duties under the contract.

The following case illustrates another form of deceptive consumer practice.

**In Re Sears, Roebuck Co.
FTC No. 712 3665, July, 1974**

The FTC intends to issue a complaint alleging that Sears, Roebuck Company, Chicago, has used deceptive bait-and-switch tactics to sell its higher priced major home appliances and that its method of compensation for appliance salesmen encouraged them to use such tactics. The matter is being handled by the commission's regional office in Chicago.

A major home appliance is one having two or more models in the product line with the most expensive model retailing at more than $50. Major provisions of the proposed remedy would:

- —Prohibit Sears from making sales offers that are not bona fide and from disparaging or refusing to sell advertised major home appliances.
- —Require Sears to clearly disclose in all advertisements that they are the subject of a commission cease-and-desist order relating to bait-and-switch tactics.
- —Forbid Sears to use any compensation system for appliance salesmen that is linked in any way to sales quota that discriminate against low-margin, advertised items; or to use bait-and-switch tactics.

The complaint alleges that [offers of major appliance sales are not] bona fide but are made to induce prospective customers to visit Sears' stores. Salesmen allegedly make no effort to sell the advertised appliances at the advertised prices but try to sell higher priced models through disparaging statements. . . .

The firm has been given the opportunity to advise the Commission whether it is interested in having the proceeding disposed of by the entry of a consent order.

Commissioner Thompson dissented, stating that he "believes that, since no effort has been made in this matter to address the question of whether the products the customer is being 'switched' *to* are themselves good buys or bad ones in relation to comparable items offered by competing outlets, there has been no showing of probable consumer injury here. In the absence of such a showing, he cannot find, as Section 5(b) of the FTC Act requires, that the 'proceeding' instituted by the filing of this complaint 'would be to the interest of the public . . .'. Given a limited budget, an expenditure of resource to stop what the staff apparently concedes is a 'victimless crime' necessarily means a comparable reduction in the number of cases this agency can bring that, unlike this one, "involve real economic injury to the consuming public."

Chairman Engman in a separate statement in which Commissioner Hanford concurred said: "In contrast to Commissioner Thompson's characterization of the violation alleged in this case, I do not believe, nor do I think the staff concedes, that a blatant bait-and-switch advertising scheme constitutes a 'victimless crime.' I would consider this to be true even if there were a showing that the products which customers are switched *to* are comparable in price and quality to those offered by competing sellers.

"Numerous prior Commission orders and the Commission's *Bait Advertising Guide* make it clear that Section 5 of the Federal Trade Commission Act is violated when a retailer advertises a low priced product to entice customers into his place of business and then, according to a preconceived selling plan, disparages the low priced item in an attempt to push a higher priced product on the customer. Such selling tactics are often accompanied by unreasonably low inventories of advertised items, high pressure sales methods once the customer is in the store, misrepresentations about the real value of the advertised items, and, as alleged in this instance, employee discipline and compensation systems which discriminate unfairly against the sale of low priced, advertised merchandise.

"The customer is victimized in bait-and-switch schemes because he or she makes the initial choice to patronize the advertiser's store rather than his competitors on the assumption that advertisements of low priced items have been made in good faith. In actuality, of course, the bait-and-switch advertiser has used the advertising as a deceptive gimmick to get the customers in his store first and thus gain unfair advantage over his competitors. If the allegations of large scale bait-and-switch advertising in this complaint are proved through the adjudicative process, I would consider entry of an appropriate order very much in the public interest."

WARRANTY

A warranty is any promise made by the seller to the buyer regarding the quality of the products sold. This promise can arise out of the negotiations between the two parties or be implied by law. The main law creating warranties in sales transactions is Article 2 of the Uniform Commercial Code (UCC), adopted by forty-nine states and the District of Columbia. In this section, we will discuss the major warranties created by this law to protect consumers.

The UCC is a comprehensive code regulating many aspects of business operations. It was written by legal scholars and business practitioners with the intent of making state business laws the same throughout the nation. They drafted ten articles regulating sales contracts, commercial paper, bank deposits and collections, letters of credit, bulk transfers, warehouse receipts, investment securities, and secured transactions. Although the code was originally the same for all states adopting it, court interpretations have changed some of its terms. Nevertheless, much of the code remains uniform throughout the nation.

Article 2 regulates sales contracts. A sales contract is the transfer of legal ownership to tangible personal property. These contracts do not include sales of land, things attached to land, services, or securities in a corporation. In every UCC sales contract, four warranties may be made by the seller. If any one of them is breached or not honored by the seller, the consumer may sue the seller for his or her damages. The four warranties are:

1. Express Warranty. An express warranty comes out of the negotiations between the parties themselves. It may be created by definite statements made orally or in writing to the buyer. Some examples of other things that can create express warranties are pictures, diagrams, blueprints, samples, models, or descriptions of the product sold. When the seller uses any of these items, then he or she makes an express warranty that the product sold will be like the item shown.

Before an express warranty becomes binding on the seller, the courts must determine if a reasonable consumer would rely on it. Opinions and overstatements by the seller should not be relied upon, according to most courts. For example, statements like "this is the best product on the market" or "this is the best for your money" are opinions, not warranties.

A new federal law requires written express warranties to contain specific information, printed in a conspicuous and understandable fashion. The warranty must include the warrantor's name and address, a description of the product warranted, a statement of what remedies the purchaser has, the time period for enforcing the warranty, and the procedures to be followed to enforce the warranty.

2. Warranty of Title. This warranty promises that the seller is the legal owner of the products sold, that he or she has the legal right to sell the products, and that they are sold free of any lien. It protects the buyer's ownership of the products from claims by others. If someone else has ownership interests in the products sold, the consumer can sue the seller for breach of warranty. A seller may exclude this warranty from a sale by using specific language disclaiming it.

3. Warranty of Merchantability. Every sales contract made by a merchant implies this warranty, according to the U.C.C. It means that the product sold must be fit for its ordinary purposes and adequately packaged, contained, and labeled. If the product is defective and that defect causes injury to a consumer, then the seller is responsible. For example, an excessively carbonated soda bottle which explodes is a breach of this warranty because of inadequate packaging. Also, foreign objects in food products violate this warranty because the food is not fit for the purposes intended. The UCC permits a disclaimer of this warranty by clear and conspicuous language. Most state courts accept the phrase "as is" as an adequate waiver of this warranty, although Massachusetts courts now reject this disclaimer.

4. Warranty of Fitness for a Particular Purpose. A seller makes this warranty when he or she knows the purpose for which the buyer is purchasing a product and the buyer relies on the seller's skill to select a suitable product. For example, a consumer who tells the seller what he or she wants and then selects the product recommended receives this warranty. But if the buyer selects the product personally or gives technical specifications to the seller, there is no reliance on the seller's skill; hence no warranty arises. This warranty can be disclaimed by conspicuous words in writing. A phrase like "there are no warranties of fitness" is adequate.

Each of these warranties extends to the purchaser, members of the purchaser's immediate family, and guests of the purchaser who are injured while using the product in the purchaser's household. Some courts are dissatisfied by these limitations. Therefore, some judges have formulated the concept of product liability. Under this theory, a consumer injured by a defective product can sue the seller if the product reaches the consumer without any substantial change from when it was first sold. It is unnecessary for the consumer to have purchased the item from the seller. The care used by the seller in making and selling its product does not affect liability under this theory.

Henningsen v. Bloomfield Motors, Inc.
161 A.2d 69 (1960)

Justice Francis.

Henningsen purchased a Plymouth from Bloomfield Motors as a gift for his wife. At the time of purchase, Henningsen signed a purchase order that included an express warranty against defects in material and workmanship. It limited the manufacturer's liability to replacing defective parts only. This warranty was in lieu of all other warranties expressed or implied. The disclaimer was made in fine print on the reverse side of the purchase order as the seventh of ten paragraphs. After the car was purchased, his wife was driving it when a loud noise sounded, the steering wheel spun in her hands, and the car crashed into a wall. The Henningsens sued Chrysler, the manufacturer, and Bloomfield, the dealer, for breach of warranty. The trial court awarded damages to the Henningsens and the defendants appealed.

Defendants argued that no implied warranties were made by Chrysler to Henningsen, that there was an effective disclaimer of any warranties, and that the wife had no contract with defendants and thus no warranties were made to her.

The claim of implied warranty against the manufacturer. Chrysler points out that an implied warranty of merchantability is an incident of a contract of sale. It concedes, of course, the making of the original sale to Bloomfield but maintains that this transaction marked the terminal point of its contractual connection with the car. Then Chrysler urges that since it was not a party to the sale by the dealer to the Henningsens, it made no warranty to them.

There is no doubt that under early common-law concepts of contractual liability only those persons who were parties to the bargain could sue for breach of it. In more recent times a noticeable disposition has appeared in a number of jurisdictions to break through the narrow barrier of contracts when dealing with sales of goods in order to give realistic recognition to a universally accepted fact. The fact is that the dealer and the ordinary buyer do not, and are not expected to, buy goods, whether they be food or automobiles, exclusively for their own consumption or use. Makers and manufacturers know this and advertise and market their products on that assumption: witness the family car, baby foods, etc. The limitations of contracts for the sale of goods developed their place in the law when marketing conditions were simple, when maker and buyer frequently knew each other and met fact to face on an equal bargaining plane, and when many of the products were simple, uncomplicated, and conducive to inspection by a buyer competent to evaluate their quality. With the advent of mass marketing, the manufacturer became remote from the purchaser, sales were accomplished through intermediaries, and the demand for the product was created by advertising media. In such an economy the consumer is the person being cultivated. Manifestly, the connotation of consumer was broader than simply buyer. He signified such a person who, in the reasonable contemplation of the parties to the sale, might be expected to use the product.

Accordingly, we hold that under modern marketing conditions, when a manufacturer puts a new automobile in the stream of trade and promotes its purchase by the public, an implied warranty that it is reasonably suitable for use as such accompanies it into the hands of the ultimate purchaser. Absence of agency between the manufacturer and the dealer who makes the ultimate sale is immaterial.

The effect of the disclaimer. What effect should be given to the express warranty in question, which seeks to limit the manufacturer's liability to that stated in the purchase order? This warranty is a standardized form designed for mass use. It is imposed upon the automobile consumer. He takes it or leaves it, and he must take it to buy an automobile. The gross inequality of the bargaining position occupied by the consumer in the automobile industry is apparent. There is no competition among the car makers in the area of warranties. Where can the buyer go to negotiate for better protection? All dealers use the same form. Such control and limitation of his remedies are inimical to the public welfare and, at the very least, call for great care by the courts to avoid injustice through application of strict common-law rules of freedom of contract. This disclaimer was not effective.

The defense of no contract with Mrs. Hennigensen. Both defendants contend that since there was no contract with the wife, she cannot recover for breach of warranty made by either of them. On the facts, as they were developed, we agree that she was not a party to the purchase agreement. Her right to maintain the action, therefore, depends upon whether she occupies such legal status thereunder as to permit her to take advantage of a breach of defendants' implied warranties.

In the present matter, the basic contractual relationship is between the husband, Chrysler, and Bloomfield. The precise issue is whether the wife, who is not a party to their respective warranties, may claim under them. We are convinced that the cause of justice in this area of the law can be served only be recognizing that she is such a person who in the reasonable contemplation of the parties to the warranty, might be expected to become a user of the automobile. Accordingly, her lack of contract does not stand in the way of prosecution of the injury suit against the defendant Chrysler.

We affirm the decision the trial court.

CASE QUESTIONS

1. *Summarize each defense raised by the defendants in this case.*
2. *Explain the reasons why the court rejects each of these defenses.*

3. To whom does a manufacturer owe responsibility when it distributes its products?

CONSUMER PRODUCT SAFETY

Giving consumers the right to sue manufacturers for product-caused injuries is not adequate to protect them. First, warranty laws do not guarantee safe products in the marketplace; they only make sellers and manufacturers liable for injuries caused by their products. Second, many people injured by defective products do not sue for their damages—either their damage is too small to justify a court case or they are unaware of their rights to sue. Third, modern products can be complicated to use or may have dangerous side effects. Consumers may be unaware of these dangers, unaware of how to use products safely, or unaware of how to assemble them safely.

To protect consumers from coming into contact with products that present an unreasonable risk of injury, Congress passed the Consumer Product Safety Act. This law attempts to protect the public from dangerous products and to assist them in evaluating product safety hazards. Also, this act encourages research into product safety standards leading toward uniform rules for product performance. It carries out these purposes by creating an independent administrative agency to regulate sales of consumer products.

Consumer Product Safety Commission

To administer the sections of this act, Congress established the Consumer Product Safety Commission (CPSC). Commissioners are appointed by the President and confirmed by the Senate. One of its members serves as chairman, and he or she can appoint other officials to carry out the commission's work. These officials may include a general counsel, scientific personnel, and a public relations expert. The CPSC has the same authority as other regulatory agencies to hold hearings, issue rules and regulations, and seek judicial enforcement of its orders.

Functions of the CPSC are divided into three major groups: establishing product safety standards, analyzing product injury data, and enforcement. Authority in these areas extends to most consumer products except tobacco, motor vehicles, agriculture poisons, aircraft, boats, drugs, cosmetics, and foods. These products are regulated by other governmental agencies.

Safety Standards. CPSC can establish any rule necessary to protect consumers from product injuries. It may establish standards for the quality of products sold, their packaging, design, performance, and construction. Also, the CPSC can require that consumer products have warnings about their hazards and instructions for proper use.

The commission develops standards through its own testing procedures, or by accepting existing safety standards developed by others. Before any standards are binding on an industry, notice of the new standard must be given to all affected persons. That notice must state why the standard is necessary, invite comments from the public on it, and allow the public to offer alternate standards. Managers should submit proposed standards for products in their industry or for those made by their company.

When the CPSC establishes a safety rule, it must show how the standard will reduce a specific risk. An estimate must be made about the likely effects this rule may have on the cost, availability, or usefulness of products affected by the standard. This requirement forces the agency to evaluate the costs of regulation compared with any benefits to the consumer. It is an important concept for preventing overregulation of business.

Procedures exist within the act so that existing safety standards can be reviewed, modified, or reversed upon a request by any interested person. This may include a consumer, manufacturer, or government representative.

Product Injury Data. The CPSC maintains an Injury Information Clearing House to collect information on death, injury, and illness caused by consumer products. Agency staff analyze this data to determine which products are causing the most serious harm to the public. Then the conclusions are made public and manufacturers are advised to take appropriate actions to reduce these hazards. Such actions may mean voluntary withdrawal of the product from the market, redesign of its components, or public boycott of it.

To prevent premature harm to a manufacturer by public reaction against one of its products, the CPSC must give prior notice to the manufacturer of its findings. Then a manufacturer can present its views to the commission, seeking to reverse these findings or modify them. If the CPSC determines a product is dangerous, it can act without giving advance notice to the manufacturer. But if the CPSC acts in error, it must reverse itself. Manufacturers receive no compensation for damages because of erroneous public warnings. Information learned by the commission from the clearing house can be the basis for establishing new safety standards.

Enforcement. The commission can determine if products are hazardous to consumers. It does this by holding hearings at which all interested parties can present their views on the safety aspects of a particular product. After this hearing, the commission can order the manufacturer or retailer to notify the public of the hazard. It can direct either party to repair the product, replace it, or refund the consumer's purchase price. The commission can prohibit the sale of hazardous products in the United States and seize any product which it feels is imminently hazardous to the public.

The CPSC can request the federal district court to enforce any of its orders. Disregard of a commission order affirmed by the court can be punished by a contempt citation. Also, any person injured by a manufacturer's or retailer's wilful disregard of a commission rule or order can sue for damages. Amounts awarded include compensation for injuries suffered, court costs, and attorney fees. Private citizens can bring suit to establish or enforce a safety rule if the commission does not. Court costs and attorney fees must be paid by the defendant. These private remedies to sue give consumers an incentive for self-enforcement of product safety laws. They act for the government when it refuses or fails to act.

TABLE 11-1. MAJOR FUNCTIONAL OFFICES IN THE CONSUMER PRODUCT SAFETY COMMISSION

Chairman and Commissioners
Executive Assistant
General Counsel
Directors:
    Public Affairs
    Congressional Relations
    Resource Utilization
    Medical
    Engineering Sciences
    Epidemiology
    Compliance
    Economic Analysis
    Standards Coordination
    Information and Education
    Biomedical Sciences
    Field Coordination
    Planning and Evaluation
    Minority Enterprise

Source: U.S. Government Manual, 1975-76 Edition.

The commission can seek civil and criminal penalties against any person who knowingly violates the law. A civil penalty not exceeding $500,000 can be imposed for each act or series of acts that violates the terms of this law. Any person who knowingly and wilfully commits any act prohibited by the CPSC is subject to a criminal penalty of a fine of not more than $50,000 or imprisonment of not more than one year or both. Injunctions can be obtained from a court to stop any act that violates this law and to stop a person from distributing a product that does not comply with a safety standard.

OTHER RELATED FEDERAL LAWS

There are other laws regulating marketing of products about which persons in business must be aware. They are briefly noted here.

1. The Federal Food, Drug and Cosmetic Act was passed by Congress to exclude from interstate commerce impure, defective, or misbranded food, drugs, and cosmetic products. This law is administered by the Food and Drug Administration, a regulatory agency located in the Department of Health, Education and Welfare. It has authority to seize any defective product within its jurisdiction, to hold hearings, and to sue for civil and criminal penalties. The FDA conducts tests to see if ingredients used in foods, drugs, and cosmetics are safe, if manufacturing procedures meet health standards established by the agency, and if processing and handling of products are satisfactory. Business must cooperate with these tests and investigations.

2. The Wool Products Labeling Act and the Fur Products Labeling Act establish requirements for stamping, tagging, and labeling wool and fur products. These laws are designed to prevent deception to the public by use of substitutes or mixtures in wool and fur products. Both laws are administered by the Federal Trade Commission and civil penalties exist for any violations. Preventive action that can be taken by the FTC to stop violations including seizing misbranded products, ordering corrective labels installed on these products, and seeking injunctions stopping future violations of the laws. Wilful violations of these laws are misdemeanors, subject to fine and/or imprisonment.

3. The Flammable Fabrics Act was passed to protect the public from bodily harm or death resulting from the use of clothing made out of highly flammable materals. This law was originally administered by the FTC but Congress transferred jurisdiction to the

CPSC. The law establishes minimum standards for clothing products, generally forbidding clothing material from exceeding a stated burning rate. Technicians use tests to determine clothing safety and garments not meeting those tests can be taken off the market. Wilful violations of the act are misdemeanors, punishable by fine and/or imprisonment.

4. Miscellaneous. The FTC administers the Truth in Lending Act, requiring any person who extends credit or loans to publish the true interest costs, finance charges and other fees. Also within the FTC's jurisdiction are the Webb Pomerene Act, exempting exporters from the antitrust laws; the Lanham Trademark Act, permitting persons to register tradenames and trademarks; and the Fair Packaging and Labeling Act, prohibiting manufacturers from using deceptively sized containers and misleading information on their products.

The Hazardous Substance Act gives the CPSC authority to require the labeling of dangerous products used by children, to ban some products so dangerous that they cannot be used safely in homes, and to prohibit sales of dangerous children's toys. The Poison Prevention Packaging Act gives the CPSC authority to require special packaging for household products with which children might come into contact. The Household Refrigerator Safety Act regulates home refrigerator designs to prevent small children from suffocating if trapped inside.

MANAGEMENT GUIDELINES

Selling a product involves pricing the item and advertising it. Employees concerned with these parts of the selling function should be made aware of the legal regulations affecting these activities. The following are some guidelines for helping employees in marketing cope with and understand their responsibilities.

1. Products of equal grade and quality should not be sold at different prices to different buyers who are in competition with each other, if that price differential gives one a marketing edge over a competitor. Price differences are valid where cost differences or the necessity to meet the lower price of a competitor exist.

2. Advertising allowances or any other promotional service must be offered to all customers on proportionally equal terms.

3. An exclusive distributorship system is legal only if competing products are available to other buyers. A company can designate a distributor as the one primarily responsible for selling its products in a certain territory and terminate the designation if the company's products are not adequately merchandised.

4. Franchise agreements are valid where the franchisor can show restrictions are necessary to maintain product quality or customer good will. Agreements can limit the purchases made by a franchisee, their resale prices and territory allocations.

5. A committee of product designers, manufacturing engineers, and marketing specialists should be formed to coordinate production in accordance with standards established by the CPSC and other testing organizations. This committee should review existing commission standards to see if products made by the company comply. It should formulate standard proposals to submit to the commission. And the committee should alert all employees to the importance of good customer relations.

REVIEW QUESTIONS

1. Explain why a marketing manager must know something about consumer protection laws.
2. Summarize the types of consumer protection laws now existing in the United States and evaluate their effectiveness.
3. Explain the six elements required for price discrimination.
4. Show some ways by which the FTC protects consumer interests.
5. Explain UCC warranties.
6. Evaluate the approach to consumer protection taken by the Consumer Product Safety Act.
7. McGanns, a leading department store, was accused by the FTC of unfair marketing practices. The store frequently mixed higher priced and better quality merchandise in with lower priced goods. A customer looking for medium priced suits was directed to a department in which higher priced products were placed, seemingly by accident. Does this practice violate Section 5 of the FTC Act?
8. Borden Corporation is a manufacturer of ice cream and other dairy products. It hired Murray Advertising Agency to film commercials for television. One commercial advertised ice cream products. During the filming, mashed potatoes were substituted for the ice cream because the hot television lights caused the ice cream to melt. Is this commercial an unfair, deceptive method of competition?

TOPICS

CHAPTER 12. COLLECTIVE BARGAINING
Introduction • Employee Rights • Employer Unfair Labor Practices • Union Unfair Labor Practices • Dispute Settlement Procedures • Review Questions

CHAPTER 13. UNION—MANAGEMENT RELATIONS
Introduction • Strikes • Picketing • Union Democracy • Union Reports • Officer Reports • Penalties • Pension Reform • Management Guidelines • Review Questions

CHAPTER 14. OCCUPATIONAL INJURIES
Introduction • Workmen's Compensation • Collection Procedures • Employer Defenses • Occupational Safety and Health Laws • Employer Duties • Employer Rights • Employee Rights and Duties • Management Guidelines • Review Questions

CHAPTER 15. EMPLOYMENT DISCRIMINATION
Introduction • Civil Rights Laws • Remedies • State Civil Rights Laws • Affirmative Action Programs • Reverse Discrimination • Management Guidelines • Review Questions

PART FOUR

LAWS AND REGULATIONS AFFECTING LABOR

A comprehensive and fair labor policy has always been one of America's goals. After numerous struggles, Congress realized that employment contracts are not just agreements between two parties. These contracts affect the public welfare as well. Employee discontent can lead to disruptions in production, civil chaos, and political unrest. Thus, for political and economic stability, it is important to have acceptable and workable labor laws.

The approach to labor peace in America is a legalistic one. Both the federal and state governments have complex systems of laws, rules, regulations, and court decisions dealing with the employer-employee relationship. Business managers must know about these laws to operate their firms effectively and to minimize civil and criminal penalties for violating these laws. In this part, we will study the three main branches of labor law: collective bargaining, occupational injuries, and employment discrimination.

Collective bargaining laws create a framework by which employers and employees can peacefully settle their disputes. The policy behind these laws is no longer controversial, although some persons still question the wisdom of certain interpretations of the law. These laws seem successful since industrial strife is now almost completely removed from our society.

Occupational safety laws are more controversial. These laws deal with job-related injuries. At first, the law was unconcerned with employee injuries, considering them largely the problems of individuals. But the social cost of such injuries soon led state governments to adopt workmen's compensation laws. Under these laws, injured workers received money to pay for their costs and disabilities. This approach did not prevent job injuries, so the federal government recently enacted the Occupational Safety and Health Act to require safer working conditions. Problems of the cost and feasibility of this law cause many people to question its value to society. Continued experimentation with this law makes judgments about its effects difficult.

Employment discrimination is part of American labor history, and recent legislative attempts to abolish it are causing many problems in the work force. Civil rights acts require an employer to give equal job opportunities to all persons. Interpretations of these laws and the application of them to the job market are causing resentment and bitterness. It is too early to tell if these laws can remedy discrimination, but a knowledge of them is important to avoid the penalties for violating them.

12

COLLECTIVE BARGAINING

Labor can do nothing without capital, capital nothing without labor, and neither labor nor capital can do anything without the guiding genius of management; and management, however wise its genius may be, can do nothing without the privileges which the community affords. (W.L. Mackenziez King, Canadian Club Speech, Montreal, March 17, 1919.)

The American legal system has comprehensive laws regulating union-management relations. In the next two chapters, we will study the important laws requiring employers and employees to negotiate their differences. But before examining these laws, we should first understand why so many laws are necessary to guarantee labor peace. This introduction gives a brief summary of labor history to show us why such laws are needed. It is not a comprehensive analysis of labor history, but only a general outline of its important concepts.

Labor history can be divided into five periods. In the first, called *the early period*, the majority of workers were serfs or slaves. They had no rights and they expected none. One law typical of these times was the Statute of Laborers, an English law requiring all people to work. Under such conditions, workers received few benefits. This period lasted through the seventeenth century. Beginning with the eighteenth century and lasting up to the nineteenth century was *the early unionization period*, during which some unions were organized in the large urban centers of America and England. These unions were merely groups of employees organized together to discuss working conditions with their employers; most were poorly organized and powerless. Courts declared them illegal criminal conspiracies against employers.

The third period, called *the industrial revolution period*, began in the nineteenth century. It was marked by rapid changes in society and in the work force. The industrial revolution brought new machines to produce products. Although this was a peaceful revolution, it drastically changed the role of the worker, the national economic system, and society itself. For example, traditional hand craftspeople were replaced by unskilled laborers; home working conditions were replaced by giant factories; rural communities were replaced by urban centers; a stable agriculture economy was replaced by a cyclical industrial economy; and owner-operators of productive facilities were replaced by hired managers. Frequently, managers treated machines better than workers, since a steady flow of immigrants made labor cheap and easily replaceable. The capital needed to finance purchases of new machines and factories came from creditors here and abroad. The way these creditors decided to channel money into the economy influenced the way recessions and depressions developed. All of these changes created social and economic pressures on workers. They demanded some protections to help them cope with these rapid transitions. In response, strong unions developed.

In *the unionization period*, labor associations developed three aims: to create a seniority system to protect members' jobs from arbitrary layoffs due to recession or replacement by cheaper immigrants; to upgrade worker status in society through wage and fringe benefit increases; and to become a constructive force in society by sponsoring laws to improve social, economic, and political conditions. The first major union formed during this period was the Knights of Labor, a union of skilled and unskilled workers organized to obtain broad social gains and economic advancement for its members. The Knights soon failed because of internal dissension among its members and because its goals were too generalized to be translated into specific policy. Next came the American Federation of Labor, a union of skilled workers seeking economic gains rather than political power. Shortly thereafter, the Congress of Industrial Organization developed to represent unskilled and semiskilled employees at large industrial factories. Both of these labor unions survived to this day because they were concerned with narrow issues directly affecting their members, not social or political causes.

The fifth period of labor history can be called the *modern period*. It is characterized by a legalistic approach to solving labor problems, and developed out of the approach employers took toward unions. Most employers filed antitrust actions against labor organizations, arguing they were restraints of trade prohibited by the Sherman Act. Courts responded favorably to this argument, stopping union growth by declaring unions illegal. The union response was strikes and economic slowdowns, then violence, and later political pressure to change the laws. Congress soon realized that labor and management needed help in solving their disputes, the public needed protection of their rights in society, and the national interest required a stable economic system. Laws now require collective bargaining, the process of negotiating for the settlement of disputes between employers and workers over working conditions. Thus our complex system of laws regulating labor came about as a result of the challenges to unions by employers.

The first major labor law passed by Congress was the Norris LaGuardia Act of 1932. It limited the power of courts to issue injunctions in labor disputes and prohibited employers from forcing workers to sign contracts not to join a union. Next came the National Labor Relations Act of 1935, simply called the Wagner Act. This law gives workers rights to join a union and to bargain with employers. It also lists certain labor practices an employer cannot follow. In 1947, Congress enacted the Labor Management Relations Act, referred to as the Taft-Hartley Act, to correct some union abuses. This law listed labor practices a union could not follow and structured the National Labor Relations Board as an administrative agency to help settle disputes. Finally, to correct union violations of its members' rights, Congress passed the Labor Management Reporting and Disclosure Act of 1959, called the Landrum Griffin Act.

With these laws, Congress created our national labor policy. This policy encourages union growth and the process of negotiation as the way of settling labor disputes. It creates a partnership among labor, management, capital, and government to foster a more orderly society for the public. It creates a workable policy toward labor relations without causing the social upheavals found in other countries. This chapter will study how this partnership works and how it affects a manager's decision-making process in the labor relations area. The Wagner Act and the Taft-Hartley Act are called the Labor Management Relations Act (LMRA) and will be discussed as a unit rather than separately.

EMPLOYEE RIGHTS

Section 7 of the LMRA gives employees five basic rights:

1. To Form or Join a Labor Organization. A labor union is a lawful assembly, protected by the First Amendment to the Constitution. Any assembly of workers has the protections of the labor laws, even if not called a union or affiliated with any conventional labor organization. Workers have the right to form a union to put them on an equal economic basis with their employer. As stated in one famous case:

> Employees have as clear a right to organize and select their representatives for lawful purposes as the employer has to organize its business

and select its own officers and agents. Discrimination and coercion to prevent the free exercise of the rights of employees to self organization and representation is a proper subject for condemnation by competent legislative authority. Long ago we stated the reason for labor unions. We said they were organized out of the necessities of the situation; that a single employee was helpless in dealing with an employer; that he was dependent ordinarily on his daily wage for the maintenance of himself and family; that if the employer refused to pay him the wages that he thought fair, he was nevertheless unable to leave the employ and resist arbitrary and unfair treatment; that union was essential to give laborers opportunity to deal with their employer on an equality. (*NLRB* v. *Jones and Laughlin Steel Corp.*, 301 U.S. 1, 1937.)

2. To Select Their Bargaining Agents. Employees have as clear a right to select their representatives for negotiating with their employer as the employer has in selecting its own officers to run the business. An employer cannot interfere with the selection of an agent by the workers. This agent may be an employee of the firm or an outsider. Whoever is selected will remain as the exclusive agent for the employees until legally removed. LMRA regulates the selection and removal of these agents. Agents have the power to negotiate on behalf of their union members but members must approve any agreements reached with the employer.

3. To Bargain Collectively with the Employer. This is a fundamental right of all workers. It means the employer must sit down with union representatives to discuss employment conditions for all workers. The discussion must be conducted by both sides with open and fair minds, each side sincerely trying to overcome all problems existing between them. There is no duty for the employer to agree with any union demand, however. But negotiators must discuss directly related employment matters, such as wages paid workers, the hours they work, and other working conditions. Some relevant issues to discuss are money, fringe benefit programs, job safety, and time for work. Some nonrelevant issues are endorsement of political candidates, positions on political or foreign policy issues, national economic conditions, and managerial matters. In carrying out this right to bargain, unions have some duties. They cannot trespass on or destroy an employer's property, commit acts of violence against other workers, or engage in any illegal act. And the basic rights of an employer to run its business cannot be interfered with.

4. To Engage in Acts of Mutual Aid or Protection. This right gives the workers power to hold union meetings, distribute literature, petition employers and government, strike, picket, and engage in any other legal acts to promote the common interests of their members.

But none of these acts are allowed unconditionally. The LMRA contains many restrictions on their use. Any of these acts can be stopped by a court if carried out in an unlawful manner. Some commonly prohibited acts are plant seizures, sitdown strikes, and violence.

5. To Refrain from Any Union Activity. The rights to join a union, select representatives, and bargain with an employer are optional. A worker is not compelled to exercise these rights; he or she has some freedom of choice. If an employee does not wish to participate in union activities, compulsion cannot change this decision. But a worker may be required to listen to union solicitation speeches, to pay union dues, and to join a union as a condition of continued employment. Some states now have right-to-work laws, prohibiting an employer from requiring workers to join a union as a condition of employment, although they must pay union dues.

EMPLOYER UNFAIR LABOR PRACTICES

Section 8(a) of LMRA defines a number of unfair labor practices that an employer cannot follow. An unfair labor practice is any activity that violates the fundamental rights of employees guaranteed in Section 7. To determine whether an unfair labor practice was committed, courts must consider the past labor history of the employer and its intent and motivation. If the employer is found guilty of committing one of the prohibited actions, courts will then issue an injunction stopping this conduct. There is no penalty and the employer is not guilty of any civil or criminal conduct. No fine or imprisonment can be imposed and no damages action can be brought. But doing one these unfair practices will bring a reprimand from the government and, if a pattern of such practices develops, a hostile attitude from government officials. Then when other sections of the LMRA with civil or criminal penalties are violated, sentencing, fines, and damages may be greater. A pattern of unfair labor practices can show a lack of good faith or an intent to violate the laws. Some employer unfair labor practices are:

1. To Interfere with or Coerce Employees in the Exercise of Their Rights. Section 8(a) (1). An employer cannot interfere with employees when they are forming a union, selecting their representatives, bargaining, voting, striking, picketing, or engaging in any other protected and legal acts. Court cases tell us what acts an employer can and cannot do. For example, an employer cannot threaten to fire or discipline a worker for union activity or promise any rewards to those who refrain from union activity. An employer violates this section if it gives a wage increase to employees discussing the formation of a union or threatens to close a plant if a union is formed. If a union exists, the employer cannot bypass it in dealing with employees.

In *American Shipbuilding Co. v. NLRB*, 380 U.S. 300 (1965), the Supreme Court ruled that it is not coercive for an employer to join a multiemployer bargaining association and lock out its employees if the union strikes another member of the association, provided the union agrees. It is never coercive for an employer to express its views, arguments, or opinions, either orally or in writing, if these words contain no unfair statements, threats, or coercive expressions. An employer can express antiunion philosophy, economic views, and convictions if they are general statements.

2. To Dominate or Interfere with the Formation or Administration of Any Labor Organization. Section 8(a)(2) makes it an unfair labor practice for an employer to form a company-run union for its employees or contribute any financial aid or incentives to one union over another. It is an unfair labor practice to harass a union with needless lawsuits, to plant spies in union meetings, to manage a union, to agree with a union that only members of its organization will be hired (closed shop), or to give lodging, food, or expense money to some union officials.

It is not an unfair labor practice for the employer to confer with employees on company time, to cooperate with employees forming a union, to insist on an election before bargaining with a union if the employer has a good-faith doubt about the employees' true desires, or to pay the dues of its employees to the union.

3. To Encourage or Discourage Membership in a Union by Discriminating in Regard to Hiring, Job Tenure, or Any Other Condition of Employment. For an employer to commit an unfair labor practice under this part, Section 8(a)(3), there must be some intentional discrimination by the employer against an employee because of his or her union membership. To become acts of discrimination, actions by the employer must result in some employees being treated differently from others because of union membership. If actions by the employer are motivated by business reasons rather than antiunion bias, then such actions do not violate the law, even though some employees are treated differently.

Under this section, it is not an unfair labor practice for an employer and union to agree on a union shop contract, requiring employees to join a union for continued employment. Some state laws permit an employee to refrain from union membership but he or she must pay dues for the benefits a union secures for all employees.

4. To Discharge or Discriminate Against an Employee Because Unfair Labor Practice Charges are Filed or Testimony Given Against an Employer. Under Section 8(a)(4), the government assumes the duty of protecting employees who have exercised their rights under the LMRA. It is an unlawful act for employers to blacklist an employee because of any charges he or she makes to the government. But the employer can discipline that employee if there are legitimate business reasons to do so. If an employer has no bad motives and has not shown any pattern of unfair labor practices, then it can discharge a worker for absenteeism or neglect of duties, even though the employee filed charges or gave testimony against the employer.

NLRB v. Scrivener
405 U.S. 117 (1972)

Mr. Justice Blackmun.

This case presents the issue whether an employer's retaliatory discharge of an employee who gave a written sworn statement to a National Labor Relations Board (NLRB) field examiner investigating an unfair labor practice charge against the employer, but who had not filed the charge or testified at a formal hearing on it, constitutes a violation of Section 8(a)(1) or Section 8(a)(4) of the act. The board held that it was, but the Court of Appeals held otherwise and denied enforcement of the board's order. We granted certiorari in order to review a decision that appeared to have an important impact on the administration of the act. We disagree with the Court of Appeals.

Robert Scrivener is a small electrical contractor in Springfield, Missouri. He does business as an individual proprietor under the name of AA Electric Company. On March 21, the union there filed charges of unfair labor practices with the NLRB. On April 17, a field examiner from the board's regional office met with Mr. Scrivener and his employees and discussed the charges that had been filed. At the end of the day, Scrivener dismissed four employees who had given statements; he did so with the explanation that he had no work for them to do.

On May 13 the union filed amendments to its charges, adding the allegation that the dismissal of the four men on April 18 was because they had given statements to the examiner in connection with the earlier charge and that this was a violation of Section 8(a)(1) and Section 8(a)(4).

Construing Section 8(a)(4) to protect employees during the investigative stage as well as in connection with the filing of a formal charge or the giving of formal testimony fulfills the section's objective. Mr. Justice Black spelled out the congressional purpose: "... Congress has made it clear that it wishes all persons with information about such practices to be completely free from coercion against reporting them to the Board. This is shown by its adoption of Section 8(a)(4) which makes it an unfair labor practice for an employer to discriminate against an employee because he filed charges. And it has been held that it is unlawful for an employer to seek to restrain an employee in the exercise of his right to file charges."

This freedom is necessary to prevent the board's channels of information from being dried up by employer intimidation of prospective complainants and witnesses. It is also consistent with the fact that the board does not initiate its own proceedings; implementation is dependent upon the initiative of individual persons.

An employee who participates in a board investigation may not be called formally to testify or may be discharged before any hearing at which he could testify. His contribution might be merely cumulative or the case may be settled or dismissed before hearing. Which employees receive statutory protection should not turn on events that have no relation to the need for protection. It would make less than complete sense to protect the employee because he participates in the formal inception of the process but not to protect his participation in the important developmental stages that fall between filing the charge and its settlement. This would be unequal and inconsistent protection.

We therefore conclude that an employer's discharge of an employee because the employee gave a written sworn statement to a board examiner investigating an unfair labor practice charge filed against the employer constitutes a violation of Section 8(a)(4). The judgment of the Court of Appeals is reversed and the case remanded for further proceedings.

CASE QUESTIONS

1. Why were the employees discharged in this case?
2. To what extent is a worker protected from discharge for participating in proceedings before the NLRB?

---

5. *To Refuse to Bargain Collectively with Representatives of the Employees.* Section 8(a)(5). An employer must negotiate with em-

ployees over wages, hours, and working conditions. There is no duty to agree to any demands, only to meet with employee representatives at reasonable times and places and to negotiate in good faith. To bargain in good faith means that an employer does not use delaying tactics, coercion against employees, or harassment against the union, and the employer discusses relevant issues willingly. It is not an unfair labor practice for an employer to refuse to bargain until the union proves it has majority status, or until it proves its representatives were selected validly. Neither party can bargain about a closed shop contract, politics, religious issues, management functions, or foreign affairs. However, an employer must negotiate about a union or agency shop contract, wages, bonuses, the effects of business changes on employees, profit sharing, grievance procedures, health programs, hours worked, housing, retirement, seniority systems, dues checkoff, strikes, subcontracting practices, vacations, insurance, and arbitration—to name just a few of the bargainable issues.

Detroit Edison Co. v. Utility Workers Local 223
218 NLRB 147 (1975)

The employer required all employees seeking promotion to higher paying positions to take an appitude test. Advancements were made based upon test scores obtained. Upon the employer's refusing to show union bargaining representatives these test results, the union filed an unfair labor practice charge against the employer. A hearing was held before an administrative law judge from the NLRB. He ruled that the scores must be turned over to the union and the actual test papers submitted to a professional psychologist for evaluation. The board modifies this order.

The employer's refusal to provide the union with copies of the aptitude tests administered to employee applicants for promotion, including the actual test papers and the actual test scores of the applicants, violated Section 8(a)(5). To remedy this violation, the employer should be required to submit the test scores to the union. But contrary to the opinion of the administrative law judge, the test papers themselves should also be submitted directly to the union, rather than to the psychologist.

The law judge required the intervention of a psychologist because he believes that the mere submission of the test to the union representatives is not likely to produce constructive results. The union may find it necessary to retain an expert to interpret the tests and to assist it in fulfilling its responsibility to its employees. But this does not mean that the union's access to this information should be conditioned upon the intervention of the expert. As the agent of the employees, it is entitled to information necessary to its role as bargaining agent. The information requested here may be beneficial to the union in fulfilling its responsibility. Its access to this information should not be conditioned upon the retention of a psychologist.

CASE QUESTION

1. On what basis could these tests be included in the bargainable issues of wages, hours, and working conditions?

UNION UNFAIR LABOR PRACTICES

In response to many cases of unions abusing their power over employers, Congress added section 8(b) to the LMRA in 1947. This section lists certain unfair labor practices for a union. Some of them are patterned after the improper labor practices of an employer, some are new for unions, and two of them apply to both unions and employers. Prohibited practices in this section are:

1. To Restrain or Coerce Employees in the Exercise of Their Rights or an Employer in the Selection of its Bargaining Agent. Section 8(b)(1). A union can prescribe rules for its internal operations and it can punish any member who refuses to follow them. But it cannot use force, violence, or intimidation against an employee. And a union cannot discipline one of its members without good cause. It can seek a union or agency shop contract requiring employees to join or pay dues to the union. It can use union hiring halls as referral agents to employers for workers if membership in the halls is open to all persons, not just union members. It is an unfair labor practice for a union to maintain a blacklist of employees who refuse to support a union, to establish a closed shop where only union members will be hired, to encourage an employee to withdraw an unfair labor practice charge, to exert pressure on an employer to withdraw charges against the union, or to refuse to bargain with an employers' association.

2. To Cause an Employer to Discriminate Against an Employee Because of Union Membership. Section 8(b)(2) makes it an unfair labor practice for a union to agree with an employer to deny promotion to, to fire, or to take away a wage increase from an employee who has refused to join a union. A union and an employer can agree that disciplinary action will be taken against any member who refuses to pay union dues.

3. *To Refuse to Bargain Collectively with an Employer.* Section 8(b)(3). Unions must come to negotiations with the same attitude as employers. Their duties parallel those of employers. For example, a union commits an unfair labor practice if it attempts to bargain without the majority support of the employees, bargains for illegal purposes, or refuses to negotiate with an employer or its representatives. It is permissible for a union to strike, picket, or engage in other legal acts and still bargain in good faith.

4. *To Encourage, Threaten, or Coerce any Individual* employed by any employer to engage in a strike or a refusal to handle or work on products where the purpose is to force an employer:

—to join a labor union or employer's association;
—to bargain with a union not yet approved as a representative of a majority of employees;
—to bargain with one union when another union is the legal representative of a majority of employees; or
—to assign work to employees in one union rather than to employees in a different union.

This section, 8(b)(4), forbids the use of primary and secondary pressures in the four types of labor disputes listed. A secondary pressure is a union tactic directed against a neutral employer to force it to harm another employer who has a dispute with the union. For example, if union A has a dispute with company B, a strike against company B is a primary tactic, permitted by law. But if the union strikes company C, a customer of B, this is a secondary tactic and may be prohibited by this section. Secondary pressures are dangerous because they involve an innocent party in a labor dispute that is not its own.

Under this section, it is an unfair labor practice for a union to strike employer A because employer B uses nonunion employees, to strike a general contractor to force it to stop dealing with a subcontractor, to ask employees of another company not to load trucks carrying products of a company the union is striking, or to refuse to work on products made by nonunion employees.

It is not an unfair labor practice for union members to strike their employer because it is doing the work of another employer shut down as a result of a strike. In this example, courts have ruled that the two employers are allies and both are involved directly in the labor dispute. Also, a union member can refuse to cross the picket line set up by another union at its place of employment, consumers can picket or boycott a neutral employer, union members can publicize their dispute with an employer and can ask other union members to boycott products made by the company.

NLRB v. Local 825, International Union of Operating Engineers
400 U.S. 297 (1971)

Mr. Justice Marshall.

In this case we are asked to determine whether strikes by Operating Engineers at the site of the construction of a nuclear power generator plant at Oyster Creek, New Jersey, violated Section 8(b)(4) of the NLRA. Although the NLRB found the strikes to be in violation of this section, the Court of Appeals refused to enforce the board's order. We believe the Court of Appeals construed the act too narrowly. Accordingly, we reverse and remand the case.

The general contractor for the project, Burns, subcontracted all of the construction work to three companies—White, Chicago, and Poirier. All three employed operating engineers who were members of Local 825. But White, unlike Chicago and Poirier, did not have a collective bargaining agreement with Local 825.

In the latter part of September, 1965, White installed an electric welding machine and assigned the job of pushing buttons that operated the machine to members of the Ironworkers Union, who were to perform the actual welding. Upon learning of this work assignment, Local 825's job steward and its lead engineer threatened White with a strike if operating engineers were not given the work. White, however, refused to agree to the demand. On September 29, 1965, the job steward and lead engineer met with the construction manager for Burns, the general contractor. They informed him that the members of Local 825 working at the jobsite had voted to strike unless Burns signed a contract, which would be binding on all three subcontractors as well as on Burns, giving Local 825 jurisdiction over all power equipment, including electric welding machines, operated on the jobsite. On October 1, after White and Burns refused to accede to the demands, the operating engineers employed by Chicago and Poirier as well as those employed by White walked off the job. They stayed out from 8:00 A.M. to 1:00 P.M., returning to work when negotiations over their demands started.

An unfair labor practice proceeding against Local 825 subsequently ensued. The board found that the union had violated 8(b)(4) by inducing employees of White, Chicago, and Poirier to strike to force White to take the disputed work away from the Ironworkers and assign it to the Operating Engineers.

Congressional concern over the involvement of third parties in labor disputes not their own prompted 8(b)(4). This concern was focused on secondary boycotts, which were conceived as pressure brought to bear not upon the employer who is a party to a dispute but upon some third party who has no concern in it, with the objective of forcing the third party to bring pressure on the employer to agree to the union's demands. Section 8(b)(4) is, however, the product of legislative compromise and also reflects a concern with protecting labor organizations' right to exert legitimate pressure aimed at the employer with whom there is a primary dispute. This primary activity is protected even though it may seriously affect neutral third parties.

Thus there are two threads to 8(b)(4) that require disputed conduct to be classified as either primary or secondary. And the tapestry that has been woven in classifying such conduct is among labor law's most intricate. But here the normally difficult task of classifying union conduct is easy. As the Court of Appeals said, the record justifies the conclusion that Burns and the subcontractors were subjected to coercion in the form of threats or walkouts or both. And as the board said, it is clear that this coercion was designed to achieve the assignment of the disputed work to the operating engineers.

Local 825's coercive activity was aimed directly at Burns and the subcontractors that were not involved in the dispute. The union engaged in a strike against these neutral employers for the specific overt purpose of forcing them to put pressure on White to assign the job of operating the welding machines to operating engineers. Local 825 was not attempting to apply the full force of primary action by directing its efforts at all phases of Burns's normal operation. It was instead using a sort of pressure that was unmistakably and flagrantly secondary.

The more difficult task is to determine whether one of Local 825's objectives was to force Burns and the other neutrals to cease doing business with White. The Court of Appeals concluded that the union's objective was to force Burns to use its influence with the subcontractor to change the subcontractor's conduct, not to terminate the relationship. That court read the statute as requiring that the union demand nothing short of a complete termination of the business relationship between the neutral and the primary employer. Such a reading is too narrow.

Some disruption of business relationships is the necessary consequence of the purest form of primary activity. These foreseeable disruptions are, however, clearly protected. Likewise, secondary activity could have such a limited goal, and the foreseeable result of the conduct could be, while disruptive, so slight that the cease-doing-business requirement is not met.

Local 825's goal was not so limited nor were the foreseeable consequences of its secondary pressure slight. The Operating Engineers sought to force Burns to bind all the subcontractors on the project to a particular form of job assignments. The clear implication of the demands was that Burns would be required either to force a change in White's policy or to terminate White's contract. The strikes shut down the whole project. If Burns was unable to obtain White's consent, Local 825 was apparently willing to continue disruptive conduct that would bring all the employers to their knees.

Certainly, the union would have preferred to have the employers capitulate to its demands; it wanted to take jobs away from the Ironworkers. It was willing to try to obtain this capitulation by forcing neutrals to compel White to meet union demands. To hold that this flagrant secondary conduct with these most serious disruptive effects was not prohibited by Section 8(b)(4) would be largely to ignore the original congressional concern.

Reversed and remanded.

CASE QUESTIONS

1. Summarize the dispute in this case.
2. Define a secondary boycott.
3. Was the union tactic in this case a prohibited secondary tactic?
4. Are all secondary tactics illegal?

5. To Require Employees Joining a Union to Pay Excessive Fees. Section 8(b)(5). It is an unfair labor practice for a union to charge its members excessively high dues, fees, and expenses. To determine what is excessive, courts consider the amounts other unions charge and the employee's wages. The law does not require that all members in the union pay the same amounts; there can be a sliding scale of fees adjusted by time in the union and other relevant factors. However, the scale cannot be set to discourage new people from joining the union or prevent part-time employees from joining.

6. To Cause an Employer to Pay or Agree to Pay for the Services That Are Not Performed or Not to Be Performed. Section 8(b)(6) was intended to eliminate featherbedding, the practice of paying employees for not working. However, courts interpret the phrase "not to be performed" as allowing contracts for extra work not actually needed. Thus it is not an unfair labor practice for a union to force an employer to make up work for employees or to force an employer to pay twice for the same service done by different employees. It is an unfair labor practice for a union to force an employer to pay for unneeded standby services.

7. To Picket or Threaten to Picket Any Employer Where the Purpose Is to Force the Employer to Accept or Bargain with a Union Representative of the Employees Unless the Union is Certified as the Representative of the Employees. Section 8(b)(7) prevents the employer from getting involved in disputes between two unions over representation of the employees. Under this section, it is an unfair labor practice for a union to picket an employer to organize its employees when the employer has already legally recognized another union as representative of its workers, or when the employees have already voted for a union within the last twelve months, or when the union pickets without seeking government certification.

However, it is not an unfair labor practice for a union to picket or use other publicity to advise the public that an employer does not employ members of its union. But if workers refuse to cross this informational picketing line, then it becomes an unfair labor practice.

8. To Enter into Any Agreement with an Employer Where the Employer Agrees Not to Handle or Deal in Any of the Products of Another Employer. Section 8(e) prohibits hot cargo contracts where unions and employers agree not to touch products of an employer with whom the union has a labor dispute. Such contracts are unenforceable and void. However, two exceptions exist. A union and employer in the construction industry can form hot cargo agreements for the contracting and subcontracting of work to be done at the construction site. Statutory language extends the same exceptions to manufacturers in the garment industry.

Connell Construction Co. v. Plumbers and Steamfitters Local 100
44 L.Ed.2d 418 (1975)

Mr. Justice Powell.

The building trades union in this case supported its efforts to organize mechanical subcontractors by picketing certain general contractors, including Connell. The union's sole objective was to compel the general contractors to agree that in letting subcontract for mechanical work they would deal only with firms that were parties to the union's current collective bargaining agreement. The union disclaimed any interest in representing the general contractors' employees. In this case, the picketing succeeded, and Connell seeks to annul the resulting agreement as an illegal restraint on competition.

Local 100 contends that the kind of agreement it obtained from Connell is explicitly allowed by the construction industry proviso to Section 8(e) and that antitrust policy must defer to the labor law. The majority of the Court of Appeals declined to decide this issue, holding that it was subject to the exclusive jurisdiction of the NLRB. This Court had held, however, that the federal courts may decide labor law questions that emerge as collateral issues in suits brought under independent federal remedies, including the antitrust laws. We conclude that Section 8(e) does not allow this type of agreement.

Local 100's argument is straightforward: the first proviso to 8(e) allows an agreement between a labor organization and an employer in the construction industry relating to the contracting or subcontracting of work to be done at the site of the construction, alteration, painting, or repair of a building, structure, or other work. Local 100 is a labor organization, Connell is an employer in the construction industry, and the agreement covers only work to be done at the site of the construction. Therefore, Local 100 says, the agreement comes within the proviso. Connell responds by arguing that despite the unqualified language of the proviso, Congress intended to allow subcontracting agreements only within the context of a collective bargaining relationship; that is, Congress did not intend to permit a union to approach a stranger contractor and obtain a binding agreement not to deal with nonunion subcontractors. On its face, the proviso suggests no such limitation.

Section 8(e) was part of a legislative program designed to plug technical loopholes in Section 8(b)(4)'s general prohibitions of secondary activities. In Section 8(e) Congress broadly proscribed using contractual agreements to achieve the economic coercion prohibited by 8(b)(4). The proviso exempts the construction and garment industries as an apparent compromise. But Congress limited the construction industry proviso to one situation, allowing subcontracting agreements only in relation to work done at a jobsite. In contrast to the latitude in the garment industry proviso, Congress did not afford construction unions an exemption from 8(b)(4) or otherwise indicate that they were free to use subcontracting agreements as a broad organizational weapon. In keeping with these limitations, the Court has interpreted the construction industry proviso as a measure designed to allow agreements pertaining to certain secondary activities on the construction site because of the close community of interests there, but to ban secondary objective agreements concerning nonjobsite work, in which respect the construction industry is no different from any other. Other courts have suggested that the proviso serves an even narrower function, namely, to alleviate the frictions that may arise when union men work continuously alongside nonunion men on the same construction site.

The union admits that it sought the agreement solely as a way of pressuring mechanical subcontractors in the Dallas area to recognize it as the representative of their employees.

If we agree with Local 100 that the construction industry proviso authorizes subcontracting agreements with stranger contractors, not limited to any particular jobsite, our ruling would give construction unions an almost unlimited organizational weapon. The unions would be free to enlist any general contractor to bring economic pressure on nonunion subcontractors, as long as the agreement recited that it only covered work to be performed on some jobsite somewhere. The proviso's jobsite restriction then would serve only to prohibit agreements relating to subcontractors that deliver their work complete on the jobsite.

It is highly improbable that Congress intended such a result. These careful limits on the economic pressure unions may use in aid of their organizational campaigns would be undermined seriously if the proviso to 8(e) were construed to allow unions to seek subcontracting agreements from any general contractor vulnerable to picketing. We therefore hold that this agreement is outside the context of the collective bargaining relationship.

CASE QUESTIONS

1. Why was the union picketing Connell?
2. Upon what basis does the union argue that its activities against Connell are legal?
3. Why does the court reject this argument?

DISPUTE-SETTLEMENT PROCEDURES

The LMRA establishes a system for helping management and labor settle their disputes without causing a major disruption in the economy or adversely affecting the public interest. The law creates five aids to the collective bargaining process:

1. National Labor Relations Board (NLRB). This administrative agency has exclusive jurisdiction to enforce the LMRA and related laws. It has five members, each appointed by the President and confirmed by the Senate. One of its members serves as chairman. Each member has a five-year, renewable term. The board can hire staff to assist it in carrying out its duties. This staff includes lawyers, investigators, administrative law judges, and clerical workers. Like most regulatory agencies, the NLRB has investigative, legislative, administrative, enforcement, and adjudicative powers. It can make its own rules of procedure, conduct investigations into unfair labor practice charges, subpoena individuals and documents, hold hearings, and issue orders. Appeals from board orders go first to the court of appeals and then to the Supreme Court.

This agency acts as a referee between labor and management, helping them settle their disputes. Most of these disputes deal with either the legal status of a union or the validity of unfair labor practice charges. Both the LMRA and the NLRB create rules and procedures to settle these types of disputes.

2. *Union Certification Procedures.* The LMRA creates a peaceful method by which a union can be recognized as the bargaining agent of employees. This procedure minimizes the conflicts over union jurisdictional disputes and guarantees stability to union existence. To become certified, six steps must be followed:

a. *appropriate unit.* Employees must form themselves into a unit for bargaining purposes. Either the workers or a labor union can begin this process. Usually workers will express their preferences to organizers, either orally or by ballot. The unit formed must be an appropriate one; that is, it must consist of workers who have common bargaining interests. A unit can have as members those employees who belong to a certain craft, a department, a plant, a multiplant system, or an entire industry. The law gives complete discretion to the workers in selecting their unit, except that it prohibits professional employees from joining with nonprofessional workers, and guards from joining the same unit as other employees. If the employer accepts the unit formed, collective bargaining can begin. If the employer, any union, or any employee objects, a petition to the NLRB can be filed.

b. *petition.* The person or organization dissatisfied with the unit formed can ask the NLRB to review the matter. This request is made by a formal petition, stating that a substantial number of employees wish to be represented by a labor union. Upon receipt of this petition, the board will conduct an investigation into the facts contained in this document.

c. *investigation.* This preliminary inquiry into the facts in the petition determines if any reasonable grounds exist for challenging the formation of the labor unit. If no reasonable grounds are found, the petition will be dismissed. Alternatively, if any doubts about the facts contained in the petition exist, a hearing will be held.

d. *hearing.* At this hearing, held before the NLRB, all interested parties can give evidence concerning the validity of the union formed for bargaining purposes. Notice of the hearing must be given to all employees, the employer, and other interested parties and unions. All can participate in the hearing. Upon completion of the evidence, the board may either certify the unit as appropriate for bargaining purposes or deny the unit's status as agent for the workers. In the latter case, the board can order an election to decide the union's status.

TABLE 12-1. MAJOR FUNCTIONAL OFFICES IN THE NATIONAL LABOR RELATIONS BOARD

Chairman and Members
Solicitor
Chief Administrative Law Judge
Director of Information
General Counsel
Administration

Source: U.S. Government Manual, 1975-76 Edition.

e. *election.* The NLRB conducts an election to remove all doubts about the representation of the workers. This election gives the employees a free choice in determining whether they will be unionized, and if so, by whom. The board will set the time and place for the election, establish electioneering rules, and settle all questions about employee eligibility to vote. Voting is by secret ballots, issued, collected, and counted by the NLRB. For the results to be valid, a substantial number of employees must vote and the union must get a majority of the votes cast. Any person or party affected by the outcome can challenge the results before the NLRB. It will either affirm the results or order a new election if any part of the balloting was improper. The NLRB will not hold any election if the employees held a valid election within the past twelve months or if there are any unsettled unfair labor practice charges.

f. *certification.* If the board is satisfied with the fairness of the election and if the union won, it will certify that union as the exclusive bargaining agent for all the employees in the unit. That union will remain as the employee's agent for at least a twelve-month period. Then employees can vote out the union. If the employees request the decertification of a union, the board will conduct an investigation and hold a hearing and perhaps another election.

3. *Unfair Labor Practice Charges.* The NLRB has the power to stop any person from committing an unfair labor practice. Any person, union, or employer can file notice with the NLRB of an alleged unfair practice within six months after it happens. The following outlines NLRB procedures upon receipt of the charge:

> Under the LMRA, the process of adjudicating unfair labor practice cases begins with the filing by a private party of a "charge." Although Congress has designated the Board as the principal body which adjudi-

cates the unfair labor practice case based on such charge, the Board may adjudicate only upon the filing of a "complaint", and Congress has delegated to the Office of General Counsel, acting for the Board, the unreviewable authority to determine whether a complaint shall be filed. In those cases in which he decides that a complaint shall issue, the General Counsel becomes an advocate before the Board in support of the complaint. In those cases in which he decides not to issue a complaint, no proceeding before the Board occurs at all. The practical effect of this administrative scheme is that a party believing himself the victim of an unfair labor practice can obtain neither adjudication nor remedy under the labor statute without first persuading the General Counsel that his claim is sufficiently meritorious to warrant Board consideration.

In order to structure the considerable power which the law gives him, the General Counsel has adopted certain procedures for processing unfair labor practice charges. Charges are filed in the first instance with one of the Board's 31 Regional Directors, to whom initial power to decide whether or not to issue a complaint resides. A member of the staff of the Regional Director's Office then conducts an investigation of the charge, which may include interviewing witnesses and reviewing documents. If, on the basis of the investigation, the Director believes the charge has merit, a settlement will be attempted, or a complaint issued. If the charge has no merit in the Regional Director's judgment, the charging party will be so informed by letter with a brief explanation of the reasons. In such a case, the charging party will also be informed of his legal right to appeal within 10 days to the Office of General Counsel in Washington, D.C.

If the charging party exercises this right, the entire file in the possession of the Regional Director will be sent to the Office of Appeals in the General Counsel's Office. The case will be assigned to a staff attorney who prepares a memorandum containing an analysis of the factual and legal issues of the case. This memorandum is called an "agenda minute" and serves as the basis for discussion at a meeting of the "Appeals Committee", which includes the Director, and the Associate Director of the Office of Appeals. At some point in this period, the charging party may make a written presentation of his case as of right and an oral presentation in the discretion of the General Counsel. If an oral presentation is allowed, the subject of the unfair labor practice charge is notified and allowed a similar but separate opportunity to make an oral presentation. In any event, a decision is reached by the Appeals Committee, and the decision and the reasons for it are set forth in a memorandum called the "General Counsel's Minute". This document is then cleared through the General Counsel himself. If the case is unusually complex or important, the General Counsel will have been brought into the process at an earlier stage and will have a hand in the decision and the expression of its basis in the General Counsel's Minute. In either event, the Minute is then sent to the Regional Director who follows its instructions. If the appeal is rejected and the Director's decision not to issue a complaint is sustained, a separate document is prepared and sent by the General Counsel's Office in letter form to the charging party, more briefly setting forth the reasons for the denial of his appeal (*NLRB v. Sears, Roebuck*, 421 U.S. 132, 1975.)

If the charge is meritorious, a complaint will be issued. Eventually, a hearing will be held before the NLRB. If the board determines that the complaint is valid, it may issue an order restoring the parties to the conditions before the unfair practice commenced. This may mean reinstatement of wrongfully discharged employees, with or without back pay. The order may require reports to see if there is continual compliance. If evidence at the hearing does not support the complaint, it will be dismissed. Either party to the hearing may appeal board action to the Court of Appeals and the Supreme Court. Any person not complying with a board order can be punished by the courts for contempt.

4. Mediation Services. The basic policy of the LMRA encourages labor and management to agree freely on the settlement of their disputes. There is no compulsory arbitration required by the act. However, the Congress realized that the parties may need expert help in solving their problems. Consequently, it has formed the Federal Mediation and Conciliation Service, to assist in negotiating settlements. This service can act by itself or upon the request of either side to a labor dispute. It acts as an intermediary between the parties, offers suggestions for settling the dispute, requires the parties to negotiate, and forces a vote by employees on management's offers. The service helps preserve labor peace and promote prompt settlements.

5. National-Emergency Strikes. Some labor disruptions in certain industries can cause severe hardship and danger to the nation. The law must have procedures to deal with these risks. The LMRA has emergency strike laws to settle such disputes. Under these procedures, the President must determine if any actual or threatened strike will affect interstate commerce or foreign trade and whether it will imperil the national health or safety. If so, the President can invoke special powers. First, a board of inquiry is appointed to determine what the strike issues are. Second, this board will report its findings to the President, who may order the Attorney General to petition a federal district court for an injunction, stopping the strike for sixty days. During this sixty-day cooling-off period, the parties must make reasonable settlement offers. At the end of this sixty-day period, the board of inquiry will report the last settlement offer of the employer. Within fifteen days, the NLRB must hold a vote by union members on this last settlement offer. The results of this election are sent to the Attorney General within five days after the balloting. Thereupon, the injunction against the strike ends and the employees are free to strike. The President submits the entire matter to Congress for their appropriate action. In effect, Congress will then write the terms of the labor contract.

REVIEW QUESTIONS

1. Explain how the industrial revolution contributed to the growth of unions. To what extent are these reasons valid today?
2. In what ways do laws encourage collective bargaining?
3. Summarize employee rights under Section 7.
4. Describe the penalties for committing an unfair labor practice. Can a law be effective with these penalties?
5. Under what circumstances can a union engage in secondary tactics? Why are there any limitations?
6. Outline union certification procedures.
7. To what extent does the General Counsel of the NLRB influence unfair labor practice charges?
8. What options does the Congress have in settling a national emergency strike?
9. To determine the majority status of a union seeking recognition as agent for employees, an employer sought to poll his employees. The union objected to this, alleging the very nature of the inquiry tends to have a coercive effect on the exercise of Section 7 rights. Do you agree?
10. An employer started a retirement plan in combination with the union. The plan provided that eligible employees had to contribute part of their wages to the plan and maintain membership in the union to receive any benefits. This plan is challenged in that it coerces employees to continue union membership even while not employed merely to avoid loss of benefits. Is the plan coercive under LMRA?

13

UNION-MANAGEMENT RELATIONS

*That the state has [the] power to regulate labor [and management] with a view to protecting the public interest is hardly to be doubted. They cannot claim immunity from regulation. Such regulation, however, whether aimed at fraud or other abuses, must not trespass upon the domains set apart for free speech and free assembly. (*Thomas v. Collins, 323 U.S. 516, 1945.*)*

Unions have various weapons in their arsenals to use against management. These weapons include strikes and picketing. Both can bring economic pressure on an employer, forcing it to give in to labor demands. If there were no limitations on labor's use of them, then these tactics could make an employer helpless when confronted by worker demands. To equalize union-management relations, Congress imposed some restrictions on employee strikes and picketing.

Even with these limitations, unions became powerful organizations. Some are as large and as strong economically as the employers of their members. With such power, abuses are inevitable. To limit such abuses, Congress enacted the Labor Management Reporting and Disclosure Act (LMRDA), commonly called the Landrum Griffin Act. This law tries to give union members democratic organizations and imposes liabilities on union officials who abuse their positions of power.

The employee pension plan is one area of potential abuse Congress singled out for special legislation. A pension is a fringe benefit for employees. It pays a sum of money to retired employees who have worked for an employer for a certain number of years. For each year an employee worked, money is paid into a fund. That money is invested until distributed to retired workers who meet the conditions established in the pension plan. Employers administer most of these plans, either directly or through an insurance company. Unions control some plans. Recently, Congress found many abuses in the way unions and management operated their pension plans. Among the abuses were bad investments, fraud, and unfair treatment of employees eligible for benefits. To remedy these abuses, Congress enacted the Employees Retirement Income Security Act. In this chapter, we will study this new law, the law guaranteeing union democracy, some legal restrictions on strikes and picketing, and pension reforms. Some guidelines for better union-management relations will conclude the chapter.

STRIKES

A strike is a temporary, concerted withdrawal of workers from an employer's service to force their demands. The right to strike is both protected and limited by law. Generally speaking, a strike is permitted if its purposes are legal and it is carried out in a legal manner. There are several types of strikes that the law either permits or limits in some ways. These are:

1. Primary Strike. Employees strike their employer. Generally, a primary strike is legal, although some collective bargaining agreements may restrict it or take it away completely. When a union negotiates away its right to strike, a court may or may not uphold the agreement. Some courts hold that the right to strike is too important for employees to give up; therefore a pledge not to strike is invalid. But most courts require unions to honor their no-strike pledge where management, union, and the employees agree to it.

Buffalo Forge Co. v. United Steelworkers of America
61 ABAJ 874 (1975)

Smith, Judge.

Here the United Steelworkers of America and two of its locals represented the production and maintenance employees of Buffalo Forge. The same international union and the two other locals represented the company's office, clerical, and technical employees. On November 16, 1974, in negotiating their first collective bargaining agreement with Buffalo Forge, the unions representing the office, clerical, and technical employees went out on strike and began picketing all three of the company's sites. On November 18 the production and maintenance employees at one of the company's sites refused to cross the picket lines. Three days later the unions representing the production and maintenance employees at the sites called a work stoppage at all the company's sites. This strike prompted Buffalo Forge to sue for damages and injunctive relief against all the unions. The district court denied the company's request for injunctive relief and this appeal followed.

Section 301 of the Labor Management Relations Act vests jurisdiction in federal courts over suits for violation of contracts between an employer and a labor organization representing employees in an industry affecting commerce. Section 4 of the Norris LaGuardia Act establishes a pre-existing nonabsolute bar to federal court injunctions in any case involving or growing out of any labor dispute.

Resolution of the central issue raised on appeal required interpretation of the *Boys Market* case decided by the Supreme Court in 1970. That case set forth a general standard for reconciling the competing demands of the two statutes in the context of a strike over a grievance that the parties are bound by agreement to arbitrate. The district court ruled that under *Boys Market,* courts are deprived of jurisdiction by the Norris LaGuardia Act to issue a preliminary injunction like the one sought by Buffalo Forge. The union's obligation under the pre-existing collective bargaining agreements to resolve disputes with management through a mandatory six-step settlement procedure culminating in arbitration and to refrain from authorizing strikes was deemed not controlling in light of Congress's stated antipathy to injunctions. This court concludes that the district court correctly construed the import of *Boys Market.*

Only strikes over a grievance that the union has agreed to arbitrate are within the scope of the Norris LaGuardia Act. The strike at issue here was not over a grievance with Buffalo Forge, the court noted, but over a manifestation of the striking workers deference to other employees' picket lines. A strike not seeking to pressure the employer to yield on a disputed issue, the court stated, is not an attempt to avoid the arbitration machinery established by the collective bargaining agreement. Accordingly, it does not violate the federal pro-arbitration policy to require federal courts to refrain from enjoining those strikes. (This case has been affirmed by the Supreme Court.)

CASE QUESTIONS

1. Contrast the policy of Section 4 of the Norris LaGuardia Act with that of Section 301 of the LMRA.
2. When does a no-strike pledge bind a union not to strike?

---

2. Secondary Strike. In this situation, employees strike one employer so that it pressures another employer to settle a union dispute. The law regarding secondary pressures was discussed in the preceeding chapter under Section 8(b)(4) of LMRA.

3. *Sympathy Strike.* Here, employees strike their employer for the benefit of other employees having a dispute with the same employer. It is a secondary pressure and restricted by law. *Buffalo Forge*, supra.

4. *General Strike.* All employees in an industry or nation strike their employers in this situation. It is not permitted by law because it is a secondary pressure and harmful to the national economy. But it is unclear how the government would deal with such a situation.

5. *Sitdown Strike.* Workers seize and occupy the employer's property when engaging in this type of strike activity. While there may be times when such actions are proper, such workers can be arrested by the police and discharged by their employer. The law often considers this action criminal trespass, not legitimate labor activity. *NLRB v. Fansteel Corp.*, 306 U.S. 40 (1939).

6. *Slowdown Strike.* Employees partially cease working, although they do not walk off their jobs. This is not a permitted action, although workers frequently accomplish the same result legally by rigidly following the employer's work rules. Employees not allowed to strike frequently use this tactic.

7. *Wildcat Strike.* Any strike not authorized from the union. Such a strike is illegal under collective bargaining agreements and employers can obtain a court order compelling the workers to return to work. *NLRB v. Draper Corp.*, 145 F.2d 199 (1944.)

8. *Government Employee Strike.* A strike by employees working for federal, state, or local government. In most civil services, this type of strike is illegal since it denies citizens services for which they voted. *Norwalk Teachers v. Board of Education*, 83 A.2d 482 (1951).

9. *National Emergency Strike.* A strike by employees against a company or industry that is so important that a strike against it harms the national health and safety. Federal law limits this type of strike.

10. *Violent Strike.* A strike characterized by force, pushing, rock throwing, fighting, or other nonpeaceful techniques. Such conduct is never permitted by law and courts can order the violence stopped. If the violence continues, the court may order the strike to stop. *Corriveau and Routhier Inc. v. NLRB*, 410 F.2d 347 (1969).

11. Economic Strike. A strike by employees for improvement in wages, hours, or working conditions. This strike is legal and a worker fired for striking can be reinstated if replacements have not been hired during the strike. *NLRB* v. *Fleetwood Trailer Co.*, 389 U.S. 375 (1967).

12. Unfair Labor Practice Strike. A strike because an employer allegedly committed an unfair labor practice listed in Section 8(a) of LMRA. It is a legal strike activity and a worker fired for striking can be reinstated even if replacements have been hired during the strike. See *Fleetwood Trailer, supra.*

PICKETING

This important labor tactic involves communication to the public by employees or outsiders who carry signs and parade at an employer's place of business. Other union members and some members of the public will refuse to cross this picket line. This line can cause some economic hardship to the employer, and induce it to settle the labor dispute. To be protected by law, picketing must be for a lawful purpose and carried out in a lawful manner.

Courts compare picketing to free speech, protected by the First Amendment to the Constitution. But as our right of free speech is not absolute, neither is labor's right to picket absolute. "Many United States and [state] court opinions have recognized constitutional protections for peaceful picketing. The courts, have, however, sustained injunctions against peaceful picketing when such picketing was counter to valid [governmental] policy...." (*United Farm Workers of America* v. *The Superior Court of Santa Cruz Cty.*, 537 P.2d 1237, 1975.)

There are several specific types of picketing that the law either permits or limits in some ways. These are:

1. Primary Picketing. Employees picket their employer with whom they have a direct dispute. In the absence of any illegal acts, this picketing is legal. *Thornhill* v. *Alabama*, 310 U.S. 88 (1940).

2. Secondary Picketing. Employees picket an employer to force it to pressure another employer. This is illegal except for those situations discussed in Section 8(b)(4) of LMRA.

3. Tertiary Picketing. Employees picket customers or suppliers of the employer with whom they have a labor dispute. This type of picketing is secondary picketing and similarly limited by Section 8(b)(4).

4. Informational Picketing. Employees publicize their dispute with an employer but allow other workers and the public to cross their picket line. It is legal if carried out in the manner specified in the discussion of Section 8(b)(4) of LMRA.

5. Mass Picketing. Great numbers of employees parade in a tight formation, thus preventing people from entering the employer's premises. It is illegal because it intimidates people and often leads to violence. *International Union* v. *Russell*, 356 U.S. 34(1958).

6. Organizational and Jurisdictional Picketing. Employees picket to force an employer to recognize and bargain with their union. This is legal unless it violates the rules dealing with union certification procedures discussed in the last chapter. In general, where a union is certified as bargaining agent for the employees, another union cannot force the employer to bargain with it. Picketing to force negotiation with the second union can be stopped by court injunction. As illustrated in *NLRB* v. *Plasterers Local Union 79*, 404 U.S. 116 (1971), "The alleged unfair labor practice in this case was the picketing of the job sites by the Plasterers and the dispute giving rise to this picketing was the disagreement over whether Plasterers or Tile Setters were to lay the final plaster coat. This dispute was a three cornered one. The Plasterers [picketed both the employer] and the Tile Setters. . . . [T]he employer's refusal to accede to the Plasterer's demands inevitably and inextricably involved him with the Tile Setters against the Plasterers. It was this triangular dispute which [the court can stop]."

7. Stranger Picketing. Picketing by people other than persons who work for the employer. It may be allowed where it is informational picketing or strangers merely join employees on a picket line. *American Federation of Labor* v. *Swing*, 312 U.S. 321 (1941).

8. Common Situs Picketing. Employees of one employer picket at a place where many different employers are working. The law restricts this type of picketing because employers not a party to the dispute are affected. *Building and Construction Trades Council*, 155 NLRB 319, 1965.

9. Ambulatory Situs Picketing. Employees picket their employer wherever it is located and move the picket line to another place as the employer moves. For example, if employees of an office cleaning company have a dispute with their employer, they can picket it. Since the employer performs its work at several different places, the workers would like to picket wherever the employer is in order to bring maximum public pressure on it. But the firms where the cleaning company works may not want to get involved in any labor dispute not their own. Consequently, the law must balance the conflicting needs of the employees and of neutral employers. Courts allow employees to picket wherever their employer is if their picket signs identify who their dispute is with and picketing lasts only as long as their employer is at the picketed site. *Truck Drivers and Helpers Local Union,* 181 NLRB 790, 1970.

UNION DEMOCRACY

The Labor Management Reporting and Disclosure Act of 1959, commonly called the Landrum Griffin Act, is an important part of national labor regulation. Congress passed this act after investigations revealed some abuses by some union officials. The act imposes duties and responsibilities on unions and their officers. Enforcement of these duties resides with the Labor-Management Relations Division in the Department of Labor. The LMRDA imposes four types of duties on unions:

1. Members' Bill of Rights. Title I of the LMRDA creates a bill of rights for all members of a union or labor organization. Union leaders must respect these rights. Some of the major ones are:

a. All members have equal rights within the union to nominate candidates for union offices, to vote in every regular or special union election, to receive notice of all regular and special meetings, to attend these meetings, and to participate in any discussions at such meetings.

Trbovich v. United Mine Workers of America
404 U.S. 528 (1972)

Mr. Justice Marshall.

The Secretary of Labor instituted this action under the Labor Management Reporting and Disclosure Act of 1959, to set aside an election of officers of the

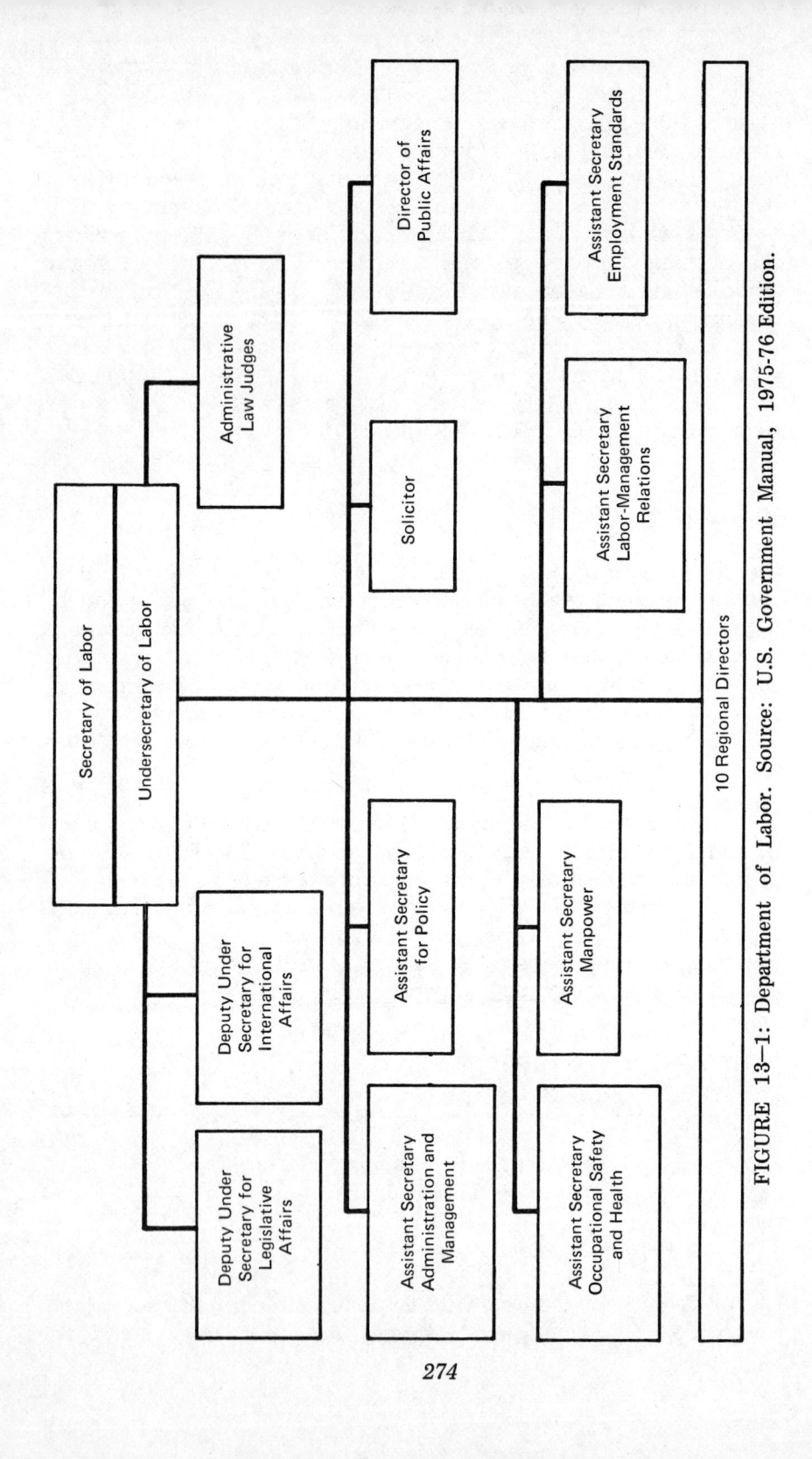

FIGURE 13–1: Department of Labor. Source: U.S. Government Manual, 1975-76 Edition.

United Mine Workers of America, held on December 9, 1969. He alleged that the election was held in a manner that violated the LMRDA in numerous respects, and he sought an order requiring a new election to be held under his supervision.

Trbovich, a member of the UMWA, filed the complaint with the secretary that eventually led him to file this suit. He now seeks to intervene in the litigation, in order (1) to urge two additional grounds for setting aside the election, (2) to seek certain specific safeguards with respect to any new election that may be ordered, and (3) to present evidence and argument in support of the secretary's challenge to the election. The District Court denied his motion for leave to intervene on the ground that the LMRDA expressly stripped union members of any right to challenge a union election in the courts and gave that right exclusively to the secretary. The Court of Appeals affirmed on the basis of the District Court's opinion. We granted certiorari to determine whether the LMRDA imposes a bar to intervention by union members in a suit initiated by the secretary. We conclude that it does not and we remand the case to the District Court with directions to permit intervention.

The LMRDA was the first major attempt of Congress to regulate the internal affairs of a labor union. Having conferred substantial power on labor organizations, Congress began to be concerned with the danger that union leaders would abuse that power, to the detriment of the rank-and-file members. Congress saw the principle of union democracy as one of the most important safeguards against such abuse and accordingly included in the LMRDA a comprehensive scheme for the regulation of union elections.

Title IV of the statute establishes a set of substantive rules governing union elections, and it provides a comprehensive procedure for enforcing those rules. Any union member who alleges a violation may initiate enforcement procedure. He must first exhaust any internal remedies available under the constitution and bylaws of his union. Then he may file a complaint with the Secretary of Labor, who shall investigate the complaint. Finally, if the secretary finds probable cause to believe a violation has occurred, he shall bring a civil action against the labor organization in federal district court to set aside the election if it has already been held and to direct and supervise a new election. With respect to elections not yet conducted, the statute provides that existing rights and remedies apart from the statute are not affected. But with respect to an election already conducted, the remedy provided by the law shall be exclusive.

The critical statutory provision in this case makes suit by the secretary the exclusive post-election remedy for a violation of election rules. This Court has held that this power prohibits union members from initiating a private suit to set aside an election. But in this case, Trbovich seeks only to participate in a pending suit that is plainly authorized by the statute: it cannot be said that his claim is defeated by the language of the act.

Intervention by union members in a pending enforcement suit, unlike initiation of a separate suit, subjects the union to relatively little additional burden. The principal intrusion on internal union affairs has already been accomplished, in that the union has already been summoned into court to defend the legality of its actions. Intervention in the suit by union members will not subject the union to burdensome multiple litigation nor will it compel the union to respond to a new and potentially groundless suit. Thus, at least insofar as Trbovich seeks only to present evidence and argument in support of the secretary's complaint, there is nothing in the language or history of the LMRDA to prevent such intervention.

The question is closer with respect to Trbovich's attempt to add to the secretary's complaint with two additional grounds. These claims have been determined by the secretary to be without merit. Hence, to require the union to respond to these claims would be to circumvent the screening function assigned to the secretary. We recognize that it is less burdensome to the union to respond to new claims in the context of the pending suit than it would be to respond to a new and independent complaint. Nevertheless, we think Congress intended to insulate the union from any complaint that did not appear meritorious to both a complaining member and the secretary. According we hold that in a post-election enforcement suit, the act imposes no bar to intervention by a union member so long as that intervention is limited to the claims of illegality presented by the secretary's complaint.

The LMRDA imposes two duties on the secretary, which are related but not identical. First, the act gives the individual union members certain rights against their union, and the Secretary of Labor in effect becomes the union member's lawyer for purposes of enforcing those rights. And second, the secretary has an obligation to protect the vital public interest in assuring free and democratic union elections that transcend the narrower interest of the complaining member. Both functions are important and they may not always dictate precisely the same approach to the conduct of the litigation. Even if the secretary is performing his duties, broadly conceived, as well as can be expected, the union member may have a valid complaint about the performance of his lawyer. Such a complaint, filed by a member who initiated the entire enforcement proceeding, should be regarded as sufficient to warrant relief in the form of intervention.

CASE QUESTIONS

1. Why does the Secretary of Labor deny Trbovich the right to intervene in this case to set aside the union election?
2. Why is the union member allowed to intervene in this suit?
3. What procedures exist for a union member to challenge union elections?

b. All members have the right to meet with other members of the union and to express their views at union meetings.

c. All dues, fees, expenses, or assessments required of members cannot be increased unless reasonable procedures are followed. The LMRDA lists the required procedures. This part of the act also prohibits union leaders from punishing a member by arbitrarily increasing his or her dues or fees.

d. Every member has the right to sue union leaders or bring legal action against them before any administrative agency. However, the member may be required to follow union procedures before suing and the member's legal action must not be financed in any way by an employer.

Hodgson v. Local Union 6799, United Steelworkers of America
403 U.S. 333 (1971)

Mr. Justice Marshall.

Petitioner, the Secretary of Labor, instituted this action under the LMRDA against Local 6799 to set aside a general election of officers conducted by the union. The lawsuit arose after Hantzis, an unsuccessful candidate for president of the local, protested the election to both the local and international union organization. His protest contained several matters, including the use of union facilities to prepare campaign materials for the incumbent president who was reelected.

After failing to obtain relief through the internal procedures of either union organization, Hantzis filed a complaint with the Secretary of Labor. The complaint repeated the charge that union facilities had been used to promote the candidacy of the incumbent president and raised for the first time an additional objection concerning a meeting attendance requirement imposed as a condition of candidacy for union office. At no time during his internal union protests did Hantzis challenge the attendance requirement.

Following an investigation of the complaint, the secretary concluded that union facilities had been used improperly to aid the reelection of the incumbent president and that the meeting attendance requirement was unreasonable and unfairly administered. The union was advised of these conclusions and was asked to take voluntary remedial action. When they failed to comply with the request, the secretary brought this proceeding in the District Court. It ordered a new election. The Court of Appeals affirmed, without discussing the reasonableness of the meeting attendance rule.

Because this case presents an important issue concerning the scope of the secretary's authority under the act, we granted certiorari. We conclude that Hantzis' failure to object to the attendance rule during pursuit of his internal union remedies bars the secretary from later challenging the rule in a court action.

The act provides that once a member challenging an election has exhausted his internal union remedies and filed a complaint with the Secretary of Labor, the secretary shall investigate such complaint, and if he finds probable cause to believe that a violation of this act has occurred and has not been remedied, he shall, within sixty days after filing of the complaint, bring a civil action against the labor organization. At the outset, petitioner contends that the language of the act empowers the secretary to investigate and litigate any and all violations of the act that may have affected the outcome of an election once a union member has exhausted his internal remedies concerning any violation that occurred during that election.

Examination of the relevant legislative materials reveals a clear congressional concern for the need to remedy abuses in union elections without departing needlessly from the longstanding congressional policy against unnecessary governmental intervention with internal union affairs. A strong, independent labor movement is a vital American institution. The shocking abuses revealed by investigations have been confined to a few unions. The overwhelming majority are honestly and democratically run. In providing remedies for existing evils, the government did not intend to undermine self-government within the labor movement nor to weaken unions in their role as the bargaining representatives of workers.

The requirement that a union member exhaust his internal union remedies before enlisting the aid of the secretary was designed to harmonize the need to eliminate election abuses with a desire to avoid unnecessary governmental interference. But petitioner contends that the congressional concerns underpinning the exhaustion requirement were in fact adequately served in this case, because the election in question was actually protested by a union member within the union and because the union was later given a chance to remedy specific violations before it was taken to court by the secretary. To accept petitioner's contention that a union member who is aware of the facts underlying an alleged violation need not first protest this violation to his union before complaining to the secretary would be needlessly to weaken union self-government. Plainly, petitioner's approach slights the interest in protecting union self-regulation and is out of harmony with the congressional purpose.

In this case, it is clear that the protesting member knew of the existence of the meeting attendance requirement provision and that his election protests to the local and international unions concerned matters wholly unrelated to the rule. We therefore hold that internal union remedies were not properly exhausted and that the secretary was barred from litigating the claim. Given this holding, we do not reach the questions whether the meeting attendance rule is reasonable.

CASE QUESTIONS

1. Why does a union member have to follow internal remedies before requesting help from the Secretary of Labor?
2. In what ways did Hantzis violate the rules concerning internal remedies?

---

e. No member of a union can be fined or penalized in any way for violating union rules unless given notice of the violation charged, a reasonable time to prepare a defense, and a hearing. However, this procedure is unnecessary if the member is charged with nonpayment of dues.

f. A union has the right to make rules for governing its affairs. These rules must be reasonable and not in conflict with any of the rights given members by the LMRDA. A member must follow these rules and can be penalized for not observing them. Courts will determine the reasonableness of any disputed rule.

UNION REPORTS

A union must adopt a constitution and bylaws for its operation and its conduct of routine business. Certain items must be included in these documents:

-the name of the labor organization, its address, and a list of current officeholders and their compensation and fringe benefits,
-the procedures for electing and removing officers and the dues, fees, fines, and assessments members may be charged,
-the qualifications for union membership, disciplinary procedures, and a list of all rules with current amendments,
-annual financial audits conducted by a certified public accountant, inquiring into all receipts and expenditures made by the union, salaries and other payments made to union leaders, and loans made by the union, and
-rules governing the takeover of a local union by the national union to which it is affiliated.

All of these rules, reports, and audits are public records, filed with the Secretary of Labor and open for inspection to union members, the government, employers, and the public.

OFFICER REPORTS

The LMRDA requires union officers to make yearly reports. These reports must state whether the person has any financial interest in the company that employs members of the union or in any supplier or customer of that company. The report must also state the financial interest any union officer has with the union or any of its customers or suppliers. This section publicizes the personal dealings by a union officer with union funds and reduces potential conflicts of interest.

PENALTIES

The LMRDA establishes criminal penalties of a fine up to $10,000 and up to one year in jail or both for any person who violates any part of this law. These penalties can be imposed on union leaders and the union itself. Union officers have a fiduciary duty to the members. This duty requires that they act in the same manner as a reasonably prudent person would act in managing his or her own property. For any violations of this fiduciary duty, officers can be sued personally by any member of the union. The suit can seek recovery of any losses incurred by the union for violations of the fiduciary duty and compensation to the individual members who may have suffered losses because of the officer's breach of fiduciary duties.

PENSION REFORM

An important issue in negotiations between unions and management is the employee pension plan. These plans have experienced rapid growth in recent years because they are popular with employees. Unions bargain for them and employers agree to these requests as one way of keeping good workers. Since these plans are so important to the collective bargaining process and to our national economy, it is necessary to keep pension plans in sound working order.

However, Congressional investigations revealed numerous abuses in the administration of pension programs. Some plans were funded inadequately so that insufficient money was available to pay retirement benefits. Other plans were administered corruptly so that workers were defrauded. And some other plans were run arbitrarily so that certain employees could not get any payments despite a lifetime of work. To remedy these abuses in pension plan operations, Congress enacted the Employee Retirement Income Security Act (ERISA). This comprehensive law establishes eligibility requirements for employee participation in retirement programs, creates formulas for funding these plans, imposes reporting requirements, and creates penalties for pension plan administrators. This section examines some of the major duties of pension plan officials and shows how the law affects union-management relationships.

1. Types of Plans. An employee pension plan is any program set up by an employer or an employee organization that provides retirement income to employees or deferral of employee income beyond his or her period of employment. ERISA recognizes that an employer may have one of several different types of pension coverage for its workers. A defined benefit plan imposes a ceiling on amounts paid to a retired worker; generally, benefits cannot exceed the lesser of $75,000 or one hundred percent of an employee's average compensation for his or her highest three years of income. By contrast, a defined contribution plan imposes a ceiling on the amounts paid into a retirement fund by an employer and employee; generally, the annual addition to an employee's retirement fund cannot exceed the lesser of $25,000 or twenty-five percent of an employee's compensation.

The pension reform act also permits an excess benefit plan for certain employees. This plan is set up by an employer solely for the purpose of giving benefits to certain employees in excess of the limits imposed on defined benefit and contribution plans. It is used mostly for giving deferred compensation to a select group of management or other highly compensated employees.

Retirement plans set up by certain employers are exempt from ERISA. For example, retirement plans set up by the federal, state, or local governments are not subject to ERISA. Plans maintained by church groups, fraternal organizations, certain labor organizations, and partnership buy-out agreements are also exempt.

2. Eligibility. No pension plan can require an employee to complete a prolonged period of work with the employer before he or she can participate in the plan. An employer can require its workers to meet two conditions: They must be at least twenty-five years of age and complete at least one year of service. These minimal require-

TABLE 13-1. MINIMUM PENSION VESTING STANDARDS

Years of Service	Nonforfeitable Percentage
5	25
6	30
7	35
8	40
9	45
10	50
11	60
12	70
13	80
14	90
15 or more	100

Source: Section 203(a)(2)(B). Employees Retirement Income Security Act.

ments eliminate one major abuse with pensions. Before this law, some employer pension programs required employees to work at least ten years before becoming eligible for pension coverage. Just before the employee completed the years in service, employers would discharge the worker and keep the money paid into the retirement plan. Employers hiring seasonal workers and workers who have reached a certain maximum age are exempt from this section.

Section 203 requires that each pension plan provide a vesting period for employee benefits. This means an employee shall be entitled to certain retirement benefits after working a certain number of years. If the employee quits or is discharged, he or she does not give up any accrued benefits. The law establishes a formula for awarding benefits. For example, an employee with five years of service gets twenty-five percent of the employer's payments and all of his or her personal payments into the plan. After fifteen years of service, an employee gets one hundred percent of his or her own and the employer's contributions. Neither the union nor the management can bargain for eligibility or vesting rules different from those established in ERISA.

2. Funding. Every employee pension benefit plan must follow certain funding formulas. This insures that an adequate amount of money will be in the pension fund to meet future disbursements to retired workers. For most pension plans, the law requires contributions that cover the normal cost of operating the plan for the year, the cost of amortizing past liabilities of the plan that were not funded adequately, the cost of amortizing the accrued liability for future retirement benefits, and the cost of any losses in investing the accumulated fund. The statute lists precise formulas for determining the amortization periods. Management and unions can bargain for different funding formulas, subject to approval by the Secretary of the Treasury.

3. *Reporting.* Retirement plans can be administered by the employer, the union, or a financial institution, such as an insurance company or bank. The administrator of each plan must file certain reports. These include:

a. Every employee and beneficiary participating in the pension plan must receive a summary of the plan. This summary must be written in simple language and contain an accurate statement of the plan's terms. It must contain the eligibility requirements, disqualification procedures, and funding techniques.

b. The government and all participants must receive an annual report. This report must include an audited financial statement of the plan's investments and an actuarial statement of its funding formulas. These reports must be signed by a certified public accountant and an enrolled actuary. The financial statement must detail the fund's assets and liabilities, and changes in the fund's balances and financial position at the end of the year. It must contain explanations about any self dealings by administrators, transactions with any parties who have an interest in the fund, and any loans in default. The act sets up auditing and actuarial standards for making these reports.

c. Each administrator shall give to participants a statement of his or her total benefits and the nonforfeitable portion of these pension benefits. Each of the reports discussed here becomes public information, available to both union and management personnel.

4. *Penalties.* Every pension plan must hire a fiduciary to control and manage the plan. Either the employer or the union can designate who this person shall be. The fiduciary must establish procedures for carrying out the plan's funding in accordance with the formulas written in the statute. In addition, the fiduciary must hire a trustee to manage the plan's assets. Both the fiduciary and trustee must perform their duties with the care, skill, and diligence that a prudent person would use in controlling his or her own property. ERISA prohibits the trustee from using the plan's assets improperly, such as investing or using the assets for the benefit of any party who has any interest in the plan. But, the act does permit the trustee to invest in the employer's business. Any person who violates this fiduciary duty

shall be personally liable to make good any losses resulting from mismanagement. For self-protection, the person acting as trustee can and should obtain insurance.

Any person who wilfully violates any part of this law may be fined up to $5,000 or imprisoned not more than one year or both. The fine may be increased to $100,000 if a financial institution controls the plan.

The government or any participant in the plan can sue to enforce any part of this law. An administrator of the plan can be ordered to pay up to $100 per day to the participant for any refusal to comply with any part of this law. If the trustee makes improper investments, then it can be penalized up to five percent of the amount involved.

Also, the Secretary of Labor has the power to investigate any aspect of the pension plan's operations. He or she has the powers of any investigative agency to inspect the records, reports, and data of any pension plan. Also, the secretary has authority to issue regulations interpreting this law.

UNION-MANAGEMENT GUIDELINES

Labor relations is one area where managers of unions and companies must consult with the law specialist for advice. Even with this expert advice, however, good employee relations require that all company and union managers know the collective bargaining laws. The following are some guidelines managers must follow to minimize employee grievances and his or her liability for violations of the law.

1. A committee should be created to help department or plant managers understand collective bargaining procedures. This committee should be composed of the company's legal counsel, personnel manager, the chief financial officer, and the chief executive of the firm. It should maintain liaison with operating managers in plants and other work centers. The principle functions of the committee should be the establishment of a uniform labor policy for the company, the coordination of information released to the news media and employees, and consultation with operating managers.

The union should form a similar committee, composed of its chief legal officer, its wage and salary analyst, and top union management. The committee should coordinate bargaining strategy and keep the public, its union stewards, and its membership informed about collective bargaining progress.

2. If a union seeks recognition as bargaining agent for employees, the management committee must determine the union's legal status. The union committee should ask the NLRB to hold an election. If the union does not, then the employer should not bargain with it.

3. The NLRB will determine the appropriate bargaining unit for employees. Restrictions prevent professional workers from joining the same unit as nonprofessional employees and guards from belonging to the same unit as other employees. Both the union and management committees must accept the unit formed by the workers, subject to these conditions.

4. Unions may conduct a campaign to enlist support among the employees. Activities by the union and management are restricted by law. Managers can state opposition to a union, list the benefits now available to workers, point out the costs and risks inherent in union membership, inform employees of their rights to reject a union, and state that the company can hire replacements if workers stage an economic

strike. However, managers cannot promise any benefits to workers for rejecting a union, threaten to take away benefits if employees approve a union, refuse to bargain with representatives, warn employees that the company will close down if they vote for a union, or issue any statement falsely linking the union with violence and crime. The company must permit employees to set up a picket line, provided it is for a legal purpose and carried out in a legal manner. The union committee should carefully monitor all management activities to see that they comply with the law. Special observers should be selected for each department or plant.

5. The committees should circulate lists of permitted and prohibited conduct by managers and hold periodic meetings to reinforce the impact of these lists.

6. Negotiations between management and the union should be carried on by a skilled team, whose members have substantial experience in collective bargaining. Outside professional staff may be needed. Certainly, members of both committees should take an active part in negotiations through policy formation, informational research, and news releases. The negotiating teams must meet at reasonable times and places.

7. The employer must negotiate over wages, hours, and other working conditions. This list of bargainable items includes wage rates, overtime pay, union recognition, union security, holidays, seniority systems, grievance procedures, fringe benefits, and arbitration procedures. The law limits bargaining over closed shop contracts, hot cargo arrangements and non-work-related issues. ERISA prohibits management and unions from bargaining over some aspects of pension programs.

8. Copies of the collective bargaining agreements negotiated between management and the union should be made available to all top-ranking employees and union officials. Summaries should be prepared for other employees. Special efforts should be taken to explain its terms to the public. Managers and union officials should be urged to follow its terms precisely and to consult with their committees if they have any doubts or questions.

REVIEW QUESTIONS

1. Define a strike, and state when courts can issue an injunction stopping it.

2. Discuss the rights of workers when engaged in each kind of strike mentioned in this chapter.

3. Explain how picketing is part of an employee's right to free speech protected under the Constitution.

4. Outline the major sections of the Landrum Griffin Act. Why was it enacted by Congress?

5. Summarize the major requirements of the federal pension reform law. Explain how this law affects union-management negotiations.

6. Explain the fiduciary duty of pension administrators.

7. Discuss some ways management can improve its relations with its union.

8. A business agent was discharged from his office because he was disloyal to the union. The facts showed that at a recent union meeting, the business agent publicly criticized the policies of the union president, who had asked the union membership to support two members under criminal indictment. Was the discharge binding on the business agent?

9. Maritime Union amended its constitution to require that all candidates for national office in the union had to hold some other office in the union. Prior to its adoption, there had been contests for almost every national office in the union. After adoption of the amendment, there was little opposition for any office. The union argues the change is necessary to assure that only qualified people hold office. Is this argument enough to uphold the amendment?

10. Is it valid for a union to strike or picket to force an employer to discharge a worker who was assessed a fine by the union but who refused to pay it? Can a union strike or picket to induce an employer to make a contribution to a union-named charity as a penalty for employing a worker who is not in good standing with the union?

14

OCCUPATIONAL INJURIES

Laborin' man an' laborin' woman
Hev one glory an' one shame;
Ev'y thin' thets' done inhuman
Injers all on' em the same.
(James Russell Lowell, The Biglow Papers, *Series I, 1848, No. 1, Stanza 10.)*

Before the industrial revolution, job-related injuries were not a serious problem. Most people worked in farming or in cottage industries. Each of these occupations employed mostly family members at or near the home. Employees were nonexistent, although a few workers might be hired on a temporary basis. The head of the family assumed financial obligations for injuries suffered by any of these workers. But with so few workers, doing simple tasks, the number and severity of injuries were small.

With the development of new machines and work methods, the size of manufacturing operations increased. New looms for weaving textiles demanded work places larger than the home. Steel making raised new hazards for workers. Assembly line operations increased the likelihood of boredom. To produce the output required to transform a rural society into an industrial one, concentrations of inexpensive laborers were needed—people who worked long hours to keep costs down. This combination of tired, bored workers doing routine tasks in large factories surrounded by fast-moving complex machinery drastically increased the number and severity of job-related injuries. A need existed for some type of legislation to remedy this situation. In response, two types of laws were passed: workmen's compensation laws and occupational safety and health acts. Each of these laws will be discussed in this chapter.

WORKMEN'S COMPENSATION

By 1900, the accident rate in American factories reached alarming proportions. Under the laws existing at that time, injured employees could sue their employers for compensation for these injuries. But the employer had two major defenses to minimize liability. First, if the employee was at fault in causing the injury, then the employer was not liable because of contributory negligence or assumption of risk. Second, if another employee was at fault in causing the injury, then the employer could escape liability by pleading the fellow-servant rule. Statistics reveal that most worker lawsuits were dismissed for one of these reasons.

A minority of the injured employees could sue their employers. However, suing required a lawyer to process the case, testimony of witnesses to support the worker's allegations, and money to pay the fees and expenses of a trial. Only wealthy factory workers could assume this burden. If the worker did sue, the employer frequently discharged those employees who testified for the worker. And the money awarded by the courts to successful plaintiffs varied with each case. A worker was never certain how much money he or she would receive. The advocacy skills of the attorney frequently were more convincing than the seriousness of a worker's injury.

For those who could not sue, a more serious fate awaited. Those who were cripled by their injuries could no longer work and they were discharged. A welfare system did not exist, so these former workers often turned to criminal activities in order to survive. Most became a burden on society and a threat to the lives and safety of other citizens. Governmental action was necessary to remove this danger. Under the inherent police powers permitting the government to pass any reasonable laws necessary for the protection of public health and safety, governments passed laws shifting the financial burden for accidental injuries from the employee to the employer. The cost of these injuries was to be treated as a business cost, to be paid ultimately by the consumer through a slightly higher price for products. An injured worker should be compensated for injuries occurring at work.

The first American law taking this approach was the Federal Act of 1908. This law awarded compensation to laborers injured while working on federal government construction projects. Compensation was paid for up to one year of disability. No moneys were paid if the injured worker was at fault in causing the injury. The first state law to compensate workers for injuries was the Massachusetts Workmen's Compensation Act of 1911. Today, all states have adopted workmen's compensation statutes, although the federal government has not adopted a comprehensive law covering all American workers. Since these laws protecting workers are different in each state, it is not possible to discuss them in any detail. But there are some basic similarities among all the state plans. We can make some general comments about the common elements and indicate the basic weakness in all state workmen's compensation laws.

A workmen's compensation law is a plan for paying workers or their dependents money for injuries or physical disabilities caused as a direct result of their employment. The plans are compensation acts, substituting for the lawsuit the employee's right to recover money at specified rates for injuries. Payments are made for all accidental injuries, regardless of the fault or negligence of the worker. These laws provide cash to an injured worker, but do not make the employer an insurer of the employees' safety. Amounts paid to workers are fixed by state law, either at a definite dollar sum for each type of injury or at a percentage of the worker's weekly wage. However, a worker receives more than lost wages. Compensation includes money for medical, doctor, hospital, and rehabilitation expenses as well as payments for diminished earning capacity as a result of the injury. No money is awarded for pain and suffering incurred as a result of the injury, disfigurement, or loss of services by the worker's spouse.

COLLECTION PROCEDURES

The procedure for recovering compensation is relatively quick, inexpensive, and perhaps more humane than having to sue. To collect damages for a job-related injury, the worker must first notify the employer of the injury. This notification gives the employer an opportunity to correct any safety hazard and to investigate the circumstances surrounding the injury. Failure to give this notice may result in a denial of any benefits from the law. After the employer's investigation, payment is often made.

If the employer refuses to make satisfactory payments to the worker, then a claim for compensation must be filed with the state's workmen's compensation board. This administrative agency exists in each state, created by the legislature to adjudicate disputes between an injured worker and the employer. The agency has several members, appointed by either the governor or the legislature. Upon receipt of the claim, the board will hold a hearing to determine the merits of the employee's case. This hearing acts in place of a trial, saving the parties the expenses of judicial delay, court costs, and attorney fees. Hearings held by the board do not follow court procedures, but more closely resemble administrative agency procedures. State law establishes these procedures, but subject to review by the courts.

At the hearing, the employee must prove his or her case by a preponderance of the evidence. The employee must show that an accident happened, directly causing an injury to the claimant while he or she was acting in the scope of employment. Next, the employee must prove the degree and amount of disability, medical expenses, and other costs incurred. The types of injuries for which a worker can receive compensation are broad. The case of *Wolf* v. *Sibley, Lindsay and Curr Co.*, 369 N.Y.S. 2d 637 (1975), is a good example. In this case, the employee suffered acute depressive reactions following the discovery of his supervisor's body immediately after the supervisor committed suicide. In a suit seeking to recover workmen's compensation benefits denied by the compensation board, the N.Y. Court of Appeals stated:

> The focus of inquiry is whether or not there has been an accidental injury within the meaning of the Workmen's Compensation Law. Since there is no statutory definition of this term, the court examines the relevant decisions. These may be divided into three categories: (1) psychic trauma that produces physical injury, (2) physical impact that produces psychological injury and (3) psychic trauma that produces psychological injury. As to the first class of injury, this court has consistently recognized the principle that an injury caused by emotional stress or shock may be accidental within the purview of the compensation law. Cases falling into the second category have uniformly sustained awards to those incurring nervous or psychological disorders as a result of physical impact. As to cases in the third category the decisions are not clear.
>
> Of those cases dealing with psychic trauma causing psychological injury, *Chernin* v. *Progressive Service Co.*, 9 N.Y. 2d 880, is the only one to have reached this court. There, a cab driver sought workmen's compensation benefits for a paranoid schizophrenic condition allegedly resulting after his cab struck a pedestrian. Benefits were denied on the ground that the claimant's psychic injury was a surfacing of prior internal emotional conflicts that he had previously been able to suppress. The opinion left unanswered the question of whether an occurrence arising out of and in the course of employment which causes psychological trauma may be compensated even though there was no physical injury.
>
> A few months later, this court decided *Matter of Klimas* v. *Trans Caribbean Airways*, 10 N.Y. 2d 209, which reinstated an award for a heart attack caused by work related anxiety and stress, and *Battalla* v. *N.Y.S.*, 10 N.Y. 2d 237, which eliminated the impact doctrine in the field of torts. These holdings have eroded the underpinnings of *Chernin*.
>
> Subsequently, *Matter of Straws* v. *Fail*, 17 A.D.2d 998, percolated

through the courts. This case involved a claim for compensation by a billiard hall porter who was asked by his employer to accompany a fellow employee to the hospital. En route the coemployee collapsed and died in the claimant's arms. As a result, the employee suffered psychoneurosis and was unable to work for a year. The court denied recovery, citing its own opinion in *Chernin*. Shortly thereafter a motion for leave to appeal was denied, thus giving rise to a degree of uncertainty.

This court holds today that psychological or nervous injury percipitated by psychic trauma is compensable to the same extent as physical injury. This determination is based on two considerations. First, there is nothing in the nature of stress or shock situation that ordains physical as opposed to psychological injury. The determinative factor is the particular vulnerability of an individual by virtue of his physical make-up. In a given situation one person may be suspectible to a heart attack while another may suffer depressive reaction. In either case the result is the same—the individual is incapable of functioning properly because of an accident—and should be compensated under the Workmen's Compensation Law.

Second, having recognized the reliability of identifying psychic trauma as a causative factor of injury in some cases and the reliability by identifying psychological injury as a resultant factor in other cases, the court sees no reason for limiting recovery in the latter instance to cases involving physical impact.

Upon presentation of the claimant's case, the employer can present any defense it has for denying the claim. Possible defenses are discussed below. The hearing officers on the board will then issue their decision. In this decision, the board will state which facts it thinks were proven by the parties and its interpretations of the law as applied to the claim, and then grant or deny money to the worker. Moneys awarded to the worker may come directly from an insurance fund operated by the employer or from a private insurance company. In some states, the money can come from the state, out of a fund into which all employers have made contributions.

Either party can appeal to the appropriate state court. The appellate court will review the board's findings and decision. As with all administrative agencies, findings of fact by the board are presumed conclusive on appeal. This means the state court can reverse the board only if it did not follow fair procedures established by the state legislature or if it did not apply the law correctly.

An injured worker generally has no other choice than to claim workmen's compensation benefits. Most states do not allow a worker to sue the employer for injuries. However, if a third party caused the employee's injuries, some states give the worker a choice. Either a lawsuit can be filed against the third part or a compensation claim can be filed against the employer. The employee cannot recover in full from both parties and any recovery from the employer permits the employer to sue the third party for indemnification.

Banks v. Chicago Grain Trimmers Ass'n
390 U.S. 495 (1968)

Mr. Justice Stewart

On January 30, 1961, shortly after returning home from work, the petitioner's husband suffered a fall that resulted in his death on February 12. On February 20, 1961, the petitioner on behalf of herself and her three minor children filed a claim against her husband's employer, the respondent, for compensation death benefits under the Worker's Compensation Act. The petitioner alleged that her husband's fall on January 30 had resulted from a work-connected injury suffered on January 26.

On September 8, 1961, the petitioner began a wrongful death action in federal court against a third party, the Norris Grain Company, alleging that her husband's fall resulted from an accident caused by it. On May 3, 1963, a jury returned a verdict of $30,000 for the petitioner in that lawsuit.

Three issues were argued in this Court, only one of which is relevant here. The Workers' Compensation Act permits an individual entitled to compensation to sue a third party for damages. If no such suit is brought and compensation is accepted from the employer under an award, the rights of the employee against the third party are assigned to the employer. If, as in this case, a suit is brought against a third party, the employer is liable in compensation only to the extent that allowable compensating benefits exceed the recovery from the third party.

EMPLOYER DEFENSES

Prior to the workmen's compensation laws, an employer could raise several objections to a suit for damages arising from a worker's on-the-job injury. First, the employer could raise contributory negligence if the worker was at fault in causing the injury. Second, the employer could assert assumption of risk if the worker knowingly worked in a hazardous area. Third, the employer could allege the fellow-servent rule if the worker's injuries were caused by a coworker.

An employer loses these defenses under workmen's compensation laws. Payments must be made even if the worker was careless in causing the injury, knowingly worked in a dangerous area, or was inured as a result of a coworker's negligence. A worker receives money regardless of fault. Workmen's compensation acts are the first "no fault" laws, a concept now advocated for automobile liability, divorce proceedings, and professional malpractice claims. Under compensation laws, an employer does have certain defenses. Some of these are:

1. Wilful. If an employee intentionally injures him or herself in order to collect benefits, then an employer has no obligation to pay. A person should not benefit from personal wrongdoing.

2. Intoxication. An employee who suffers an injury because he or she is drunk, from either drugs or alcohol, will be denied benefits. But if an employer knows or should know that a worker is intoxicated yet still assigns work, liability may exist.

3. Exempt Worker. The compensation laws do not cover all workers. Volunteers, temporary workers, and independent contractors are not covered by the typical state workmen's compensation law. Also, some workers are covered by different laws. For example, motor carrier employees, railroad workers, seamen, longshoremen, members of the armed forces, and federal employees have different statutes protecting them.

4. Scope of Employment. An injured worker must be acting in the scope of his or her employment when injured to receive benefits under the law. To determine when an employee is working for the employer, the employment contract must be examined to see what duties the employee has and how those duties can be carried out. If the worker is acting for the benefit of the employer at the time of injury, then he or she is acting in the scope of employment and money can be awarded. Acts that some courts consider to be within the scope of employment are lunch time, commuting time, and wash-up time. The facts of each situation must be analyzed carefully to see if the injury-causing activity is covered by compensation.

O'Leary v. Brown-Pacific-Maxon, Inc. (BPM)
340 U.S. 504 (1951)

Mr. Justice Frankfurter.

This is an action against the deputy commissioner of compensation by BPM to enjoin enforcement of a compensation award for the death of one of its employees. The employee drowned while attempting to rescue endangered swimmers at an employer-owned and operated recreational area for its employees on Guam. The District Court sustained the award, but the Court of Appeals reversed, stating the employee was not engaged in the scope of his employment when death occurred.

Workmen's compensation is not confined by the common law concepts of scope of employment. The test of recovery is not a causal relation between the nature of employment and the accident. Nor is it whether the employer is benefited by the act causing the injury. All that is required is that the obligation or condition of employment create the zone of special danger out of which the injury arose. A reasonable rescue attempt at an employer-owned recreational facility especially operated for employees, near a shoreline declared dangerous for swimmers, is a covered act in the scope of employment.

CASE QUESTIONS

1. Define the scope of employment as used in workmen's compensation acts.
2. Contrast this definition of scope of employment with that used in agency law. In the case, this definition is referred to as coming from the common law.

An example of a typical state workmen's compensation plan is that of the state of Connecticut. (Connecticut General Statutes, Secs. 31–284, 307, 309.)

Basic rights and liabilities

(a) An employer shall not be liable to any action for damages on account of personal injury sustained by an employee arising out of and in the course of his employment or on account of death resulting from personal injury so sustained, but an employer shall secure compensation for his employees as follows, except that compensation shall not be paid when the personal injury has been caused by the wilful and serious misconduct of the injured imployee or by his intoxication. All rights and claims between employer and employees, or any representatives or dependents of such employees, arising out of personal injury or death sustained in the course of employment as aforesaid are abolished other than rights and claims given by this chapter, provided nothing herein shall prohibit any employee from securing, by agreement with his employer, additional benefits from his employer for such injury or from enforcing such agreement for additional benefits.

(b) Each employer who does not furnish to the compensation commissioner satisfactory proof of his solvency and financial ability to pay directly to injured employees or other beneficiaries compensation provided by this chapter shall insure his full liability in one of the following ways: (1) By filing with the insurance commissioner in form acceptable to him security guaranteeing the performance of the obligations of this chapter by such employer; or (2) by insuring his full liability under this part in such stock or mutual companies or associations as are or may be authorized to take such risks in this state; or (3) by such combination of the above-mentioned two methods as he may choose, subject to the approval of the insurance commissioner. If the employer wilfully fails to conform to any provision of this subsection, he shall be fined not more than one thousand dollars for each such failure. In case of an alleged noncompliance with the provisions of this subsection, a certificate of noncompliance under oath, by the chairman of the commission, shall constitute prima facie evidence of noncompliance.

Compensation for total incapacity

If any injury for which conpensation is provided under the provisions of this chapter results in total incapacity to work, there shall be paid to the injured employee a weekly compensation equal to sixty-six and two-thirds per cent of his average weekly earnings at the time of the injury; but the compensation shall in no case be more than the maximum weekly benefit rate set forth in section 31–309 for the year in which the injury occurred, or less than twenty dollars weekly; and such compensation shall not continue longer than the period of total incapacity. The following-described injuries of any person shall be considered as causing total incapacity and compensation shall be paid accordingly:

(a) Total and permanent loss of sight of both eyes, or the reduction to one-tenth or less of normal vision;

(b) the loss of both feet at or above the ankle;

(c) the loss of both hands at or above the wrist;

(d) the loss of one foot at or above the ankle and one hand at or above the wrist;

(e) any injury resulting in permanent and complete paralysis of the legs or arms or of one leg and one arm;

(f) any injury resulting in incurable imbecility or mental illness; but an employee who has suffered the loss or loss of the use of one of the members of his body, or part of one of the members of his body, or the reduction of vision in one eye to one-tenth or less of normal vision, shall not receive compensation for the later injury in excess of the compensation allowed for such injury when considered by itself and not in conjunction with the previous incapacity except as hereinafter provided.

Maximum weekly compensation. Determination of average weekly earnings of production and related workers in manufacturing

The weekly conpensation received by an injured employee under the provisions of this chapter shall in no case be more than sixty-six and two-thirds per cent, raised to the next even dollar, of the average weekly earnings of production and related workers in manufacturing in the state as hereinafter defined for the year in which the injury occurred. The average weekly earnings of production and related workers in manufacturing in the state shall be determined by the labor commissioner on or before the fifteenth day of August of each year, to be effective the following October first, and shall be the average of the manufacturing production and related workers' weekly earnings for the year ending the previous June thirtieth and shall be so determined in accordance with the standards for the determination of average weekly earnings of production and related workers in manufacturing established by the United States department of labor, bureau of labor statistics.

OCCUPATIONAL SAFETY AND HEALTH LAWS

More than thirty years experience with state workmen's compensation laws allows us to evaluate their effectiveness. Their main objective was fulfilled. A quick and inexpensive way of giving compensation to injured employees exists. But the amounts awarded often do not reflect the costs of an injury and amounts vary from state to state for the same type of injury.

A more serious problem is with the injuries themselves. These laws did nothing to stop worker injuries. The number of such injuries continued to grow into unacceptable proportions. Workmen's compensation paid for injuries after they happened. These laws did not prevent job injuries. Some of the larger employers did institute safety programs to cut accident rates and thereby lower insurance premiums. But not all employers took enough action. New laws were needed. However, it was not until the 1970s that such new laws were adopted. Then Congress enacted the Occupational Safety and Health Act to reduce the alarming accident rate in the work place.

Studies conducted by special congressional committees showed that employee injuries and diseases caused by unsafe working conditions resulted in $1.5 million yearly in lost wages. On-the-job injuries caused the nation's gross national product to decline by $8 billion in 1969. Fifteen thousand deaths and over 200,000 injuries occurred each year to American workers. Between the years 1965 and 1970, ten times as many work days were lost to job injuries as to strikes. As the study pointed out, there was an elaborate machinery to prevent labor disputes yet nothing to reduce job injuries. To halt the spread and cost of job-related injuries, to reduce the medical disability expenses, and to prevent lost production, Congress enacted the Occupational Safety and Health Act (OSHA). This comprehensive act encourages employers and employees to reduce job hazards through voluntary cooperation. To aid in this cooperative effort, the federal law establishes some rights and duties for each group.

EMPLOYER DUTIES

OSHA imposes a number of costly duties on employers:

1. General Duty. Every employer covered by the act is to furnish each of its employees a work place free from recognized hazards that may cause death or serious harm. Congress left this general duty vague because it thought precise standards covering all situations leading to injury or death could not be defined in advance. Thus, the employer has an affirmative duty to act on its own to remedy safety violations. Also, this duty exists in addition to any obligation under state workmen's compensation laws and state safety acts.

2. Safety Standards. Every employer subject to the act is to comply with safety and health standards established by the Occupational Safety and Health Administration, also referred to as OSHA. This administration is a regulatory agency reporting to the Secretary of Labor, responsible for creating, reviewing, and enforcing safety standards for the work place. (See the organizational chart for the Department of Labor on page 272.) Most of these standards come from national safety organizations, such as the National Fire Protection Association and the National Standards Institute. Others come from standards formulated in other federal laws, such as the Walsh Healy Construction Safety Act. OSHA standards have the force and effect of law and are therefore enforceable as any other law. However, compliance with these standards can be difficult for employers. Standards are written in technical language, often unclear even to experts in the safety field. Consider the definition of an "exit" required by OSHA standards for all work places. This definition must use the word exit to define an exit.

> "... that portion of a means of egress between the termination of an exit and a public way, ... a continuous and unobstructed way of exit travel from any point in a building or structure to a public way and consists of three separate and distinct parts: the way of exit access, the exit, and the way of exit discharge. A means of egress comprises the vertical and horizontal ways of travel and shall include intervening room spaces, doorways, hallways, corridors, passageways, balconies, ramps, stairs, enclosures, exits, escalators, horizontal exits, courts and yards. (quoted in *Tax Review*, August, 1975.)

3. Record Keeping. Employers must maintain several types of records relating to job safety. They are necessary so the government can check on employer compliance with the law and to indicate needed revisions in safety standards. Employers must keep a log of occupational injuries and a supplementary record on each specific injury suffered by a worker while on the job and publish an annual summary of all injuries. These reports are filed with the Department of Labor and are open to public inspection. Any accident causing death or resulting in injury to five or more persons must be reported. Employers must give notices advising workers of their rights under this law. Reports on worker physical examinations must also be kept to see if their exposure to dangerous conditions exceeds safety standards.

4. Safety Programs. The law encourages an employer to conduct periodic inspections of its work places to discover job hazards. This means that a top management person should establish a safety program. This program must evaluate an employer's current state of compliance with the safety standards, determine what improvements are needed, and make all necessary changes. A safety checklist should be developed for each work activity and utilized to monitor continually the work place for compliance with safety standards. Well-defined safety rules should be established and employees must be educated in safety procedures.

5. Inspections. Inspection of the work place by an OSHA compliance officer is of critical importance for the act's effectiveness. Each employer must admit this officer to any work area, without delay but at reasonable times, to conduct inspections and to interview employees. The employer must give this officer all relevant records, reports, safety programs, and safety rules. The officer can inspect the work place, issue citations for any violations of safety standards, and review proposed remedies with the employer. An employer must cooperate with the inspection or face legal sanctions. Most inspections are made without prior notice to the employer.

The inspection officer may need a search warrant to make an investigation if the employer does not permit it. The Supreme Court will have to decide this issue. In one recent case, *Brennan* v. *Gibson's Products, Inc.*, 407 F. Supp. 154 (1976), a federal district court in Texas overruled a warrantless inspection of a manufacturing plant. The judge stated: "OSHA's sweep is broad. Made subject to its warrantless inspections is every private concern engaged in business affecting commerce.... As a basis for imposing [inspections], Congress found that work injuries and illnesses burden commerce substantially in various evident ways. This [right of inspection], based upon such generalized conclusions does not comply with 4th Amendment standards. There is no need to invalidate the OSHA inspection procedures. The statute authorizes entries without delay, it does not explicitly authorize warrantless searches.... This court believes Congress intended to authorize objected to OSHA inspections only when made by a search warrant issued by a U.S. magistrate or other judicial officer ... under probable cause standards appropriate to administrative searches." See *In Re Accu Namics, Inc.* (below) for a conflicting view.

6. Penalties. The act imposes both civil and criminal penalties for violations of its sanctions or standards. An employer can be fined up to $10,000 for each wilful or repeated violation of safety standards. If the employer fails to correct a violation or fails to publish required notices, it can be fined up to $1,000. For wilful violations of this act resulting in death to an employee, an employer can be criminally fined up to $10,000 and/or imprisoned up to six months. For second offenses, the fines and jail terms double. Any person who informs an employer about a planned inspection by a compliance officer can be fined up to $1,000 and/or imprisoned up to six months. These penalties are in addition to those established in state safety laws. But Congress did not give workers any rights to sue an employer for safety violations.

In setting the amount of the penalty, the law requires the OSHA to consider four factors: the size of the business, the seriousness of the violation, the good faith of the employer, and the prior history of previous violations by the employer.

EMPLOYER RIGHTS

The act gives the employer certain rights:

1. Creation of Standards. Safety standards must be developed by the Occupational Safety and Health Administration in cooperation with other sources. It relies upon advice from government agencies, private testing laboratories, and the National Advisory Committee on Occupational Safety and Health. This committee has twelve members representing labor, management, the public, and the safety profession. Through this committee, an employer can present views on any existing or proposed safety standard. Also, all proposed standards must be published in the Federal Register before they can become effective. Employers have an opportunity to comment on them. They may request a public hearing. Employers should use this method for presenting their opinions on safety standards.

2. *Variances.* If an employer determines it is unable to comply with a particular safety standard, then it may request a variance. If OSHA grants the variance, then the employer does not have to comply with the disputed safety standard. To obtain a variance, the employer must show that it is unable to comply with the standard, that it is taking all available steps to safeguard employees against the hazards covered by the standard, and that it has an effective program for coming into compliance with the standards. Variances may be granted for up to one year and can be renewed. Any variance necessary for national defense reasons can be granted for up to six months.

3. *Inspections.* During an inspection of the work place, an employer has several rights. First, the employer can insist the compliance officer time his or her visit at a reasonable hour. Second, the employer can require the officer to conduct the inspection in a reasonable manner with due regard for production. Third, the employer can review the officer's identification and other credentials before permitting the inspection. Fourth, the employer can present evidence of its good faith compliance with the act, citing its existing safety programs and rules. Fifth, the employer or its representative can accompany the officer on the inspection and explain any aspects of existing safety procedures. Sixth, after the inspection, the employer can request copies of the officer's findings. Each violation of a safety standard discovered by the officer must be discussed with the employer and a time period established for its remedy. Within six months, the employer will be advised if a citation will be issued. This citation must be in writing, describing the violation, stating the proposed remedy, and notifying the employer of any penalty to be imposed.

In Re Accu Namics, Inc.,
17936 CCH Employment Safety and Health Guide (1974)

Cleary, Commissioner.

Accu Namics is a Texas corporation engaged in the business of installing underground water and sewer pipes. The primary piece of protective equipment used by the corporation was a portable steel frame and steel sheeted box, referred to as a trench shield. On the afternoon of January 18, a cave-in occurred in which four workers were killed. About one hour after the cave-in, a compliance officer who was in the area and had heard about the accident came over to the worksite which was along a public street. A large crowd had gathered at the site and a general state of confusion existed. The compliance officer did not identify himself to the superintendent when he first arrived, but later in the afternoon he did inform the superintendent who he was.

On January 27, 1972, the corporation was cited for an alleged serious violation. A hearing was convened on May 30, 1972, at which time the parties were given an opportunity to present evidence as to the existence of the alleged violation. On October 25, the administrative law judge, James Burroughs vacated the citation and proposed penalty, finding that the secretary did not comply with the act as well as with his own regulations and procedural guidelines by failing to advise the corporation of the inspection until it was completed. The secretary appealed to the Occupational Safety and Health Review Commission (OSHRC).

The commission holds that a search warrant is not required where the premises are open to the public, since merely observing what is open to the public does not constitute a search. In the present case trenching operations were being conducted along a public street in order to lay a sewer pipe. The work area was accessible to the public view. Under these circumstances, the corporation had no reasonable expectation of privacy and the compliance officer did not need a warrant to enter the work place. Once on the work place, he merely observed what any other person could have observed.

We construe the section concerning the presentation of credentials to be mandatory only when the Fourth Amendment would bar a warrantless search and thus when notice of authority is required. Inasmuch as the workplace was open to the public, there was no mandatory requirement that credentials be presented and there was no abuse in discretion in failing to do so.

Even if there were a requirement that credentials be presented in the present case, in our view, the compliance officer substantially complied with this requirement. The obvious purpose of presentation of credentials is identification. The record indicates that within about one hour after arriving at the jobsite, the compliance officer verbally identified himself to the foreman. The mechanical task of displaying one's official credentials merely constitutes the corroboration of a verbal identification. Although presentation of credentials is the express statutory term, it is only one means of identification. The essential objective of identification at the earliest practical opportunity has been satisfied.

Upon a thorough examination of the record, we conclude that the corporation was in serious violation of the act. In so doing, we specifically adopt the judge's finding of fact. We also agree with the secretary's determination that the violation be characterized as serious. Four of the corporation's employees were fatally injured as a result of the cave-in. In addition, the corporation knew or should have known that the trench shield alone was an inadequate means of protection and that the soil was unstable and a cave-in could result. Thus the criteria for a serious violation have been met.

With respect to the penalty, we have considered the four factors established in the act and we accept the advice of the secretary and assess a penalty of $500.

CASE QUESTIONS

1. Describe how the inspection was made in this case.
2. The employer has a right to be informed of an inspection and can insist on identification of the compliance officer. How was that statutory right fulfilled in this case?

---

4. Trade Secrets. During the inspection, the employer should be prepared to identify the areas in its establishment that contain trade secrets. Once these areas have been identified to the compliance officer, all information pertaining to the trade secrets must be kept confidential.

5. Contesting the Citation. After the employer receives the citation, it has fifteen working days to notify OSHA that it intends to contest the citation, the proposed penalties, or the proposed time period for remedying the violation. If not so notified within the fifteen day period, the government will finalize the terms of the citation and impose the penalties. If the employer decides to contest the citation, it must post a copy of the citation near the place of the alleged violation and notify employees and OSHA of its decision to contest. Shortly thereafter, lawyers for the Department of Labor will file a complaint against the employer with the Occupational Safety and Health Review Commission (OSHRC). This commission is an independent regulatory agency set up to adjudicate citation contests and employee safety complaints. It consists of three members, appointed by the President and confirmed by the Senate. OSHRC has those powers and limitations of adjudicatory agencies discussed in Part I of this book.

The employer must answer the complaint filed by the Department of Labor. The commission will set a date for a hearing before an administrative law judge assigned by the commission. At this hearing, the government must prove that a violation of some safety standard occurred and that employees were exposed to the hazardous condition. Lawyers for the employer can challenge the reason-

TABLE 14-1. MAJOR FUNCTIONAL OFFICES IN THE OCCUPATIONAL SAFETY AND HEALTH REVIEW COMMISSION

Chairman
Commissioners
Chief Legal Counsel
Administrative Law Judges
Executive Director
Executive Secretary
Chief Review Counsel
Directors: Management Systems
           Information and Publication

Source: U.S. Government Manual, 1975-76 Edition.

ableness of the standard, explain the precautions taken to minimize the hazard, or protest the reasonableness of proposed penalties. During the hearing, each party may call its own witnesses, introduce evidence, and cross-examine witnesses.

After the hearing, the law judge will issue his or her findings, either upholding the citation or dismissing it. Either side may appeal these findings to OSHRC. That body will review the entire proceeding. Following action by this Commission, either party may appeal to the federal court of appeals and the Supreme Court. As with other administrative agencies, its findings of fact are presumed valid on appeal.

In Re Luther Marvin Robbins
17,045 CCH Employment Safety and Health Guide (1975)

Moran, Chairman.

On September 19, 1972, Judge Dern issued his decision and order in this case holding that the company had violated the Occupational Safety and Health Act of 1970 in that it failed to comply with Occupational Safety and Health standards. He assessed a penalty of $900 for the violation.

On October 18, 1972, that decision was directed for review by the commission. The commission has reviewed the entire record in this case including the briefs filed by the parties. Based upon that review we affirm the decision and order of the judge.

In our opinion the judge properly raised the penalty proposed by the Secretary of Labor from $750 to $900, giving heavy weight to the gravity of the violation—using an aluminum ladder close to an energized power line and making no effort to eliminate the electrical hazard. When a proposed penalty is contested, the secretary's proposed penalty has advisory force only; the commission is not bound by the advisory action of the secretary. Accordingly, the judge's decision and order are affirmed in all respects.

Dissent. The Court of Appeals does not support the commission's conclusion that a penalty can be assessed in an amount higher than that proposed by the Secretary of Labor. On the contrary, it holds only that the commission can reduce or vacate the proposed penalty. When an employer contests an enforcement action initiated against him under this act, he is seeking relief from a certain penalty which will inexorably and automatically be imposed upon him if he fails to contest within the fifteen-day period prescribed in the act. If the facts of the matter developed at a hearing do not warrant any relief, then the penalty proposed by the complainant should stand unchallenged. An employer who exercises his statutory and constitutional right to a hearing should not thereby subject himself to a larger penalty than could be imposed upon him had he not invoked his rights. If this order is allowed to stand, no employer would risk an appeal.

CASE QUESTIONS

1. Explain the safety standard violated by the employer.
2. What effect would this case have on an employer's right of appeal?

---

6. Defenses. In its answer to the complaint filed with the review commission, the employer can raise defenses to the citation. Several are available. First, it may argue that the standards established by OSHA are too vague or technical to apply in its work place. Second, an employer could argue the violation was only a minor one, causing little danger to employees. Third, an employer could assert that existing safety procedures followed by it were adequate to protect employee safety. Last, the employer could contest the reasonableness of the procedures followed by the compliance officer, the penalties assessed, or the time period for remedying the violation. Some employers have tried to argue that employees, customers, or a subcontractor were responsible for a safety violation, not the employer. Courts have rejected this defense, deciding that employers have a duty to require employees, customers, and others to follow safety rules. The employer is responsible even if others fail to observe the rules. Arguments against the constitutionality of the act have also been rejected. The following case from the 5th Circuit U.S. Court of Appeals rejects several such defenses.

Atlas Roofing Co. v. OSHRC
518 F.2d 990 (1975)

Brown, Judge

An employer seeks review of an order of the Occupational Safety and Health Review Commission affirming a penalty assessed by the Secretary of Labor under OSHA. The employer challenges the order not only on the issues of substantive compliance with the federal regulations, but also on the grounds that the basic structure of OSHA is constitutionally defective because (1) the civil penalties under OSHA are really criminal in nature and call for the constitutional protections of the Sixth Amendment and Article III, (2) even if found to be a civil penalty, OSHA violates the Seventh Amendment because there is no jury trial.

The enforcement procedures of OSHA have three stages: citation, administrative hearing, and court review. Each is distinct because unless the employer initiates the next level of review, the penalty becomes final and unreviewable.

The citation procedure begins with an inspector determining that the employer has violated a specific safety standard or the general duty provision requiring the employer to provide a safe working environment. Within a reasonable time thereafter, the Secretary of Labor assesses the penalty and so notifies the employer. For initial violations, an employer may be subject to a $10,000 penalty for wilful violations or for violations that are determined to be serious. Alternatively, criminal proceedings may be triggered by conditions that the secretary considers both wilful and serious, and the employer, upon conviction, is subject to a fine of up to $10,000 and six months in jail.

On receipt of the secretary's citation, an employer has fifteen days to notify the secretary that he intends to challenge the penalty. Once a challenge is made, the secretary is required to initiate the administrative hearing by notifying OSHRC. An administrative law judge conducts the hearing and thereafter makes a report that will itself become the final decision of OSHRC unless the parties seek and the commission grants discretionary review.

The final stage is review in the court of appeals and thereafter the discretionary review by the Supreme Court. The court of appeals review is based on the Administrative Procedures Act "substantial evidence on the record considered as a whole" standard. In *Kennedy v. Mendoza Martinez,* 372 U.S. 144 (1963), the Supreme Court set forth the test for determining when Congress can impose civil rather than criminal sanctions, thus avoiding the constitutional requirements.

The Court summarized seven factors to be considered: (1) whether the sanction involves an affirmative disability or restraint, (2) whether it has historically been regarded as a punishment, (3) whether it comes into play only on a finding of intent, (4) whether its operation will promote the traditional punishment aims of retribution and deterrence, (5) whether the behavior to which it applies is already a crime, (6) whether the sanction has another purpose, and (7) whether it appears excessive in relation to its purpose.

The Supreme Court was aware that this test might point in divergent directions, but each element of the test was considered relevant to a determination of the character of a statute's sanctions. While the civil penalties of OSHA are subject to scrutiny under several of these tests, the court feels that, taken as a whole, they demonstrate that Congress meant the statute to regulate rather than to reprimand. The focus of the statute, the control of jobsite safety practices and health conditions, has a demonstrable and legitimate government concern. When Congress has characterized the remedy as civil and the only consequences of a judgment for the government is a money penalty, the courts have taken Congress at its word.

Failing the Sixth Amendment and Article III hurdle, the employer further argues that even if the penalty is civil, the Seventh Amendment requires that Congress provide a system of enforcement that gives employers the opportunities to put their case before a jury in federal district court. Where adjudicative responsibility rests only in the administering agency, jury trials would be incompatible with the whole concept of administrative adjudication and would substantially interfere with the agency's role in the statutory scheme.

That the civil sanction is in the form of a dollar penalty is not a sufficient distinction to deny the power of Congress to prescribe an administrative rather than a judicial mechanism. To so hold would produce the absurd spectacle of Congress, having full power to prescribe an administrative structure with sanctions of denial or revocation of a life or death license, being denied the power to prescribe a money fine of a single dollar.

CASE QUESTIONS

1. On what constitutional basis does the employer appeal?
2. Explain the Sixth and Seventh Amendments.
3. Explain each of the seven factors the Supreme Court holds important in determining whether a civil penalty is valid.
4. Why is a jury trial not allowed in administrative proceedings?

Note. The Supreme Court has yet to decide if the elaborate civil penalty provisions of OSHA are constitutional.

EMPLOYEE RIGHTS AND DUTIES

Employees have many rights but few duties under the act. The following summarizes these rights and duties:

1. Compliance with Standards. Each employee must comply with all safety standards, rules, regulations, and orders issued by either the government or the employer. This is the only requirement imposed on employees under the act. But an employee incurs no penalties for violating these standards or rules. However, an employer can use traditional disciplinary measures in dealing with any employee who refuses to comply with safety procedures.

2. Safe Work Place. The act guarantees each employee a work place free from recognized hazards that cause or are likely to cause death or serious harm. The act promises workers that employers will comply with established safety standards and that warnings of health hazards at the job site will be posted. Also, the act protects employees from dangerous conditions on the job for which no safety standard has yet been set.

3. Inspections. Employees and their representatives may request an inspection of their work areas if they suspect a violation of the act. They have the right to accompany the compliance officer on the inspection tour and present evidence of safety violations. A copy of any citations issued to an employer must be given to the employees. Prominent warnings must be given employees for any violations found during the inspection.

4. Job Protection. The act forbids discrimination against an employee because he or she has filed a complaint or instituted proceedings under this act. Retaliation against or discharge of an employee who gives evidence against the employer or encourages others to do so is forbidden. An employee may refuse to perform assigned tasks that could subject the person to the danger of serious harm or death due to a safety violation. If an employer wrongfully discharges or discriminates against an employee, then the government will conduct an investigation and order appropriate relief to remedy the employer action. This may mean reinstatement with back pay and fringe benefits.

5. Appeals. An employee and its representative have the same rights as an employer to contest actions by the compliance officer, findings of the administrative law judge, orders of the review commission, and rulings of the courts. Also, an employee can file written objections and request hearings on existing or proposed safety standards. Furthermore, employees can protest the amount of time given an employer to remedy a safety violation. Finally, employees can bring legal action against OSHA for its failure to take action on a safety violation that results in an illness, injury, or death.

MANAGEMENT GUIDELINES

Worker injuries are expensive. The injured worker suffers physical pain, emotional damage, and financial expenses. The employer loses the services of the worker, incurs medical costs, and may have to pay higher insurance premiums under workmen's compensation laws. Managers may incur civil and criminal penalties under OSHA laws for persistent safety violations. And the economy suffers from lost production due to job-related injuries. For these reasons, every employer should establish a procedure for minimizing job-related injuries. The following are some guidelines managers should consider:

1. A member of the highest level of management should be designated as job safety officer, with responsibilities for coordinating all company activities in this area. This officer will probably be associated with the personnel or employee relations department. But he or she should create liaison employees in each plant, department, factory, or work area. To help this officer, a committee composed of the corporate attorney, an engineer, the medical officer, and supervisors from each major work area should be formed. Its function should be advisory, supplying the job safety officer with technical information on safety standards, job-related diseases and injuries, and compliance statistics.

2. An informational flow network should be established whereby liaison employees report unsafe and unhealthy work environments in their areas to the committee. Upon receipt of this information, the committee should promptly investigate the affected areas and make safety recommendations to the liaison employee. Their recommendations should be binding on the manager of the affected work areas, subject to reversal by the highest level of management in the firm. Noncompliance with the recommendations should be reported immediately to the highest management level.

3. A reporting system for job injuries should be established. The OSHA law requires all employers to maintain three types of records. These must include a log of occupational injuries, a supplementary record, and an annual record of such injuries. Liaison employees in the work areas should be instructed on how to keep these records and what type of injuries to record. These reports should be centralized with

the committee. They must be shown to the OSHA compliance officer and submitted to the OSHA area director if a serious injury occurs. An analysis of these records by the committee can reveal a safety hazard before any serious injury occurs.

4. The committee should coordinate the company's position on safety standards. An employer can submit its recommendations on safety standards to the appropriate government office. The committee should initiate proposals for new safety standards within the company and present its views on behalf of the company to the government.

5. A training program for the liaison officers should be established, preparing them for OSHA inspections. An employer has certain rights when visited by an OSHA inspector. Since it may not be possible for the job safety officer to accompany the inspector, the liaison officers can be designated to accompany the inspector. They must be acquainted with the act and safety standards established under it. Also, they must be able to explain company procedures and safety rules.

6. It is imperative for the company to conduct job safety programs for its employees engaged in any task likely to cause harm, injury, or disease to the workers. Some jobs are inherently dangerous, others made so by employees who are not aware of the risks or fail to take precautions. An intensive, repetitive program to enforce voluntary compliance with safety rules is essential. Such programs can minimize job-caused injuries, reduce workmen's compensation insurance premiums, and perhaps negate criminal and civil penalties under OSHA laws.

7. Adequate facilities for dealing with employee injuries should be established. This includes medical facilities, equipment, and trained personnel to administer emergency aid. Sufficient funding to enable the medical personnel to function must be provided.

REVIEW QUESTIONS

1. Contrast workmen's compensation laws with Occupational Safety and Health laws.

2. Explain the changes in employer defenses made by state workmen's compensation laws.

3. Summarize employer rights and duties under the Occupational Safety and Health Act.

4. Summarize employee rights and duties under the Occupational Safety and Health Act.

5. Discuss the various ways by which a company and its managers can reduce liability for worker injuries.

6. Mildred was employed as a clerk in a large drug manufacturing company. Frequent work assignments required her to travel to different parts of the city in which her office was located. On one day, while she was delivering small packages for her employer, her car was struck by another vehicle which failed to yield the right of way at a stop sign. Although not injured, Mildred did become quite upset after the accident. She requested workman's compensation benefits but her employer refused them. On appeal to the state workmen's compensation board, the employer defended its action, arguing that Mildred must sue the other motorist for her injuries and that no liability exists for emotional injuries. Is the employer liable for paying any benefits to Mildred?

7. Jones, a maintenance employee at Arco Steel Corporation, was injured in the steel storage yard. Evidence showed that Jones was not authorized to be in this yard, that he was sleeping at the time of his inquiry, and that he was not wearing proper safety equipment. A recent OSHA safety inspection revealed several dangerous conditions in the storage area and ordered improvements to be made. These improvements were not made. Is Jones entitled to any workmen's compensation benefits for his injury?

8. In the facts above, what actions, if any, can Arco take against Jones?

9. Safety inspectors from OSHA ordered important safety improvements to be made at a tunnel construction project. The project supervisor requested funds from the contractor to make these changes, but was refused. Shortly thereafter, an explosion oc-

curred, killing several workers and injuring others. What is the extent of the project supervisor's liability in this case?

10. As part of its national safety program for the steel industry, OSHA established standards for steel blast furnaces. To carry out these standards, the industry was required to spend substantial sums of money. The standards were adopted without a formal hearing although industry representatives did submit their views when the standards were first proposed. Can the industry enjoin enforcement of these standards?

15

EMPLOYMENT DISCRIMINATION

When Lorillard introduced Erik cigars several years ago, the ads featured a blond Nordic boatman. Today the Viking sailor is gone from some TV commercials. His replacement is a black haired Puerto Rican, romping on the beach of San Juan. ("Minorities Market," Barrons, September 3, 1973, p. 8.)

Laws and customs permitted discrimination against certain groups of people in the United States. Blacks were brought to this country in slavery, freed in the 1860s to live the next one hundred years in ghettos. Native Americans were forced to surrender their lands to settlers in return for desolate reservations, where they subsisted on meager funds provided by an uninterested government. Puerto Ricans, Mexican-Americans and Chinese-Americans were victims of equally harsh social treatment. Japanese-Americans were held in relocation camps at the start of World War II because their loyalty was in doubt. German- and Italian-Americans were not, however, similarly treated.

In neighborhoods where these racial and ethnic groups predominated, states spent less money for the operation of school systems. Consequently, residents of these areas received inferior educational opportunities. This reduced their ability to compete in the job market. Employers, perhaps not intentionally discriminating, hired only the best qualified. This practice eliminated most minority group members from the better paying jobs. Since their education remained inferior and job opportunities were denied them, minority group members remained in a depressed economic condition for generations. A study of national employment and income statistics for blacks illustrates the consequences of employment discrimination. The unemployment rate for blacks is at least twice the rate for white workers. Of those employed, over one-half of the white workers hold managerial or office positions but only one-quarter of the blacks hold such positions. Blacks represent only a small portion of the skilled craftsmen in America, yet constitute a near majority of those employed in service jobs.

Discrimination in American life is not always intentional. Frequently it is the result of tradition based upon the historical patterns of American settlement. When voters realized the harshness and waste of discrimination, they responded by urging their representatives to adopt laws to remedy this problem. Such laws are collectively referred to as civil rights laws. Among other things, these laws guarantee equal employment opportunities to all people. Since the passage of these laws, minorities have made substantial economic progress. For example, income for blacks has doubled since 1969 and two times as many blacks now hold managerial positions.

This chapter will discuss the laws and court rulings prohibiting employment discrimination. It is important for persons planning a career in management to know about these laws because violations of civil rights laws can be expensive. Recently, one company had to pay $75 million in damages to minority employees for past discrimination. Also, legal actions can be brought against managers who discriminate. Consequently, most companies now are committed to changing discriminatory practices. In many companies, a manager's performance review evaluates progress toward equal employment in his or her department. Industry changes are more fundamental than the Erik TV commercial suggests and future managers must be aware of them.

CIVIL RIGHTS LAWS

A civil right means some privilege given to citizens by the Constitution, Congress, a state or local government. Some legal scholars say a civil right is one of the natural rights of persons, giving them the means of happiness. Whatever their source, these rights are expressed through civil rights laws. A civil rights law prohibits the denial of equal enjoyment of any accommodation, facility, common carrier, place of amusement, voting, and employment opportunity on the basis of a person's race, creed, color, sex, or national origin.

The Constitution of the United States contains four parts important to civil rights laws: The Thirteenth Amendment abolishes slavery and establishes universal freedom for all citizens; the Fourteenth Amendment extends all rights and privileges of citizenship to the freed slaves and guarantees the equal protection of the laws to all citizens; the Fifth Amendment states that no person can be deprived of life, liberty, or property without due process of law; and Article I,

TABLE 15-1. SUMMARY OF THE CIVIL RIGHTS ACTS RELATING TO EMPLOYMENT

PROHIBITION: It shall be an unlawful employment practice for an employer, union and employment agency to—
- refuse to hire,
- discharge, or
- restrict employment status

of any individual because of
- race,
- color,
- religion,
- sex, or
- national origin.

EXEMPTION: It shall not be an unlawful employment practice to discriminate if—
- a bona fide occupational qualification justifies the discrimination,
- an educational institution or religious order requires persons of a particular religion or sex,
- the person is a member of the Communist Party,
- national security justifies discrimination,
- objective ability tests exclude certain minority groups,
- laws give preferential status to veterans, or
- laws give preferential status to Indians.

ENFORCEMENT: Equal Employment Opportunity Commission
- Investigates
- Prosecutes
- Adjudicates
- Remedial Relief—hiring
  promotion
  wage adjustment
  seniority adjustment
  damages

Attorney General
- Conciliation
- Civil Suit

Private Action
- civil suit

PENALTIES: Civil Suit by discrimination victims
Affirmative Action Program ordered
Civil Damages
Criminal Penalties

Source: 42 U.S.C. 1911 *et seq.*

Section 8, gives Congress the power to regulate interstate commerce.

Pursuant to these constitutional powers, Congress enacted several significant civil rights laws. The first came immediately after the Civil War. One, a law gave all persons in the United States the same rights as those of white citizens to make and enforce contracts and to sue and be sued in court, and the full benefit of all laws for the protection of persons and property. Another law extended the rights of white citizens to inherit, purchase, lease, or sell property to all persons. A third law passed in 1875, gave all persons in the United States equal rights to use places of public accommodation. For various reasons, these laws did not bring about the equal treatment of all persons. Public apathy toward the plight of minorities, narrow interpretations of the laws, and a lack of vigorous enforcement by the government all contributed to their failure.

It was not until eighty-two years later that Congress enacted the next major civil rights law. The Civil Rights Act of 1957 states that citizens cannot be deprived of their voting rights because of their race, creed, or national origin. This act also created the Civil Rights Commission to investigate discrimination in America. Seven years later, Congress passed the Civil Rights Act of 1964. This act prohibits segregation in places of public accommodation, although private clubs and small guesthouses are exempt. Title VII of this act makes it unlawful for any employer acting in interstate commerce who employs fifteen or more regular employees to practice discrimination in hiring or employment practices on the basis of an individual's race, religion, color, sex, or national origin. This title prevents an employer from restricting the employment opportunities of any worker on discriminatory grounds listed above. These prohibitions apply to employment agencies referring workers to employers and to labor organizations. Thus a union cannot discriminate against any person regarding membership in or expulsion from a union. Nor can the union persuade an employer to discriminate.

Victims of discrimination can sue for their damages. Also, there are penalties for anyone who conspires to violate the civil rights of any worker. For example, a recent consent decree orders nine major steel companies and the United Steel Workers Union to pay $30.9 million to 46,000 black, Spanish-surnamed, and women workers for past acts of discrimination by the companies and the union. Any person who wilfully interferes with the civil rights of another may be fined or jailed. In one recent case, a court assessed $4 million in fines against an employer and $250,000 against a union for malicious discrimination against some employees.

REMEDIES

Civil rights laws create several remedies for discrimination.

1. Civil Suit. The federal district court has original jurisdiction to hear civil rights cases arising under any of the civil rights acts. In this court, persons can sue for monetary damages and other relief to compensate them for acts of discrimination against them. The suit can be filed against anyone or any organization participating in the civil rights violation. This includes those who may have failed to prevent the violation. Damages include money sums for emotional, physical, and economic losses suffered because of the discrimination. Punitive damages to punish an employer may be awarded also. The district court also has the power to change any law or practice that permits discrimination and to order corrective action to offset the effects of past discriminatory practices. Under this last power, the court can order an employer to reinstate, hire, promote, or increase the salary of any discrimination victim. Also, courts can modify the terms of any collective bargaining contract that perpetuates discrimination. For example, in the case of *Franks* v. *Bowman Transportation Company* (47 L. Ed.2d 444, 1976), the Supreme Court recently ordered a firm to hire a black person and award him seniority as of the date he was first refused a position because of his race.

United States v. Sheet Metal Workers Local 36
416 F.2d 123 (1969)

Heaney, Circuit Judge.

The Attorney General brought this action against the union, charging it with a pattern or practice of discrimination against blacks on account of their race in violation of Title VII of the Civil Rights Act of 1964. The trial court found the union had discriminated before the act was passed, but had ceased from discriminatory activities after its passage, and that the union made an effort to recruit blacks. No complaints had been received by the government alleging discrimination by the union. The court added that the Civil Rights Act was not intended to penalize unions for past discrimination or to destroy the seniority system and that there must be intentional patterns of discrimination before there is a violation of the act. The court dismissed the complaint and the government asks this court to reverse.

We first must consider the general question of whether it was necessary for the government to prove that the union discriminated after the enactment of the Civil Rights Act. We answer in the negative. Until 1967, the union had no black members, it did not organize employees working for black contractors, and it discouraged its members from working on jobs with black craftsmen. The union employment referral system operated in a discriminatory manner. Persons are referred for employment on the basis of discriminatory hiring patterns in effect before the act was passed. The system established four priority groups:

> First job priority—workers with four years experience under the union's collective bargaining contract.
> Second job priority—workers with four years construction experience.
> Third job priority—workers with one year experience in construction.
> Fourth job priority—high school graduates or college students.

Under the collective bargaining agreement with employers, blacks could never get above the fourth group because they had been denied construction job opportunities before enactment of the Civil Rights Act. The plan carries forward the effects of former discrimination and therefore violates the act.

The hiring plan must be changed. The experience requirement must allow blacks with experience in construction to move into group one, and reasonable steps should be taken to inform the black community that all persons are now permitted to use the referral system without regard to race, color, or creed. We impose no quotas and we grant no preferences. Reversed and remanded.

CASE QUESTIONS

1. *Explain how the union discriminated after passage of the act.*
2. *Why can the court change the collective bargaining agreement between the employer and the union?*
3. *Describe the remedies ordered by the court.*
4. *Explain the effects of this case on the integrity of the collective bargaining process.*

A class action suit makes it easier to sue when the persons discriminated against are so numerous that separate suits are too expensive or time consuming. But before the class action can be maintained, the remedies sought by the members of the class must be the same and the facts giving rise to the action must be similar for each person in the class. For example, in *Sylvester v. U.S. Postal Service*, 393 F. Supp. 1334 (1975), the U.S. District Court for the Southern District of Texas ruled that some black employees could sue on behalf of all black employees in a post office. They alleged racial discrimination against black supervisors in a local post office, yet their complaint was on behalf of all black workers in the local post office. Since all black employees could be supervisors, the court ruled that current black supervisors could represent them in a class action. And discrimination against supervisors now could affect non-supervisory personnel in the future, according to the court ruling.

2. Criminal Action. Upon complaint by any member of the public, the government may start criminal action against any persons or organization conspiring to deprive others of their civil rights. In this criminal proceeding, it is not necessary to identify the discrimination victim nor to prove that any particular act deprived the person of civil rights. The government must prove some acts were done wilfully that resulted in discrimination against the person. An example of a recent conviction concerned a defendant who gave false reports to police about some blacks. That information caused the police to arrest them. Such harassment constituted a violation of the act. A fine of $1,000 and imprisonment of six months can be imposed.

3. Administrative Proceeding. Title VII of the act creates a special alternative procedure for dealing with employment discrimination cases. It creates the Equal Employment Opportunity Commission (EEOC), a five-member administrative agency, appointed by the President and confirmed by the Senate. The EEOC investigates charges of unlawful employment discrimination brought by any person. This commission has the power to eliminate any improper practice by informal and formal means. For example, it can persuade an employer to stop its unfair practices, sue in court for an injunction restraining discriminatory practices, and negotiate back pay for workers discriminated against.

If the commission refuses to act on a complaint, a person can sue in court. Proceedings before the EEOC cost nothing to the person making the complaint since the act specifies that either the employer or the government shall pay all expenses.

The commission is an independent regulatory agency, having all the traditional powers of an administrative agency, including subpoena powers, power to require testimony of witnesses under oath, and power to compel employers to keep appropriate records and to submit them to the commission upon demand. Its procedures are similar to agencies discussed in prior chapters.

Complaints must be filed with the EEOC in writing, under oath, within ninety days after the employer committed the alleged discriminatory act. The complaint must set out a full description of

TABLE 15-2. MAJOR FUNCTIONAL OFFICES IN THE EQUAL EMPLOYMENT OPPORTUNITY COMMISSION

Chairman
Commissioners
Executive Directors
General Counsel
Directors: Program Planning
   Congressional Affairs
   Public Affairs
   Management
   Equal Employment Opportunity
   Intergovernmental Relations

Source: U.S. Government Manual, 1975-76 Edition.

what occurred, naming all parties complained against. Upon receipt of the complaint, field officers of the EEOC will investigate. Their findings will be submitted to the commission. Then, commission attorneys will attempt to negotiate an informal compromise. Within fifteen days after the investigation findings are submitted to the EEOC, either party may appeal to the full commission for a hearing.

At this hearing, both sides may present evidence to prove there was or was not an act of discrimination. Each side has the power to cross-examine the witnesses and evidence submitted. But the commission may limit this right to protect the complainant and other persons. Also, each side may contest the remedies proposed by the investigator as well as any damages awarded. The EEOC will dismiss, modify, or affirm the investigator's findings. Parties can appeal within thirty days to the court of appeals and the Supreme Court for review of the commission's actions.

Johnson v. Railway Express Agency, Inc.
42 L. Ed. 2d 305 (1975)

Mr. Justice Blackmun.

Petitioner, Willie Johnson, Jr., is black. He started to work for respondent, Railway Express Agency, Inc., (REA). On May 31, 1967, petitioner with others, filed with the EEOC a charge that REA was discriminating against its black employees with respect to seniority rules and job assignments. He also charged the respondent unions, Brotherhood of Railway Clerks TriState Local and Brotherhood of Railway Clerks Lily of the Valley Local, with maintaining racially segregated memberships. Three weeks later, on June 20, REA terminated petitioner's employment. Johnson then amended his charge to include an allegation that he had been discharged because of race.

The EEOC issued its final investigative report on December 22, 1967. The report generally supported petitioner's claims of racial discrimination. It was not until more than two years later, however, on March 31, 1970, that the commission rendered its decision finding reasonable cause to believe petitioner's charges. But EEOC decided not to prosecute. And nine and a half more months went by before EEOC, on January 15, 1971, gave petitioner notice of his right to institute a Title VII civil action against the respondents within thirty days.

On March 18, 1971, counsel for the petitioner filed a supplemental complaint against REA and the two unions, alleging racial discrimination on the part of defendants in violation of Title VII of the 1964 Act and of 42 U.S.C. 1981 (Civil Rights Act of 1866). The district court dismissed the Section 1981 claims as barred by the Tennessee one-year statute of limitations. In his appeal to the Court of Appeals, petitioner argued that the running of the one-year period was suspended because of his complaint with the EEOC. The Court of Appeals rejected this argument and we granted right of appeal.

Title VII of the Civil Rights Act of 1964 was enacted to assure equality of employment opportunities by eliminating those practices and devices that discriminate on the basis of race, color, religion, sex, or national origin. It creates statutory rights against invidious discrimination in employment and establishes a comprehensive scheme for the vindication of those rights. Anyone aggrieved by employment discrimination may lodge a charge with the EEOC. That commission is vested with the authority to investigate individual charges of discrimination, to promote voluntary compliance with the requirements of Title VII, and to institute civil actions against employers or unions named in a discrimination charge. Thus, the commission itself may institute a civil action. If however, the EEOC is not successful in obtaining voluntary compliance and, for one reason or another, chooses not to sue on the claimant's behalf, the claimant, after the passage of 180 days, may demand a right-to-sue letter and institute the Title VII action himself without waiting for the completion of the conciliation procedures.

In the claimant's suit, the district court can appoint counsel for him, to authorize the commencement of the action without the payment of fees, costs, or security, and even allow an attorney's fees. If intentional unlawful discrimination exists, the court may award back pay and order such affirmative action as may be appropriate. The back pay, however, may not be for more than the two-year period prior to the filing of the charge with the commission. Some district courts have ruled that neither compensatory nor punitive damages may be awarded in the Title VII suit.

Despite Title VII's range and its design as a comprehensive solution for the problem of invidious discrimination in employment, the aggrieved individual clearly is not deprived of other remedies he possesses and is not limited to Title VII in his search for relief. The legislative history of Title VII manifests a congressional intent to allow an individual to pursue independently his rights under both Title VII and other applicable state and federal statutes. In particular, Congress noted that the remedies available to the individual under Title VII are coextensive with the individual's right to sue under the provisions of the Civil Rights Act of 1866, 42 U.S.C. 1981, and that the two procedures augment each other and are not mutually exclusive.

The Civil Rights Act of 1866 relates primarily to racial discrimination in the making and enforcement of contracts. Although this Court has not specifically so held, it is well settled among the federal courts of appeals, and we now join them, that this act gives a federal remedy against discrimination in private employment on the basis of race. An individual who establishes a cause of action under this act is entitled to both equitable and legal relief, including compensatory and punitive damages. And a back-pay award under this act is not restricted to the two years specified for back-pay recovery under Title VII.

Congress has clearly retained Section 1981 as a remedy against private employment discrimination separate from and independent of the more elaborate and time-consuming procedures of Title VII. Petitioner freely concedes that he could have filed his Section 1981 action at any time after his cause of action occurred; in fact, we understand him to claim an unfettered right to do so. Thus, in a very real sense, petitioner has slept on his Section 1981 rights. The fact that his slumber may have been induced by faith in the adequacy of his Title VII remedy is of little importance inasmuch as the two remedies are truly independent. Moreover, since petitioner's Title VII court action now also appears to be time barred because of the peculiar procedural history of this case, petitioner, in effect, would have us extend the Section 1981 cause of action well beyond the life of his Title VII cause of action. We find no policy reason that excuses petitioner's failure to take the minimal steps necessary to preserve each claim independently. Judgment of the Court of Appeals is affirmed.

CASE QUESTIONS

1. Contrast the remedies available to petitioner under Title VII and Section 1981.
2. What considerations should an individual evaluate in selecting the court or the EEOC as the place for settling a civil rights violation?

4. Government Action. The Civil Rights Act of 1964 authorizes the Attorney General of the United States to file a lawsuit against any person or organization wherever there is a pattern of resistance to granting full employment rights. Also, the Attorney General can join in any lawsuit brought by an individual.

5. Private Settlement. A person can use informal methods to remedy discrimination. The person can submit a grievance to arbitration under a union contract. Findings and decisions made by the arbitrator are binding on the courts. Alternatively, the person may ask for assistance from a mediator, some respected member of the community. The mediator may be able to negotiate a satisfactory solution. Unlike arbitration, courts are not required to accept mediation as binding results.

STATE CIVIL RIGHTS LAWS

State fair employment practice laws generally prohibit job discrimination by either an employer or labor organization. But state laws vary considerably in the type of relief granted for discrimination and in the procedures for obtaining relief. Some state laws give rights to sue for damages, others allow suits to obtain better job opportunities, and still other state laws apply criminal penalties against employers who discriminate. Most states allow class action suits to obtain whatever remedies are available. Suits can be started by either an individual victim of discrimination or by the state attorney general on behalf of all workers discriminated against. Many states have a human relations commission, with authority to hear employment discrimination cases and order appropriate remedies. Some of the major cities have civil rights laws that parallel those of federal and state governments. Thus an employer may find agencies from three levels of government interested in its employment practices.

AFFIRMATIVE ACTION PROGRAMS

The government now realizes that discrimination in employment cannot be eliminated immediately. Passing laws guaranteeing civil rights makes it illegal to discriminate. But such laws do nothing to help those persons who have been the victims of discrimination for generations. Those individuals who have few skills and little formal education have no effective job opportunities even though legal restraints have been removed. Others may have education but do not know where to look for better jobs. To solve these problems, the government developed the affirmative action program.

Executive Order 11246, first issued in 1965 but amended periodically, states that in all contracts in excess of $10,000 with the federal government, employers must promise not to discriminate against any employee on the basis of race, color, sex, religion, or national origin. Furthermore, the employer must take affirmative action to see that employees are hired and treated in a nondiscriminatory manner. Employers must actively solicit job applications from members of recognized minority or disadvantaged groups. Currently, officially recognized minority and disadvantaged groups are Hispanic, Asian or Pacific Islanders, Blacks not of Hispanic origin, American Indians, Alaskan Natives and women. An employer must not discriminate against persons who belong to one of these racial or ethnic groups. Also, the employer must take affirmative action in favor of those persons.

Classifications of citizens into ethnic groups could be unconstitutional since it denies all persons the equal protections of the laws. Although the Supreme Court has not ruled directly on this argument, the next case indicates the Court's answer to part of the questions raised by racial classifications.

Morton v. Mancari
417 U.S. 535 (1974)

Mr. Justice Blackmun.

Section 12 of the Indian Reorganization Act provides: "The Secretary of the Interior is directed to establish standards of health, age, character, experience, knowledge, and ability for Indians who may be appointed, without regard to civil service laws, to the various positions maintained, now or hereafter, by the Indian Office, in the administration of functions or services affecting any Indian tribe. Such qualified Indians shall hereafter have the preference to appointment to vacancies in any such positions."

In June, 1972, pursuant to this provision, the Bureau of Indian Affairs, with the approval of the Secretary of Interior, issued a directive stating that the BIA's policy would be to grant a preference to qualified Indians not only, as before, in the initial hiring stage, but also in the situation where an Indian and a non-Indian, both already employed by the BIA, were competing for a promotion within the bureau. The record indicates that this policy was implemented immediately.

Shortly thereafter, appellees, who are non-Indian employees of the BIA at Albuquerque, instituted this class action, on behalf of themselves and other non-Indian employees similarly situated, in the District Court for New Mexico, claiming that the so-called Indian Preference Statutes were repealed by the Equal Employment Opportunity Act and deprived them of rights to property without due process of law, in violation of the Fifth Amendment. Named as defendants were the Secretary of the Interior, the Commissioner of Indian Affairs, and the BIA directors.

After a short trial, the District Court concluded that the Indian Preference Statute violated the Civil Rights Act of 1964, prohibiting discrimination in most federal employment on the basis of race. The court enjoined the government from implementing any policy in the BIA that would hire, promote, or reassign any person in preference to another solely for the reason that such person is an Indian. The government appealed to this Court.

Determining whether the statute constitutes invidious racial discrimination in violation of the due process clause of the Fifth Amendment depends on the unique legal status of Indian tribes under federal law and on the power of Congress, based upon a history of treaties and the assumption of a guardian status, to legislate on behalf of federally recognized tribes. The full power of Congress to deal with the special problems of Indians is drawn both explicitly and implicitly from the Constitution. It gives Congress the power to regulate commerce with the Indian tribes, and thus, to this extent, singles Indians out as a proper subject for separate legislation. The Constitution also gives the President the power to make treaties with the Indian tribes. This power has been used by the government to create a special relationship with the various tribes.

Literally every piece of legislation dealing with the Indian tribes and reservations singles out the Indians for special treatment. If these laws, derived from historical relationships and explicitly designed to help only Indians, were deemed invidious racial discrimination, an entire title of the United State Code would be effectively erased and the solemn commitment of the government toward Indians would be jeopardized.

It is in this historical and legal context that the constitutional validity of the Indian preference is to be determined. In 1934, Congress determined that proper fulfillment of its trust required turning over to the Indians a greater control of their own destinies. The overly paternalistic approach of prior years had proved both exploitative and destructive of Indian interests. Congress was united in the belief that institutional changes were required. An important part of the Indian Reorganization Act was the preference issue here in question.

Contrary to the characterization made by appellees, this preference does not constitute racial discrimination. Indeed, it is not even a racial preference. Rather, it is an employment criterion reasonably designed to further the cause of Indian self-government and to make the BIA more responsive to the needs of its constituent groups. It is directed to participation by the governed in the governing agency. The preference is similar in kind to the constitutional requirement that a Senator must be an inhabitant of that state from which he shall be elected, or that a member of a city council reside within the city governed by the council. Congress has sought only to enable the BIA to draw more heavily from among the constituent group in staffing its projects, all of which affect the lives of tribal Indians. The preference is granted to Indians not as a discrete racial groups, but rather as members of quasi-sovereign tribal entities whose lives and activities are governed by the BIA in a unique fashion. There is no other group of people favored in this manner. Furthermore, the preference applies only to employment in the Indian service. The preference does not cover any other government agancy or activity, and we need not consider the obviously difficult question that would be presented by a blanket exemption for Indians from all civil service examinations. Here, the preference is reasonable and directly related to a legitimate nonracially based goal. This is the principal characteristic that generally is absent from proscribed forms of racial discrimination.

CASE QUESTIONS

1. Describe the preference given Indians in this case.
2. Do these preferences constitute a form of reverse discrimination against non-Indian employees of the BIA?
3. On what legal basis can Congress permit some citizens to be treated differently from others?

A company subject to Executive Order 11246 must notify its union that both must comply with its terms. If the employer or union refuse to follow the terms of the order, all contracts with the federal government can be revoked and suit can be started to force compliance.

To see how affirmative action works in practice, we should consider one interpretation of it by the Secretary of Labor, called the Philadelphia Plan. This plan required building contractors to submit an affirmative action program specifying definite goals for hiring minority construction workers in the Philadelphia area. First, the contractors had to determine the number of minority members in the various building crafts and trades in the city area. Next, they were required to find out how many minority group members were available for work. Then contractors had to establish goals to bring minority workers into the work force. For example, if one hundred employees are required on a job and the black construction worker population of the area is five percent of the total worker population, then the contractor must try to hire five percent black construction workers. If these persons are not trained for their jobs, then contractors must bring them into union-operated training programs. According to the secretary's interpretation, the plan takes priority over union contracts. It is designed not to favor one group over another, but to remedy the effects of past discriminatory activities.

In 1971, the Department of Labor established a new interpretation of Executive Order 11246. Its rules now require any employer with fifty or more employees and a federal contract in excess of $50,000 to formulate a written affirmative action plan. In this plan, an employer must survey each of its departments to see if disadvantaged groups are represented in proportions similar to their availability in the job market. If they are not, the employer must create a program to bring minority and women employment in each of its departments up to the percent of their availability in the market. To do this, the employer must determine the relevant job qualifications for each of its positions, then find out the number of minorities and women having those qualifications, and finally establish a goal for hiring a proportionate number of disadvantaged persons. For example, if a college degree in economics is required for a particular job, the employer must determine the number of women, blacks, Hispanic, Orientals, and Native Americans who have that degree. If ten percent of all economics degrees are held by blacks, then an employer should set as its goal the hiring of ten percent blacks for that type of position. The Departments of Labor and Commerce can supply statistics on people having certain qualifications. The affirmative action plans do not require rigid goals. They can be flexible targets to reach, in a reasonable manner, by good-faith methods. Employers must develop plans for hiring goals even if there are no present job openings or even if there has been no discrimination practiced in the past. If the employer was guilty of past discrimination, then specific remedial action may be ordered to correct immediately the racial and ethnic imbalance.

The current affirmative action programs can be summarized as follows:

1. Recruitment for employment must be undertaken without regard to race, sex, or ethnicity. An employer can establish qualifications for its positions and hire the most qualified person, if the qualifications are relevant to the job. The employer must prove the relevance of each job qualification.

Philips v. Martin Marietta Corporation
400 U.S. 542 (1971)

Per Curiam.

Petitioner, Mrs. Ida Philips, commenced an action in the District Court under Title VII of the Civil Rights Act of 1964 alleging that she had been denied employment because of her sex. The District Court granted summary judgment for Martin Marietta on the basis of the following: (1) in 1966 Martin Marietta informed Mrs. Philips that it was not accepting job applications from women with preschool-age children; (2) as of the time of the motion for summary judgment, the company employed men with preschool-age children; (3) at the time Mrs. Philips applied, seventy to seventy-five percent of the applicants for the position she sought were women and seventy-five to eighty percent of those hired for the position, assembly trainee, were women; hence no question of bias against women as such was presented.

The Court of Appeals affirmed and denied a rehearing. We granted certiorari.

The Civil Rights Act of 1964 requires that persons of like qualifications be given employment opportunities irrespective of their sex. The Court of Appeals therefore erred in reading this section as permitting one hiring policy for women and another for men—each having preschool-age children. The existence of such conflicting family obligations, if demonstrably more relevant to job performance for a woman than for a man, could arguably be a basis for distinction in the act. But that is a matter of evidence tending to show that the condition in question is a bona fide occupational qualification reasonably necessary to the normal operation of that particular business enterprise. The record here is not adequate for resolution of these important issues. Summary judgment was therefore improper and we remand for fuller development of the record and for further consideration.

Concurring. While I agree that this case must be remanded for a full development of the facts, I can not agree with the Court's indication that a bona fide occupational qualification reasonably necessary to the normal operation of the company's business could be established by a showing that some women, even the vast majority, with preschool-age children have family responsibilities that interfere with job performance and that men do not usually have such responsibilities. That exception has been construed by the EEOC to be applicable only to job situations that require specific physical characteristics necessarily possessed by only one sex. When performance characteristics of an individual are involved, even when parental roles are concerned, employment opportunity may be limited only by employment criteria that are neutral as to the sex of the applicant.

330 Laws and Regulations Affecting Labor

CASE QUESTIONS

1. What is a bona fide occupational qualification?
2. Give some examples of such qualifications that would allow an employer to refuse to hire on account of a person's race, sex, creed, or national origin.

---

2. Employment policy must be structured to expand the number and types of applicants for a position. If the policy does not do this, then the recruitment period must be extended to allow minorities to apply. An employer must develop a nondiscriminatory pool of applicants from which hiring decisions will be made. Failure to do this constitutes a violation of the law.

3. Job requirements must be applied uniformly to all candidates. Standards for evaluation of candidates must be nondiscriminatory, but standards should not be diluted to favor one particular group of applicants. Any job requirement that excludes members of a disadvantaged group is valid only if it is a factor necessary for the job. An example of an improper job requirement is a minimal height requirement for firemen that is not based on scientific, analytical, or statistical study of the importance of the height requirement. According to a recent federal District Court ruling, such height requirements are invalid because there is no rational connection between job performance and employment requirements. (*Fox* v. *Washington*, 396 F. Supp. 504, 1975.) The next case shows how educational requirements can be discriminatory.

Griggs v. Duke Power Co.
401 U.S. 424 (1971)

Mr. Chief Justice Burger.

We granted the right to appeal in this case to resolve the question whether the Civil Rights Act of 1964, Title VII, prohibits an employer from requiring a high school education or passing of a standardized general intelligence test as a condition of employment in or transfer to jobs when (a) neither standard is shown to be significantly related to successful job performance, (b) both requirements operate to disqualify blacks at a substantially higher rate than white applicants, and (c) the jobs in question formerly had been filled only by white employees as part of a longstanding practice of giving preference to whites.

Congress provided in Title VII for class action suits for enforcement of provisions of the Civil Rights Act of 1964, and this case was brought by a group of incumbent black employees against Duke Power Company. All the petitioners are employed at the Company's Dan River Steam Station. At the time of this action, the Company had ninety-five employees at the Station, fourteen of whom were black.

The District Court found that prior to July 2, 1965, the effective date of the 1964 Act, the company openly discriminated on the basis of race in the hiring and assigning of employees at its Dan River plant. The plant was organized into five operating departments: labor, coal handling, operations, maintenance, and laboratory and test. Blacks were employed only in the labor department, where the highest paying jobs paid less than the lowest paying jobs in the other four departments, in which only whites were employed. Promotions were normally made within each department on the basis of job seniority. Transferees into a department usually began in the lowest position.

In 1955 the company instituted a policy of requiring a high school education for initial assignment to any department except the labor and for transfer from the coal handling to other departments. When the company abandoned its policy of restricting blacks to the labor department in 1965, completion of high school was made a prerequisite to transfer from labor to any other department. From the time the high school requirement was instituted to the time of the trial, however, white employees hired before the time of the high school education requirement continued to perform satisfactorily and achieve promotions in the other departments. Findings on this score are not challenged.

The company added a further requirement for new employees on July 2, 1965, the date on which Title VII became effective. To qualify for placement in any but the labor department, it became necessary to register satisfactory scores on two professionally prepared aptitude tests as well as to have a high school education. Completion of high school alone continued to render employees eligible for transfer to the four desirable departments from which blacks had been excluded if the incumbent had been employed prior to the time of the new requirement. In September, 1965, the company began to permit incumbent employees who lacked a high school education to qualify for transfer from labor to a better job by passing two tests—the Wonderlie Personnel Test, which purports to measure general intelligence, and the Bennett Mechanical Aptitude Test. Neither was directed or intended to measure the ability to learn to perform a particular job or category of jobs. The requisite scores used for both initial hiring and transfer approximated the national median for high school graduates.

The District Court found that while the company had followed a policy of overt racial discrimination in the period prior to the act, such conduct had ceased. The court also concluded that Title VII was intended to be prospective only, and consequently the impact of prior inequities was beyond the reach of corrective action by the act.

The objective of Title VII is plain from the language of the statute. It was to achieve equality of employment opportunities and remove barriers that have operated in the past to favor an identifiable group of white employees over other employees. Under the act, practices, procedures, or tests neutral on their face, and even neutral in terms of intent, cannot be maintained if they operate to "freeze" the status quo of prior discriminatory employment practices.

The Court of Appeals opinion stated, "whites fare far better on the company's alternative requirements" than blacks. This consequence would appear to be directly traceable to race. Basic intelligence must have the means of articulation to manifest itself fairly in a testing process. Because they are black, petitioners have long received inferior education in segregated schools and this Court expressly recognized these differences. There, because of the inferior education received by blacks in North Carolina, this Court barred the institution of a literacy test for voter registration on the ground that the test would abridge the right to vote indirectly on account of race. Congress did not intend by Title VII, however, to guarantee a job to every person regardless of qualifications. In short, the act does not command that any person be hired simply because he or she was formerly the subject of discrimination, or because he or she is a member of a minority group. Discriminatory preference for any group, minority or majority, is precisely and only what Congress has prescribed. What is required by Congress is the removal of artificial, arbitrary, and unnecessary barriers to employment when the barriers operate invidiously to discriminate on the basis of racial or other impermissible classification.

Neither the high school completion requirement nor the general intelligence test is shown to bear a demonstrable relationship to successful performance of the jobs for which it was used. Both were adopted without meaningful study of their relationship to job-performance ability. Rather, the requirements were instituted on the company's judgment that they generally would improve the overall quality of the work force.

The evidence, however, shows that employees who have not completed high school or taken the tests have continued to perform satisfactorily and make progress in departments for which the high school and test criteria are now used. The promotion record of present employees who would not be able to meet the new criteria thus suggests the possibility that the requirements may not be needed even for the limited purpose of preserving the avowed policy of advancement within the company. In the context of this case, it is unnecessary to reach the question whether testing requirements that take into account capability for the next succeeding position or related future promotion might be utilized upon a showing that such long range requirements fulfill a genuine business need. In the present case the company has made no such showing.

The Court of Appeals held that the company had adopted the diploma and test requirements without any "intention to discriminate against Negro employees." We do not suggest that either the District Court or the Court of

Appeals erred in examining the employer's intent; but good intent or absence of discriminatory intent does not redeem employment procedures or testing mechanisms that operate as "built-in headwinds" for minority groups and are unrelated to measuring job capability.

The company's lack of discriminatory intent is suggested by special efforts to help the undereducated employees through company financing of two-thirds the cost of tuition for high school training. But Congress directed the thrust of the act to the *consequences* of employment practices, not simply the motivation. More than that, Congress has placed on the employer the burden of showing that any given requirement must have a manifest relationship to the employment in question.

The facts of this case demonstrate the inadequacy of broad and general testing devices as well as the infirmity of using diplomas or degrees as fixed measures of capability. History is filled with examples of men and women who rendered highly effective performance without the conventional badges of accomplishment in terms of certificates, diplomas, or degrees. Diplomas and tests are useful servants, but Congress had mandated the common sense proposition that they are not to become masters of reality.

The company contends that its general intelligence tests are specifically permitted by the act, which authorizes the use of any professionally developed ability test that is not designed, intended, or used to discriminate because of race.

The EEOC, having enforcement responsibility, has issued guidelines to permit only the use of job related tests. The administrative interpretation of the act by the enforcing agency is entitled to great deference. Since the act and its legislative history support the commission's construction, this affords a good reason to treat the guidelines as expressing the will of Congress. Nothing in the act precludes the use of testing or measuring procedures; obviously, they are useful. What Congress has forbidden is giving these devices and mechanisms controlling force unless they are demonstrably a reasonable measure of job performance. Congress has not commanded that the less qualified be preferred over the better qualified simply because of minority origins. Far from disparaging job qualifications as such, Congress has made such qualifications the controlling factor, so that race, religion, nationality, and sex become irrelevant. What Congress has commanded is that any tests used must measure the person for the job and not the person in the abstract.

The judgment of the Court of Appeals is, as to that portion of judgment appealed from, reversed.

CASE QUESTIONS

1. In what ways was the employer discriminating against blacks?
2. What was the relationship between the test scores and job performance?

3. Does the Civil Rights Act require that persons be hired just because they were discriminated against in the past?

4. Employers must obtain information on the religion, race, sex, and ethnic identity of job applicants. This data will be turned over to the government for monitoring compliance with the law. This information cannot be used for any discriminatory purposes and the employer must keep such information confidential.

5. Employment policies on job tenure, promotion, and discharge must be nondiscriminatory. An employer cannot discriminate against a worker at any time during his or her career with the employer. Three cases show how discrimination can arise in a company during the career of an employee.

The first case deals with an employer who discharged a worker who refused to work on Saturday due to his religious convictions. Title VII also prohibits discrimination on the basis of religion. In *Cummins* v. *Parker Seal Co.*, 516 F.2d 544 (1975), the U.S. Court of Appeals for the Sixth Circuit ruled that a discharge of an employee who refused to work on a religious day was a violation of the act. Before an employee can be fired for this conduct, the employer must first show some undue hardship on itself. Complaints from other workers who are forced to work extra hours on Saturday must yield to the single worker's right to practice religion.

In the next case, an employer was found guilty of maintaining a discriminatory disability plan. This plan paid benefits to workers who were injured. It denied benefits to women employees who missed work days because of pregnancy. The court ruled this plan violated Title VII. Any company benefit that denies a benefit to women is illegal. Since pregnancy is unique to women, a plan that does not provide for paid days off work for pregnancy prevents a woman from acting like a woman and is discriminatory. (*Gilbert* v. *General Electric Co.*, 519 F.2d 661, 1975.)

The final case deals with union seniority systems. Such plans can be discriminatory, as shown in the following case.

Myers v. Gilman Paper Corporation
392 F.Supp.2d 413 (1975)

Alaime, Judge.

Prior to the effective date of Title VII, blacks were hired into relatively low paying lines of progression and were prohibited from entering into higher paying ones. While some blacks were hired into formerly all-white jobs between 1965 and 1972, few transferred into formerly all-white lines of progression. From 1965 to 1972 blacks who transferred to traditionally all-white lines of progression forfeited previously earned seniority. Thus a black employee transferring to a formerly all-white line of progression had less seniority than a white employee who was hired the same day but who was initially assigned to that line.

The essence of the claim against the union is that the collective bargaining agreements tended to perpetuate past discrimination through job seniority provisions and through the absence of provisions for the posting of job vacancies. This court finds that the job seniority provisions and practices were at least a concurrent, if not prevailing, cause of the perpetuation of the past discrimination.

The international union, however contends that even if its local union is found liable for perpetuating past discrimination, it cannot be. The locals, according to the international, are not agents of the international union. Assuming this argument is correct, the mandate of Title VII is not limited by principles of agency or contract. This mandate places an affirmative duty on unions to end present discrimination and the effects of past discrimination. By failing to show that it has taken any steps to assure its local's compliance, the union becomes liable for its own unreasonable inaction.

CASE QUESTIONS

1. *Explain how the seniority system continued past discrimination.*
2. *Explain the effects of this case on company layoff policies when blacks lack the seniority of white workers because of past discrimination.*

REVERSE DISCRIMINATION

An unsettled issue is the role of white males under the Civil Rights Act and the affirmative action programs. In one recent case, the U.S. District Court for Connecticut ruled that a white citizen could sue a company that gave preferential hiring to minorities and women for its summer internship program. (*Hollander* v. *Sears, Roebuck and Co.*, 392 F. Supp. 90, 1975.) The suit was brought under the Civil Rights Act of 1866. The court held that this law was not intended to allow only nonwhite citizens to sue. Rather, the law allows suits by any person who was deprived rights to make a contract. Some whites may be denied rights enjoyed by most other white persons.

One way by which white males can be discriminated against is through the goals of the affirmative action program. Such goals require an employer to set targets for hiring females and minorities. These targets may exclude qualified white males from employment. Also, the white male may suffer discrimination through the disuse of the seniority system. Courts have ruled that company and union seniority systems may be discriminatory. Such systems can discriminate against newly hired females and minority workers since those with less employment time will be layed off first. Some courts have considered adjusting the seniority system so that workers are removed in a way to maintain a proper racial, ethnic and sex balance among the work force. Whether the use of affirmative action programs in these ways constitutes a denial of equal protection of the laws must be decided by the Supreme Court.

MANAGEMENT GUIDELINES

Strict enforcement of antidiscrimination in employment laws is new. These laws are undergoing continued interpretation by the courts and evaluation by the voters. Nevertheless, a manager of a business must comply with the spirit of the regulations and laws. The following is a guide for management compliance.

1. All managers and personnel officials must make a commitment to end intentional and institutional discrimination in their organizations. The cost of not complying with these civil rights laws can be great. One company paid over $100,000 in legal fees to defend itself and up to $1 million in back pay for just one department's discrimination practices.

2. Managers responsible for hiring must survey their existing work force to determine the number of minority and women presently employed and in what capacity and at what wage rate. If a statistical survey shows that minorities and women are not working in a business at all levels in reasonable proportions to their numbers in the work force, then the burden is on the employer to prove it is not discriminating.

3. Those managers should then be instructed to survey the effects of their existing personnel policies concerning hiring, promotion, work assignments, compensation, layoffs, discharges, and other aspects of these policies. Policies not apparently discriminatory may be having discriminatory effects.

4. Every qualification or requirement for hiring, promotion, work assignments, compensation, layoffs, or discharge of a worker should be evaluated for discriminatory consequences. Employers can use race, sex, creed, or national origin of a person as a basis of personnel action if such a factor is a bona fide occupational qualification or if honoring it becomes an excessive burden to the employer. For example, an employer can discharge an employee who refuses to work on the Sabbath if no other employee has the skills to substitute for this worker or excessive employee discontent over the one worker's refusal to work reaches chaotic proportions or the employee's absence makes working conditions unsafe for others.

5. Managers should determine the number of minorities and women that can be employed in the types of jobs available.

6. Managers should then establish objectives or goals for hiring minorities and women so that the workers generally reflect the racial and sex composition of the community in which the employer operates. Quotas are not legal under the Civil Rights Act but goals for hiring are permitted.

7. Definite recruitment methods for attracting qualified minority and women workers to the business should then be established. Announcements of job openings and job searches should be conducted directly among minority group and women's organizations.

8. An active recruitment effort should be started. A good faith effort to comply with the civil rights acts is not an excuse for falling short of company goals. Managers should be aware that their performance on this task is just as critical as reaching company goals for production, sales, or profit. Appropriate rewards should be made to those managers who fulfill their goals.

9. All managers and supervisors involved in the selection of job applicants should be advised of permitted and prohibited questions to ask job applicants. For example, any questions about a person's age, sex, race, or religion may indicate bias to the applicant unless they are asked in such a way that the identity of the respondent is concealed. Questions about an applicant's criminal record or past wage garnishments can be improper since several courts have ruled they can lead to discrimination against blacks. But managers can explain that the need for a security clearance requires a "clean record." Also, the company can request information about a person's family, health, age, and sex for insurance purposes, but only after the person is hired. If a job requires physical exertion, a medical exam can be required before employment to see if the applicant can perform the job.

10. Managers should establish a training program for new and existing minority and female employees to see that they are qualified to move into higher levels of responsibility in the company.

11. One high-ranking officer of the business, with authority over other managers, should be appointed to coordinate and carry out the affirmative action program. This

manager should be compensated adequately so that he or she can carry out the purposes of the law as well as acquire insurance to indemnify against possible suits. One large company now spends $3 million annually to guarantee that it complies with all federal and state civil rights laws and court rulings.

REVIEW QUESTIONS

1. Explain the constitutional and statutory authority for the federal government's regulations of employment discrimination.
2. Outline the remedies available to a worker who is the victim of employment discrimination.
3. Discuss the social and political consequences of treating some groups of citizens differently from others in employment.
4. Explain the affirmative action program.
5. Explain the circumstances when an employer can refuse to hire a job applicant on the basis of race, religion, sex, or national origin.
6. Discuss the ways by which a manager can avoid or minimize liability for job discrimination.
7. Williams sued his employer for discrimination. The complaint alleged that he was denied promotion because of his race, but it was filed in court before the laws made such practices illegal. With the filing of the suit, Williams was discharged. Subsequently, the Civil Rights Act was amended to include employers like Williams's. Williams now sues his former employer, alleging he was discharged in retaliation for his antidiscrimination suit filed earlier. The Civil Rights Act prohibits the discharge of any employee who files complaints of discrimination against an employer. Has the employer violated the law?
8. The EEOC instituted discrimination charges against an employer for practicing acts prohibited by Title VII. At a court trial, the commission charge was dismissed. The employer now asks the EEOC to pay fees and court costs. The employer based its demand on that part of the act which gives a court discretion in awarding court costs and fees to the prevailing party. Can the EEOC be liable for court costs if its complaint is dismissed?
9. O'Malley filed suit against her employer for discrimination. The suit was dismissed by the court because she failed to prove any acts of discrimination. Subsequently, the EEOC instituted suit on behalf of O'Malley alleging the same facts as in the earlier suit. The employer requests the court to grant a summary judgment in its favor. Should the motion be granted?
10. Several postal service employees filed a charge of discrimination against their employer, the U.S. Postal Service. It was filed with

the Civil Service Commission, which held a hearing to investigate the allegations. At this hearing, evidence was submitted, witnesses examined, and conclusions of fact made. The commission dismissed the complaint, and the employees appeal to the federal district court. At trial, is the court limited by the evidence and findings made by the Civil Service Commission?

TOPICS

CHAPTER 16. ETHICAL PROBLEMS IN AMERICAN BUSINESS
Introduction • Criminal Conduct • Altruistic Crimes • Abuse of Position • Misuse of Power • Social Irresponsibility • Multinational Power • Summary • Review Questions

CHAPTER 17. SOCIAL RESPONSIBILITY OF BUSINESS
Introduction • Criminal Enforcement • Civil Remedies • Self-Regulation • Enforcement Techniques • Professional Liability • Social Responsibility • Summary • Review Questions

PART FIVE

BUSINESS AND SOCIETY

The modern business firm must satisfy the diverse needs of several different groups of people. For example, employees demand higher wages for their work, customers look for better products for their money, owners expect higher returns on their investments, and society requires behavior responsive to community problems. These groups are the four publics every business firm must serve.

Traditionally, business satisfied the needs of each public through maximizing profit. Achieving the highest possible profit margins encouraged owners and potential investors to channel more money into firms. This new money enabled business to make better products for their customers, pay higher wages to employees, and turn in more tax revenue for use by government to solve community problems. Managers considered profits as the key to fulfilling the four publics' needs.

But reliance on profits as the only way to satisfy its publics is no longer adequate for today's managers. Each of the publics now expects every business and its managers to act properly as well as profitably. Business managers must view their firms as part of an interdependent society, not as autonomous entities. As part of this larger society, managers owe duties to that society as well as to their firms. If managers ignore their obligations to society, then society will take actions against all business firms.

Society can express its antibusiness attitude in three ways. First, it can propose more business regulatory laws like the ones discussed in this book. Each of these regulations require conduct that should have been voluntarily performed by managers. Each regulation also affects business profits. If business managers do not seem to act voluntarily for the community's interest, the community will sponsor new laws to force action.

Second, society can change the economic system under which business operates. American business acts in a profit-oriented capitalistic environment. But some people claim the profit motive encourages unplanned development of land and exploitation of human and natural resources. If business managers do not act properly, then society may create a nonprofit, socialistic economy.

Third, society can react with violence against what it considers improper business conduct. Environmentalists can deny access to raw materials, workers may damage the employer's property, or mobs can attack plants or equipment. Business firms and managers must prevent these actions by acting in a way society approves.

Thus the challenge facing business seems apparent. To keep society's good will, business must redefine its role in our society.

Managers and their employees must avoid any conduct that society considers improper, in addition to making an adequate profit to satisfy the four publics' needs. Good business citizenship requires this but business survival demands it. In the final part of this book, we will discuss some ethical problems facing the modern business manager and offer some suggestions for making business more socially responsible.

16

ETHICAL PROBLEMS IN AMERICAN BUSINESS

Merchants have no country. The mere spot they stand on does not constitute so strong an attachment as that from which they draw their gains. (Thomas Jefferson, 1814.)

The public often criticizes business for not living up to the ethical standards expected of it. To counteract business's failure to maintain those standards, legislatures pass new regulatory laws, so that managers are required to conform to expected standards. So, to minimize new government regulations, persons in business must make sure that their conduct conforms to accepted ethical principles. But talking about ethics is difficult because it means so many different things to different people.

The dictionary defines ethics as standards for human behavior. Philosophers and theologians determine proper standards as guides for everyday activities. These guides become objective measures by which all human actions are judged acceptable or unacceptable. The standards are rigid, not changeable according to the circumstances or the person acting.

While it is easy to define ethics, it is not so easy for people to accept and follow ethical guides. Scholars do not agree among themselves what ethical guides should be in every instance. Also, the guides that are agreed to are not adopted like a statute. They are accepted by each individual through his or her personal analysis of life. This personal formulation of ethical rules of conduct creates differing standards for evaluating specific business actions. The person in business must conform to these differing standards. Following good ethical conduct in business becomes difficult when so many different ethical standards exist among the public. Perhaps as a minimum, the manager should determine the ethical standards of most people in the community in which the business operates and then conform business conduct to them.

This chapter outlines four areas in which business managers can be faced with ethical problems: activities that violate criminal laws, acts that conflict with a community's standard of fairness, conduct that abuses corporate power, and actions that do not utilize corporate power for the public's welfare. Summaries of actual case histories illustrate these problem areas. In each of these situations, the public expects the business manager to act in a proper manner. If the manager does not, then citizens will look for ways to punish that manager, the firm, and perhaps business generally.

In each of the case histories summarized here, you should put yourself in the manager's role. Ask yourself what you would do in a similar situation. To focus your attention on key ethical problems in each case, some questions follow each summary. In aswering these questions, do not look for right or wrong answers. Ethical problems often present dilemmas for which there are no clear-cut answers, only alternatives. You should outline the alternatives a manager has and evaluate the consequences of each. Then you can select that alternative which has the most acceptable consequences or the least undesirable consequences.

CRIMINAL CONDUCT

A proportionately small but constant source of ethical difficulties for the modern business manager is the direct and clear violation of criminal law by personnel in the organization. Many managers have found themselves involved in legal problems with prosecutors because they went along with illegal behavior committed by their superiors or by their subordinates. For covering up another's criminal behavior, a person becomes a co-conspirator, subject to criminal penalties. The following two cases illustrate the problems for some managers.

A. In a recent case, evidence shows that the nation's forty-fifth largest financial services corporation was founded and operated in an illegal manner. A few of its managers entered false financial figures on its annual reports, giving outsiders the impression that the company was growing and prosperous. Some examples of their illegal conduct included making loans without recording them on company accounts, registering fraudulent sales of life insurance policies, and forging corporate securities. The managers of this company also manufactured

56,000 fictitious life insurance policies, worth more than $2 billion and sold them to unsuspecting reinsurance firms. Profits made from this operation were skimmed off by the managers. Although a growing number of the company's managers and employees knew of the fraud practiced by the company and of its deception on investors, not one reported this criminal activity. Finally, one employee who was fired told news reporters in retaliation for his discharge. Within two months after the fraud was reported, the company was bankrupt, and the public suffered about $10 million in damages.

The interesting aspect of this case is not the fraudulent schemes of the managers. Their actions were not original or unique, just practiced on a wider scale than prior frauds. The unusual aspect is that the fraud was practiced over several years despite repeated audits by reputable certified public accounting firms and yearly reports made to federal and state regulatory agencies. The fraud continued because of official negligence and with the cooperation of numerous company employees, each of whom failed to report it. The employee who did reveal the plot did so out of discontent, not moral outrage.

B. A different type of criminal behavior developed in another recent case. Here, a study of the airline industry revealed that fifteen major international airlines gave kickbacks, discriminatory discounts, and special travel services to ticket agents who then directed customers to one of these airlines. Rebates went to foreign and domestic travel agents by American and European air carriers. Industry representatives testified that the agents asked for this money. Had the airlines refused, agents would write tickets on competing airlines that paid the money. To remain competitive, the companies felt it necessary to violate the law and go along with the requests for payments.

CASE QUESTIONS

1. *If you were an employee or manager working for either of the companies mentioned in these cases, what would you do upon learning of the illegal activities by your superiors?*
2. *Why would employees of the financial services company or the airlines not reveal to authorities the illegal acts of their superiors and companies?*
3. *Of what use are criminal and business regulatory laws prohibiting conduct as described in these cases if the illegal acts can be performed for a long period of time without detection?*
4. *Enforcement of laws depends primarily upon the honesty of people. How is this statement verified by the prior cases?*
5. *How is the employer's profit affected by the criminal activity in each of these cases?*

ALTRUISTIC CRIMES

Perhaps more common ethical problems for managers arise in the situations where personnel knowingly violate the law for the best interests of their employer. Their purpose is not to gain any financial advantage for themselves but merely to advance the firm's profits. These crimes are altruistic, committed for some greater good, not personal greed. Such illegal acts are performed at the request of some person in a position of power over the company who uses that power to threaten the company. Employees or managers will then commit crimes for the benefit of their employers. The following recent cases illustrate several examples of this type of ethical business problem.

A. A large United States food manufacturer sought to purchase farms for crop production in a Central American country. The government denied its requests to purchase the land. Finally, a government official suggested to management that if a certain consultant were employed by the firm, negotiations might proceed more satisfactorily. The company employed the person suggested, paying him $500,000. Shortly thereafter, the land was sold to the company. The company knew that the money paid to the consultant was used to bribe government officials. It paid the money in order to get the land, which could then be used for profitable purposes by the company.

B. A major international oil company paid in excess of $4 million to officials of an oil-producing country. A government leader demanded the money as his price for not nationalizing company-owned property. Refusing to pay this money would cost the company substantially more in lost assets. Acknowledging that money was paid to prevent expropriation would subject the company and others to similar demands from other countries.

C. Information available from the special prosecutor's office in the Department of Justice indicates the practice of making illegal payments to American political and government officials is common. More than eighty American companies have admitted making illegal campaign contributions to political candidates, elected officials, and appointed civil servants in responsible positions of authority over the companies. Company representatives said that in most cases the recepient asked for the money. Refusal to give could subject the company to legal harassment from the public official.

CASE QUESTIONS

1. Recent evidence indicates these practices have been going on for many years. Business executives, politicians, and governmental

authorities knew of these practices. None revealed them to the public. Why?
2. What effect does disclosure of this inaction have on public confidence in the integrity of our regulatory system?
3. What is the personal obligation of a manager when asked to make an illegal payment of the type mentioned in the above cases?
4. What is the personal obligation of a manager when asked to make a payment to a foreign government official that is legal in the country where it is requested but illegal in the United States?
5. Do bribery, kickbacks, or other payments to foreign officials violate American law? (Consider Section 5 of the Federal Trade Commission Act and the disclosure requirements of the Securities Act of 1933.)
6. Should a manager of a corporation doing business in a foreign country conform to ethical standards of the host country or to those of America? One philosopher states there are three levels of ethics: what is ethical in the host country according to their culture and history; what is ethical in the United States; and what is ethical according to a minimum code of human conduct. To which standard should the manager conform? What consequences arise when a person violates his or her personal code of ethics even though the community's ethics are not violated?
7. What effect does making of an illegal payment to a foreign official have on profits? Does it protect a business or merely "whet their appetites" for more?
8. One company has issued guidelines to its employees regarding foreign political payoffs. The guides state: "Business will be conducted in strict observance of both the letter and the spirit of the applicable law of the land wherever we operate. Where a situation is not governed by statute, business will be conducted in such a manner that we would be proud to have the full facts disclosed." To what extent will these guidelines be effective? How can they be enforced?
9. In the securities regulations section, we saw situations where corporate executives and employees learned confidential information about their companies and used it to benefit themselves financially by trading in the stock of their company. In some cases, they disclosed this inside information to their friends. Such conduct violated the law. But is it asking too much to expect a manager to remain passive when he or she sees an opportunity to make substantial profit? Explain the consequences on the trading public of permitting such trading.

ABUSE OF POSITION

Managers of American corporations have considerable flexibility in operating their firms. Most shareholders in large, publicly held firms are not interested in the affairs of the corporation. They prefer to vote their proxies in favor of management as long as the dividends are good and the market price of their securities increases. Knowledge of this shareholder apathy enables top corporate managers to use some corporate assets for themselves. Managers refer to use of these assets as part of their compensation. If reasonable, there is no violation of the law or waste of corporate assets. But when the cost of these benefits is revealed, the public becomes suspicious about their necessity and dismayed to learn who pays for them. In a cost-conscious consumer society, the public may consider such benefits an abuse of a manager's corporate position. The following three case histories illustrate this point.

A. A top manager of a leading manufacturing concern nearly brought his company to financial ruin. He merged the company with unprofitable firms, he hired poor assistants who permitted the company to neglect proper inventory control, and he funded quality control operations poorly, causing inferior production. The board of directors became dissatisfied with his performance only after a lively shareholder's meeting revealed so much discontent that he had to be removed. The board allowed the executive to resign rather than be fired. Also, it paid him a $2 million bonus. Some observers commented that this payment was a reward for incompetency and wondered how much the company would pay to a competent manager. In a similar case, an executive made illegal political contributions of corporate money to political candidates. He was fined for this action and his company penalized, and numerous shareholders filed suits against the company for mismanagement. Adverse publicity prompted the manager to resign, yet the company paid him pension benefits totalling more than $100,000 a year.

B. Some corporate executives materially enhance their living standards at company expense. In one recent lawsuit against a corporate president, a stockholder alleged that the executive acquired three chauffeur-driven cars, two jet aircraft, and a hunting lodge in the Canadian northland. The corporation purchased each of these items, but they were used for the personal enjoyment of the president, his wife, and family. Evidence showed that the planes transported his wife on shopping trips around the country and his son to college. His family spent vacations at the lodge. In each situation, the president always discussed business with some corporate officials to justify the corporate payment for these items.

CASE QUESTIONS

1. Do these activities violate criminal laws?
2. How does each of these activities affect the firm's image in the minds of consumers, employees, investors, and the public?
3. What obligations would you have, as an employee of the company in case B, to reveal the president's use of corporate assets to stockholders or to the SEC?
4. How do the actions in these cases affect corporate profits? Why?

C. Corporations must buy substantial amounts of raw materials inventory, supplies, equipment, and other commodities to operate. The purchasing manager is in charge of making most or all of these acquisitions. This manager must solicit bids from various suppliers, each of whom is anxious to get all the business it can. Their anxiety raises possibilities for abuse of position. Selling agents may offer bribes or gifts to purchasing managers to get orders. To put some restrictions on this conduct, the National Association of Purchasing Managers has drafted guidelines for its members. The guidelines state:

> Unnecessary sales and purchasing expense is an economic waste—a tax on legitimate industry. Its elimination will assure satisfactory profits to the producer, economy to the consumer, and greater efficiency in commercial relations.
>
> We recognize that the concern which buys must also sell, that buying and selling are companionate functions, that sound commercial transactions must be mutually profitable, and that cooperation between buyer and seller will reduce the cost to purchasing, sales, and distribution with consequent benefits to industry as a whole.
>
> In furtherance of these principles, we subscribe to the following standards in our buying and selling: . . .
>
> 3. To avoid misrepresentations and sharp practices in our purchases and sales, recognizing that permanent business relations can be maintained only on a structure of honesty and fair dealing. . . .
>
> 9. To provide or accept no gifts or entertainment in the guise of sales expense, where the intent or effect is to unduly prejudice the recipients in favor of the donor as against legitimate competitors.
>
> 10. To give or receive no bribes, in the form of money or otherwise, in any commercial transaction and to expose commercial bribery wherever encountered for the purpose of maintaining the highest standards of ethics in industry.

CASE QUESTIONS

1. What is meant by sharp practice?
2. Does Standard 9 prevent gifts to purchasing managers?
3. To what extent are these standards enforceable? Are they realistic? Why should a company adopt them?

MISUSE OF POWER

A corporation has the right to run its own affairs. The laws of most states gives the corporate manager the right to follow policies that may seem bad management provided a majority of shareholders ratify these actions. But, financial risk and legal penalty can result from irresponsible use of a manager's power. Evaluate the ethical conduct of the managers in the following cases. Their use of power raises serious questions about the fairness of their actions and invites public criticism.

A. A large manufacturer of food products anticipated a rise in the cost of sugar, one of its important raw materials for food processing. It bought large amounts of this commodity and stockpiled it pending the increases. Other companies did not purchase bulk supplies. Shortly, the price of sugar tripled. Competitors were now forced to buy their supplies at the higher market price. This made the cost of their finished products higher for consumers. The company that prepurchased sugar was not faced with the same cost increases as its competitors. Nevertheless, it increased its prices on products made from sugar to meet the competitors' prices. The company received a substantial windfall profit. Intense consumer reaction followed. Various groups argued that the consumer actually paid higher prices than costs justified.

B. In another context, some managers displayed disregard for the public's interest. In the 1960s, the stock markets in America boomed. Many small, close corporations decided to sell their securities on the public market to ride the crest of the exchange trading. They fulfilled all legal requirements for registering securities. Then they sold the stock to investors at substantially higher prices than what current members of the corporation had originally paid for the stock. In the 1970s, the economy entered the post-Vietnam recession and the stock markets declined. Shares of these formerly private corporations declined at a greater pace than the market as a whole. Managers of these companies decided to repurchase company stock with corporate funds at substantially reduced prices. By this transaction, the managers will be using stockholder money to reacquire private control of the business. The public investor stands to lose not only stock values but any potential for recouping the investment.

CASE QUESTIONS

1. Describe the effects of these managerial actions on consumers and investors.

2. In what ways can either of these groups protect themselves from such actions.
3. Explain the ethical problems presented to the manager when faced with the necessity to act in these cases. Would a failure to raise prices in case A be mismanagement?
4. Describe the effect on future profits when companies act as in the above cases.

SOCIAL IRRESPONSIBILITY

The public has an image of American business. That image comes from the amount of economic power modern corporations have. The public sees business as composed of many organizations owning substantial assets and employing many trained personnel. These people appear to possess substantial power to influence elected officials and government employees. Yet some members of the public also view the corporation as not interested in the problems facing the country. They see corporations as opposed to any proposals to remedy them. The corporation thus appears antisocial in its behavior, that image encourages resentment of corporate power and lends support for new laws forcing the corporations to be more responsive to society's needs. Consider some examples of how business needlessly encouraged public resentment by appearing socially irresponsible to the public.

A. Consumers are demanding more protections for themselves and new rights to receive the best products at the lowest prices. To assure that consumers are paying the lowest prices for products, some groups proposed legislation that unit prices be put on all packaging or labels. This pricing method informs the consumer how much he or she pays for each ounce, gram, or unit of measurement in each different sized container. More informed buyers and improved purchasing power for the consumer dollar were expected from this pricing policy. Despite the minor cost to companies for complying with this request, most food manufacturers opposed it. They used many of the same arguments advanced against earlier social legislation—an unconstitutional attack on their right to run their business, needless intrusion of government into private business, and the belief that consumers should determine for themselves the true costs of items being purchased.

These arguments were made again when consumer groups demanded dating on food products to show freshness of things sold and proposed special consumer protection agencies to police business sales practices. Despite business opposition, most of these proposals became law. The public considered them beneficial to society, and business opposition only raised fears in the minds of some consumers that industry was taking advantage of them.

B. Employees can suffer severe job injuries in American work places. Some of these injuries are not preventable as they arise from the dangerous nature of the jobs performed. Others, probably most of them, can be prevented by taking reasonable safeguards. When Congress considered the job safety law discussed in a prior chapter, business representatives opposed the proposed legislation. They argued the cost of complying with the proposals was too great in view of the few benefits from a safer work environment. To many employees, this argument appeared callous. To them, business objections to the safety law seemed to center on the proposition that it was cheaper to pay for worker injuries than to pay to eliminate or reduce them. A worker who risked being deformed by an occupational injury considered this argument irresponsible, if not criminal. The safety laws were passed and business suffered not only legislative defeat but public scorn as well.

CASE QUESTIONS

1. Should the business manager assume a more active role in community affairs?
2. How does social inaction or opposition to socially beneficial laws create public animosity toward the corporation?
3. What ethical problems are presented to a manager when the corporation adopts positions on social problems contrary to the manager's viewpoint?
4. How will profits be affected by business conduct in each of the prior cases?

MULTINATIONAL POWER

Some corporations become so large that they begin doing business in more than one country. They amass considerable political and economic influence in several countries. The use of this power creates new problems for the government of the countries in which the companies operate and ethical problems for the managers of these multinational enterprises. Consider the following case problems involving international business.

A. The United States has determined cigarette smoking is harmful to a smoker's health. Government regulations insist that manufacturers inform consumers of these health dangers by displaying prominent warnings on cigarette packaging. Other nations do not require such warnings. Should a manager of a cigarette company that sells its products in America and abroad distribute the products in foreign markets without the health warning? Since human body composition is similar throughout the world, would the manager and the company risk charges that they were insensitive to the health of foreigners? On the other hand, if the warnings were added, what effect would it have on sales if foreign competitors did not add similar warnings? Can you draw a parallel with automobile safety standards and pollution control systems?

B. Traditional hostilities between nations can involve the multinational business manager in ethical disputes. Consider the case of an international company that does business in two countries, A and B. It makes certain products in country A that the leaders of country B consider harmful to their country's security. Should the manager continue production of these products in country A? To do so would encourage reaction by country B; not to do so would risk retaliation by country A. Either alternative raises questions about the loyalty of the international corporation.

The loyalty of the multinational corporation was questioned during the oil embargo of the United States by certain oil-producing nations. At the request of Arab oil producers, American oil corporations allegedly reduced and later eliminated oil supplies to American military forces. The companies argued the military embargo was necessary to avoid offending the Arab leaders. If the embargo was not carried out, serious damages may have resulted to their oil-producing equipment. The dilemma facing the international manager is to determine to whom loyalty is owed: to the company, to the nation that created the company, to the nation where the individual manager happens to be working, or to the nation where the individual manager was born or raised.

C. Occasionally, the voters in one country will elect a regime that is hostile to the interests of the multinational firm. In such a case, the managers must determine what their reaction should be. Passive acceptance may result in a forfeiture of substantial assets. Involvement in the country's political affairs may create further opposition to the company's existence in that country. A similar problem arises when a corporation does business in a nation having a political or social system opposed by people in other countries where the firm does business. Numerous groups in the United States insist that American multinational firms should cease doing business in the Union of South Africa because of its racial policies. These groups demand the companies use their power to change the South African system. But managers claim involvement in South African affairs will encourage the companies to become involved in the internal affairs of other countries. Managers do not know how to select the "good" and "bad" nations in which to intervene.

D. Multinational organizations operate their business firms to derive the maximum profit from their operations, without regard to national frontiers. Managers will locate plants where costs justify the most profitable location, not where political loyalties dictate. American managers will locate facilities where labor costs are lowest, often taking jobs away from American workers. Some people call these practices union-busting tactics, and others consider them sound business practices.

CASE QUESTIONS

1. What are the limits of the powers of a national government over the activities of a multinational organization?
2. Should a manager surrender national identity when he or she accepts a position with a multinational firm?
3. Ethical standards of behavior not only differ among people in the same countries but among different cultures as well. What the public will accept in one nation may not be tolerated in another. How does a manager cope with variations of ethical standards? Complying with standards in one country may subject the manager to criticism or sanctions in other countries. Show how this statement is true.
4. The acceptability of profit varies in different countries. How does a manager justify profit motives in socialistic countries?

SUMMARY

Most problems of ethical behavior stem not from criminal violations of the law, but from actions that are performed without proper regard for the interests of consumers, employees, stockholders, or the public. A manager faced with the dilemma of doing what he or she thinks correct and what the employer requires has an ethical problem. The individual must develop a personal value system enabling him or her to function as an employee of the organization and as a person. If the individual cannot develop these standards, job performance will suffer and self-resentment will grow. Profits of the organization may decline.

Companies have an obligation to help their employees become more ethical in their actions and to be more conscious of the correctness of their actions. Employees must be aware of all the publics served by the company and how they can fulfill the conflicting needs of each public. Employees cannot rely only on business regulatory laws. They must develop personal ethical principles. But these should not be overly moralistic, seeking to convert society to their views of righteousness. Rather, the standards adopted should merely reflect community standards in which the managers do business. If business managers fail to do this, the public will demand legislation to require them and their companies to do it.

The problems of insuring ethical behavior in organizations may seem minor compared with the other problems facing the management. But if we consider the amount of executive attention spent on image building and the number of corporate dollars spent on image advertising and public relations, we can begin to realize how important ethical action is to business. One corporate or manager action viewed as unfair, wrong, socially irresponsible, or abusive to the public can nullify all the money spent on advertising. The public will realize business has no commitment to good citizenship and fair practices. They will then seek out other ways of protecting themselves from business conduct.

REVIEW QUESTIONS

1. Define the word "ethics," and show how ethical rules are derived.
2. Are ethical rules clear and unambiguous to all persons?
3. Why is the study of ethics important to persons planning a career in business?
4. State several situations in which ethical dilemmas confront a manager. On what basis should he or she reconcile this problem?
5. How can an individual develop a personal ethical value system enabling the person to function successfully in the modern business organization?
6. A corporation executive proposed an idea that other managers considered illegal. Management directed the executive to seek the advice of the corporate attorney. When he presented the idea to the lawyer, the executive deleted the illegal aspects of the plan, hoping the lawyer would endorse it. Then the executive could implement it with the illegal aspects restored. As a subordinate of the executive proposing the plan, what obligations do you have to inform the lawyer of the executive's intentions?
7. A building inspector asks a restaurant owner for a bribe. Without the payment, the inspector will issue a summons to close the

premises for safety violations. The owner directs you to make the payment. Should you do it?

8. As part of an audit of your company's personnel policies, you discover that the employer is intentionally discriminating against black persons. It employs them, but never gives them adequate training for advancement. Should you report this policy to the government? If you do, many white employees may not be promoted to higher paying positions so that blacks may be promoted as a remedy for past discrimination. What are your duties in this situation?

9. An artificial sweetener was banned in the United States because it could cause cancer if consumed in large quantities. Under American law, such products cannot be sold to consumers. A regulatory agency orders your company to destroy the food made with this ingredient. Upon hearing of this order, officials of an Asian country ask for the food. Without this food, the officials claim many persons will starve. American tests show the food could cause cancer. What actions should you recommend to your company?

17

SOCIAL RESPONSIBILITY OF BUSINESS

> ...*[T]his is an age when there is much talk about the social responsibilities of business. It is said that corporations should involve themselves in the communities where they are located; and this includes financial support of civic groups, many of whom will become involved in political issues. The state of the law in this area is murky.... Either the use of corporate funds for such purposes should be permitted, or permitted subject to regulation and reporting or barred. It is patently unfair to subject the business world to the charge of "copping out" on civic responsibilities when the penalty for not "copping out" may be criminal prosecution...* (Stephen H. Fletcher, "Corporate Political Contributions," The Business Lawyer, Vol. 29 (July, 1974), 1089.)

In the preceding chapter, we saw several situations when business managers find themselves in difficult moral dilemmas. Some of these situations call for an easy answer—the law should not be violated. Other situations are more difficult to answer—when does an abuse of corporate or individual power become unethical? It is unrealistic to expect that all managers and employees will always do the right thing in every situation. Not all persons will analyze ethical duties in the same way, so different solutions will emerge. And some managers will make mistakes when carrying out their solutions to ethical questions, while a few individuals will be dishonest and attempt to defraud others.

Because of these factors, some authority must create standards for business conduct and impose sanctions if they are violated. These standards should help individuals in business act more ethically in business dealings and encourage corporations to become more socially responsible. This chapter will discuss some ways by which ethical conduct can be enforced: criminal prosecution, civil actions, and self-regulation. Next, we will suggest an alternative method for policing business and we will conclude this chapter with a brief discussion of business's role in solving national social problems.

CRIMINAL ENFORCEMENT

Business leaders should support vigorous enforcement of criminal laws against white collar crimes as well as more violent street crimes. Some activities of business executives and managers are more harmful to society than the muggings, rapes, or burglaries so often condemned by corporate executives. Conspiracies to fix prices and securities frauds cost the American consumer more each year than a decade of street crime. Such activities are not apparent because they are done in secret surroundings, without physical injury to anyone. Yet the higher consumer prices caused by these actions are costly to our economy. Political payoffs and illegal contributions to candidates are also costly to our society. These crimes rob Americans of their democratic institutions. Honest business leaders should condemn such activities and urge state and federal prosecutors to bring criminal prosecutions against those few who violate the law. These acts, if left unpunished, will prompt the public to demand new business regulatory laws.

But business leaders should demand prosecution of all persons involved in the illegal transations. For example, the prior chapter illustrated problems with illegal contributions to candidates and government officials. Corporate executives gave this money out of fear. They were fearful of the tremendous power the government could bring against their organizations if the anger of some officials was raised. To them, the use of this power frequently seemed unfair and arbitrary. Thus, when a government official having this power asked for financial payments, executives were afraid not to give. The consequences of alienating one official in a key decision-making position could be disastrous for the company. Consequently, officials requesting the money as well as executives who give it should be penalized. Also, business leaders should encourage prosecutors to investigate the "crime" of centralizing excessive governmental authority without adequate checks on its use in the offices of a few persons.

There are dangers for business leaders who urge better enforcement of criminal laws. They may become the subject of prosecution themselves. For example, in one recent case, the Department of Justice brought criminal action against the president of a large food distributing company because he failed to learn rats had entered the firm's warehouse and contaminated food stored there. Both the

TABLE 17-1. ANNUAL COST OF WHITE COLLAR CRIME
(Billions of Dollars)

Bankruptcy Fraud	$ 0.08
Bribery, Payoffs	3.00
Computer Related Crime	0.10
Consumer Fraud, Illegal Competition, Deceptive Practices	21.00
Credit Card and Check Fraud	1.10
Embezzlement and Pilferage	7.00
Insurance Fraud	2.00
Receiving Stolen Property	3.50
Securities Fraud & Thefts	4.00
Total (billions)	$41.78

Source: "White Collar Justice," *BNA Securities Regulation & Law Report*, No. 348, April 14, 1976, p. 3.

president and the government admitted that this executive had no personal knowledge of the rodents, but the government relied upon an earlier case to prosecute the official. This case held that the Food, Drug and Cosmetic Act imposes liability on persons in corporations even without awareness of any wrongdoing. In that case, the Supreme Court held that the larger good of society required liability of top executives to force them to take more care in preserving the purity of food products.

This case shows the dangers in supporting a vigorous enforcement of our criminal laws. Government prosecutors may seek to hold top managers in corporations responsible for the unethical or criminal behavior of their managers and employees. But the consequences of remaining silent to criminal and ethical violations by others in business may be even more dangerous. The public may assume business's passive attitude is an endorsement of such behavior.

CIVIL REMEDIES

Responsible business leaders should support strong citizen's rights laws. It is good public relations in this age of consumerism and it is good business practice to penalize the few executives who produce inferior products or act socially irresponsibly or unethically.

Recent federal legislation gives the government rights to sue companies and managers who wilfully violate the terms of some business regulatory laws. For example, the Attorney General can sue firms practicing racial or ethnic discrimination in employment, the

Consumer Product Safety Commission can sue to enjoin the sales of harmful products, and the Securities and Exchange Commission can suspend trading in securities when necessary to protect investors. Sanctions for violations of any of these laws can be a civil fine in varying amounts. Although these fines do not bring in much revenue to the government, they do show to the managers that continued violations may bring criminal prosecution. And fines show to citizens that government is concerned over their welfare, not in conspiracy with business. By supporting the concept of civil fines, executives and managers show their concern for the public and their willingness to pay a price for any violations of the public's welfare. Opposition to fines encourages the antibusiness attitude some citizens already have.

Another type of civil remedy that business leaders should support is the class action suit by shareholders, employees, consumers, or competitors. Often executives and managers view these suits as harassments or nuisance suits against wealthy corporations. In some cases, that may be true. But this may not be sufficient reason to oppose the concept of class action remedies. The cost of this opposition may be greater than the settlement costs of the few improper class actions.

Some company policies result in conduct that injures many people. Most of those injured can not afford the expense and time involved in suing for damages resulting from these wrongful actions. Often the amount of injury to one person is not significant enough to warrant a lawsuit. But the cumulative impact on the economy of the corporation's wrongful conduct may be tremendous. Unless some procedure exists whereby the injured parties can obtain relief, their resentment will grow. Other improper policies by the companies will add to their discontent. Eventually, a breakout of this accumulated resentment will occur. It may manifest itself in support for new business regulatory laws, restrictions on profits, or nationalization of corporate assets. The class action suit can serve as a vent for releasing frustrations.

Managers should also support laws to improve defects in the class action procedures. Instead of opposing group legal actions, managers should propose better group representation. Reform of court rules should be considered to guarantee adequate notice to all parties interested in the case. Ways to permit greater individual participation in the class suit should be considered. More equitable methods of paying the legal expenses should be developed. The question of penalizing any person who uses the class action for improper purposes should be explored.

One area where business can make a contribution to reform of the class action suit is in the area of state responsibility. Present law does not permit a state to sue on behalf of its citizens for injuries they may have suffered because of improper actions by a business. Each citizen injured must sue individually or through a class action commenced by one of the persons injured. One action by the state could simplify the entire matter. Money recovered by the state can be distributed to injured citizens of the state or kept by the state for future expenditure.

SELF-REGULATION

Reliance on criminal penalties and civil remedies is inadequate to guarantee ethical conduct among business managers. Not all unethical actions are illegal, so prosecution would be useless. Imposition of civil remedies requires public knowledge of the improper behavior and sufficient public outrage to enforce its remedies. These conditions may be lacking in many cases of ethical violations. And it is better for business to condemn its own improper dealings as one way of preventing tougher business regulatory laws. So business must regulate itself. Two possible methods of self-regulation would be creating ethical standards boards and using outside directors.

"Ethics and Earnings: Profit Minded Chief At Bendix Tries To Set A Businessmen's Code," *Wall Street Journal,* November 11, 1975, Vol. 186, No. 99.

W. Micheal Blumenthal of Bendix Corp. proposed the idea of establishing a professional watchdog group that would devise and police an ethical code for American businessmen.

Exactly how far the project would go isn't clear. Indeed, considering the meager results of past attempts to devise broad codes of business ethics skeptics think Mr. Blumenthal will be wasting his time. But others who know the Bendix chief say that if anyone has a chance of making it work, he does.

Mike Blumenthal is one of the small though growing number of corporate leaders who seem willing to plunge voluntarily into the nebulous subject of the social and moral responsibilities of big business. In recent years, of course, many executives have found themselves grappling with such issues, but often not without prodding from consumer activists, theologians, environmentalists or other gadflies. And action has often been slow to follow, partly because changes often conflict with traditional profit-making goals.

As Mr. Blumenthal sees it, changes are needed. "We're operating in a much more complicated environment, and business leaders are confronted with more difficult choices than ever before," he says. "You used to be able to make decisions on the basis of the greater return for the least dollars. But now you must spend time and money on things that don't seem efficient in terms of profits. The old ways won't work anymore. Today, a guy like Henry Ford (the tough-minded founder of Ford Motor Co.) would either be in jail or his company would be on strike."

Mr. Blumenthal himself contends that the stakes in the growing debate over business ethics are nothing short of corporate survival.

"If the businessmen are ethically strong and morally clean, why should they not be the first to denounce the abuses and malpractices which, far more than the critics in the media, threaten the survival of the free enterprise system?" he asks.

The idea of a code of business ethics isn't new, of course. For instance, the electrical equipment price-fixing scandals of the early 1960's triggered a barrage of criticism from the press and public and soon afterward an ethics advisory council of top business leaders was set up under the Commerce Department. In 1962 the group presented a proposed code to President Kennedy. But after his assassination, the Johnson administration, seeking business support, let the code die.

What, if anything, Mr. Blumenthal's report will produce remains to be seen. He speculates, for example, in terms of "a black book that would show what a panel of experts on business ethics says about a particular problem." Foreign bribes might be a topic about which a consensus on proper conduct could be reached, he suggests. He also mentions political contributions and the handling of sensitive issues such as layoffs, pensions and safety.

"There's nothing in business life which corresponds to the bar associations, the American Medical Association or the American Institute of Architects," he notes. "Business people should set up an association dedicated to defining and maintaining the standards of their profession." An ethical code devised by this group, he says, could correspond to the standards of other such associations and could be enforced by some type of censure.

Theologians and academic experts generally applaud the idea and believe many top executives agree. But even some sympathetic observers wonder how many corporations are really ready to embrace a code of ethics and make it stick. Many of them remain optimistic, however.

"Many companies are getting more defensive as the social and moral pressures increase," says Charles W. Powers, director of public responsibility for Cummins Engine Co., Columbus, Ind. "Some will emerge to provide leadership, and hopefully that group will be powerful."

Others question whether codes of ethics do much good. "Canons of ethics generally end up being canons of profit," argues Mark Green, an attorney with Ralph Nader's Corporate Accountability Research Group. "You end up with self-policing codes that are inadequate. We need stricter criminal penalties."

And a few regard the whole idea as foolish. Ultimately a businessman has to have his own set of standards, "so why set up a body to tell you what's right and wrong?" asks an executive with an Ohio-based auto parts concern that competes with Bendix.

Source: Reprinted with permission of The Wall Street Journal, © Dow Jones & Company, Inc. 1975. All rights reserved.

1. Ethical Standards Boards. Within each industry corporate leaders should create special boards. These boards should be composed of prominent executives, labor leaders, educators, and community representatives. After careful deliberations, these members should create standards for the guidance of all managers and employees in each industry. A staff should be employed to review corporate actions and executive behavior among firms in its industry. The staff should also receive and investigate complaints from members of the public, competitors, and government officials. Any serious violations of the board's ethical standards should be reported to the board.

Upon receipt of evidence showing the possibility of a violation of its standards, the board should hold a hearing. At this hearing, the members should review evidence collected by its staff and listen to testimony submitted by the complainant and the accused. Hearings should be conducted according to rules guaranteeing fair procedures. When the hearing is completed, the board should issue an opinion, either upholding the complaint or dismissing it. If the board finds the executive or the corporation did violate its ethical standards, an order correcting the violation should be issued. It may direct the offender to reform its actions or make restitution to persons injured by the violation.

To prevent any premature harm to the person or organization complained against, publicity about the hearing should be minimal. Announcements to the news media should be made if the person or organization refuses to comply with the board's recommendations. A summary of its activities could be released in an annual report.

The activities and procedures of the ethical standards boards recommended here seem to resemble those of government administrative agencies. Some of the procedures of these agencies were criticized because of the power they had over corporations and managers. Does the ethical standards board recommended here duplicate the abuses of administrative agencies? Hopefully not. The agencies are governmental bodies. They have the power to harm the reputation and property of business and managers subject to their authority. Agencies can seek criminal penalties. Political considerations frequently enter into agency actions. Members are appointed through the political process, often without the support of industry leaders whom they will regulate.

But the recommendations made here for ethical standards boards for each industry remove many of the worst aspects of the agency form of regulation. The boards would have no criminal authority, only powers of moral persuasion. Executives would have a right to make significant input into standards formulations. Members of the boards would be appointed because of their national or industrial prominence, not their political connections. Pro-industry bias is reduced with the addition of representatives of labor and the community. In short, the boards would seek to perform for business the same functions accounting societies and bar associations perform for their members—a system of internal self-enforcement of established ethical guidelines. Their purpose should not be to act as vigilante groups, but merely as ethical watchdogs for the economy, separate from governmental and criminal authorities.

2. Outside Directors. Directors are elected by shareholders to supervise the operations of a corporation. In large, publicly owned corporations, shareholders are distributed over wide geographic areas and unable to communicate effectively with each other. Most communications to shareholders come directly from management and are returned to it. For want of any better alternative, shareholders accept what managers tell them and vote their stocks in accordance with management's wishes. This enables incumbent management to run the corporation and remain responsible only to themselves. Given this power, managers often have themselves elected to the board of directors and think more of their personal welfare than of the welfare of the shareholders, consumers, or society. Shareholder apathy enables managers to commit many abuses of power and misuses of position. To remedy this problem, independent voices must be heard on the corporation's board of directors. Outside directors should be considered.

An outside director is one elected to a corporate board of directors to serve as a representative of shareholder interests. This person does not assume a management role in the corporation as either an officer or manager. According to theory, if the director is not part of the management, then he or she may be more critical of company policy. The outsider can be more alert to any abuses of power and position by the insiders. If there are a significant number of independent and impartial representatives on the board of directors, then more opinions contrary to management's will be expressed and evaluated. These opinions may encourage managers to evaluate the morality of their conduct.

To be effective directors, the outsiders must be selected because of some expertise in finance, management, or corporate affairs. Additionally, the person should have some national prominence, which would enable him or her to gain a national forum to criticize corporate policy if it is irresponsible. Each of these outside directors serving on the corporation's board of directors should be funded adequately so that they can employ a competent staff to investigate corporate policy, actions, procedures, and recommendations made to the directors. Without a staff independent of management, the directors will be helpless, having to rely on management studies and reports to evaluate its actions. This circumstance will not allow them any intelligent or independent voice in management.

"Debate On Outside Directors," Arthur J. Goldberg, *New York Times,* October 29, 1972

More than three dozen suits have been filed by disgruntled shareholders of the Penn Central Transportation Company against the members of its board of directors who served prior to its receivership. These suits are based on the rule of law imposing the ultimate legal responsibility for the management of a corporate enterprise upon its board of directors.

Yet, the question arises, in light of the complexity of the operation of any large company of how even the most conscientious outside board members can meet their basic duty of serving responsibly as directors. In addition to this legal obligation, the modern board of directors is properly being called upon to meet the economic and social challenges of the society at large.

The major problem in the corporate director system is the gap between what the law decrees to be the governing role of the corporate director and the reality of management control of the corporation.

Contrary to legal theory, the boards of directors of most of our larger companies do not in fact control and manage their companies, nor are they equipped to do so. Instead, the management hired by the board, presumably to execute decisions of the board, in fact generally decides the course of operations and periodically requests the board to confirm the determinations of the management.

Thus, the board is relegated to an advisory and legitimizing function that is substantially different from the role of policy maker and guardian of shareholder and public interest contemplated by the law of corporations.

At the very best, outside directors of almost all large corporate enterprises under the present system cannot acquire more than a smattering of knowledge about any large and far-flung company of which they are directors. As a result, outside directors often are even unable to ask discerning questions when presented with a complex management decision for approval at the board meetings.

This can result in the outside director not fulfilling his fiduciary responsibility to the shareholders. As one former Penn Central director frankly admitted: "I don't think anybody was aware that it was that close to collapse."

Factors that may be deemed as illustrative of negligence or mismanagement on the part of directors include:

¶ Ignoring signs of mismanagement and failing to take affirmative action after learning facts sufficient to put a prudent man on notice of possible mismanagement.

¶ Disregard of duties by indifference to responsibilities.

¶ Acting as figureheads with no genuine attempt to oversee the administration of corporate affairs.

¶ Failure to examine and review carefully the books and records of the corporation and management's major policy decisions.

The lack of adequate and persistent investigation by a board of directors of areas of decision such as product-line development, consumer relations, ecology and social issues within the corporate structure can properly lead to charges of corporate irresponsibility against the board itself as well as the corporation as a whole.

As commentators have noted, a corporation with tens of millions of dollars in sales is no longer merely a business with private goals, but is also a social institution with resulting responsibilities. Indeed, everyone has the right to be concerned with the effect of a company's products or practices if they are dangerous, harmful or deceptive in any way.

The dilemma of the corporate director and indeed of the corporation as a whole is how to meet these responsibilities to the shareholders, to the enterprise of the corporation and to the public at large.

It is difficult, if not impossible, under the present director system for the most dedicated director to have much impact on policy decisions. The outside director is simply unable to gather enough independent information to act as a watchdog or sometimes even to ask good questions.

When presented with the agenda of the board meeting, the director is not basically equipped to provide any serious input into the decision. Realistically, it has already been made by management. This mode of operation, however, leaves the director open to justifiable criticism and legal recriminations.

It would be the counsel of wisdom and in the interest of shareholders and the public to provide outside directors with the means whereby they could discharge their fiduciary responsibilities in the conduct of corporate affairs.

To assure that the board of directors of a typical large company is performing its duties by using its best and independent judgment in the interest of the stockholders and the public at large, one of the possible solutions is for the board to establish a committee of overseers of outside directors (the exact name is not important, but the function is).

Such a committee would be generally responsible for supervising company operations on a broad scale and make periodic reports to the board.

To perform these duties adequately this committee would need authorization to hire a small staff of experts who would be responsible only to the board and would be totally independent of management control. In addition, the committee should also be empowered to engage the services of consultants of the highest competence.

As the eyes and ears of the directors, these independent experts and their staff assistants and consultants would look into major policy questions and report to the committee and through them to the board as a whole before decisions are taken on management recommendations.

The fundamental responsibility of these experts, staff and consultants would be to provide an independent source of expertise for the board. This would help enable the board members to fulfill the due diligence requirements of a reasonable independent investigation of company operations.

In addition, it would reassert the position of the board as a focal point for creative policy input for corporate decisions.

The experts, staff assistants and consultants would in turn have to be assured of full and complete cooperation from management and from lower-level corporate employees in filling requests for information. This right to information, of course, is one of the rights as well as a responsibility of corporate directors.

The membership of this group of expert advisers should include representatives from widely divergent areas of expertise.

For technical aspects of product-line development, scientific advisers should be recruited. For a look at future markets and the desires of the public, a demographic expert and consumer adviser should be consulted. To ensure compliance with truth-in-advertising standards, an outside advertising consultant might be utilized.

Other possible experts might include an independent auditor to assure the soundness of the accounting techniques used by the corporation and a disinterested independent financer (for example, a retired executive of an investment banking house) to ascertain whether the operations are being frugally financed.

Finally, some employee representatives might be consulted for their independent view of the performance of the corporation from their perspective. Permanent staff assistants to the overseer committee could perform most of the investigative work necessary for the use of the experts.

Source: © 1972 by The New York Times Co. Reprinted by permission.

ENFORCEMENT TECHNIQUES

Legal action to enforce ethical behavior among business employees and managers in addition to self regulation, may be necessary to improve the moral climate of American industry. But for any type of legal remedy to be effective, it must be enforceable. Some suggestions for structuring an ethical enforcement system can be developed by examining congressionally created enforcement methods. Congress has been experimenting with different ways of enforcing its business regulatory laws. By observing these, we can develop a system for regulating business ethics.

1. Direct Court Action Against Wrongdoers. Under some laws, Congress gives injured parties the right to sue in court those who caused their damages. For example, antitrust laws permit a competitor to sue for triple damages any person whose anticompetitive practices cause it damages. Shareholders can sue their corporation or its officers for violations of the securities acts. Direct court action by the damaged party is effective where that person has the experience to know when to sue and the financial resources to afford to sue.

2. Administrative Action on Behalf of an Injured Party. Some laws passed by Congress create an administrative agency with powers to sue on behalf of an injured party who may file a complaint with it. Any money recovered from the person violating the law goes to the complainant. Recent legislation gives the Federal Trade Commission power to sue business firms that damage consumers by unfair or deceptive methods of competition. The Equal Employment Opportunity Commission can sue on behalf of a worker claiming discrimination in employment. This enforcement method seems effective where the injured person may be unaware of his or her rights in court or unable to afford court costs and attorney's fees.

3. Direct Government Intervention. Congress gives some government agencies and departments power to sue any person violating regulatory laws without waiting for complaints to be filed. The Securities and Exchange Commission can stop the sale of any stock or bond it thinks harmful to investors, and the Federal Trade Commission can remove advertisements it deems deceptive to consumers. If a pattern of racial, ethnic, or sex discrimination appears in any industry, the Attorney General of the United States has powers to file suit seeking an injunction against such conduct. And the Occupational Safety and Health Act gives the power to halt safety violations only to an administrative agency, not to workers or their representatives. Direct government action seems effective where issues are likely to be so complex that only specific expertise of professionals can settle them.

4. Specific Enforcement Remedies to Individuals. Under some federal laws, individuals have powers to sue specific parties that fail to carry out their duties under the law. For example, if the Consumer Product Safety Commission does not set safety standards for certain products, any consumer can file suit in court to compel the Commission to act. Participants in pension plans are entitled to certain reports. If they are not furnished, the individuals can sue the plan administrators to force compliance with the law and to obtain $100 for each day the required reports are overdue. This enforcement technique becomes a spur for action when bureaucratic delays inconvenience the public or nullify the purpose of a law.

5. Indirect Actions. Finally, some laws act indirectly to obtain compliance. The Environmental Protection Act of 1969 states that national policy requires a productive harmony between man and his environment. Every part of government must consider the environmental impact of its actions. Environmental considerations of any project are now as important as economic factors in decision making. However, Congress does not give the Environmental Protection Agency (EPA), government, or anyone else any direct rights under this law. Instead, the EPA can set standards and policy for industry and government agencies. The EPA can cooperate with other government regulatory agencies as they determine the environmental impact of their actions. And the EPA can recommend that a particular agency deny a permit or license to any firm whose actions could harm the environment. For example, a company wishing to build a power plant may need the permission of the Federal Power Commission before starting construction. Before giving that permission, the FPC must consider the effect on the environment of that project. The EPA will study this power plant project and then advise the FPC to give or deny permission to build. EPA recommendations are advisory and government agencies have discretion to accept or reject them.

This enforcement technique is more subtle than the others discussed. It can be effective where public policy so strongly supports the objectives of the law that rejection of EPA recommendations is unlikely because of hostile political reaction. Environmental destruction is so obvious to citizens today that most politicians will support any action to prevent further abuses or clean up existing ones. This support makes forced compulsion less necessary. Also, indirect action may be the only possible enforcement tool where the goals and means to fulfill them are unclear or in dispute. With environmental matters, no one knows the dollar cost of preserving a clean environment, the effect on employment of some pollution standards set by

EPA, the impact on export sales of environmental policies, or the technology available to remedy pollution. Thus, any enforcement of this law must be generalized, adaptable to a variety of different conditions, to be workable.

6. Ethical Enforcement System. For any ethical enforcement system to work, procedures must be flexible and adaptable to many different situations. There are several reasons for this approach. First, the average citizen wronged by an ethical violation may not know about the principles established by law or by the ethical standards boards suggested before. Consequently, giving only private parties the right to sue for such violations may not be adequate to halt these abuses. However, direct action by individuals should exist as an alternative to other enforcement techniques. Second, government agencies and the ethical standards boards' investigators will uncover ethical violations. They should be allowed to bring legal action to halt the violations and to seek restitution for injured persons.

Not all situations involving ethical problems for business employees and managers could be covered by a law or rule. Enforcement in these situations will be impossible. Yet most people in society would condemn a business decision that runs counter to community ethical or moral values. Consequently, merely requiring disclosure of the circumstances surrounding a business action that may violate ethical rules may be sufficient to bring public pressure to reform.

Taking these factors into consideration, a possible ethical enforcement technique for business could consist of a threefold procedure: permit any individual suffering injury because of another's violation of established ethical guidelines to sue in court to recover money for any losses suffered; give each government agency responsible for regulating an industry authority to inquire into the ethical aspects of any business decisions; and encourage each agency and standards board to publish any business violations of community- or industry-accepted ethical rules, thus stimulating public pressure to eliminate future violations and correct existing ones.

PROFESSIONAL LIABILITY

Ethical guides are necessary for either the ethical standards boards or the government to enforce. These guides should be prepared by the boards. In drafting these guidelines, the boards should consider the ethical principles that now exist in most industries, for example, the purchasing managers' guides. These principles are created by trade association for use by their members and their employees. But these principles are optional and incomplete, and do not recognize the professional nature of business in modern America. Standards created by the ethical standards boards must be mandatory and drafted for professionals.

The traditional definition of a profession is any vocation requiring specialized training in a field of learning whose members are held accountable to certain standards. Two traditionally recognized professions closely allied with business management are law and accounting. In each of these fields, practitioners must enroll in special education programs. These programs prescribe a rigorous study of technical rules and principles of good conduct. Regulatory boards supervise lawyers and accountants. These boards apply ethical standards to assure client protections. Business should be recognized as a profession. It requires managers and their employees to study unique problems of organizing and controlling business organizations. Business practitioners have accountability to owners, employees, customers, and society. What is now lacking is complete guidelines for measuring their accountability. That omission can be remedied by formation of ethical standards by the boards suggested here.

Since business is a profession, its members should be treated like any other professionals. In accounting and law, professional regulatory boards license and supervise the practice of the professions. Members are held accountable for their negligent or improper conduct by boards which apply established ethical rules for appropriate disciplinary action. Adoption of some of these guidelines for business managers and employees can be a start toward drafting standards for industry.

Consider some of the ethical duties professional agents owe to their clients. Each owes a duty of loyalty to the client while representing his or her interests. That duty requires the professional to act honestly in all dealings on behalf of the client. The professional must use best efforts to further the client's business and there must be no conflict of interests while acting on behalf of the client. The professional agent may not use any confidential information acquired while acting for a client for personal benefit or disclose it to others. In general, the professional agent has a fiduciary duty to perform all actions with the exercise of due care and diligence which a reasonably prudent person would use in managing his or her own property.

Clients of a business manager are the public. For business managers, the public consists of consumers, employees, owners, and society. To each of these publics, the manager owes certain duties in the same manner that a professional owes responsibility to his or her

TABLE 17-2. NATIONAL ASSOCIATION OF PURCHASING MANAGEMENT

STANDARDS AND ETHICS OF BUYING AND SELLING

1. To buy and sell on the basis of value, recognizing that value represents that combination of quality, service, and price which assures greatest ultimate economy to the user.

2. To respect our obligations and neither expressly nor impliedly to promise a performance which we cannot reasonably expect to fulfill.

3. To avoid misrepresentation and sharp practice in our purchases and sales, recognizing that permanent business relations can be maintained only on a structure of honesty and fair dealing.

4. To be courteous and considerate of those with whom we deal, to be prompt and businesslike in our appointments, and to carry on negotiations with all reasonable expedition so as to avoid trespassing on the rights of others to the time of buyers and salesmen.

5. To avoid statements tending to injure or discredit a legitimate competitor, and to divulge no information acquired in confidence with the intent of giving or receiving an unfair advantage in a competitive business transaction.

6. To strive for simplification and standardization within the bounds of utility and industrial economy, and to further the development of products and methods which will improve industrial efficiency.

7. To recognize that character is the greatest asset in commerce, and to give it major consideration in the selection of customers and source of supply.

8. To adjust claims and settle disputes on the basis of facts and fairness, to submit the facts to arbitration if a mutual agreement cannot be reached, to abide by the decisions of the arbiters and to resort to legal measures in commercial disputes only when the preceding courses prove ineffective.

9. To provide or accept no gifts or entertainment in the guise of sales expense, where the intent or effect is to unduly prejudice the recipients in favor of the donor as against legitimate competitors.

10. To give or receive no bribes, in the form of money or otherwise, in any commercial transaction and to expose commercial bribery wherever encountered for the purpose of maintaining the highest standard of ethics in industry.

Source: Purchasing Handbook, 3rd Edition, McGraw Hill Co., New York, 1973.

---

clients. Thus a business manager owes his or her fiduciary duty to consumers, shareholders, employees, and society. To this broad group, whose members would appear to have conflicting interests, the manager must act with loyalty and honesty to benefit each public.

Admittedly, this may be difficult to accomplish. Consider the plight of an executive of a large utility company. The community may want less noticeable power transmission lines, requiring the expenditures of capital to bury cables. Customers will object to the higher rates charged to cover the expenses and owners may be reluctant to advance the capital for the project without some indications of a payback period. Reconciling these conflicting interests is an essential part of a manager's job; representing each interest with integrity should be a mandatory obligation.

Certainly, these broad aspects of a fiduciary duty will have to be defined to cover specific activities involving a manager's responsibilities in the same manner that professional accounting and law societies adapt their ethical rules to everyday activities of their professional members. This can be the responsibility of the ethical standards boards. These boards may have to modify the standards for different industries or interpret them differently for different levels of employee responsibility in the organization. But developing ethical standards for American business and enforcing them fully can be a starting point for restoring and preserving the public's confidence in business integrity.

SOCIAL RESPONSIBILITY

A study of contemporary American society reveals numerous problems facing the public. Each demands a solution and the public expects its institutions to solve them. Consider just two examples. (1) Housing appears to be inadequate to meet the needs of families. Recent studies show that the rate of inflation in new housing prices exceeds the rate of savings by the average family. This prevents them from acquiring the capital necessary to purchase homes. (2) Numerous workers in society lack the basic educational skills even to qualify for company training programs. They are condemned to a lifetime of unemployment.

When American business ignores these problems or argues against governmental solutions for them, the image of business as "greedy profitmakers" is reinforced. Business managers should reevaluate their positions regarding the role of their enterprises in solving such national social ills. American business firms have the economic resources to finance programs to correct our national problems. They have the personnel trained in management techniques, capital formation, and control policies needed to make these corrective actions successful. Also, business has a record of success in producing an abundance of quality products at reasonable prices, enabling most people in society to achieve a comfortable standard of living. The knowledge that produced this record of accomplishment could be adapted to society's needs, hopefully with the same results.

But management sees another side to the questions of business's role in solving national social problems. Some would argue that business should exist simply to make a profit. Government should then tax these profits and spend its revenues to solve national problems in accordance with voters' preferences. Allowing business managers to solve such problems transfers control over the nation's expenditures from citizens to an elite of corporate managers. The democratic process could be subverted. Also, some would argue that management expertise cannot be transferred automatically to public policy areas. It has limits, shown by the economic reversals of conglomerate mergers made during the 1960s. In addition, stockholders may object to the types of projects in which the corporate managers spend their money. Courts could consider such expenditures as a waste of corporate assets. Finally, community organizations funded by the corporation may act contrary to the shareholders' wishes. Such organizations may become politically active, indirectly involving the corporation in illegal political funding.

The question of whether business should become more socially responsible is a complex one. Business firms may feel it is improper for them to engage in such activities, but many segments of the public expect some response from business. Managers may feel compelled to act. In that situation, the firm should develop a strategy for meeting its social responsibilities in the most efficient manner possible. A few basic steps should be followed by the manager:

1. The entire organization should make a commitment to accept its role as social benefactor. This means management should decide upon a specific plan of action, with the approval and concurrence of the board of directors and the stockholders. Without this commitment, any social action by the firm may be so controversial as to divide the members into warring camps, making normal business operations impossible.

2. The firm should concentrate on narrow objectives rather than attacking a complete list of social ills. Concentrating on narrow objectives can enable the firm to allocate its resources and personnel more efficiently and in degrees or amounts where some success is possible.

3. The firm should use the same techniques and energies to fulfill its social objectives as it employs to market its products, raise capital, meet production quotas, or operate other elements of its business. This means the firm must make a long-term commitment to reach its goals, establish subgoals necessary to attain the objectives, and formulate detailed plans of action to accomplish each of its targets.

4. A monitoring system should be established, enabling managers to verify performance and initiate corrective actions where needed. Individual managers should be held accountable for successfully fulfilling company social objectives as are other managers who ac-

complish objectives in the traditional areas of responsibility. Rewards should be paid on an equal basis.

By following these brief steps, management may help improve the image of business, accomplish some worthy project for society, and satisfy the public's concern about the legitimacy of business operations.

SUMMARY

Business must develop a new way for measuring the success of a company. Success must not be measured simply in production goals achieved, financial targets reached, or sales increased. A firm's financial statement must reflect its social commitment and ethical behavior. Today, a company that spends money to reach goals in either of these areas creates negative effects on profits and assets. Such treatment is unfortunate because failure to make progress in these areas may depress profits in the long run. For example, neglecting to build a community park may save corporate money now but may so enrage the local populace that they boycott company products or damage its property. Yet any company expenditure for the community's welfare to prevent these possibilities cannot be treated as a legitimate benefit to business.

A new accounting technique must be developed to reflect the true costs and benefits to the company of these expenditures. Various suggestions have been made:

1. Classify company expenditures for its social responsibility or improving the ethical behavior of its employees as actual benefits rather than costs to the firm. The benefits may be recorded as amounts saved by not being fined for some unethical practice that violates the law.
2. Record expenses as benefits to company good will.
3. Record such expenses as a part of its public relations costs.
4. Create a new item on the asset side of a company's financial statement known as "social responsiveness." Expenditures in this area would be recorded as amounts spent to acquire or improve upon this asset.

REVIEW QUESTIONS

1. Describe the different techniques for enforcing ethical behavior in business.

2. Discuss the benefits of business self-regulation of ethical behavior over government enforcement.

3. Professionals are licensed and conform to legally sanctioned standards. Should business managers be licensed and regulated in a similar way?

4. Evaluate the use of outside directors as a way of enforcing ethical and morally responsible behavior in business.

5. Discuss the benefits and dangers to business managers and society of having business become more involved in solving national social problems. Is the risk worth taking?

6. A company improved a neighborhood playground by spending $15,000. Local children now have a pleasant place to play. How should this company expenditure be treated by corporate accountants? Describe the effects of this expenditure on shareholders.

7. A corporation encourages employees to become politically and socially active in local community affairs. It does not encourage any particular political or social group. The corporation allows employees to take time off from work as paid leave time to run for and serve in public offices. Does this constitute unlawful or unfair participation of the corporation in politics? Consider the consequences of this corporate policy on political opponents of company employees who do not receive paid leave.

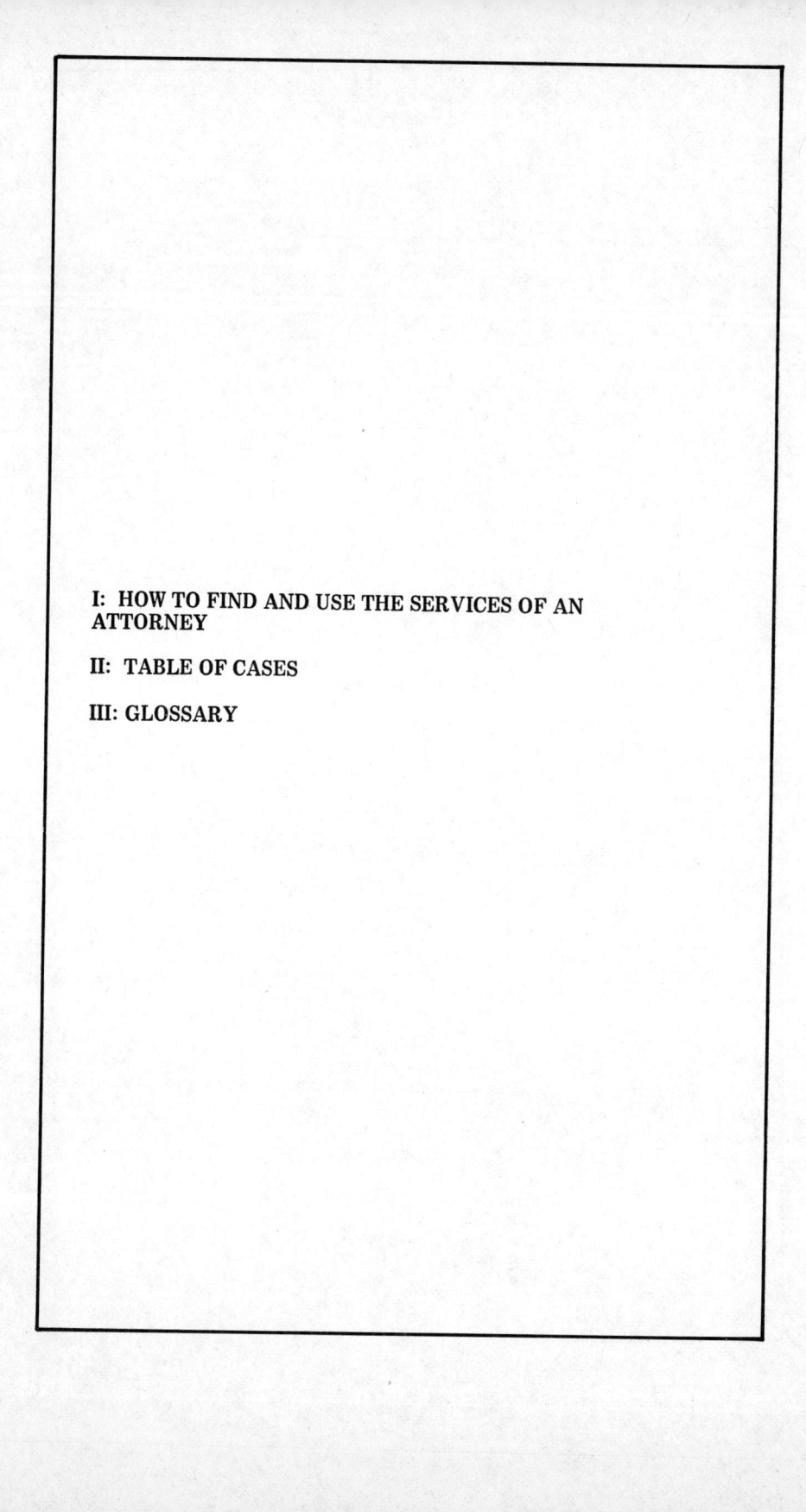

I: HOW TO FIND AND USE THE SERVICES OF AN ATTORNEY

II: TABLE OF CASES

III: GLOSSARY

APPENDIXES

I

HOW TO FIND AND USE THE SERVICES OF AN ATTORNEY

In this book, we studied some of the legal aspects of business regulation. We acquired a basic understanding of law, court procedures, and some major federal regulatory laws. At one time in our society, this amount of knowledge was adequate to carry on business. But today, law is more complex and the consequences of violating law are more severe. Consequently, we may sometimes find that we must hire an expert in law to advise us of our legal rights and duties. This brief section explains when hiring a lawyer might be necessary, how to find a competent one, the payment plans available, what the lawyer will expect from you, and what you can expect from the lawyer.

WHEN TO HIRE A LAWYER

A course in basic law should alert you to the benefits of practicing preventive law. Knowing about law can tell you when to call upon the services of a lawyer before it is too late for this person to be of any real help to you in minimizing legal problems. Many lawyers spend most of their time counseling clients on how to avoid legal trouble rather than representing them in court. Hence, you should consult a lawyer before legal problems become too burdensome and costly to solve.

Generally this means your lawyer should become an integral part of your business planning from the inception of an idea through its implementation to its conclusion. At each stage of an idea's life cycle, the lawyer can advise you on the idea's legal effects on competitors, customers, employees, shareholders, and the government. This advice may cause you to alter strategy but it may save costs in the long run.

Some specific problems for which you should consult with a lawyer are:

1. Business Structure. Your lawyer can review existing state and federal laws relating to business organization and operation. Laws continually change. Your attorney can advise you on the best way to structure your business to get maximum advantages from the law. The lawyer can review a firm's articles of incorporation to see if other states offer more advantages to the business. Some states offer tax incentives for incorporation, other states offer corporations greater flexibility of management. The lawyer also could advise your organization to shift to a different type of business organization. For example, recent changes in state law permit professionals to incorporate and possibly save some tax dollars by doing so.

2. Document Preparation. When a business is started, forms must be prepared. Some of these are the incorporation articles, perhaps partnership agreements, taxpayer identification reports, and others. During the business's operation, numerous other forms must be filed, pertaining to employee wages, production, product safety, shareholder meetings, tax returns, job safety reports, and others. Expert advice from a lawyer can make it easier to fill out these reports and reduce potential liability for inadvertent errors in recording information.

3. Strategy. Some business actions require an evaluation of alternatives. The lawyer can advise you on the legal aspects and consequences of each alternative. For example, a decision to merge with another business involves antitrust considerations as well as financial, managerial, and marketing ones. Also, a competitor, customer, or labor organization may threaten legal action as a way of inducing you into some agreement. A lawyer's opinion can confirm or deny the potential of this threat.

4. Personal. A successful person wants to save expense and time in his or her personal life. An attorney can be as helpful in your personal planning as in your business operations. For example, advice on estate planning can minimize your tax burden while transferring maximum benefits to your heirs. Advice on family relations matters can remedy legal problems stemming from divorce, separation, or child custody. Tax advice can simplify audit proceedings before state and federal agencies.

ATTORNEY SELECTION

Assuming we need the services of a lawyer, the next problem is hiring one. This decision is not always an easy one to carry out. Lawyers do not advertise in the same way as a person selling products or services. This limitation on advertising attempts to protect the integrity of the legal profession. However, a lawyer's reputation is his or her best advertisement. We should hire an attorney who has a good reputation for solving the types of problems we expect in our business or personal life. We can discover a lawyer's reputation in the same way that any other person's reputation is learned: look at what the lawyer has done, and at how the public has evaluated his or her work.

This can be done in several ways. First, examine the news reports about various lawyers. Periodic newspaper and television stores about certain attorneys will appear. These reports may indicate the types of cases a particular lawyer handles and the degree of success for the clients. Second, listen to word-of-mouth advertising. If friends or relatives have used a lawyer, ask their opinions. Third, look at the membership list of any clubs or associations to which you belong. No doubt several attorneys will be members and you can evaluate each according to your personal contacts. Lastly, you could consult with business associates or your employer. During the course of their careers, they will probably have used a lawyer and may recommend one to you.

DUTIES OF A LAWYER

Law is a profession and those engaged in its practice are professionals. This means lawyers profess detailed knowledge and apply that knowledge to advise, represent, and guide others. They should act for the welfare of others. The law profession requires that lawyers have expertise and use that expertise in a proper fashion. To guarantee this expertise, the courts require that those wishing to become lawyers must fulfill certain conditions. Some of these conditions include four years of college study, followed by three years of full-time law school. After obtaining a law degree, the person becomes qualified only for the bar examination. This is a comprehensive test on the law's major areas. It is prepared and administered by the state in which the potential lawyer wishes to practice. The bar examination determines if the applicant has acquired sufficient legal knowledge and developed adequate legal analytical abilities to advise and represent others.

If the bar examination is passed, the applicant must then submit to an investigation into his or her background to see if anything detracts from the moral integrity required of an attorney. Upon successful completion of this moral character investigation, the applicant is admitted as an attorney, to practice law in the state that administered the bar examination. The court continually supervises the professional conduct of members of the bar. If at any time, an attorney violates court rules, the code of professional responsibility of the American Bar Association, or any duty owed to clients, the attorney will be reprimanded by the court. This reprimand may involve a warning, suspension from practice for a period of time, or disbarment from practice.

The attorney has obligations to the public, and to assure that these obligations are followed, the American Bar Association has established a code of conduct to govern the attorney. Similar codes have been adopted by courts in each state. Some major rules of the American Bar Association are:

> 1. Judicial hearings ought to be conducted through dignified and orderly procedures designed to protect the rights of all parties. Although the lawyer has the duty to represent his client zealously, he should not engage in any conduct that offends the dignity and decorum of proceedings. While maintaining his independence, a lawyer should be respectful, courteous, and above-board in his relations with a judge, or hearing officer before whom he appears. He should avoid undue solicitude for the comfort or convenience of judge or jury and should avoid any other conduct to gain special consideration.
> 2. The professional judgment of a lawyer should be exercised, within the bounds of the law, solely for the benefit of his client and free of compromising influences and loyalties. Neither his personal interests, the interests of other clients, nor the desires of third persons should be permitted to dilute his loyalty to his client.
> 3. A lawyer shall not knowingly: reveal a confidence or secret of his client; use a confidence or secret of his client to the disadvantage of the client; use a confidence or secret of his client for the advantage of himself or of a third person, unless the client consents after full disclosure.
> 4. A lawyer shall not enter into an agreement for, charge, or collect an illegal or clearly excessive fee. A fee is excessive when after a review of the facts, a lawyer of ordinary prudence would be left with a definite and firm conviction that the fee is in excess of a reasonable fee.

(Source: American Bar Association, 1970.)

ATTORNEY COMPENSATION

Perhaps no question presents greater confusion to potential clients than that of how to pay for attorney services. Some guidelines can be helpful to remove some doubts. First, the client should discuss in advance the fee arrangements for handling a legal problem. If the fee seems too high, visit another lawyer to see what competitors charge. Most lawyers will consider the difficulty of the problem the primary factor in setting a fee. This will indicate the amount of time and research necessary to solve the problem.

If a client anticipates using an attorney on a regular basis, a retainer method of compensation should be considered. Under this payment plan, a client pays a regular monthly fee to the lawyer and the lawyer promises to perform stipulated legal services without further cost to the client. This system may be less costly in the long run than paying an attorney for each separate transaction performed.

The contingency fee system is an alternate financing arrangement. The lawyer agrees to charge a minimum fee for representing the client in court. If the client wins the case, the lawyer will take a percentage of any money awarded. If the client loses the case, the lawyer will take only the minimum fee. This payment system is advantageous where the client has a right to sue but is unwilling or unable to invest substantial sums to sue.

Some laws passed by Congress now establish the fees that lawyers can charge for representing clients before some government agencies. Often the government pays attorney fees if it loses the case. Also, courts have the power to award a successful plaintiff costs and attorneys' fees if the plaintiff wins in court. Such fees are paid in cases of corporate mismanagement, antitrust suits, and consumer injury cases. The client's lawyer can charge more than court-awarded fees, however.

A new idea for compensating lawyers is the prepaid legal services plan. This plan operates much like medical insurance coverage. A certain amount of money is deposited into a fund, operated by an insurance company or bar association. Persons belonging to the fund can consult a lawyer, and the lawyer's fee is paid in whole or in part by the fund. Money for the plan comes from employer contributions and employee deductions from wages. It usually exists as a fringe benefit under some employment contracts. If this type of plan becomes popular throughout the country, it could enable the middle-class person to have more access to legal advisors without having to pay fees that seem excessive to the wage earner.

DUTIES OF A CLIENT

A person should learn how to be a client. For a good client, the amount of litigation the person becomes involved in may be reduced, the costs for legal services can be lower, and the lawyer can represent the person more effectively. The suggestions here are some guidelines for being a better client.

1. Make an Objective Evaluation. Every person who becomes involved in a law proceeding invariably thinks his or her views are the right ones. The litigant is a combatant and must have enthusiasm for the battle. To sustain the legal struggle, the person must have loyalty to his or her cause. But that loyalty can be a hindrance to becoming a good client. At each stage in the legal proceeding, the client must fairly and objectively analyze the situation and study the facts surrounding an issue and the consequences of each alternate plan of action. The client must balance the costs of an action against the benefits from that action. This cost-benefit analysis is important in evaluating compromise proposals. An open and objective mind not blurred by the emotions of a particular moment is the first requirement for a good client.

2. Understand the Risks. Law is not an exact science. Automatic formulas do not exist. The outcome of any case depends on many variables, for example, the judge's rulings on legal issues, the witness's ability to convince the jury, the attorney's impact on the court, the jury's analysis of the facts, and the actions of an appellate court. Since a case outcome cannot be predicted with any degree of certainty, a client must understand the risks of suing even where the case seems like a "sure bet." A client must understand that no definite answer can be given to every legal problem. Realizing and accepting this uncertainty can help you appreciate the work of your lawyer.

3. Be Precise. Whenever a claim arises against a person, or whenever a legal problem begins, the natural tendency is to panic. For example, being cited by a government inspector for violations of the safety law can be traumatic for someone not accustomed to such procedures. Similar experiences can arise when you are audited by a tax collector, involved in an automobile accident, or forced to open your employment or corporate records to an inspector from an administrative agency.

In each of these situations, the person must not panic. Being a good client means the person recovers immediately from any shock, analyzes the facts carefully to determine what basic rights are involved, and gathers all evidence that may have importance in any subsequent proceeding. Until legal help can be consulted, the good client refrains from making any damaging statements or turning over any damaging evidence to investigators. Of course, to do all of these things properly requires confidence in yourself and in your knowledge of the law. To be a good client requires a precise study of law.

4. Keep Evidence. If any legal dispute against you proceeds to a trial, evidence will be needed to establish your case and your rights. That evidence will be helpful to your attorney in deciding what your action should be. Your attorney will be able to help you only to the extent that evidence exists. Since no person knows in advance what evidence will be important to a later proceeding, a good client preserves all factual materials pertaining to a legal problem. For example, names, addresses, identifications, and other data about each person involved in the dispute should be recorded; copies of all reports and documents should be kept in several different locations; written summaries of each conversation should be noted; and photographs of property in dispute should be made. Some business managers keep this evidence in a diary maintained while they are in key positions in their companies. A good client should take equal care in keeping evidence.

5. Be Brief. Both you and your attorney are or should be busy persons. Your attorney will be billing you at an hourly rate unless you have agreed upon a different method of compensation. Thus, the longer it takes you to communicate the important facts of your problem, the more it could cost you for legal services. Accordingly, you should tell the attorney only what he or she needs to know to solve your problem. Anything more or less than that will delay your attorney's work. A client must be brief.

6. Remember Your Liability. Even though you hire a good lawyer, remember that a client is responsible for the mistakes, errors and omissions of the attorney. Improper actions by the lawyer can affect your liability to the court and to the other parties in the legal proceeding. Consider the following case. Several black individuals sued the officers and directors of a swimming pool association. These managers voluntarily voted to exclude blacks from the pool. They did so on the advice of their lawyer who said the private, nonpublic nature of the association exempted it from the civil rights laws forbidding discrimination in public places. The federal Court of Appeals disagreed. The court said the managers acted improperly in excluding blacks and are liable for penalties established in the law. It added that the managers are not relieved from liability merely because they acted on the advice of their lawyer and even though they did not know their actions were illegal. Ignorance of the laws is not a defense to a lawsuit to enforce these laws. Officers and directors must use due diligence in running a business. They must use their own best judgments and not rely on an attorney's judgment. Their ignorance of the law, though caused by their lawyer's advice and corroborated by some courts, is no defence. Each person was held personally liable and required to pay money damages to those blacks discriminated against.

Of course, these managers can sue their attorney for malpractice. But that can be difficult to do, costly, and time consuming. A good client remembers that he or she has ultimate liability and acts in awareness of that fact.

II

TABLE OF CASES

Accu Namics, Inc., In Re, 301
American Column and Lumber Co. v. United States, 188
American Federation of Labor v. Swing, 272
American Shipbuilding Co. v. NLRB, 250
Atlas Roofing Co. v. OSHRC, 306

Banks v. Chicago Grain Trimmers Ass'n, 293
Battalla v. N.Y.S., 291
Benson v. 1120 St. Charles Co., 95
Berger v. Amana Society, 93
Birnbaum v. Newport Steel Corp., 142
Blue Chip Stamps v. Manor Drug Stores, 141
Bogosian v. Gulf Oil Corp., 190
Boys Market, 269
Brennan v. Gibson's Products, Inc., 299
Brown Shoe Co. v. United States, 207
Buffalo Forge Co. v. United Steelworkers of America, 268
Building and Construction Trades Council, In Re, 272

California v. Byers, 74
Central Credit Collection Corporation v. Grayson, 162
Chernin v. Progressive Service Co., 291
Citizens to Preserve Overton Park, Inc. v. Volpe, 64
Connell Construction Co. v. Plumbers and Steamfitters Local 100, 259
Corriveau and Routhier Inc. v. NLRB, 270
Cummins v. Parker Seal Co., 334

Detroit Edison Co. v. Utility Workers Local 223, 253
Dowdell v. United States, 70

Eisen v. Carlisle and Jacquelin, 38
Electrolux Corp. v. Val-Worth, Inc., 204

Ernst and Ernst v. Hochfelder, 136
Escott v. Barchris Construction Corp., 123

Federal Power Commission v. Florida Power and Light Co., 62
Federal Trade Commission v. Anheuser Busch, Inc., 223
Federal Trade Commission v. Morton Salt Co., 226
Federal Trade Commission v. Procter and Gamble Co., 202
Federal Trade Commission v. Sperry and Hutchinson Co., 205
Flood v. Kuhn, 210
Fortner Enterprises, Inc. v. United States Steel Corp., 189
Fox v. Washington, 330
Franks v. Bowman Transportation Company, 318

General Foods, In Re, 228
Gideon v. Wainwright, 69
Gilbert v. General Electric Co., 334
Goldfarb v. Virginia State Bar, 209
Gottschalk v. Benson, 170
Greguski v. Oyster Bay, 27
Griggs v. Duke Power Co., 330

Hannah v. Larche, 68, 70
Hannigan v. Sears, Roebuck and Company, 160
Hanover Shoe, Inc. v. United Shoe Machinery Corp., 191
Hawaii v. Standard Oil Company of California, 206
Henningsen v. Bloomfield Motors, Inc., 233
Hill York Corporation v. American International Franchises, Inc., 118
Hodgson v. Local Union 6799, United Steelworkers of America, 277
Hollander v. Sears, Roebuck and Company, 335
Hysler v. Florida, 70

International Union v. Russell, 272
Interstate Commerce Commission v. Chatsworth, 43

Jaquith Company v. Island Creek Coal Co., 106
Jennings v. Connecticut Light and Power Company, 47
Johnson v. Railway Express Agency, Inc., 321
Jones v. Ahmanson and Company, 93

Kansas v. Colorado, 17
Katzowitz v. Sidler, 97
Kennedy v. Mendoza Martinez, 306
Klor's Inc. v. Broadway Hale Stores, Inc., 186

Luther Marvin Robbins, In Re, 304

Mallory v. United States, 69
Malloy v. Hogan, 70
Mapp v. Ohio, 69
Maternally Yours v. Your Maternity Shop, 164
Matter of Klimas v. Trans Caribbean Airways, 291
Matter of Straws v. Fail, 291
Matthews v. Eldridge, 76
Miranda v. Arizona, 69
Mogul v. McGregor, 179
Morton v. Mancari, 325
Muller Corporation v. Gazocean International, 36
Myers v. Gilman Paper Corporation, 334

National Labor Relations Board v. Draper Corporation, 270
National Labor Relations Board v. Fansteel Corporation, 270
National Labor Relations Board v. Fleetwood Trailer Company, 271
National Labor Relations Board v. Jones and Laughlin Steel Corporation, 248
National Labor Relations Board v. Local 825, International Union of Operating Engineers, 256
National Labor Relations Board v. Plasterers Local Union 79, 272
National Labor Relations Board v. Scrivener, 251
National Labor Relations Board v. Sears, Roebuck and Company, 264
National Labor Relations Board v. Wyman Gordon Company, 59
Northern Pacific R. Company v. United States, 182
Norwalk Teachers v. Board of Education, 270

O'Leary v. Brown-Pacific-Maxon, Inc., 294

Perlman v. Feldmann, 102
Pharmaceutical Manufacturers Association v. Finch, 57
Philips v. Martin Marietta Corporation, 329
Powell v. Alabama, 70

Ramsey v. United Mine Workers, 208
Reliance Electric Co. v. Emerson Electric Company, 135
Rhodes Pharmacal Company v. Federal Trade Commission, 56
Roan v. Connecticut Industrial Building Commission, 46, 47
Robinson v. California, 70

Sears, Roebuck and Company, In Re, 229
Securities Exchange Commission v. Datronics Engineers, Inc., 122

396 Appendix

Securities Exchange Commission v. Howey, 113
Securities Exchange Commission v. Manor Nursing Centers, Inc., 116
Securities Exchange Commission v. McDonald Investment Co., 120
Securities Exchange Commission v. Medical Committee for Human Rights, 134
Securities Exchange Commission v. National Student Marketing Corporation, 147
Securities Exchange Commission v. Texas Gulf Sulpher, 132, 138
Sierra Club v. Morton, 60
Smith v. Brown-Borhek Company, 105
Standard Oil Company of California v. United States, 194, 196
Standard Oil Company of New Jersey v. United States, 179
Sterling Drug, Inc., In Re, 211
Superintendent of Insurance v. Bankers Life and Casualty, 136
Sylvester v. U.S. Postal Service, 319

Telex Corporation v. IBM, 170, 171
Testing Systems Inc. v. Magnaflux Corporation, 159, 168
Thomas v. Collins, 267
Thornhill v. Alabama, 271
Toombs v. Citizens Bank of Waynesboro, 95
Trbovich v. United Mine Workers of America, 273
Truck Drivers and Helpers Local Union, In Re, 273

United Farm Workers of America v. The Superior Court of Santa Cruz County, 271
United Housing Foundation Inc. v. Forman, 112
United States v. American Tobacco Company, 180
United States v. Arnold, Schwinn Company, 186
United States v. Container Corporation, 183
United States v. National Association of Securities Dealers, 208
United States v. Oregon State Medical Society, 209
United States v. Phillipsburg National Bank, 199, 201
United States v. Sealy, Inc., 185
United States v. Sheet Metal Workers Local 36, 318
United States v. Topco, 180, 181

Vecki v. Sorensen, 27

Wabash Ry Co. v. Barclay, 100
Williams v. Illinois, 70
Williams v. New York, 70
Wolfe v. Sibley, Lindsay and Curr Company, 291
Woodward v. Wright, 111

III

GLOSSARY

A

abrogate. To repeal; to make void.

abuse of discretion. A power that has not been justly and properly exercised under the circumstances of the case.

abuse of process. Irregular use of legal proceedings.

access to courts. The right to use judicial remedies to enforce rights in actions of every kind.

accountant. A person who is skilled in, keeps, or adjusts accounts.

accounting. The act or system of recording or summarizing business and financial transactions in books and analyzing, verifying, and reporting the results.

accrual of cause of action. The coming into existence of a right to sue.

acquit. To discharge an accusation completely.

acquittal. The discharge of an accusation by verdict, sentence, or other legal process.

action. An ordinary proceeding in a court by which a party sues another party for the enforcement or protection of a right.

actual damages. Damages in satisfaction of or in recompense for loss or sustained injury.

actuary. One who calculates insurance risks and premiums.

adjudication. A solemn or deliberate determination of an issue by the judicial power.

administrative agency. A governmental commission that carries out certain legislation.

administrative law. The branch of public law that deals with the various governmental agencies, prescribing their procedures.

Administrative Procedures Act. A federal statute, passed by Congress in 1946, that provides a basic and comprehensive regulation of procedures before federal agencies.

administrative process. Any proceeding in or before an administrative body as distinguished from a proceeding in a court.

adversary trial. A trial in which there are opposing parties before the court who have had full opportunity to present and establish their opposing contentions.

advertisement. Bringing to the public information contained in a notice.

affidavit. Any voluntary statement in writing and sworn to or affirmed before some person legally authorized to administer an oath.

affirm. To confirm a former judgment or order of a court.

affirmative action. The process by which the federal government encourages employers to hire certain classes of persons as a remedy for past discrimination against those groups.

ambulatory. Capable of being altered.

amendment of judgment. The correction of the record of the judgment.

answer. A plea made by a defendant to a complaint.

antitrust act. A statute prohibiting all combinations and arrangements in the form of trusts or pools; or otherwise among individuals, partnerships, and corporations that operate to establish or maintain a monopoly in the manufacture, production, or sale of any commodity; or that restrain trade or commerce.

appeal. A proceeding by which a case is brought from an inferior court to a superior court for reexamination, review, reversal, or modification.

appellant. A person who files an appeal.

appellee. A party against whom an appeal is taken, also called the respondent.

arbitrary decision. A decision, rendered by a court, judge, or other officer exercising judicial power, that is based upon the will of the officer alone, and not upon reason or exercise of judgment.

arbitration. The submission of some disputed matter to selected persons, and the substitution of their decision for the judgment of the established tribunals of justice, thus avoiding the formalities and delay of ordinary litigation.

articles of incorporation. The document that forms a corporation, stating its name, the purposes for which it is formed, the stock to be issued, and such other matters as required by state law, and which is filed in some public office.

assumption of risk. A common law docrine that an employee accepts the dangers of injury when working in a hazardous occupation.

attachment. A writ ordering property of a debtor to be taken by a court official for the benefit of a creditor.

attorney. A person who is licensed as an officer of the courts and who is empowered to appear, prosecute, defend, represent, and advise others.

Attorney General. The chief legal officer of the United States or of a state, who represents the government in litigation and serves as its principal legal advisor.

audit. The verification of accounting figures and computations.

authorization cards. Statements made by employees giving their preferences regarding the formation of a union at the place of their employment.

B

bailiff. A sheriff's deputy.

bargaining agent. A representative of employees who negotiates the terms of the employment contract with the employer.

beneficial use. The legal title of property held by one person while the right to the use it is held by another.

bias of judge. As a ground for disqualification of a judge, bias is the same as prejudice and implies such ill-will or hostility toward a party to the proceeding to prevent a fair trial.

blacklisting. The practice among employers of listing employees discharged for union activities and agreeing not to employ such persons.

blue sky laws. A popular name for state statutes enacted to protect the public against securities frauds. Such laws regulate corporations' finances and the conduct of their business in issuing, selling, and distributing their securities.

board of directors. The body responsible for conducting the business of the corporation.

bona fide occupational qualification. A good faith requirement for employment with an employer, not acting as a subtle way of preventing certain classes of persons from qualifying for employment.

boycott. A concerted refusal to have dealings with an individual, organization, or product to express disapproval or to force acceptance of certain conditions.

brand. A mark used to identify an owner's property.

breach. A break; a breaking.

breach of duty. The failure or omission to do that which a person is bound by law to do.

brief. A detailed statement of a party's case.

broker. One who buys, bargains, or carries on negotiations in behalf of another. For these services, a commission is charged.

burden of proof. The duty of establishing the truth of a given proposition or issue by such evidence as the law demands in the case in which the issue arises.

bylaw. A rule or law of an organization for its government.

C

©. A designation accompanied by the initials, monogram, mark, or symbol of a copyright proprietor, affixed to books, maps, drawings, pictures, etc., to give notice of the existence of the copyright.

capital. That portion of the assets of a corporation used to conduct the corporate business and for the purpose of deriving gains and profits.

capitalization. The total amount of the various securities issued by a corporation. Capitalization may include bonds, debentures, preferred and common stock, and surplus.

capital stock. All shares representing ownership of a business, including preferred and common.

carrier. A transporter of passengers or freight.

case. A contested question in a court of justice.

case law. The law as laid down in the decisions of the courts.

cash dividend. A dividend paid in money.

cause. An action or suit.

cause of action. A right of action at law.

caveat emptor. A Latin phrase meaning let the buyer beware—the general rule that the buyer purchases products at his peril.

cease and desist. An order by an administrative agency requiring that certain practices be stopped.

certificate of stock. The actual piece of paper that is evidence of ownership of stock in a corporation. The document states that the person to whom it is issued is entitled to all the rights and subject to all the liabilities of a stockholder in the company.

certification. The legal assent by the National Labor Relations Act (NLRB) that a union has fulfilled the legal requirements to qualify as bargaining agent for the employees at a particular work site.

Certified Public Accountant. A title conferred on those persons who have met a state's legal requirements for the practice of the profession of accounting.

charge. The court instructions to the jury as to the essential law of the case.

charter. Authority from the government giving permission for a corporation's existence.

checks and balances, system of. A constitutional principle that enables one branch of government to limit the operations of the other branches of government.

chief justice. The presiding justice of the court.

citation. A writ issued out of a court of competent jurisdiction, commanding a person to appear on a day named to do something mentioned in the writ.

city court. A court whose jurisdiction is confined to the limits of a city.

civil law. The law of the Roman Empire, as comprised in the institutes, the code, and the digest of the Emperor Justinian. The law established by a nation or state for its own jurisdiction.

civil rights acts. Statutes prohibiting the denial of equal enjoyment of any facilities on the basis of race, religion, sex, or national origin and giving the party aggrieved a right to recover a penalty for the offense.

Civil Rights Commission. An administrative agency created by Congress to make findings of fact and recommendations concerning discrimination in American society.

class action. A court case brought on behalf of other persons similarly affected by the case.

Clayton Act. A law passed by Congress in 1914 that attempts to prevent monopolies by prohibiting mergers that may lessen future competition, price discrimination, tying arrangements, and certain interlocking directorates.

clerk of court. A ministerial officer of the court who has custody of its records and seals.

closed shop. A shop where only members of a labor union are permitted to work.

code. A system of law; a systematic and complete body of law.

coercion. Compulsion, actual or presumed.

collective bargaining. The good faith meeting between representatives of employees and employer for purposes of discussing the terms and conditions of employment.

collusion. An agreement between two or more persons to defraud another of his rights, or to secure an object forbidden by law.

commerce. Every species of commercial intercourse, including the making, purchase, sale, and exchange of commodities, the transportation of persons and property, and all the instruments by which such activities are done.

commerce clause. The third clause of the eighth section of the first article of the United States Constitution providing that Congress shall have power "to regulate commerce with foreign nations, and among the several States, and with the Indian tribes."

commission. A group of persons authorized and appointed to perform some public service or duty.

commodity. Any article of trade that can be transported.

common carrier. One who agrees, for compensation, to transport the goods of another.

common law. A system of elementary rules and of general judicial declarations of principles that are continually expanding with the progress of society; in its broad sense it is that great body of unwritten law, founded upon general custom, usage, or common consent, and in natural justice or reason.

common law of England. The general system of law that prevails in England, and in most of the United States by derivation from England.

compensatory damages. Damages awarded as a recompense for actual injury to the person or property, caused by the defendant's wrongful act.

competition. The act of seeking or endeavoring to gain what another is trying to gain at the same time.

complaint. A form of legal process consisting of a formal allegation or charge against a party.

conscious parallelism. Acts performed by one company that imitate the actions followed by its competitor.

consent decree. A means of settling court cases by agreement of the parties, having the binding effect of a judicial decree.

conspiracy. A secret agreement of two or more persons for the purpose of using criminal or unlawful means to achieve some end.

constitution. A system of fundamental laws or principles for the government of a nation, society, corporation, or other aggregation of individuals, which may be either written or unwritten.

constructive notice. Notice imputed to a person not having actual notice.

constructive service. A substituted service or process, made by leaving a copy of the process at the defendant's residence when he is absent, or by posting or publishing notice of the suit and mailing a copy of the posted or published notice to the defendant.

consumer legislation. A generic term applying to laws passed by governments to give and protect the rights of purchasers of goods and services.

Consumer Product Safety Commission. An independent administrative agency set up by Congress in the Consumer Product Safety Act in 1972 to carry out the terms of that act.

contempt. Disorderly, contemptuous, or insolent language or behavior in the presence of a legislative or judicial body, tending to disturb its proceedings, or impair the respect due to its authority.

contract. An agreement by which a person undertakes to do or not to do a particular thing.

contract clause. That clause contained in the first paragraph of the tenth section of the first article of the U. S. Constitution, providing that "no State shall pass any law impairing the obligation of contract."

contributory negligence. A common law rule that carelessness on the part of any employee relieves the employer from responsibility for injuries to the employee resulting from that carelessness.

controller. An officer who has charge of the financial affairs of an organization.

controversy. The claims of litigants brought into the courts for adjudication by regular proceedings.

cooperative. An association of persons formed to buy or sell without a middleman; the profits are distributed in accordance with the labor or capital contributed.

copyright. The exclusive legal privilege to publish and sell artistic, literary, or musical works.

corporate bonds. Debentures, certificates of indebtedness, and all other instruments issued by any corporation that pay interest and are registered.

corporation. A body formed by several persons but authorized by law to act as a single person with various rights and duties.

counterclaim. A cause of action existing in favor of the defendant against the plaintiff.

county court. A court with jurisdiction confined to a single county.

court. A place where justice is judicially administered; persons officially assembled under authority of law, at the appropriate time and place, for the administration of justice.

court not of record. An inferior court, or court of limited or special jurisdiction.

court of claims. A federal tribunal for the investigation of suits against the United States.

court of competent jurisdiction. A court having power and authority of law at the time of acting to do the particular act.

court of general jurisdiction. A court of record, a superior court, having the authority to hear all types of cases.

court of king's bench. A court which was formerly the supreme English common-law court but later became a department of the high court of justice.

court of limited jurisdiction. Courts that are inferior or not of record, or not having general authority to hear cases.

court of probate. A court with jurisdiction over wills and the administration of the estates of deceased persons.

court of record. A court whose acts and proceedings are kept on permanent record.

crime. A wrong against society because it has elements of evil that affect the public as a whole and not merely the person whose property or person have been invaded.

criminal conspiracy. A concerted action by two or more persons to accomplish some criminal or unlawful purpose, or to accomplish some purpose not in itself criminal by criminal or unlawful means.

cumulative dividends. Dividends paid on stocks that have the provision that if one or more dividends are omitted, the omitted dividends must be paid before dividends may be paid on the company's common stock.

cumulative voting. A method of voting, by which an elector entitled to vote for several candidates for the same office may cast more than one vote for the same candidate, distributing among the candidates as he chooses a number of votes equal to the number of candidates to be elected.

D

damages. Indemnity to the person who suffers loss or harm from an injury.

dealer. An individual or firm in the securities business acting as a principal rather than as an agent. A dealer buys for his own account and sells from his own inventory. The dealer's profit or loss is the difference between the price he pays and the price he receives for the same security. The same individual or firm may function, at different times, either as broker or dealer.

debenture. A promissory note backed by the general credit of a company and usually not secured by a mortgage or lien on any specific property. Debentures are bought and sold as investments.

decision. The judgment of a court. The opinion represents the reasons for that judgment.

declaratory judgment. A judgment establishing the rights of the parties and making binding determinations of their respective rights.

decree. An order or sentence of a court of equity determining some right or adjudicating some matter affecting the case; a sentence or order of the court, corresponding to the judgment of a court of law.

defamation. The injury of the name or reputation of another person by slander or libel.

defendant. The person against whom a suit is brought.

defraud. All acts, omissions, or concealments that involve a breach of legal or equitable duty, trust, or confidence injurious to another.

degree of proof. The grade or measure of the proof that the law requires for the establishment of the truth of an alleged fact.

de jure. By right; complying with the law in all respects.

delegation of legislative power. The conferring by a legislature upon some other body the power to make laws.

demurrer. A pleading by a party that assumes the truth of the matter alleged by the opposite party and proposes that it is insufficient in law to sustain the claim, or that there is some other defect in the pleading or a legal reason why the opposing party should not be allowed to proceed further; an objection.

Department of Justice. The branch of the United States government that is under the direction of the Attorney General, responsible for enforcing all federal laws.

deposition. The written testimony of a witness.

derivative. Taken, received, or delegated from a specified source.

dictum. The opinion of a judge that does not affect the settlement or determination of the court.

directed verdict. A verdict that a jury returns as directed by the court. The court may thus withdraw the case from the jury whenever there is no competent, relevant, and material evidence to support the issue.

director. One of the shareholders who is elected to serve on the managing board of a corporation. The director may be an officer of the corporation (insider) or not (outsider.)

discretion. The power of free decision or choice within certain legal bounds.

discrimination. The act of not treating all persons equally, often because of their race, sex, color, national origin, or religion.

dismissal. An order for the termination of an action without a trial of any of the issues.

disparagement. To depreciate indirectly (as by degrading comparison).

dispute. Any contention made by one party and denied by the other.

dissolution. The termination of the existence of a business, a remedy for violation of antitrust merger laws.

district courts. Courts of limited jurisdiction; also the trial courts of the United States.

diverse citizenship. The jurisdiction of the Federal courts extending to controversies between citizens of different states.

divestiture. The act of taking away part of a business as a remedy for violation of antitrust merger laws.

dividend. The payment designated by a board of directors to be distributed pro rata among the shares outstanding. On preferred shares, it is generally a fixed amount. On common shares, the dividend varies with the fortunes of the company and may be omitted if business is poor or if the directors determine to withhold earnings for purposes of investment.

docket. An abstract or digest of court cases; a register of actions.

doctrine of stare decisis. The policy of following rules or principles laid down in previous judicial decisions.

doing business in the state. The transaction within the state of some substantial part of a party's ordinary business, which must be continuous, not occasional, and creates some form of legal obligation.

due diligence. That amount of care that a reasonable and prudent person would exercise under the circumstances.

due process of law. Law in the regular course of administration through courts of justice, according to those rules and forms that have been established for the protection of private rights; law according to the settled course of judicial proceedings.

E

economy. The system which deals with the creation of goods and services to satisfy the needs and wants of a society.

employ. An agreement by one person to perform a service in return for compensation.

Employees Retirement Income Security Act. A statute passed by Congress in 1974 to regulate pension programs in the United States.

employer's liability insurance. Insurance taken out by an employer to protect him against loss on account of injury to his employees while they are working.

Equal Employment Opportunity Commission. An administrative agency created by Congress in the Civil Rights Act of 1964, as amended, to carry out the terms of Title VII of that Act which prohibits discrimination in private employment.

equal protection of the laws. A constitutional guaranty that "no person or class of persons shall be denied the same protection of the laws which is enjoyed by other persons or other classes in like circumstances, in their lives, their liberty, and their property, and in pursuit of happiness."

error. A mistake of law or fact; a mistake of the court in the trial of an action; a writ to review a judgment of an inferior court in a higher court for errors appearing on the face of the record.

ethical. Conforming to accepted professional standards of conduct.

evidence. That which makes clear or ascertains the truth of the fact or point in issue; those rules of law courts use to determine what testimony is to be admitted and what rejected in each case, and what is the weight to be given to the testimony admitted.

exchanges. Associations, organized for the purpose of giving their members convenient places to transact their business.

exchequer. A very ancient court of record, intended principally to order the revenues of the crown, and to recover the king's debts and duties.

execution. A remedy in the form of a writ for the enforcement of a judgment.

expert. One who is familiar with an art or science, or possesses skill in a given field.

F

face value. The nominal or par value of the instrument as expressed on its face.

fact. That which is true.

fair trial. A legal trial; a trial conducted in all material things in substantial conformity to law.

featherbedding. Union rules allegedly made to make jobs or to require more employees to be assigned to a given job than are needed.

federal. Pertaining to the United States.

Federal courts. Courts which form a part of the national judicial system of the United States.

Federal question. Some right, title, privilege, or immunity claimed under the Constitution or laws of the United States.

Federal Register. An official publication containing executive orders, and rules and regulations of all federal departments and agencies.

Federal Trade Commission. A commission established under the Federal Trade Commission Act to carry out the provisions of the act.

fellow servant rule. The common law doctrine that if the employer has provided safe and suitable tools, machinery, and appliances, he is not to be held accountable for an injury resulting to one of his employees from the carelessness of other employees.

felony. As a general rule, all crimes punishable by death or by imprisonment for longer than one year.

fiduciary. One who holds a thing in trust for another; a trustee.

final. Terminating all controversy, doubt, or dispute; the end, ultimate, or last; not subject to appeal.

final decision. A term that includes a decision determining all the issues presented by the pleadings.

franchise. The grant of an exclusive territory to a sales agent by a private corporation.

fraud. Deceit, deception, or trickery.

free competition. A market system in which there are many traders of the same product, no one of them able to control the demand, supply, or price of the product.

Freedom of Information Act. A statute passed by Congress to permit individuals to inspect records maintained on them by an administrative agency.

full faith and credit. The constitutional requirement (article four, section one) stating that "the public acts of every state shall be given the same force and effect by the courts of another state that they have in the home state."

G

garnishment. A writ from a court ordering a person owing money to a judgment debtor to pay part of it to a court officer for the benefit of a judgment creditor.

general restraint of trade. An agreement not to carry on a certain business or occupation anywhere.

general strike. A strike against all the employers, participated in by the workmen irrespective of the persons for whom they are working.

good faith. An honest intention to abstain from taking any unfair advantage of another.

government. Management, administration, control, power, or authority to check or restrain.

guaranteed dividends. Distributions on preferred stock that are assured by the corporation.

guilds. An association of persons organized to pursue some common purpose, formed for the mutual aid and protection of the members.

H

harmless error. An error committed in the trial of an action but which is not sufficiently prejudicial to the rights of the losing party to warrant a reversal of the judgment.
hazardous occupation. An occupation having a great risk.
hearing. The argument and consideration of a case.
hundred court. A larger court-baron that was held for all the inhabitants of a particular hundred, instead of a manor.

I

ignorance of fact. Either when some fact which really exists is unknown, or some fact is supposed to exist which really does not exist.
illegal contracts. Contracts that are contrary to law, morality, or public policy.
inalienable rights. The natural or fundamental rights that belong to all men, as distinguished from the artificial rights or privileges of citizens and other classes of persons.
incorporation. The act or process of forming a corporation.
indemnification. The process of being secure against some hurt, loss, or damage.
industrial revolution. The social and economic conditions that resulted from changes made in production procedures.
inferior courts. Courts of special and limited jurisdiction.
infringement of copyright. A copying, in whole or in part, by any mode of reproduction, whether by printing, writing, photography, or by some other method not yet invented, would constitute a copying but it must come so near to the original as to give to every person seeing it the idea created by the original.
infringement of patent. The adoption by an inventor of the substance of a device or process already patented.
infringement of trademark. The use or imitation by another of his goods in such manner that the purchasers are deceived.
infringement of tradename. Imitation of a tradename that the general public, in the exercise of reasonable care, might think that it is the name of the one first appropriating it.
injunction. A restraining order issued by a court.
injury. A wrong for which the law provides a remedy.
in personam. Against the person.
in rem. Against a thing and not against a person.
insider. An officer, director, a shareholder owning ten percent or

more of the outstanding stock of a corporation and anyone possessing confidential information about the corporation.

insolvent corporation. A corporation whose assets are insufficient to pay its debts.

intent. The purpose to use a particular means to accomplish a certain result.

interference with economic relations. A tort for violations of the right of another to be secure in his business and contractual relations.

interstate commerce. The transportation of persons and property; navigation of public waters; the production, purchase, sale, and exchange of commodities and services between inhabitants or businesses of different states.

Interstate Commerce Commission. An administrative agency created by Congress to carry out the terms of the Interstate Commerce Act, which regulates interstate commerce.

issuer. A person who places his name on a security to show that it represents a share in his property or a duty to perform some obligation.

J

judge. One who performs judicial functions, and presides at the trial of cases involving justiciable matters.

judgment. The sentence of the law upon the record; the application of the law to the facts and the pleadings.

judicial process. The power to adjudicate; that is, the power to hear, consider, and determine rights of parties and render a judgment.

jurisdiction. The right to adjudicate concerning the subject-matter in a given case.

jury. A body of laymen, to ascertain, under the guidance of a judge, the truth in questions of fact arising either in civil or criminal processes.

K

kings bench. The supreme English common law court.

Kings Council. A term applied to the king's court.

knowingly. A knowledge of the essential facts, from which the law presumes a knowledge of the legal consequences arising from that knowledge.

L

labor. A factor of production involving manual or mental exertion for which compensation is received.

Labor Management Relations Act. An act of Congress passed in 1947 amending the National Labor Relations Act. Also referred to as the basic law governing labor relations in the United States, specifying procedures for employee organization, employee rights, employer and union unfair labor practices, and dispute settlement procedures.

Labor Management Reporting and Disclosure Act. A statute passed by Congress in 1959 regulating the internal operations of labor organizations.

Lanham Act. A statute passed by Congress permitting owners of trademarks to register them with the Federal government.

law. A statute; the whole body or system of rules of conduct, including both decisions of courts and legislative acts.

law of nature. A specific principle held to be derived from nature and binding upon human society in the absence or addition of other laws; natural law.

law of the case. A term applied to an established rule that when an appellate court passes on a question and remands the case for further proceedings, the question there settled becomes the law of the case.

lawsuit. An action or a proceeding in a court.

lawyer. A person licensed to practice the profession of law.

legal. According to the principles of law.

legislature. The law-making branch of government.

liability. A broad term referring to every kind of responsibility; in its legal sense, it signifies the consequences for violating a law.

license. A personal privilege to do some act or acts.

life, liberty, and property. Representative words derived from the Constitution intending to cover every right to which a person is entitled under the law.

lockout. An attempt by an employer in a labor dispute to pressure employees by closing the work site.

M

magistrate. A word commonly applied to a lower judicial officer.

management. A factor of production involving the organization and coordination of the other factors of production. Also, the word refers to the officers and employees of an organization who are responsible for running a business.

manipulate. To force prices up or down by illegal means.

margin. The percentage of the purchase price paid by the customer when he uses a broker's credit to buy a security.

market value. The price at which a thing may be sold when there is a demand and an ability to sell it at a time when a sale is desired.

marshall. An officer of a judicial district responsible for carrying out court orders.

material evidence. Evidence offered in a case, when it is relevant and goes to the substantial matters in a dispute, or has a legitimate and effective influence or bearing on the decision of the case.

material fact. A fact that influences a person to act.

measure of damages. The rule established by law or decision for arriving at the amount of the plaintiff's damages and which he is entitled to recover in a given case.

mediation. A procedure for settling disputes where parties bring their case before a board that makes non-binding recommendations.

merger. A situation resulting when a corporation buys the stock or assets or another corporation for purposes of control.

ministerial act or duty. Some act or duty imposed expressly by law, involving no discretion in its exercise, but mandatory and imperative.

misrepresentation. A misstatement of fact, which, if accepted, leads to an apprehension of a condition other and different from that which actually exists.

mistrial. An erroneous trial on account of some defect caused by the persons participating in the trial.

money judgment. A judgment that can be fully satisfied by a payment of money.

monopoly. In its broadest sense, the word means the sole power of dealing in an article; the modern meaning is any combination, organization, or entity so extensive, exclusive, and unified that its tendency is to prevent competition, with the power to control prices and cause the public some harm.

morals. Principles of right and wrong behavior.

motion. An application made to a judge or court, for the purpose of obtaining a rule or order directing some act to be done in favor of the person requesting it. Some examples of motions are motion for a directed verdict, motion for a nonsuit, motion for judgment on the pleadings, motion for a new trial, and a motion to strike.

N

National Labor Relations Act. An act of Congress, passed in 1935, that guarantees employees the right to organize into labor organizations, bargain collectively with their employer and creates some labor practices to protect these rights.

necessary and proper. A constitutional phrase from Article I, Section 8, giving Congress the power to enact all laws appropriate to carrying out its specific powers.

net earnings. The gross receipts less the expenses of operating the business to earn such receipts.

new trial. A re-examination of an issue of fact in the same court after a trial.

noncumulative dividends. Dividends on preferred stock which are dependent upon the profits of the particular year only. Unpaid (omitted) dividends of noncumulative preferred stock do not accrue.

O

oath. Any form of attestation by which a person signifies that he is bound in conscience to perform an act faithfully and truthfully.

occupational safety. A generic term meaning that the work environment should be free of hazards that may cause death, disease, or injury to workers.

Occupational Safety and Health Act. A statute passed by Congress in 1970 to provide a safe work environment for employees.

Occupational Safety and Health Review Commission. An administrative agency created by Congress in 1970 to carry out the terms of the Occupational Safety and Health Act.

opening statement. A full and fair statement of the plaintiff's case and of the facts that the plaintiff intends to prove.

open shop. A plan or policy stating that there shall be no discrimination for or against an employee on account of any affiliation or nonaffiliation with a labor union.

opinion. The reasons for a court's judgment.

order. A written directive of a court or judge determining some matter pertaining to the proceedings.

ordinances. A legislative rule enacted by a municipal corporation such as a city, town, county, or some specially created government district.

outstanding stock. Shares that have been authorized and issued and therefore are effective obligations against the corporation.

P

par. In the case of common stock, a dollar amount that appears on the face of the share and assigned to it by the company's charter. Par value may also be used to compute the dollar amount of the common shares on the balance sheet. Par value has little significance so far as the market value of common stock is concerned. A company may issue no-par stock but give a stated per-share value on the balance sheet.

In the case of preferred stock, par often signifies the dollar value upon which dividends on preferred stocks or interest on bonds are figured. For example, the issuer of a 6-percent bond promises to pay that percentage of the par value annually.

partnership. A combination by two or more persons of their capital labor or skill for the purpose of their common benefit.

party. Anyone who is directly involved in the subject matter of a case.

patent. The exclusive ownership of any new, useful invention of a machine, art, or process, granted by the federal government under Article I, Section 8 of the Constitution.

penalty. A punishment for the nonperformance of an act or the performance of an illegal act.

pension. Payments from a fund contributed to by either the employer or employee or both and made to a person after retirement from the employer's service.

per se. By or through itself.

personal service. The actual delivery of the process to the individual to be served.

petition. A pleading that requests some relief.

picketing. Stationing persons for observation, patrol, and demonstration at a work site as part of employee pressure on an employer.

plaintiff. A person who initiates a suit.

pleadings. The allegations made by the parties in a lawsuit, for the purpose of presenting the issues to be tried.

plea of nolo contendere. A formal declaration by the accused that he will not contest charges filed against him. When accepted by the court, it becomes an implied confession of guilt, and, for the purposes of the case only, equivalent to a plea of guilty but

different in that it cannot be used against the defendant in any civil suit for the same act.
preemptive. A right associated with some stock issues giving the holder the option of purchasing additional shares of newly issued stock in the same proportion to that percentage of the existing stock that the shareholder owns.
preferred stock. A class of stock that has a claim on the company's earnings before payment may be made on the common stock and usually entitled to priority if the company liquidates. Preferred stocks are often entitled to dividends at a specified rate.
prejudice. Judgment formed beforehand without examination.
pre-trial procedure. A conference between the judge and counsel to simplify the issues of a case before trial.
primary pressure. Economic or social action brought directly against the person or group with whom the dispute exists.
private law. That branch of law administered between persons as distinguished from that part of the law pertaining to government.
privilege and immunity clause. A constitutional term prohibiting the states from enacting any laws taking away rights of United States citizens.
probable. Supported by evidence strong enough to establish presumption but not truth; likely to be or become true or real.
procedural law. That branch of law that sets up a method for enforcing rights.
profit. A term meaning the increase in wealth resulting from the operation of a business.
prospectus. A written or oral statement describing a security offered for sale.
proxy. An authorization to one person to act for another in transacting some business.
prudence. Such care and diligence as an ordinary person would use under the same or similar circumstances.
public law. The branch of law that is concerned with government organization and operation.

Q

quasi. Relating to, or having the character of.
quasi-judicial functions. Those functions which lie midway between the judicial and ministerial ones.
quorum. The number necessary to lawfully transact business at a meeting.

R

ratification. The act by which one person confirms an action done on his behalf by another.

reasonable. Not immoderate or excessive, but suitable, fair, or rational.

record. A written history of the proceedings from the beginning to the end of the case.

red herring prospectus. A preliminary prospectus used after the filing of the registration statement but prior to its effective date, to inform prospective buyers of the nature of the securities to be sold.

referee. A person appointed by a court to perform certain tasks in the progress of a case.

regulatory laws. See administrative laws.

relevant. Directly touching upon the issues in the pleadings.

reservation Indians. Indians living on Indian reservations; the jurisdiction of the federal government over their tribes, and over the members of such tribes, is exclusive.

res judicata. The doctrine that a matter has been finally decided on its merits by a court having competent jurisdiction and not subject to litigation again between the same parties.

respondent. The defendant in an action.

restitution. Restoration of the specific thing, or its equivalent.

restraining order. A temporary order preventing the doing of some act during the time that an application for a preliminary injunction is pending.

restraint of trade. Combinations and arrangements for the creation of a monopoly, the control of prices, and the suppression of competition.

reversal. The annulment or setting aside of a decision.

reversed and remanded. To set aside the judgment of the lower court with instructions for further proceedings.

S

safe place to work. All the safeguards and precautions that ordinary prudence would suggest are taken to prevent injuries to employees.

scope of employment. The regular duties of an employee that are of some benefit to the employer and not entirely personal to the employee.

secondary meaning. A generic word that signifies a special activity because of long use by a person in connection with that activity.

secondary pressure. Economic or social action brought against a person or group with whom no labor dispute exists but who may be indirectly involved in the dispute.

securities acts. A broad term referring to laws enacted by Congress to help protect investors—(the Securities Act of 1933, the Securities Exchange Act of 1934, the Trust Indenture Act, the Investment Company Act, the Investment Advisers Act, and the Public Utility Holding Company Act).

Securities and Exchange Commission. An independent agency created by Congress to carry out the federal securities acts.

segregation laws. Statutes authorizing separation of races.

seniority. A person's length of service in a place of employment.

separation of powers. A constitutional concept calling for divided executive, legislative, and judicial powers among the three branches of government.

set aside. Annulled; made void.

sheriff. The officer of a county court responsible for upholding the laws.

Sherman Antitrust Act. An act passed by Congress in 1890 to prohibit combinations in restraint of trade.

short sales. Sales on margin; sales of stock not yet owned.

short swing profit. A gain made on the sale of securities held for only a brief time after purchase.

situs. Location.

slander. Speaking false, defamatory words tending to harm another's reputation.

social compact. A theory of the origin of society, stating that law resulted from the combination of persons who agreed, for mutual protection, to surrender individual freedom of action.

social responsibility. The broad concept that business employees and managers should adhere to an ethical code in their dealings with the various publics with whom they come into contact.

sole proprietorship. A form of business organization in which one person owns and manages an enterprise and assumes all risks.

specific performance. A court order compelling a defendant to carry out some obligation.

standing. A judicial term requiring an individual to show some personal injury caused by the defendant before being allowed to sue.

state antitrust laws. State statutes of the same general nature as the Sherman Antitrust Act prohibiting corporations the power to enter into illegal combinations in restraint of trade.

statute. An act of the legislature.

stock. The invested capital of a corporation.

stock dividend. A dividend payable to the stockholders of a corporation in shares of stock in that corporation.

stockholder. One who holds shares that are registered on the books of the corporation.

stockholder's liability. The statutory and judicially created liability of a stockholder in a corporation making him individually answerable for debts of the corporation and for acts of mismanagement.

strike. The concerted stoppage of work by employees as a means of enforcing a demand made on their employer.

substantive. An essential part; relating to what is essential.

supreme law of the land. The Constitution of the United States and the laws enacted under it together with any treaties made under the authority of the United States.

surplus. The sum of the assets less the sum of the liabilities. Surplus may be either paid in (arising from sources other than profits), or earned, (undistributed profits gained through regular operation of the business).

surrogate court. A court with jurisdiction in guardianship and probate matters.

sympathetic strike. A strike called in support of another strike.

T

taxing power. A power inherent in government to raise revenues.

temporary injunction. A restraining order effective until the trial of the action to which it is issued.

tender. An offer to security holders to purchase their securities.

territorial jurisdiction. The geographic boundaries of a district within which a judge or other judicial officer has authority to act.

tombstone ad. A brief announcement in the newspapers stating that a particular security is registered with the SEC, giving the name of the issuer, underwriter, and dealer, but not for the purpose of offering the security for sale.

tort. An injury or wrong committed, either with or without force, to the person or property of another.

trademark. A sign, device, or symbol by which the articles produced or dealt in by a person or firm are distinguishable from those produced or dealt in by rival manufacturers or dealers.

tradename. A name under which a person, firm, or corporation has carried on a business, trade, or occupation.

trade secret. Secrets of any character peculiar and important to the business of the employer that have been communicated to an employee in the course of a confidential employment.

treaty. A compact made between two or more independent nations.

treble damages. Triple damages provided for by statute as compensation for injuries caused by a violation of certain statutes.

trial. An examination before a competent tribunal, according to the law of the land, of the facts or law put in issue in a case, for the purpose of determining such issues.

trust. A legal form by which property is held and administered by one person for the benefit of another.

U

underwriter. One who purchases for resale a large block of a new security issue; also known as an investment banker.

unfair labor practice. An improper employment practice of either an employer or union prohibited by the Labor Management Relations Act.

unfair methods of competition. An imprecise term determined on a case by case basis in light of particular competitive conditions and by what is found to be in the public interest.

Uniform Commercial Code. A law formulated by the National Conference on Uniform State Laws and the American Law Institute dealing with most aspects of commercial transactions.

union. An organization of employees to act on behalf of all employees in negotiations with the employer regarding terms of their employment contract.

unwritten law. The common law is often referred to as the unwritten law, as distinguished from the written or statutory law.

V

venue. The place in which a case is to be tried.

verdict. The answer of a jury given to the court concerning the matters of fact committed to them.

void. Not binding on either party.

W

wages. The payment made for manual labor, or other labor of menial or mechanical kind, as distinguished from "salary" and from "fee," which denote compensation paid to professional persons.

wanton. A reckless disregard of the rights of others, a reckless indifference to the rights of others.

warranty. A promise by the seller to the buyer regarding the nature of the property sold.

willfully. An action done knowingly but not maliciously.

workmen's compensation acts. Statutes passed by states to pay money to workers injured in the scope of their employment, ending those technicalities from the common law that denied compensation for injuries.

writ. An order from a court compelling a person to do some act.

written law. The law which is passed by legislatures as statutes, ordinances, laws, treaties and constitutions; statutory law.

Z

zoning. The separation of commercial and residential districts of an area.

INDEX

Affirmative action, 324-25
  bona fide occupational qualifications, 329-33
  employee classifications under, 325-27
  Executive Order 11246, 325, 327-28
  occupational surveys, 328
  recruitment, 328
Adjudicative administrative agency, 52, 76-77
  constitutional limitations on, 78-79
Administrative agency, 16
  advantages of, 45-47
  definition of, 42
  development of, 43-45
  effects of, 43
  operations of, 52-54
  powers of, 47-49
  problems with, 68-87
    constitutional, 69-80
    economic, 81-83
    errors, 83-84
    political, 80-81
  procedures followed by, 55-65
  types, 49-52
Administrative law, 16
Administrative Procedures Act (APA), 55
Administrative process, 42-65
Adversary system, 34-35
Advertising:
  corrective, 214
  discriminatory allowances, 227
  labeling, 238
  unfair method of competition, 205, 228-30
  warranties, 230-35
Agriculture, Department of, 50
Alcoholic Beverage Control, 51
American Bar Association, professional ethics, 388
American Federation of Labor, 246
Anii, Wisdom of, 26

Antitrust (*see also* Sherman Act, Clayton Act, and Federal Trade Commission Act)
  actions by state on behalf of citizens, 206, 365
  state laws, 179
Appeal:
  grounds of, 35
  procedures, 36
Attorney:
  compensation of, 389
  duties of client toward, 390-92
  duties to client by, 387-88
  selection of, 385, 387
Attorney General, discrimination suits, 324

Bankruptcy court, 28
Barrons, 314
Biglow Papers, 288
Blumenthal, W. Michael, 365
Bone fide occupational qualification, 329-33
Boycott, 186
Brahmanic law, 12
Brokerage, 227
Business Lawyer, 361
Business regulations:
  enforcement techniques, 371-74
  sources of, 15-22

California, court organization, 31
Cease and desist order, 214
Center for the Study of American Business, 84
Civil Aeronautics Board (CAB), 50
Civil Court, 28
Civil Law, 12
Civil rights:
  acts, 317

421

Civil rights: *(continued)*
  constitutional basis for, 315
  definition of, 315
  enforcement of, 318-24
  penalties under, 317
  state laws, 324
Civil Rights Commission, 70
Class action suit:
  definition of, 37
  ethical considerations, 364
  job discrimination cases, 319
  notice requirements, 38-39
  stockholder suits, 104
Clayton Act:
  brokerage payments, 227
  enforcement of, 210-16
  exclusive dealings, 195-98
  exemptions, 207-210
  generally, 15, 156, 194-98
  liabilities, 206
  mergers, 198-204
  price discrimination, 221-27
Collective bargaining:
  definition of, 253
  employee right of, 248
  generally, 245-66
Commerce, Department of, 51
Common law, 12, 17
  business regulation under, 159-69
  job injuries under, 289, 293
  monopoly regulations under, 179
Complaint, 33
Comptroller of the Currency, 50
Computer, 166-67, 169-77
  fraud in use of, 176-77
  interference with employee contracts, 175-76
  patent and copyright protections, 166-67, 169-70
  trade secret protections, 170-75
Confucian law, 12
Congress of Industrial Organization (CIO), 246
Connecticut:
  court organization, 31
  Workmen's Compensation Act, 295-97
Conscious parallelism, 189-90
Consent decree, 210-11
Conspiracy:
  conscious parallelism, 189-90
  implied, 185

  interdependent consciously parallel behavior, 190
Constitution:
  basis of business regulations, 18-22
  civil rights amendments, 315-17
  due process clause, 69-76
  equal protections clause, 80
  federal court system, 29, 36
  freedom of contract clause, 77
  occupational safety laws, 306-307
Consumer Product Safety Act (CPSA), 235-37
Consumer Product Safety Commission (CPSC), 51, 83, 235-38, 373
  enforcement powers, 237
  functions, 235
  organization of, 235
  powers of, 236
Consumer protection:
  advertising, 214, 228-30
  Consumer Product Safety Act, 235-38
  Consumer Product Safety Commission, 235-38
  enforcement, 214
  price discrimination, 221-27
  product liability, 232
  sales practices, 228-29
  warranties, 230-34
Contracts, 13
Copyrights, 22
  common law of, 165
  computer programs, 169-76
Corporation:
  definition of, 93
  directors, 93
  misuse of powers by, 354
  multinational, 356-58
  nonresident, jurisdiction over, 32
  securities, regulation of, 93 (*see also* Securities Act and Securities Exchange Act)
  stockholders, 93-108
  social responsibilities of, 377-79
Corrective action, 214
County Court, 29
Court:
  classifications of, 28
  citations of, 22-25
    federal, 32
    state, 23

definition of, 27
  enforcement methods, 36-37
  participants in, 27
  role of, 39-40
  structures, 28-31
  trial procedures, 33-37
Court of Appeals, 29, 31
Court of Claims, 29, 31
Crimes:
  definition of, 13
  ethical aspects of, 348-51
  enforcement, 362-63
  penalties (*see* liabilities under civil rights acts, Clayton Act, Employee Retirement Income Security Act, Labor Management Reporting and Disclosure Act, National Labor Relations Act, Occupational Safety and Health Act, Securities Act, Securities Exchange Act, and Sherman Act)
Criminal conduct:
  by managers, 348-51
  total costs of managerial, 363
Criminal Court, 28
  due process within, 69-79
Customs and Patent Appeals Court, 29, 31

Deceptive sales practices, 204-205, 228-30
Decisions, 17
  precedent in, 17-18
  briefing, 22-25
Dependent administrative agency, 52
Derivative action, 104
Directors, 93
  inside information, use of, 135, 138-41
  insider reports, 134-35
  liabilities of, 123, 125, 146
  outside, 368-71
  Rule 10 (b) (5), responsibilities under, 135-43
  short swing trades by, 135
Discrimination:
  civil rights acts, 315-17
  in employment, 314-15
  remedies for, 318-24
  reverse, 335-36
  union membership, 250-51, 254
Disparagement, 168-69
Dissolution, 214
District Court, 29
Divestiture, 214
Due process, 69-77
  in administrative agencies, 70-73, 75-76, 78-79
  criminal, 69, 78-79
  procedural, 69-70
  substantive, 70
Dunne, Peter Finley, 40

Economic resources, allocation of, 156
Employees Retirement Income Security Act (ERISA), 281-84
  eligibility requirements, 281-82
  funding, 282-83
  penalties, 283-85
  reports, 283
  types of plans, 281
  vesting, 282
Environmental Protection Act (EPA), 51, 80
  enforcement, 373
Equal Employment Opportunity Commission (EEOC), 50, 320-23
  functions of, 320
  procedures, 321-23, 372
Equal protections clause, 80
Equity, 18
Ethical guidelines, managers, 374-77
Ethical Standards Boards, 367-68
  distinguished from administrative agencies, 368
  enforcement procedures, 374
  organization of, 367
  procedures, 367-68
  self regulatory device, 374-77
Ethics, 347-68, 374-77
  and corporate power, 352-58
  and criminal conduct, 348-51
  enforcement of, 374-77
  remedies, 362-68
Exclusive dealings arrangements, 195-98
Executive Order 11246, 325-35

Federal Act of 1908, 289
Federal Aviation Administration
  (FAA), 50
Federal Courts:
  jurisdiction of, 30
  organization of, 29
Federal Deposit Insurance
  Corporation (FDIC), 50
Federal Energy Administration
  (FEA), 50
Federal Maritime Commission
  (FMC), 50
Federal Mediation and Conciliation
  Service (FMCS), 50, 265
Federal Power Commission (FPC),
  50, 62
Federal Register, 57, 86
Federal Reserve System (FRS), 50
Federal Trade Commission (FTC),
  51, 52, 73
  enforcement procedures, 206, 373
  organization of, 215
Federal Trade Commission Act, 156,
  204-206
  advertising, 228-30
  enforcement, 210
  liabilities, 206
  unfair methods of competition,
    204-206
Fiduciary duty:
  of majority stockholders, 102-104
  of managers, 375-77
  of officers and directors, 103-104
  of pension administrators, 283
Flammable Fabrics Act, 238-39
Fletcher, Stephen H., 361
Food and Drug Administration
  (FDA), 51, 57-58
Food, Drug, and Cosmetics Act, 238
Franchise agreements, 186-88
Free competition, 156
Freedom of Information Act
  (FOIA), 84-87
  disclosure requirements, 84-85
  exemptions from disclosure, 85
  inspections, 86
  safeguards, 85-86
  penalties, 87
Freedom of contract clause, 77
Full faith and credit clause, 36
Fur Products Labeling Act, 238

Garnishment, 36
Goldberg, Arthur, 369-71
Government regulations, impact of, 4

Hazardous Substances Act, 239
Health, Education, and Welfare,
  Secretary of, 76-77
Hot cargo, 259-61
Household Refrigerator Safety Act,
  239
Hundred Court, 28

Independent administrative agency,
  52
Industrial revolution, 245-47, 288
Injunction, 37
Inside information, 138-41
Interdependent consciously parallel
  behavior, 190
Interference with business relations,
  159-61, 175-76
Internal Revenue Code (IRC), 15, 29
Internal Revenue Service (IRS), 52,
  82
Interstate commerce clause, 18, 22
Interstate Commerce Commission,
  (ICC), 50, 52, 54
Investigative administrative agency,
  56-59
  constitutional limits on, 69-80
Investment Advisors Act of 1940,
  149
Investment Company Act of 1940,
  148
Islamic law, 12

Jefferson, Thomas, 347
Jurisdiction, 30-33
  appellate, 28
  federal, 30
  nonresident, 31-32
  original, 28
  personal, 31
  over property, 31
  state, 30

Jury, selection of, 35
Justice, Department of:
  antitrust actions, 210
  criminal actions, 362-63
Justice of the Peace, 28

King, W.L. Mackenzie, 245
Knights of Labor, 246

Labor, 245-337
  dispute settlement procedures, 261-66
  government policy toward, 244
  history of, 245-47
  job discrimination (see Discrimination and Civil Rights)
  job safety (see Occupational Safety)
  pension rights (see Pension and Employees Retirement Income Security Act)
  rights of, 247-49
  unfair practices, 251-61
  union democracy (see Labor Management Reporting and Disclosure Act)
  weapons of (see Strikes and Picketing)
Labor, Department of, 50
  organizational chart, 274
  pension laws, 284
  Philadelphia Plan, 327-28
Labor Management Relations Act (LMRA), 247 (see also Labor, National Labor Relations Act, Picketing, Strikes, Unfair Labor Practices)
Labor Management Reporting and Disclosure Act (LMRDA), 267, 273-80
  bill of rights, 273-79
  officer reports, 280
  penalties, 280
  union reports, 279-81
Landrum Griffen Act (see Labor Management Reporting and Disclosure Act)

Lanham Act, 163-64
Law:
  classifications of, 13-15
  definition of, 6-8
  functions of, 8-10
  limits to, 10-11
  origins of, 8
  sources of, 15-18
Long arm statute, 33
Lowell, James Russell, 288

Magistrates Court, 28
Management guidelines:
  antitrust laws, 216-17
  consumer laws, 240
  job discrimination laws, 339-41
  job safety acts, 310-11
  securities acts, 128-29, 151
  social responsibility, 377-79
  union management relations, 285-86
Marlin Toy Products Co., 83
Merger:
  Clayton Act, 198-204
  Sherman Act, 180
Monopoly, 156, 180
Motions, 34
Motor Vehicles, Department of, 51
Multinational corporations, ethical aspects of, 356-58
Municipal corporations, 16

National Commission on Productivity and Work Quality, 82-83
National Labor Relations Act (NLRA), 15, 247
  employee rights under, 247-49
  National Labor Relations Board (NLRB), 261-63
  picketing, 271-73
  strikes, 268-71
  unfair labor practices, 249-54
National Labor Relations Board (NLRB), 50, 52, 261-63
  functions of, 263
  organization of, 261
Natural law, 8

Necessary and proper clause, 22
New York, court organization, 31
New York Times, 5, 176, 369-71
Norris LaGuardia Act, 247, 268-69
Nuclear Regulatory Commission (NRC), 50

Occupational safety, 244, 297-309
Occupational Safety and Health Act (OSHA), 50, 81, 84, 297-309
  appeals from, 303-305, 308-309
  citations under, 299
  constitutional objections to, 300, 306-307
  defenses against, 305-306
  employee rights and duties under, 308-309
  employer rights and duties under, 298-307
  inspections, 299-300, 301-303
  justifications, 373
Occupational Safety and Health Review Commission (OSHRC), 304
Ordinances, 16

Parker, Donn, 176
Patents, 22, 29
  common law of, 165-67
  computers and, 169-70
Pensions, 267, 280-84
Peoples Republic of China, 12
Philadelphia Plan, 327-28
Picketing:
  ambulatory situs, 272
  common situs, 272
  definition of, 271
  free speech and, 271
  informational, 272
  jurisdictional, 255
  mass, 271
  primary, 271
  recognitional, 259
  secondary, 272
  stranger, 271
  tertiary, 271
Pleadings, 33-34
Poison Prevention Packaging Act, 239

Pretrial conference, 34
Price discrimination, 221-27
Price fixing, 37, 182-84
Private law, 14, 18
Probate courts, 29
Procedural law, 14
Product extension mergers, 202-204
Product liability, 232
Production quotas, 188
Professional agents:
  duty to clients, 375
  managers, 376-77
Prospectus, 115
Proxy, 95, 133
Public law, 14
Public Utility Board, 51
Public Utility Holding Company Act of 1935, 149

Red herring prospectus, 116
Registration statement, 115
Regulatory agency (*see* Administrative Agency)
Religious laws, 12-13
Res judicata, 36
Restraint of trade, 161-63, 180
Rule 10 (b) (5):
  definition of, 136
  examples of, 136-43
  intent, 136
Rural Electrification Administration, (REA), 50

Secondary pressures, 255-58
Security:
  definition of, 112-14
  federal regulations of, 115-26, 132-49
  registration statements for, 115
  state regulations of, 150
  trading rules for (*see* Securities Exchange Act)
Securities Act, 15, 111-29
  exemptions from, 118-23
  liabilities, 123-27
  management guidelines, 128-29
  registration requirements, 115-18
  security, definition of, 112-14
  stop orders, 118

Securities Exchange Act, 15, 132-49
   liabilities under, 146-48
   proxy rules, 133
   registration requirements, 132-34
   reporting requirements, 132-34
   trading rules:
      insiders, 134-35
      margin rules, 135
      Rule 10 (b)(5), 134-43
      short swing trades, 135
      tender offers, 135
Securities Exchange Commission, 50, 143-46
   investigations by, 143-45
   organization of, 144
   powers of, 145
   remedies of, 146
   structure of, 143
Self incrimination, 69, 73-75
Separation of powers doctrine, 42
Service of process, 34
Sherman Act, 15, 179-92
   conspiracy to violate, 189
   distinguished from Clayton Act, 194
   enforcement of, 210-14
   exemptions from, 207-10
   importance of, 180
   liabilities under, 190-91
   per se violations of, 182-88
   proving violations of, 189-90
   rule of reason, 180-82
Slander of title, 168
Small Business Administration, (SBA), 50
Social compact theory, 8
Social responsibility:
   of corporations, 377-79
   ethical problems, 355-56
Social Security Act, 76-77
Specific performance, 37
Stanford Research Institute, 176
Statutes, 15-16
Statute of Laborers, 245
Statute of Limitations, 26, 37
Stockholder liabilities:
   for corporate acts, 108
   under federal securities laws, 108, 111-29
   fiduciary duties, 102-104
   illegal dividends, 108
   unjust advantages, 108

Stockholder rights:
   appraisal, 106-108
   class actions, 104-106
   dividends, 99-102
   derivative actions, 104
   inspections, 94
   meetings, 94-95
   minority, 102-104
   preemptive, 97-99
   voting, 95-97
Strikes:
   definition of, 268
   economic, 271
   general, 270
   government employee, 270
   national emergency, 270
   primary, 268
   restrictions on, 270
   secondary, 269
   sitdown, 270
   slowdown, 270
   sympathy, 270
   unfair labor practice, 271
   violent, 270
   wildcat, 270
Subpoena, 34
Substantive law, 14
Summons, 34
Supreme Court, 29

Taft Hartley Act (*see* Labor Management Relations Act)
Tax Court, 29
Tax Foundation, 81
Tax Review, 298
Taxing power, 22
Tennessee Valley Authority (TVA), 50
Territorial restrictions, 184-85
Title VII, 317
Tombstone ads, 116
Torts, 13, 159
Trade Associations, 181-82
Trade conference, 212-13
Trade regulation rule, 213-14
Trade secrets, 167
   computers and, 170-75
Trade marks and trade names:
   acquisition of, 163-65
   definition of, 163
   registration of, 164

Transportation, Department of, 50, 64-65
Treasury, Department of, 50
Treaty, 15
Treble damages, 191, 372
Trial:
  appeal from, 35
  definition of, 34-35
  evaluation of, 39-40
  execution, 36-37
  jurisdiction of, 33
  pleadings, 33-34
  pretrial, 34
  procedures, 33-37
Trust Indenture Act of 1939, 148-49
Truth in Lending Act, 239
Tying agreements, 188-89

Unfair labor practices:
  employer, 249-54
  hearings, 263-65
  union, 254-61
Unfair methods of competition, 204-206
Uniform Commercial Code (UCC):
  general, 16
  holder in due course, 213-14
  warranties, 230-35
Union certification, 262-63
Unwritten law, 14

Wagner Act (*see* National Labor Relations Act)
Wall Street Journal, 365-67
Warranty:
  definition of, 230
  disclaimer of, 231-32
  express, 231
  of fitness, 232
  of merchantability, 232
  of title, 231-32
Weidenbaum, Dr. Murray L., 84
West Publishing Company, 24
Witena Gemote, 28
Wool Products Labeling Act, 238
Workmen's compensation:
  collection procedures, 290-93
  common law background, 289
  Connecticut statute, 295-97
  definition of, 290
  emotional injuries, 291-92
  employer defenses, 293-95
Workmen's Compensation Board, 51, 290
World legal systems, 11-13
Written law, 14

Zoning, 16, 51